*Everyman, I will go with thee,*
*and be thy guide*

## THE EVERYMAN
## LIBRARY

*The Everyman Library was founded by J. M. Dent*
*in 1906. He chose the name Everyman because he wa*
*to make available the best books ever written in eve*
*field to the greatest number of people at the cheapest pos*
*price. He began with Boswell's 'Life of Johnson';*
*his one-thousandth title was Aristotle's 'Metaphysics*
*by which time sales exceeded forty million.*

*Today Everyman paperbacks remain true to*
*J. M. Dent's aims and high standards, with a wide rang*
*of titles at affordable prices in editions which address*
*the needs of today's readers. Each new text is reset to giv*
*a clear, elegant page and to incorporate the latest thinking*
*and scholarship. Each book carries the pilgrim logo,*
*the character in 'Everyman', a medieval mystery play,*
*a proud link between Everyman*
*past and present.*

# THE DISCOURSES
# OF EPICTETUS

*Edited by*
**CHRISTOPHER GILL**
*University of Exeter*

*Translation revised by*
**ROBIN HARD**

*Consultant Editor for this Volume*
**RICHARD STONEMAN**

**EVERYMAN**
J. M. DENT · LONDON
CHARLES E. TUTTLE
VERMONT

Introduction and other critical apparatus
© J. M. Dent 1995

*Moral Discourses* first included in Everyman in 1910
This edition first published in Everyman in 1995

21

J. M. Dent
Orion Publishing Group
Orion House
5 Upper St Martin's Lane
London WC2H 9EA
and
Tuttle Publishing
Airport Industrial Park, 364 Innovation Drive,
North Clarendon, VT 05759-9436, USA

Typeset in Sabon by CentraCet Ltd
Printed in Great Britain by
Clays Ltd, St Ives plc

British Library Cataloguing-in-Publication Data is available
upon request.

ISBN-13 978-0-4608-7312-3

www.orionbooks.co.uk

# CONTENTS

## THE DISCOURSES OF EPICTETUS

### BOOK I

# NOTE ON THE AUTHOR,
# EDITOR AND TRANSLATOR

EPICTETUS (c. AD 55–c. 135) was one of three men from whom significant writings on Stoic philosophy survive from the first to second centuries AD, the others being Seneca (c. 4 BC–AD 65) and Marcus Aurelius (AD 121–80). Unlike Seneca, adviser to the emperor Nero, and Marcus Aurelius, the emperor, Epictetus was born a slave, in Hieropolis in Phrygia (now Turkey), a Greek-speaking province of the Roman empire. He came to Rome and was the slave of Epaphroditus, an immensely powerful and wealthy freedman of Nero, who eventually gave Epictetus his freedom. While still a slave, Epictetus studied Stoic philosophy with Musonius Rufus, and became at some point a Stoic teacher himself in Rome. When the emperor Domitian banished philosophical teachers from Rome in AD 89, Epictetus set up a philosophical 'school' or study-centre in Nicopolis in Greece. Nicopolis, on the Adriatic coast, was on the main route between Rome and Athens; and many distinguished Greeks and Romans visited his school. One of these was Arrian (full name Lucius Flavianus Arrianus Xenophon), a Roman citizen from Bithynia who studied with Epictetus c. 107–9 before becoming a leading Roman politician and historian. He is best known for his histories of the campaigns of Alexander the Great. Epictetus wrote nothing; the *Discourses* are Arrian's written version of Epictetus' teachings. Epictetus' school became famous, the emperor Hadrian visited him, and Marcus Aurelius, after Epictetus' death, placed high value on his written teachings. Apart from his teachings, little is known of his life, except that he became crippled, probably from rheumatism, lived a life of great simplicity, and married at a late age to help bring up a child who would otherwise have been left to die.

CHRISTOPHER GILL is Reader in Ancient Thought at the University of Exeter. He has published widely on Greek and Roman philosophy and literature; his publications include *Plato: The*

*Story of Atlantis*, ed. (Duckworth, London, 1980), *The Person and the Human Mind: Issues in Ancient and Modern Philosophy*, ed. (Oxford University Press, Oxford, 1990), *The Self in Dialogue: Personality in Greek Epic, Tragedy, and Philosophy* (Oxford University Press, Oxford, 1996) and *The Structured Self in Hellenistic and Roman Thought* (Oxford University Press, 2006).

ROBIN HARD (PhD, Reading University, 1993) wrote his doctoral thesis on Plato, and is presently preparing a book on Diogenes the Cynic, and a translation of Apollodorus' *Library* for World's Classics (Oxford University Press, Oxford).

# CHRONOLOGY OF EPICTETUS' LIFE

Epictetus' birth and death dates are not known for certain; the only relatively definite date is his exile in 89. All dates are AD.

| Year | Age | Life |
| --- | --- | --- |
| 55 | | Epictetus born in Phrygia |
| 57 | 2 | |
| 59 | 4 | At dates unknown |
| 60 | 5 | Epictetus comes to Rome, becomes a slave of Epaphroditus, a powerful freedman of Nero, studies with Musonius Rufus, and is freed by Epaphroditus |
| 62 | 7 | |
| 65 | 10 | |
| 66 | 11 | |
| 68 | 13 | |
| 69 | 14 | |
| 70 | 15 | |

# CHRONOLOGY OF HIS TIMES

| Year | Literary and Intellectual Context (*Roman Empire*) | Historical Events (*Roman Empire*) |
|---|---|---|
| 54 | | Nero becomes emperor |
| 55 | Seneca writes *On Mercy* for Nero | |
| 57 | | Nero orders senators and knights to participate in his Games |
| 59 | | Nero murders his mother, Agrippina |
| 60 | Musonius Rufus goes into exile in Asia Minor (Turkey) | |
| 62 | Musonius Rufus returns to Rome | Seneca loses his position as Nero's adviser. Nero banishes his former wife Octavia (who is then murdered) and marries Poppaea Sabina |
| 65 | Musonius Rufus exiled to Gyaros | Conspiracy of Piso against Nero Plautius Lateranus, Seneca forced to commit suicide |
| 66 | | Thrasea Paetus executed; Helvidius Priscus exiled |
| 68 | Musonius Rufus returns to Rome | Nero deposed and commits suicide; Galba becomes emperor |
| 69 | | Year of Four Emperors: Galba, Otho, Vitellius, Vespasian |
| 70–9 | Musonius Rufus exiled again at some point | |

| Year | Age | Life |
|------|-----|------|
| 79 | 24 | |
| 80 | 25 | |
| 81 | 26 | |
| 89 | 34 | Epictetus exiled: goes to Nicopolis in Greece and sets up school |
| 96 | 41 | |
| 98 | 43 | |
| 100 | 45 | |
| c. 107–9 | 52–4 | Arrian studies with Epictetus in Nicopolis |
| 113 | 58 | |
| 115 | 60 | At date unknown |
| 117 | 62 | Epictetus marries to help bring up an orphan child |
| 120 | 65 | |
| 121 | 66 | |
| 126 | 71 | |
| 135 | 80 | Epictetus dies |

| Year | Literary and Intellectual Context (Roman Empire) | Historical Events (Roman Empire) |
|---|---|---|
| 79 | Pliny the Elder dies | Vespasian dies; Titus becomes emperor. Vesuvius erupts |
| after 79 | Musonius Rufus returns to Rome | |
| 80–100 | Gospels of Matthew, Luke written | |
| 81 | | Titus dies; Domitian becomes emperor |
| c. 89 | Arrian born | Domitian banishes philosophers from Rome |
| 96 | | Domitian assassinated; Nerva becomes emperor |
| 98 | | Nerva dies; Trajan becomes emperor |
| c. 100 | Musonius Rufus dies | |
| c. 113 | Pliny the Younger dies | |
| c. 115 | Dio Chrysostom dies | |
| 117 | | Trajan dies; Hadrian becomes emperor |
| 120 | Tacitus dies; Lucian born | |
| 121 | | Marcus Aurelius born |
| 126 | Plutarch dies | |
| 138 | | Hadrian dies; Antoninus Pius, father of Marcus Aurelius, becomes emperor |
| 140 | | Marcus Aurelius holds consulship for first time |

This chronological table is based on those in *The Cambridge Ancient History*, vols 10 and 11 (Cambridge University Press, Cambridge, 1934, 1936)

# INTRODUCTION

1 Epictetus was one of the best-known Stoic philosophers in the priod of the Roman empire. His teachings, preserved by Arrian, combine compelling directness with moral rigour in a way that has commanded interest from his own day to the present. He aims to provide philosophically based guidance on fundamental human problems. Above all, he gives forceful expression to the Stoic view of how to confront pain, disaster, and death without loss of peace of mind.

## The Form and Purpose of the 'Discourses'

2 All the writings in this volume are based on Arrian's versions of Epictetus' philosophical teachings. Four books of *Discourses* (Greek title *Diatribai*) survive intact (out of at least eight thought to have been written by Arrian). The *Handbook* (Greek title *Encheiridion*) is a selection by Arrian of extracts from these versions of Epictetus' teachings; about half of them are drawn, with small modifications, from the four surviving books of *Discourses*. The *Fragments* are short passages drawn from other ancient works, which also seem to derive from Arrian's writings.

3 Arrian tells us why he prepared these writings in the letter which was attached in ancient times as a preface to the *Discourses* (p. 1 below). Despite what he says there, they are probably not word-for-word reports of specific conversations, but rather Arrian's own attempts to recreate the characteristic form and style of Epictetus' mode of teaching. They are written in *koine*, the everyday Greek used widely throughout the eastern part of the Roman empire at this time, rather than in the educated Greek used by Arrian in his other works. The compressed, jagged and urgent style, punctuated by commands and questions, is also unlike Arrian's style elsewhere, and is clearly designed to let readers hear Epictetus' own voice.[1]

**4** Epictetus presumably offered formal instruction in logic, physics and ethics, which were seen by the Stoics as three interconnected branches of philosophical study. His discourses refer to the writings of Zeno (334–262 BC), Cleanthes (331–232 BC), and Chrysippus (c. 280–c. 206 BC), the Greek thinkers who laid the basis of Stoicism as a systematic philosophy. But the *Discourses* are not based on this type of formal instruction. They represent half-formal talks, sermons or counselling sessions, in which Epictetus summed up the practical implications of living a life shaped by Stoic ethical principles. These talks were given in the school, but visitors are sometimes presented as taking part, consulting Epictetus or being questioned by him; so they constitute semi-public forms of discourse, tackling ethical issues relevant to all human beings.[2]

**5** All Greek and Roman thinkers saw ethical philosophy as designed, ultimately, to have a practical effect, that of helping people to lead better lives; and some of them developed special types of discourse to draw out the practical implications of their philosophy. Socrates (469–399 BC), the first Greek thinker to focus wholly on ethics, used a unique method of systematic cross-examination, by which he induced his partners in dialogue to rethink the beliefs on which they based their lives.[3] The character and teaching-method of Socrates served as an ideal for many ancient thinkers. These included the Cynics, the first of whom was Diogenes (c. 400–c. 325 BC), who rejected conventional lifestyles and lived as street-teachers or preachers, communicating their ethical message in public places. The Cynic lecture or 'diatribe' used vivid examples, quotations and pointed sarcasm to convey its ethical message. Epictetus presents both Socrates and the Cynic teachers as ideal figures, and his *Discourses* ('Diatribes' in Greek) are clearly inspired by the Cynic and Socratic modes of teaching. But Epictetus' discourses also reflect the systematic and dogmatic character of Stoic philosophy; they state and restate a limited set of key themes in a powerful, reiterative manner.[4]

**6** In the Hellenistic Age (323–31 BC) and under the Roman empire (31 BC onwards), ancient philosophers often drew an analogy between ethical philosophy (in its practical role) and medicine. For instance, Philo (c. 110–c. 79 BC) subdivides practical ethics into protreptic (persuading someone to engage in philosophy), therapy (removing the false beliefs which cause distress), and advice (giving instructions about how to live), and compares each of these functions to aspects of the work of the doctor.[5] If we apply this framework to Epictetus, most of the discourses count as therapy (doing what Philo calls 'removing beliefs which cause disease in the critical faculties of the mind and implanting healthy beliefs') and advice (providing instructions about what counts as a 'healthy' life). In ancient philosophy, the use of the medical analogy is typically combined with the assumption that it is the doctor of the mind and not the patient who is competent to decide what counts as sickness and health. It is also combined with the idea that the crucial factor in gaining health of the mind (i.e. happiness, *eudaimonia* in Greek) lies in forming a correct understanding of the proper goal of human life, which can then shape the whole pattern of a person's beliefs, emotions and desires. Epictetus' discourses are clearly designed to be 'therapeutic' or 'advisory' in a way that reflects this understanding of philosophy as the medicine of the mind.[6]

## Epictetus and Stoicism

7 Stoic philosophy had a long history (from the early third century BC onwards), and, although there was a clearly defined overall framework, different thinkers took up different positions within this framework. Epictetus is a generally orthodox Stoic, maintaining the standpoint of the three founders of Stoicism: Zeno, Cleanthes and Chrysippus. He also offers a relatively tough, idealistic version of orthodox Stoicism.[7] His attitude comes out clearly if we look at his views on human freedom and responsibility, on what is valuable, and on doing appropriate acts:

8 Some things are up to us and others are not. Up to us are opinion, impulse, desire, aversion and, in a word, whatever is our own action. Not up to us are body, property, reputation, office and, in a word, whatever are not our own actions.

(*Handbook* 1)

No theme is more emphasized in Epictetus than that our actions are 'up to us'. In claiming this, Epictetus takes for granted the following model of human psychology. All animals (human and non-human) are motivated by 'impressions' or 'appearances' (*phantasiai*), but those of rational animals (human beings) differ in two ways from those of non-rational animals. One is that the rational impression has 'propositional content', that is, a meaning which can be expressed in a statement, such as 'this act is right'. The other is that the impression requires 'assent' (*sunkatathesis*, literally 'saying yes') before it stimulates the impulse to action (*horme*).[8] Assuming this model, Epictetus emphasizes these two ideas: (1) that, as rational animals, we can examine the content of our impressions; (2) that we can and should withhold 'assent' ('saying yes') to our impressions until we are sure that they are correct. These human capacities constitute our capacity for choice (*prohairesis*), make it 'up to us' (*eph' hemin*) how we act, and thus give us the kind of 'freedom' that only rational animals can have.[9]

**9** Epictetus' insistence that our actions are 'up to us' (like other Stoic expressions of this idea) seems to be open to a major criticism. It seems to be inconsistent with the Stoic belief that all events are determined by a seamless web of causes, sometimes called 'fate'. The early Stoic Chrysippus responded to this problem by distinguishing between 'internal' and 'external' causes. The internal cause of human actions was the capacity to assent (or not to assent) to impressions; and, in so far as we have this capacity, our actions are still 'up to us'. However, Chrysippus acknowledged that the way in which we form impressions and give assent is itself partly caused by external factors (including upbringing and social influences); and to that extent our characters, which determine our actions, are not fully up to us.[10]

**10** Because of the non-technical, practical nature of Epictetus' discourses, these issues are not examined analytically, as they are in more theoretical Stoic writings. But it is possible to see a response to this problem implied in Epictetus' practical advice. In general, he accepts that people tend to give assent in a way that reflects their (typically misguided) impressions. Thus Medea, for instance, acted in line with her (misguided) impression that it was more important to take revenge on her husband than to spare the lives of her children (*Discourses* 1.28.5–7). (All further references in this Introduction not otherwise identified are to the books, chapters and paragraphs of the

*Discourses.*) But Epictetus' repeated theme is that we can and should examine and modify the impressions that we form: for instance, by redescribing situations to ourselves (1.12.20–1; 4.4.26–8). To be human is to be capable, in principle, of 'using' impressions correctly, and of 'attending' to the way we use them (1.1.7, 12–13; 1.6.13; 2.18.24–6). His claim, in effect, is that we can, at least, rehearse, practise and 'make progress' towards the point where our impressions and assent are completely correct and fully virtuous (1.4.18–21). To this extent, all that is important about our actions (i.e. whether they express virtuous choice) is, after all, 'up to us'.[11]

11 Epictetus sometimes expresses this idea in the form of the statement that 'the god' or 'the gods' have given human beings the power to examine, and make correct use of, their impressions (1.1.7, 17; 1.6.13; 2.1.1–8). Elsewhere, he stresses the importance of recognizing that everything which happens and which is not 'up to us' is subject to the wishing and planning of 'the god' or 'Zeus'; and that a key part of human rationality lies in recognizing this truth (4.4.29–48). He does not have in mind the gods of conventional Greek and Roman religion, but rather the god of Stoic theory, who stands for the order and rationality that are inherent in the universe. The Stoics maintain that everything that happens is an expression of the providential rationality of this (non-personal) god, and that everything works out 'for the best', even if it is not obvious to human beings how this is so. Epictetus stresses the point that it is a key part of our human rationality to accept that this is so, and that making this response is 'up to us', even when the events concerned are not 'up to us' (1.6.37–43; 2.10.5–6; fragment 4).[12]

12 We can also see in Epictetus' discourses (despite their non-technical character and practical orientation) signs of a distinct position on other subjects of debate in Stoic philosophy. The central Stoic ethical claim is that virtue is the only thing that is really good, the only proper object of choice, and that it alone constitutes human happiness. The other so-called 'good things' of human life, such as health, wealth and social position, are 'matters of indifference' (*adiaphora*) by contrast with the supreme value of virtue. However, this claim is also typically combined with the idea that the other so-called 'good things' are at least 'preferable' (*proegmena*), and that their opposites,

such as sickness and poverty, are non-preferable (*apoproegmena*). Also, the process of 'selection' between 'indifferents' is generally presented as ethically valid in itself and as a means of 'making progress' towards the development of virtue (or 'wisdom', the Stoic norm of virtue). Some Stoic writings of a practical kind – such as Cicero's *On Duties*, based on a work by Panaetius (*c.* 185–*c.* 110 BC) – emphasize the importance of the process of selection between indifferents, and its role in acquiring virtue, and offer detailed advice about this.[13] In Epictetus, this theme shrinks into insignificance. He focuses almost wholly on the stark contrast between virtue, which depends on assent and choice, and is fully 'up to us', and the indifferents (which are presented, emphatically, as 'matters of indifference'), which are not 'up to us' and which are described as mere 'externals'.[14]

13 Epictetus makes a similar move regarding another set of distinctions. It is standard Stoic doctrine that people make progress towards virtue by performing 'appropriate acts' (*kathekonta*), including acts which are in line with conventional rules about fulfilling the roles of family and communal life. But they draw a sharp distinction between the ethical status of an appropriate act performed by an imperfect person (*kathekon*) and that of a completely right act performed by a perfectly wise person (*katorthoma*). Also, they do not think that any rules can be laid down (except perhaps by the wise themselves) for the performance of such perfect acts.[15]

14 Epictetus also sometimes emphasizes the importance of performing appropriate actions, as a crucial part of making progress towards virtue (3.2),[16] and advises that we take notice of what is required by the family and social roles (*prosopa*) that we possess (2.10.7–13; *Handbook* 30). However, he also emphasizes the ethical limitations of this criterion: the good (virtue) must sometimes be put before family ties, or at least must determine how we respond to these ties (3.3.5–10). He also sometimes presents the roles of family and communal life as, in effect, just a means of training ourselves to become perfectly wise, rather than as being ethically significant in themselves. The only role that really matters is that of the human being (*anthropos*), taken to be the ideal, fully virtuous human being. Epictetus uses exemplars such as Socrates, the

figure of the Cynic teacher, or political 'martyrs', like Helvidius Priscus, to represent this ideal role (1.2; 2.10, 14–23; 3.22). Again, as in the case of the distinction between virtue and 'indifferents', the effect of this move is to give a picture of ethical life as a series of stark contrasts. To live the properly 'human' life is to act as if we were wise (or at least to rehearse for this), by focusing wholly on what is 'up to us' and thus within the scope of virtue (1.4.18–20). By contrast, the side of ethical life discussed in Cicero's On Duties 1–2, the selection of 'preferable things' in line with conventional social rules and roles, is given much less emphasis by Epictetus.[17]

## The Influence of Epictetus

15 Epictetus' austere moralism and his idealistic self-concern have attracted interest from Antiquity to the present day. He was a major influence on the thought and style of Marcus Aurelius' Stoic philosophical diary (Meditations) and was regarded as a significant thinker by leading intellectuals of the second century AD such as Gellius and Lucian. The Neoplatonist philosopher Simplicius (sixth century AD) wrote a substantial commentary on the Handbook.[18]

16 Although Epictetus wrote at a time when Christianity was becoming well known in the Roman empire, his thinking is in no way influenced by this.[19] However, his severe idealism attracted early Church Fathers such as Clement of Alexandria, Origen and John Chrysostom. The Handbook was twice adopted with small modifications by medieval Christian ascetics as a guide to the self-scrutiny and discipline of monastic life. The references to the Stoic idea of god seem to have been reinterpreted in the light of the Judaeo-Christian idea of God as a person.[20] A later period of significant influence is that of the sixteenth and seventeenth centuries; those influenced include the Flemish Neo-Stoic Justus Lipsius as well as the French essayists Montaigne and Pascal. In the nineteenth century, Epictetus attracted the admiration of Matthew Arnold in Britain; and in the early twentieth century the inclusion of selections of Epictetus in two well-known American anthologies gave his thought a certain currency there.[21] The apparent similarity between his attitudes and American ethical individualism

(shaped partly by Protestant Christianity) may have helped to give his work added appeal in the USA.

17 Epictetus' practically orientated mode of writing and his unambiguous moral stance have attracted politicians and military figures, including Frederick the Great and, recently, the US Admiral James Stockdale, who has acknowledged Epictetus' influence in helping him to maintain inner strength and continuing resistance as a prisoner of war in the Vietnam War.[22] Michel Foucault has presented Epictetus' 'care of the soul', alongside Christian practices of self-scrutiny (which, as noted earlier, Epictetus helped to shape), as anticipating modern practices of self-analysis such as those of psychoanalysis.[23] Among contemporary academics, A. A. Long, a leading scholar of Hellenistic philosophy, also sees Epictetus' focus on the internal structure of human agency as marking a new level of awareness of what we call 'the self'.[24] Current interest in Hellenistic and Roman philosophy, and especially in practical ethics and the philosophical therapy of the emotions, gives Epictetus' therapeutic discourses renewed importance in academic life at the present time.

CHRISTOPHER GILL

## Bibliographical References to the Introduction

The Discourses are referred to by book, chapter and paragraph alone. All other ancient and modern references are identified. The following books are referred to in these notes by author and date alone; all other scholarly references are given in full form.

W. A. Oldfather, Epictetus: The Discourses, with a translation. Loeb Classical Library, 2 vols (Harvard University Press, Cambridge, Mass., 1946).

A. A. Long, 'Epictetus and Marcus Aurelius', in J. Luce, ed., Ancient Writers: Greece and Rome (Charles Scribner's Sons, New York, 1982), 985–1002; to be reprinted in A. A. Long, Stoic Studies (Cambridge University Press, Cambridge).

A. A. Long and D. N. Sedley, The Hellenistic Philosophers, 2 vols (Cambridge University Press, Cambridge, 1987) [= LS; numbers denote sections].

A. A. Long, ed., *Problems in Stoicism* (Athlone Press, London, 1971).

S. Everson, ed., *Psychology*. Companions to Ancient Thought, 2 (Cambridge University Press, Cambridge, 1991).

B. Inwood, *Ethics and Human Action in Early Stoicism* (Oxford University Press, Oxford, 1985).

J. M. Rist, ed., *The Stoics* (University of California Press, Berkeley, 1978).

M. Burnyeat, ed., *The Skeptical Tradition* (University of California Press, Berkeley, 1983)

## Notes to the Introduction

1 *See* P. A. Stadter, *Arrian of Nicomedia* (University of North Carolina Press, Chapel Hill, 1980), ch. 2, esp. 26–8.

2 *See* Oldfather (1946), Introd., xiii–xiv.

3 On Socrates, *see* W. K. C. Guthrie, *A History of Greek Philosophy*, vol. 3, part 2 (Cambridge University Press, Cambridge, 1971); G. Vlastos, *Socrates: Ironist and Moral Philosopher* (Cambridge University Press, Cambridge, 1991); and, on his questioning-method, G. Vlastos, 'The Socratic Elenchus', *Oxford Studies in Ancient Philosophy* 1 (1983), 27–58. *See also* A. A. Long, 'Socrates in Hellenistic Philosophy', *Classical Quarterly* 38 (1988), 150–71,

4 On Cynics and Stoicism, *see* J. M. Rist, *Stoic Philosophy* (Cambridge University Press, Cambridge, 1969), ch. 4; on the structure of Epictetus' discourses and their relationship to the Cynic diatribe, see Long (1982), 990–3, 995–6.

5 *See* John Stobaeus, *Anthologium*, ed. C. Wachsmuth (Berlin, 1958), vol. 2, 39–41; I am grateful to Malcolm Schofield for drawing my attention to this passage.

6 *See* C. Gill, 'Ancient Psychotherapy', *Journal of the History of Ideas* 46 (1985), 307–25, esp. 320–2. For the analogy between philosophy and therapy in Epictetus, see, e.g., 3.21.20; 3.23.27–32.

7 See F. H. Sandbach, *The Stoics* (Cambridge, 1975), esp. 164–70; also A. Bonhöffer, *Epiktet und die Stoa* (Frommann, Stuttgart, 1968), and *Die Ethik des Stoikers Epictet* (Frommann, Stuttgart, 1968).

8 See LS 33C and 33I; Inwood (1985), ch. 3; C. Gill, 'Is There a Concept of Person in Greek Philosophy?', in Everson (1991), ch. 9, esp. 185–8.

9 On *prohairesis*, see 1.1, esp. 7–13, 23; 1.12.9–12; 1.22.10; 3.5.7; on the use of impressions, see paras 10–11 of introduction. Epictetus' conception of *prohairesis* ('capacity for choice') is sometimes compared to the modern idea of the 'will': *see*, e.g., C. Kahn, 'Discovering the Will', in J. M. Dillon and A. A. Long, eds, *The Question of Eclecticism: Studies in Later Greek Philosophy* (University of California Press, Berkeley, 1988), ch. 9, esp. 252–5. It is perhaps better compared to contemporary philosophical ideas about human beings as motivated by 'reasons'; *see* Gill (ref. in n. 8 above). *See also* R. Dobbin, '*Prohairesis* in Epictetus', *Ancient Philosophy* 11.1 (1991), 111–35.

10 See LS 62C and D; also A. A. Long, 'Freedom and Determinism in the Stoic Theory of Human Action', in Long (1971), ch. 8; and C. Stough, 'Stoic Determinism and Moral Responsibility', in Rist (1978), ch. 9.

11 See A. A. Long, 'Representation and the Self in Stoicism', in Everson (1991), ch. 6, esp. 111–20.

12 On Stoic ideas about god, *see* LS 54; and Cicero, *On the Nature of the Gods* 2–3. On Epictetus' ideas on god and human freedom, *see* D. E. Hahm, 'A Neglected Stoic Argument for Human Responsibility', *Illinois Classical Studies* 17 (1992), 23–48, esp. 39–42.

13 See LS 58 and 63; Cicero, *On Duties*, ed. and tr. M. T. Griffin and E. M. Atkins (Cambridge University Press, Cambridge, 1991); and I. G. Kidd, 'Stoic Intermediates and the End for Man', in Long (1971), ch. 7.

14 *See*, e.g. 1.1, and *Handbook* 1.

15 See LS 59; also Kidd (ref. in n. 13 above); and G. B. Kerferd, 'What Does the Wise Man Know?', in Rist (1978), ch. 5.

16 In 3.2.1–4, paying attention to appropriate actions is presented as an integral element in a threefold programme of ethical training; *see also* 1.4.11; 3.12.12–15.

17 *See* C. Gill, 'Personhood and Personality: The Four-*Personae* Theory in Cicero, *De Officiis* I', *Oxford Studies in Ancient Philosophy* 6 (1988), 169–99, esp. 187–92.

18 *See* R. B. Rutherford, *The Meditations of Marcus Aurelius: A Study* (Oxford University Press, Oxford, 1989), ch. 6; Oldfather (1946), xxvii.

19 Epictetus refers, glancingly, to Jews (2.9.19–21) and Galileans (4.7.6), apparently meaning Christians. But there is no sign of Christian influence in his thought: *see* A. Bonhöffer, *Epiktet und das Neue Testament* (Töpelmann, Giessen, 1911).

20 *See* M. Spanneut, article on 'Epiktet', in T. Klauser, ed., *Reallexikon für Antike und Christentum* (Hiersemann, Stuttgart, 1962), vol. 5, 599–681, esp. 633–41, 647–50, 664–7.

21 *See* Oldfather (1946), xxvii–xxix; Long (1982), 985.

22 J. B. Stockdale, 'Courage under Fire: Testing Epictetus' Doctrines in a Laboratory of Human Behavior', text of a speech given at King's College, London, 15 November 1993, Hoover Essays, 6 (Hoover Institution, Stanford University, Stanford, 1993); *see also* J. B. and S. Stockdale, *In Love and War* (US Naval Institute Press, Annapolis, 1991), J. B. Stockdale, *Thoughts of a Philosophical Fighter Pilot* (Hoover Institution Press, Stanford, California, 1995).

23 M. Foucault, in L. H. Martin, H. Gutman and H. Hutton, eds, *Technologies of the Self* (University of Massachusetts Press, Amherst, 1988), 37–8.

24 Long (*see* n. 11 above).

# NOTE ON THE TEXT

The translation of Epictetus in this edition is based on Elizabeth Carter's translation of 1758 (Everyman edition, J. M. Dent, London and New York, 1910, reprinted 1926). This has been extensively revised by Robin Hard, following, except in a few minor points, the Greek text printed in the Loeb Classical Library edition (Greek text with English translation) prepared by W. A. Oldfather (Harvard University Press, Cambridge, Mass., 1925, reprinted 1946). Oldfather's Greek text is based substantially on that of H. Schenkl (second edition, Teubner, Leipzig, 1916). The fragments given here are those included by Schenkl. These have been generally accepted by scholars as the ones most likely to be based on Arrian's account of Epictetus. This selection differs significantly from that of Elizabeth Carter.

# DISCOURSES

---

## Arrian to Lucius Gellius, greeting

*I did not write these discourses of Epictetus as a literary composition, in the way that one normally writes works of such a kind, nor did I myself release them to the public, for, as I say, it was not my intention to write a book. Rather, I tried to note down whatever I heard him say, so far as possible in his own words, to preserve reminders for myself in future days of his cast of mind, and frankness of speech. These are, then, as you would expect, the kind of discourses that one person would address to another as the moment demands, and not such as he would compose formally for people to read in the future. And being of such a nature, they have, I know not how, fallen without my consent or knowledge into the hands of the general public. Yet to me it is no great matter if I shall be thought incapable of writing a proper book, and to Epictetus it will not matter in the slightest if anyone views his discourses with disdain, since at the time he was actually delivering them it was plain that his single aim was to move the minds of his listeners towards what is best. So if these present discourses should achieve that effect they would be having, I believe, precisely the effect that a philosopher's discourses ought to have; but if they fail to do so, those who read them should understand that when Epictetus himself delivered them his listener was induced to feel just what Epictetus wanted him to feel. If, however, the words on their own fail to accomplish this, perhaps the fault lies with me, or perhaps that must inevitably be the case.*

*Farewell*

# BOOK I

# CHAPTER I

# On What Is In Our Power, And What Is Not

1. Of the arts and faculties in general, you will find none that contemplates, and consequently approves or disapproves, itself.
2. How far does the contemplative power of grammar extend?

As far as the judging of language.

Of music?

As far as the judging of melody.

3. Does either of them contemplate itself, then?

By no means.

Thus, when you are writing to a friend, grammar will tell you that this is the way you should write: but whether or not you are to write to your friend at all, grammar will not tell you. The same is true of music, with regard to melodies; but whether it be proper or improper at any particular time to sing or play the lyre, music will not tell you.

4. What will tell you, then?

The faculty which contemplates both itself and all other things.

And what is that?

The reasoning faculty; for that alone of the faculties that we have received comprehends both itself – what it is, what it is capable of, and with what valuable powers it has come to us – and all the other faculties likewise. 5. For what else is it that tells us gold is beautiful? For the gold itself does not tell us. Evidently the faculty that can deal with impressions. 6. What else distinguishes grammar, and the other arts or faculties, and inspects the use that is made of them, and points to the proper occasions for their use?

Nothing but this.

7. It was fitting, then, that the gods have placed this alone in our own power, the most excellent faculty of all which rules all the others, the power to deal rightly with our impressions, whilst all the others they have not placed in our power. 8. Was it

indeed because they did not want to? I rather think, that if they could, they would have entrusted us with those also: but there was no way in which they could. 9. For seeing that we are on earth, and confined to an earthly body, and amongst earthly companions, how was it possible that in these respects we should not be hindered by external things?

10. But what says Zeus? 'Oh Epictetus, if it were possible, I would have made this poor body and property of yours free, and not liable to hindrance. 11. But as things are, you must not forget that this body is not your own, but only cleverly moulded clay. 12. Since, then, I could not give you this, I have given you a certain portion of myself, this faculty of exerting the impulse to act and not to act, and desire and aversion, and, in a word, making proper use of impressions. If you attend to this, and place all that you have in its care, you will never be restrained, never be hindered; you will not groan, will not find fault, will not flatter any man. 13. Well then, do all these advantages seem small to you?' Heaven forbid! 'Are you then satisfied with them?' I pray so to the gods.

14. But as it is, although it is in our power to take care of one thing alone, and devote ourselves to that, we choose instead to take care of many, and to encumber ourselves with many; body, property, brother, friend, child, and slave; 15. and being thus bound to a multiplicity of things we are burdened by them and dragged down. 16. Thus, when the weather does not happen to be fair for sailing, we sit fussing ourselves, and perpetually looking out. – Which wind is blowing? – The north wind. – What have we to do with that? – When will the west blow? – When itself, friend, or Aeolus pleases; for Zeus has not made you dispenser of the winds, but Aeolus.

17. What, then, is to be done?

To make the best of what is in our power, and take the rest as it naturally happens.

And how is that?

As god pleases.

18. What, am I to be beheaded now, and on my own?

Why, would you have all the world, then, lose their heads for your consolation? 19. Are you not willing to stretch out your neck, like Lateranus at Rome, when Nero ordered him to be beheaded? For he stretched out his neck and took the blow, but when that blow was too weak, after shrinking back for a moment, he stretched out his neck again. 20. And, before that, when Epaphroditus, the freedman of Nero, approached somebody and asked him why he was in conflict with the emperor, he said, 'If I have a mind to say anything, I will tell it to your master.'

21. What, then, should we have at hand upon such occasions? Why, what else than to know what is mine, and what is not mine, what is within my power, and what is not? 22. – I must die: and must I die groaning too? – Be fettered. Must it be lamenting too? – Exiled. Can anyone prevent me, then, from going with a smile and good cheer and serenity? – 'Betray the secret.' 23. – I will not betray it; for this is in my own power. – 'Then I will fetter you.' – What are you saying, man? Fetter *me*? You will fetter my leg; but not even Zeus himself can get the better of my choice. 24. 'I will cast you into prison.' My wretched body, rather. 'I will behead you.' Did I ever tell you, that I alone had a head that cannot be cut off? 25. – These are the things that philosophers ought to study; it is these that they should write about each day; and it is in these that they should exercise themselves.

26. Thrasea used to say, 'I would rather be killed today than banished tomorrow.' 27. How, then, did Rufus answer him? 'If you prefer that as the heavier misfortune, how foolish a preference! If as the lighter, who has put it in your power? Why do you not study to be contented with what is allotted to you?'

28. And so, what was it that Agrippinus used to say? 'I will not become an obstacle to myself.' News was brought to him: 'Your case is being tried in the Senate.' 29. – 'May good fortune attend it. But the fifth hour has arrived' (the hour when he used to exercise and have his cold bath): 'let us go off and take our exercise.' 30. When he had taken his exercise someone came and told him, 'You are condemned.' To exile, he asked, or death? 'To exile.' – What of my property? – 'It is not confiscated.' – Well, then, let us go to Aricia, and eat our meal there.

31. This is what it means to have studied what one ought to study; to have rendered one's desires and aversions incapable of being restrained, or incurred. 32. I must die. If instantly, I will die instantly; if in a short time, I will dine first, since the hour for dining is here, and when the time comes, then I will die. How? As becomes a person who is giving back what is not his own.

## CHAPTER 2

# How Is One To Preserve One's True Character In Everything?

1. To a rational creature, only what is contrary to reason is unendurable: but everything rational he can endure. 2. Blows are not by nature unendurable. – 'How so?' – See how the Spartans bear a whipping, after they have learned that it is a reasonable thing. 3. 'But to be hanged – is that not unendurable?' Even so, when a man feels that it is reasonable, he goes off and hangs himself. 4. In short, we shall find by observation, that by nothing is the rational creature so distressed as by the irrational, and, conversely, to nothing is he so drawn as to the rational.

5. But it happens that these concepts of rational and irrational, as well as good and bad, and advantageous and disadvantageous, mean different things to different people. 6. This is the principal reason why we need an education, to teach us to apply our preconceptions of rational and irrational to particular cases in accordance with nature. 7. But to judge what is rational and irrational, we make use not only of a due estimation of the value of external things, but of what relates to each person's particular character. 8. Thus, it is reasonable to one man to hold another's chamber-pot for him, since he considers only that if he does not submit to this, he will be beaten and lose his dinner, whereas if he does hold it, he will have nothing harsh or distressing to suffer; 9. whilst to some other man it appears insupportable, not merely to hold the pot himself, but to allow anyone else to do so. 10. If you ask me, then, 'Shall I hold the pot or not?', I will tell you, it is a more valuable thing to get a dinner than not; and a greater disgrace to be given a thrashing than not to be: so that, if you measure yourself by these things, go off and hold the pot.

11. 'Yes, but that would be beneath me.'

It is you who are to consider that, not I: for it is you who know yourself, and what value you set upon yourself, and at what rate you sell yourself: for different people sell themselves at different prices.

12. Hence Agrippinus, when Florus was considering whether he should go to Nero's shows, so as to perform some part in them himself, said to him, 'Go.' 13. – 'So why do you not go yourself?' said Florus. 'Because', replied Agrippinus, 'I do not even consider doing so.' 14. For as soon as a person even considers such questions, comparing and calculating the values of external things, he draws close to those who have lost all sense of their proper character. 15. Now what are you asking me? 'Is death to be preferred, or life?' I answer, life. 16. 'Pain or pleasure?' I answer, pleasure. – 'But if I do not act a part in the tragedy, I shall lose my head.' 17. Go and act it then, but I for my part will not. – 'Why?' – Because you regard yourself as just a single thread of the many that make up the garment. – 'And then?' – You should give thought as to how you can be like all other men, as one thread desires not to be distinguished from the others. 18. But I want to be the purple, that small and shining band, which gives lustre and beauty to all the rest. Why do you bid me resemble the multitude, then? In that case, how shall I still be the purple?

19. Helvidius Priscus saw this too, and acted accordingly: for when Vespasian had sent word to him not to attend the Senate, he answered, 'It is in your power not to allow me to be a senator; but as long as I am one, I must attend.' 20. – 'Well, then, if you do attend, at least be silent.' – 'Do not ask for my opinion, and I will be silent.' – 'But I must ask it.' – 'And I must say what seems right to me.' 21. – 'But if you do, I will put you to death.' – 'Did I ever tell you that I was immortal? You will do your part, and I mine: It is yours to kill, and mine to die without trembling; yours to banish me, mine to depart without grieving.'

22. What good, then, did Priscus do, who was but a single person? Why, what good does the purple do to the cloak? What else than standing out in it as purple, and setting a fine example to others? 23. Another man perhaps, if Caesar had told him in such circumstances not to go to the Senate, would have said, 'I am obliged to you for excusing me.' 24. But Caesar would not have tried to prevent such a man from going in the first place, well knowing that either he would sit there like a jug or, if he spoke, he would say what he knew Caesar wanted him to say, and then pile on still more.

25. In this manner also did a certain athlete act, who was in

danger of dying unless his genitals were amputated. His brother, who was a philosopher, came to him and said, 'Well, brother, what do you intend to do? Are we going to cut this part of you off, and return again to the gymnasium?' He would not submit to that, and awaited his death with courage.

26. Someone asked: 'How was it that he did so? As an athlete or as a philosopher?' As a man, said Epictetus; but as a man who had contended at Olympia and been proclaimed a victor; who had spent a good deal of time in such places, and not merely been rubbed with oil in Bato's training-school. 27. Yet another person would have had his very head cut off, if he could have lived without it. 28. This is what I mean by respect for one's true character; and such is its power with those who have acquired the habit of deliberately introducing this consideration when examining how they should behave.

29. 'Come now, Epictetus, shave off your beard.' – If I am a philosopher, I answer, I will not shave it off. – 'Then I will have you beheaded.' – If it will do you any good, behead me.

30. Somebody asked, 'How shall each of us perceive what is appropriate to his true character?' How is it, replied Epictetus, that the bull alone, when the lion attacks, is aware of its own powers, and puts itself forward to protect the entire herd? Is it not clear that the possession of these powers is at the same time accompanied by an awareness of them also? 31. And with us, too, whoever has such powers will not be ignorant of them. 32. But neither a bull nor a noble-spirited man comes to be what he is all at once: he must undertake hard winter training, and prepare himself, and not propel himself rashly into what is not appropriate to him.

33. Only consider at what price you sell your own will and choice, man: if for nothing else, that you may not sell it cheap. But what is great and exceptional perhaps belongs to others, to Socrates and those who resemble him.

34. Why, then, if we are born to this, do not all or many of us become like him?

Why, do all horses become swift? Are all dogs keen at the scent? 35. What, then: because I am not naturally gifted, shall I neglect all care of myself? Heaven forbid! 36. Epictetus will not be better than Socrates; but if I am not worse, that is enough for me. 37. I shall never be a Milo, and yet I do not neglect my body; nor a Croesus, and yet I do not neglect my property: nor, in general, do we cease to take pains in any area, because we despair of arriving at the highest degree of perfection.

## CHAPTER 3

# What Should We Conclude From The Principle That God Is The Father Of Mankind?

1. If a person could be persuaded of this principle as he ought, that we are all first of all children of god, and that god is the father of gods and men, I think that he would never conceive a single abject or ignoble thought about himself. 2. Now if Caesar were to adopt you, there would be no bearing your haughty looks: so will you not be elated on knowing yourself to be the son of Zeus? 3. Yet, in fact, we are not elated; but since in our birth we have these two elements mingled within us, a body in common with the animals, and reason and intelligence in common with the gods, many of us incline towards the former kinship, miserable as it is and wholly mortal, and only some few to the divine and blessed one. 4. And since of necessity every man must deal with each thing according to the opinion that he holds about it, those few who think they are born to fidelity, and honour, and a securely grounded use of their impressions, will harbour no abject or ignoble thought about themselves, whilst the multitude will think the opposite. 5. 'For what am I? A poor miserable man', they say, and 'This poor wretched flesh of mine.' 6. Wretched indeed. But you have something better too than this paltry flesh. So why do you cast that aside and hold fast to what is mortal?

7. Because of this kinship with the mortal, some of us deviate towards it to become like wolves, faithless and treacherous and noxious; others, like lions, wild and savage and untamed; but most of us become like foxes, the most roguish of living creatures. 8. For what else is a slanderous and ill-natured man than a fox, or something yet more wretched and mean? 9. Look, then, and take care that you do not become one of these roguish creatures.

## CHAPTER 4

# On Progress

1. The man who is making progress, having learned from the philosophers, that desire has good things for its object, and aversion bad things, and having also learned that peace of mind and serenity can only be attained by a man if he achieves what he desires and does not fall into what he wants to avoid – such a man has either rid himself of desire altogether or put it off to another time, and applies aversion only to things that are within the sphere of choice. 2. For if he should try to avoid anything that lies outside the sphere of choice, he knows that he will sometimes fall into it despite his aversion, and be unhappy. 3. Now if virtue promises happiness, an untroubled mind and serenity, then progress towards virtue is certainly progress towards each of these. 4. For whatever is the definitive end to which the perfection of a thing leads, progress is always an approach towards it.

5. How does it happen, then, that when we agree that virtue is something of this kind, we yet seek progress, and show it off, in other things? What does virtue achieve?

Peace of mind.

6. Who is making progress, then? The person who has read many treatises by Chrysippus? 7. Why, does virtue consist in this, in having gained a thorough knowledge of Chrysippus? For if that is the case, we must agree that progress is nothing other than knowing many works by Chrysippus. 8. But now we are admitting that virtue brings about one thing, and yet declaring that progress, the approach to virtue, brings about another.

9. 'This man here', someone says, 'is already able to read Chrysippus, even by himself.' – By the gods, that is good progress you are making, man. What progress! 10. 'Why do you make fun of him?' – And why do you distract him from an awareness of his deficiencies? Are you not willing to show him what virtue brings about, so that he may know where to seek his progress? 11. Seek it in that place, wretch, where your task lies. And where does your task lie? In desire and aversion, that you may neither fail to attain what you desire, nor fall into what

you want to avoid; in exerting your impulse to act and not to act, that you may not be liable to error; in assent and the withholding of assent, that you may not be liable to be deceived. 12. The first areas of study are the first and most necessary. But if, trembling and lamenting all the while, you seek never to fall into misfortune, how, I ask you, are you making progress?

13. Show me then your progress in this point. It is as if I were talking to an athlete and said, 'Show me your shoulders', and he then replied, 'Look at my jumping-weights.' That is quite enough of you and your jumping-weights: what I want to see is what the jumping-weights serve to achieve.

14. 'Take the treatise *On Impulse*, and see how thoroughly I have read it.'

That is not what I am looking for, slave, but how you exercise your impulse to act and not to act, how you manage your desires and aversions, how you approach things, how you apply yourself to them, and prepare for them, and whether in harmony with nature or out of harmony. 15. For if you are acting in harmony with nature, give me evidence of that, and I will say that you are making progress; but if you are acting out of harmony, go your way, and do not merely comment on these treatises, but even write such works yourself. And what will you gain by it? 16. Do you not know that the whole book sells for five denarii? So is the person who expounds it, do you suppose, worth more than five denarii? 17. Never look for your work in one place and your progress in another.

18. Where is progress, then?

If any of you, withdrawing himself from externals, turns to his own faculty of choice, working at it and perfecting it, so as to bring it fully into harmony with nature; elevated, free, unrestrained, unhindered, faithful, self-respecting: 19. if he has learned too, that whoever desires, or is averse to, things outside his own power can neither be faithful nor free, but must necessarily be changed and tossed back and forth with them; must necessarily too be subject to others, who can procure or prevent what he desires or wants to avoid: 20. if, finally, when he rises in the morning, he observes and keeps to these rules; bathes and eats as a man of fidelity and honour; and thus, in every matter that befalls, puts his guiding principles to work, just as the runner does in the business of running, or the voice-trainer in the training of voices: 21. this is the man who is truly making progress, this is the man who has not travelled in vain. 22. But if he is wholly intent on reading books, and has laboured at that only, and gone abroad for the sake of that: I bid him go home immediately, and not neglect his domestic affairs; 23. for what he has travelled for is nothing. No, what matters is studying how to rid his life of lamentation, and complaint, and cries of 'Alas!' and 'How miserable I am!', and misfortune, and disappointment; 24. and to learn what death, what exile, what prison, what hemlock is, so that he may be able to say in prison, like Socrates, 'My dear Crito, if that is what pleases the gods, so be it', and not 'Wretched old man that I am, is it for this that I have kept my grey hairs!' 25. Who says such things? Do you suppose I will mention to you some mean and despicable person? Does not Priam say such things? Does not Oedipus? Nay, how many kings do so? 26. For what else is tragedy but a portrayal in tragic verse of the sufferings of men who have devoted their admiration to external things? 27. If one had to be taught by fictions that things external and outside the sphere of choice are nothing to us, I, for my part, should wish for such a fiction as would enable me to live henceforth in peace of mind and free from perturbation. What you on your part wish for is for you yourselves to consider.

28. What, then, does Chrysippus offer us?

'That you may know that those things are not false on which serenity and peace of mind depend', he says, 29. 'take my books, and you will see how true and in harmony with nature are the things which give me peace of mind.' O great good fortune! And how great the benefactor who shows the way! 30. To Triptolemus all men have raised temples and altars, because he gave us cultivated crops; 31. but to him who has discovered, and brought to light, and communicated, the truth to all, not merely of living, but of living well – who among you ever raised an altar, or dedicated a temple or statue to him for this, or bows down to god on that account? 32. We offer sacrifices because the gods have given us corn or the vine; yet because they have produced such a wonderful fruit in a human mind, with the intention of showing us the true doctrine of happiness, shall we neglect to offer thanks to god for that?

# CHAPTER 5

## Against The Academics

1. If a person opposes very evident truths, it is not easy to find an argument by which one may persuade him to alter his opinion. 2. This arises neither from his own strength, nor from the weakness of his teacher: but when a man after being reduced to contradiction in the course of argument, becomes as hard as a stone, how shall we deal with him any longer by reason?

3. Such petrification takes two forms: the one, a petrification of the understanding, and the other of the sense of shame, when a person has obstinately set himself neither to assent to evident truths, nor to abandon the defence of contradictions. 4. Most of us fear the deadening of the body, and would make use of every means possible to avoid falling into that condition: but the deadening of the soul concerns us not a bit. 5. And, by Zeus, when the soul itself is in such a condition that a person is incapable of following a single argument or understanding anything, we think him in a sad condition: but if a person's sense of shame and modesty is deadened, we go so far as to call this strength of mind.

6. Do you understand that you are awake? – 'No', he replies, 'any more than I do in my dreams when I have the impression that I am awake.' – Is there no difference, then, between that impression and the other? – 'None.' 7. – Can I argue with this man any longer? And what fire or steel shall I apply to him to make him aware that he has become deadened? He is aware of it, but pretends that he is not; he is even worse than a corpse.

8. One man does not see the contradiction; he is in a bad state. Another does see it, but he is not moved, nor does he improve; he is in an even worse state. 9. His sense of shame and modesty have been completely extirpated. His reasoning faculty, indeed, has not been extirpated, but brutalized. 10. Am I to call this 'strength'? By no means; unless I am also to call by that name the quality which enables catamites to do and say in public whatever comes into their heads.

## CHAPTER 6

# On Providence

1. For everything that happens in the universe one can readily find reason to praise providence, if one has within oneself these two qualities, the ability to see each particular event in the context of the whole, and a sense of gratitude. 2. Without these one man will not see the usefulness of what has happened, and another man, even though he does see it, will not be grateful for it. 3. If god had made colours, and had not made the faculty of seeing them, what would have been their use?

None.

4. If, on the other hand, he had made the faculty, but not made objects in such a way that they fell under the faculty of vision, what would have been the use of that?

None.

5. Again: if he had made both the faculty and the objects, but had not made light?

6. Neither in that case would they have been of any use.

Who is it, then, that has fitted each of these to the other? Who is it that has fitted the sword to the scabbard, and the scabbard to the sword? Is it no one? 7. From the very structure of such completed products, we generally infer that they must be the work of some artificer, and that they were not produced by mere chance. 8. Does every such work, then, demonstrate its artificer, whilst visible objects and vision and light do not? 9. And male and female, and the desire of each for intercourse with the other, and their power to make use of the organs that have been provided for this purpose, do these things not demonstrate their artificer? Most certainly they do.

10. But further: this constitution of our understanding, such that we are not simply impressed by sensations but choose amongst them, and add to them and subtract from them, and thus make combinations of them, and by Zeus, substitute some for others which are in some way connected with them, is not even this sufficient to move certain people and dissuade them from leaving an artificer out of their scheme? 11. If not, let them explain to us what it is that brings all this about, and how it is

possible that things so wonderful, and which carry such marks of craftsmanship, should come into being of their own accord and at random.

12. What then, do these things come to pass in us human beings alone? Many in ourselves only, as things that the rational creature specifically required; but you will find many that we share with the irrational animals. 13. Do they also have understanding, then, of what comes to pass? By no means; for use is one thing, and understanding another. God had need of animals as creatures that make use of sense-impressions, and of us as beings who can understand that use. 14. It is sufficient, therefore, for them to eat and drink and rest and breed, and perform other such functions as belong to each of them; but for us, to whom god has granted in addition the faculty of understanding, 15. these functions are no longer sufficient. For if we do not act in a proper and orderly manner, and each of us in accordance with his nature and constitution, we shall no longer attain our end. 16. For where the constitution of beings is different, their offices and ends are different likewise. 17. Thus where a being's constitution is adapted only to use, there use is alone sufficient; but where understanding is added to use, unless that too be duly exercised, the end of such a being will never be attained.

18. Well then: each of the animals is constituted by god for a purpose, one to be eaten, another for husbandry, or for the production of cheese, and the rest of them for some other comparable use; and for these purposes what need do they have to understand impressions and be able to distinguish between them? 19. But god has introduced man into the world as a spectator of himself and of his works; and not only as a spectator, but an interpreter of them. 20. It is therefore shameful that man should begin and end where irrational creatures do. He ought rather to begin there, but to end where nature itself has fixed our end; 21. and that is in contemplation and understanding and a way of life in harmony with nature. 22. Take care, then, not to die without ever being spectators of these things.

23. You take a journey to Olympia to behold the work of Pheidias, and each of you thinks it a misfortune to die without experience of such things; 24. so will you have no desire to understand and be spectators of those works for which there is no need to take a journey, but in the presence of which you are

already standing? 25. Will you never perceive, then, either what you are or what you were born for; nor for what purpose you have received the gift of sight?

26. But there are some unpleasant and difficult things in life.

And are there no such things at Olympia? Do you not suffer from the heat? Are you not short of space? Do you not have trouble washing? Are you not soaked when it rains? Do you not get your share of uproar and shouting and other irritations? 27. But, I suppose, by setting these off against the remarkable nature of the spectacle, you bear and endure them. 28. Well, and have you not received faculties which give you the power to endure everything that happens? Have you not received greatness of soul? Have you not received courage? Have you not received endurance? 29. What concern to me is anything that happens, while I have greatness of soul? What shall disconcert or trouble me, or seem grievous to me? Shall I fail to make use of my faculties to that purpose for which they were granted me, but lament and groan at what happens?

30. Oh, but my nose is running.

And what have you hands for, slave, but to wipe the rheum away with?

31. But is there, then, any good reason that there should be this rheum in the world?

32. And how much better it would be for you to wipe it away than complain! Pray, what figure do you think Heracles would have made if there had not been a lion like the one they tell of, and a hydra, and a stag, and unjust and brutal men, whom he drove off and cleared away? 33. And what would he have done if nothing like these had existed? Is it not plain that he would have wrapped himself up and slept? In the first place, then, he would never have become a Heracles by slumbering his whole life away in such delicacy and ease; or if he had, what good would he have been? 34. What would have been the use of those arms of his, and his strength overall; of his endurance, and greatness of mind, if such circumstances and opportunities had not stirred him to action and exercised him?

35. What, then, should he have provided these for himself, and sought to introduce a boar, a lion, and a hydra, into his country?

36. That would have been madness and folly. But as they did exist and could be found, they were of service to reveal Heracles'

nature and exercise him. 37. Now that you realize these things, you also should look to the faculties that you have, and say as you behold them, 'Bring on me now, O Zeus, whatever difficulty you will, for I have the means and the resources granted to me by yourself to bring honour to myself through whatever may come to pass.' 38. – No; but you sit trembling, for fear that this or that might happen, and lamenting, and mourning, and groaning at what does happen, and then you find fault with the gods. 39. For what is the consequence of such meanness of spirit, but impiety? 40. And yet god has not only granted us these faculties, which enable us to endure everything that happens without being humiliated or broken by it, but, like a good king, and a true father, has given them to us free of all restraint, compulsion, or hindrance, and has put them under our complete control, not even reserving any power for himself to hinder or restrain them. 41. Possessing these faculties in freedom and as your own, will you make no use of them, nor consider what it is that you have received and from whom, 42. but sit groaning and lamenting, some of you blind to him who gave them and not acknowledging your benefactor, and others basely resorting to complaints and accusations against god? 43. Yet I undertake to show you that you have the equipment and resources for greatness of soul and a courageous spirit: you show me what occasion you have for complaint and reproach!

## CHAPTER 7

# On The Use Of Arguments Resting On Equivocations, And Hypothetical Arguments, And The Like

1. It escapes most people, that the study of arguments which have equivocal or hypothetical premises, and those which are developed by questioning, and, in a word, all such arguments, has a connection with how we should behave in our lives. 2. For what we seek in every matter is how the virtuous man may find the path he should follow and the way he should behave with

regard to it. 3. Let them say, therefore, either that the man of virtue will not engage in question and answer, or that, if he does, he will take no care to avoid behaving casually and at random in questioning and answering; 4. or if they accept neither alternative, they must concede that some examination ought to be made of those topics with which question and answer are principally concerned. 5. For what is required in reasoning? To establish what is true, to reject what is false, and to suspend judgement in doubtful cases. 6. Is it enough, then, to learn merely this? – It is enough, say you. – Is it enough, then, for him who wants to avoid any mistake in the use of money, merely to have heard that we are to accept genuine drachmas and reject those that are counterfeit? 7. – It is not enough. – So what must be added besides? Surely, that faculty which tests and distinguishes what coins are good, and what bad. 8. – Therefore, in reasoning too, mere speech is not enough, but it is necessary that we should become able to test and distinguish between the true and the false and the doubtful? – It is necessary.

9. And what else is required in reasoning? Accept the consequences of what you have properly granted. 10. Well; and here, too, is it enough merely to know this particular thing? It is not; but we must learn how such a thing follows from certain other things, and how sometimes it follows from one single thing, and sometimes from several together. 11. Is it not, then, necessary that a person should acquire this skill in addition if he is to behave intelligently in discussion, and prove each of his points in succession, and follow the demonstrations of others, and not be deceived by those who put forward sophistries in the guise of demonstrative arguments? 12. This has given rise among us to the study and practice of inferential arguments and the logical figures, and shown them to be necessary.

13. But it may sometimes happen, that from premises which we have properly granted, there follows such and such a conclusion, which, though false, nevertheless follows. 14. What, then, ought I to do? Admit the falsehood? 15. And how is that possible? Then should I say that I was wrong to grant the premises? No, that is not allowable either. Or that the consequence does not follow from the premises? But that is not allowable either. 16. What, then, is to be done in these circumstances? Is it not this? Just as once having borrowed money is not enough to make a person still a debtor, unless he continues to owe money

and has not paid off the loan, so having granted the premises is not enough to make it necessary to grant the inference, unless we continue to accept the premises. 17. If the premises remain to the end such as they were when they were granted, it is absolutely necessary to hold to our acceptance of them, and to admit what follows from them. 18. But if the premises do not remain as they were when they were granted, it is equally necessary for us to abandon our concession of the premises, and no longer accept what is inconsistent with the premises. 19. For, according to our present point of view, the inference does not follow or affect us, since we have revoked our acceptance of the premises. 20. We ought then to examine premises of this kind, and their changes and modifications, because if in the actual course of questioning or answering or drawing conclusions or anything of the kind, the premises undergo these modifications, they will become a cause of trouble to the ignorant, who cannot see what follows. Why ought we to do so? 21. So that in this area we may not behave inappropriately, or randomly, or confusedly. 22. And the same is true of hypotheses and hypothetical arguments. For it is sometimes necessary to assume some hypothesis, as a kind of step to the following argument. 23. Is every given hypothesis to be granted, then, or not every one; and if not every one, which? 24. And must the person who has granted a hypothesis abide by it and maintain it for ever? Or must he sometimes depart from it? And as for its consequences, must he accept them and reject those that conflict with it? – Yes – 25. But someone says, 'If you admit a hypothesis of what is possible, I will drive you in argument to admit an impossibility.' Will a prudent young man refuse to engage in argument with such a person, and avoid all examination and discussion with him? 26. And yet who besides the man of prudence is capable of developing an argument, and expert in question and answer, and incapable of being deceived and imposed on by sophistry? 27. Or will he indeed engage in argument, but without taking care not to behave casually and randomly in it? And if so, can he still be such a man as we are supposing him to be? 28. But, without some such exercise and preparation, is it possible for him to maintain consistency in his argument? 29. Let them show that he can, and all these considerations will be superfluous and absurd, and inconsistent with our preconception of the virtuous man.

30. Why, then, are we still indolent and slothful, and sluggish, seeking excuses to avoid labouring or staying awake over our efforts to perfect our own reason? 31. – 'But suppose, after all, I should make a mistake in these points, I have not killed my father, have I?' – Slave! Why, in this case, where had you a father to kill? What is it, then, that you have done? The only fault that you could commit in this instance you have committed. 32. This is the very thing that I myself said to Rufus, when he reproved me for not finding the single missing step in some syllogism. Why, said I, have I burned down the Capitol, then? Slave, answered he, what was missed out here *is* the Capitol! 33. Or are there no other faults, but burning down the Capitol, or killing one's father? And is it no fault to treat the impressions presented to our minds in a random, senseless and haphazard manner, and to be unable to follow an argument, a demonstration or a sophism, in short, to be unable to see in question and answer what is in accordance with one's own position and what is not – is there no fault in any of these?

## CHAPTER 8

# That For The Uneducated Our Reasoning Capacities Are Not Free Of Danger

1. In as many ways as equivalent terms may be interchanged, in just so many may the forms of arguments and enthymemes be varied in reasoning. 2. As for instance: 'if you have borrowed, and not repaid, you owe me money. But you have not borrowed, and not repaid, therefore you do not owe me money.' 3. And nobody is better equipped to do this skilfully than the philosopher. For if an enthymeme is indeed an imperfect syllogism, he who has been trained in the perfect syllogism must be equally capable of handling the imperfect one.

4. Why, then, do we not exercise ourselves and one another in this manner? 5. Because even now, although we do not train ourselves in these matters, and are not diverted, by me at least, from the study of morality, we nevertheless make no advance in virtue. 6. What is to be expected, then, if we should adopt this

pursuit in addition? And especially as it would not only be a further pursuit to distract us from more necessary studies, but also provide exceptional occasion for conceit and vanity. 7. For the power of argument and persuasive reasoning is great; and, particularly, if it be developed by training and receive an additional plausibility through the application of language. 8. For in general every faculty is dangerous to weak and uninstructed persons, as being apt to render them presumptuous and vain. 9. For by what method can one persuade a young man who excels in these kinds of study that he ought not to be an appendage to them, but they to him? 10. Will he not trample upon all such advice; and walk about conceited and puffed up, not bearing that any one should undertake to remind him of what he is lacking and where he is going wrong.

11. What, then, was not Plato a philosopher?

Well, and was not Hippocrates a physician? But you see how Hippocrates expresses himself. 12. Yet is it by virtue of being a physician that Hippocrates expresses himself so well? Why, then, do you confuse qualities which are accidentally united in the same persons? 13. If Plato was handsome and strong, must I also set to and toil to become handsome and strong, as if this was necessary to philosophy, because a certain person happened to be at once handsome and a philosopher? 14. Why will you not perceive and distinguish what are the things that make men philosophers, and what belong to them on other accounts? Pray, if I were a philosopher, would it be necessary that you should be lame too?

What then? Do I reject these faculties? 15. By no means. For neither do I reject the faculty of seeing. 16. Nevertheless if you ask me what is the good of man, I can only reply to you that it consists in a certain disposition of our choice.

## CHAPTER 9

# What Should We Conclude From The Doctrine Of Our Kinship To God?

1. If what philosophers say about the kinship between god and man is true, what else is left for men than to follow the example of Socrates, and when one is asked where one is from, never to say 'I am an Athenian', or 'I am a Corinthian', but rather 'I am a citizen of the universe'? 2. For why do you say that you are an Athenian, and not a native of that corner on which your paltry body was thrown down at birth? 3. Or is it not plain that you take your name from some more sovereign domain, which embraces not only that corner, and your whole household, and, in general, that land from which the race of your ancestors has come, from your forebears down to yourself, and that it is after some such place as this that you call yourself an 'Athenian', or a 'Corinthian'? 4. Why may not the man, then, who understands the administration of the universe, and has learned that the greatest and most important and comprehensive of all things is this system in which men and god are associated, and that from him the seeds of being are descended, not only to my father or grandfather, but to all things that are begotten and grow on earth, and especially to rational creatures, 5. as they alone are qualified by nature to associate with god, being connected with him by reason: 6. why should not a man who understands this call himself a citizen of the universe? Why not a son of god? And why shall he fear anything that happens among men? 7. Shall kinship to Caesar, or any other amongst those who hold great power at Rome, enable a man to live safely, and secure against contempt, and void of all fear whatever; and shall not having god for our maker, and father and guardian free us from griefs and terrors?

8. 'But how shall I feed myself?' somebody says. 'For I have nothing.'

Why, how do slaves, how do runaways? To what do they trust when they run away from their masters? Is it to their land, their servants, their silver-plate? No, to nothing but themselves. Yet, all the same, they do not fail to get food. 9. And must our philosopher when he travels away from home, place his confidence in others and rely upon them, and not take care of himself? Must he be baser and more cowardly than the irrational beasts, each of which is self-sufficient, and lacks neither its proper food, nor the way of life appropriate to itself and its nature? 10. I for my part think that there should be no need for an old fellow to sit here devising how to prevent you from having a mean opinion of yourselves, or arriving in your discussions at abject or ignoble ideas about yourselves; 11. but that his business should be to take care that there may not arise amongst you young men of such a spirit, that, when they learn of their affinity to the gods, and that we have, as it were, these fetters attached to us, namely the body and its possessions, and whatever is necessary to us on their account for the management and commerce of life, they may wish to throw them off, as both burdensome and useless, and depart to their kindred. 12. This is the work, if any, that ought to employ your teacher and trainer, if he really was one; and as for you, you might come to him, and say, 'Epictetus, we can no longer bear to be fettered to this paltry body, feeding and resting and cleaning it, and because of it having to associate with these people and those. 13. Are these things not indifferent, and nothing to us, and is not death no evil? Are we not akin to god, and did we not come from him? 14. Suffer us to go back again to the place from which we came; suffer us, at last, to be delivered from these fetters, that are fastened to us and weigh us down. 15. Here thieves and robbers, and courts of law, and those who are called tyrants, are thought to have some power over us, because of our poor body and its possessions. Suffer us to show them, that they have power over nobody.'

16. And in this case it would be my part to answer, 'My friends, wait for god, till he shall give the signal, and release you from this service; then depart to him. For the present, be content to remain in this place where he has stationed you. 17. The time of your abiding here is short, and easy to such as are disposed like you. For what tyrant, what robber, what thief, or what courts of law are formidable to those who thus account the body and its possessions as nothing? Stay. Do not depart without reason.'

18. Something like that is what should pass between a teacher and gifted young men. 19. But what comes to pass now? Your

teacher has no life in him: you have none either. When you have had your fill today, you sit weeping about tomorrow and how you shall get food. 20. Why, if you get it, slave, you will have it: if not, you will depart this life. The door is open: why do you lament? What room is left for tears? What occasion for flattery? Why should any one envy another? Why should he be struck with admiration for those who have great possessions, or are placed in positions of power, especially if they are strong and quick to anger? 21. For what will they do to us? The things they have the power to do will be of no concern to us: the things we care about they cannot affect. Who, then, will ever be master over a person who is thus disposed? 22. How did Socrates feel about these matters? How otherwise than a man ought to feel when he is convinced of his kinship to the gods? 23. 'If you tell me', says he to his judges, 'we will acquit you on condition that you shall no longer discourse in the manner you have hitherto, nor cause annoyance to the young or old among us, 24. I will answer: "It is absurd for you to think that if your general had stationed me in any post, I ought to maintain and defend it, and choose to die a thousand times rather than desert it, but if god has assigned us to a certain place and way of life, we ought to desert that."'

25. This is what it means for a man to be truly akin to the gods. 26. But as for us, we consider ourselves as a mere assemblage of stomach and entrails and genitals, and we fear and desire accordingly, and we flatter those who can help us in these matters, and dread the very same persons.

27. A person once asked me to write to Rome on his behalf. He had met with what most people regard as misfortune, and, after previously being eminent and wealthy, he had subsequently lost everything, and was living here. And I wrote on his behalf in a submissive style. 28. But after reading my letter, he returned it to me and said: 'I wanted your assistance, not your pity; for no evil has befallen me.'

29. Thus Rufus too was in the habit of saying, to test me, 'Your master is going to do this to you or that', 30. and when I answered him, 'Such is man's lot', he said, 'Why, then, should I intercede with him when I can get the same things from yourself?' 31. For, in truth, it is superfluous and vain to try to get from another what one has from oneself. 32. Shall I, then, who can get greatness of soul and a noble spirit from myself, try

to get an estate, or a sum of money, or a position from you? Heaven forbid! I will not be so insensible of my own possessions. 33. But if a person is cowardly and abject, what else is necessary but to write letters for him as if he was dead? 'Pray oblige us with the corpse of so-and-so and his pint of paltry blood.' 34. For, in fact, such a person is corpse and a pint of paltry blood, and nothing more. For if he was anything more, he would be aware that one man is not rendered unfortunate by another.

## CHAPTER 10

# To Those Who Have Devoted Their Efforts To Advancement At Rome

1. If we had applied ourselves as heartily to our own work as the old men at Rome do to their schemes, perhaps we too might have achieved something. 2. I know a man older than myself who is now superintendent of the grain supply at Rome. When he passed through this place on his return from exile, what things he said to me as he ran down his former life and proclaimed that for the future when he got back, he would apply himself to nothing other than spending the remainder of his days in peace and tranquillity. 'For how few have I now remaining!' 3. – You will not do it, said I. As soon as you get even a smell of Rome, you will forget all this.' And I said to him that if he was granted the least access to court, he would push his way in, offering hearty thanks to god. 4. 'If you ever find me, Epictetus', said he, 'putting one foot inside the palace, think of me whatever you please.' 5. Now, after all, how did he act? Before he entered Rome he was met by dispatches from Caesar. On receiving them he forgot all his former resolutions, and has ever since been heaping up one encumbrance upon another. 6. I should be glad now to have an opportunity of putting him in mind of his discourse as he passed through, and of saying, How much more clever I am as a prophet than you!

7. What then do I say? That man is an animal made for an inactive life? No, surely. But why are we not men of action? For my own part, as soon as it is day, I remind myself a little what I

am to read over with my pupils. And then all at once I say to myself, What is it to me how So-and-so reads? The first thing I want is to get some sleep.

9. But, indeed, what similarity is there between the business of those other men and our own? If you consider what they do, you will see. For what else do they do all day but vote on resolutions, discuss things together, consult about a bit of grain, or a patch of land, or other sources of profit? 10. Is there any similarity, then, between receiving and reading a little petition from somebody such as this: 'I beg you to allow me to export a little corn'; and this, 'I beg you to learn from Chrysippus what the administration of the universe is, and what place a rational creature holds in it; and learn, too, who you are, and where your good and evil lies.' 11. Are these things at all alike? Do they require an equal degree of application? 12. And is it as shameful to neglect the one as the other?

Well, then, are we teachers the only idle dreamers? 13. No; it is you young men who are much more so. For, indeed, we old men, when we see young ones at play, are keen to join in that play ourselves. Far more so, then, if I saw them wide awake and keen to join us in our studies, should I be eager myself to join with them in serious work.

## CHAPTER 11

# On Family Affection

1. When a government official came to visit him, Epictetus, after inquiring into various particulars, asked him whether he had a wife and children. 2. When he replied that he had, Epictetus asked further, How do you get on in this regard? – Very miserably, says he. – How so? 3. For men do not marry and beget children in order to be miserable, but rather to be happy. 4. But I am so very miserable about my poor children, that the other day, when my little daughter was sick and was considered to be in danger, I could not bear even to be with her, but ran away, until somebody told me that she had recovered. – What, and do you think you were right to act in such a way? 5. – I was

acting naturally, said he. – Well: do but convince me that you were acting naturally, and I will convince you that everything natural is right. 6. – All, or at least most, of us fathers are affected in the same way. – I do not deny the fact, but the question between us is whether it be right. 7. For, if we are to follow your reasoning, we would have to say that tumours develop for the good of the body, because they do develop and even that errors are natural, because all or the most part of us are guilty of them. 8. You must show me, then, how such behaviour as yours is natural.

I cannot; but rather, you should show me how it is not natural and not right.

9. If we were disputing about black and white, what criterion should we call in to distinguish between them?

Sight.

If about things hot and cold, and hard and soft, what then?

Touch.

10. Well then, when we are debating about what is natural and unnatural, and right and wrong, what criterion are we to take?

I cannot tell.

11. And yet, to be ignorant of the criterion for colours, or smells, or tastes, might perhaps be no very great loss. But do you think that he suffers only a small loss who is ignorant of what is good and evil, and natural and unnatural, to man?

No. The very greatest.

12. Well, tell me: Are all things which are judged good and proper by some, rightly judged to be so? Is it possible that the various opinions of Jews and Syrians and Egyptians and Romans concerning food should all be right?

How can it be possible?

13. I suppose, then, it is absolutely necessary, that if the opinions of the Egyptians are right, those of the others must be wrong: and that if those of the Jews are good, those of the others must be bad.

How can it be otherwise?

14. And where there is ignorance, there is likewise want of knowledge and instruction in essential matters.

Yes indeed.

15. So you, then, now that you are aware of this, will in future apply yourself to nothing other, and think of nothing

other than how to discover the criterion of what is in accordance
with nature, and to apply that in judging each particular case.

16. For the time being, I can assist you towards what you
desire to the following extent. 17. Does family affection seem to
you to be a good and natural thing?

How should it be otherwise?

Well; can it be the case that family affection is natural and
good, whilst that which is reasonable is not good?

By no means.

18. So there is no conflict between family affection and that
which is reasonable?

I think not.

Otherwise, when two things conflict and one of them is in
accordance with nature, the other must be contrary to nature. Is
that not the case?

It must be.

19. Whatever, then, we find to be at once affectionate and
reasonable, that we may safely pronounce to be right and good.

Agreed.

20. Well, then, you will not deny that to run away and leave
a sick child is contrary to reason. It remains for us to consider
whether it be consistent with affection.

Let us consider it then.

21. So was it right for you, when you were affectionately
disposed towards your child, to run off and leave her? And has
the child's mother no affection for her?

22. Yes; surely she has.

Would it have been right, then, that her mother too should
have left her, or would it not?

It would not.

What of the nurse? Does she love the child?

She does.

Ought she then to have left her?

By no means.

And her attendant? Does he not love her?

He does.

23. Should he not also, then, have gone away and left her, so
that in consequence the child would have been left all alone and
helpless because of the great affection of you her parents and
those around her, or would have died, perhaps, in the hands of
people who neither loved her nor cared for her?

Heaven forbid!

24. But is it not unreasonable and unfair, that what you think right in yourself, on account of your affection, should not be allowed to others, who have the very same affection as you?

It is absurd.

25. Pray, if you were sick yourself, should you be willing to have your relatives, and children themselves and your wife, so very affectionate as to leave you alone and desolate?

By no means.

26. Or would you wish to be so loved by your own that, because of their excessive affection, you would always be left alone when you were sick? Or would you not rather wish on this account to be loved, if it were possible, by your enemies so that it would be they who left you alone? If so, we can only conclude that your behaviour was by no means affectionate. 27. Well, then: was it nothing at all that moved and induced you to desert your child?

How is that possible?

No; but it would have been much the same motive as induced somebody at Rome to hide his face while a horse which he backed was running, and then, when it won against all expectation, he needed sponges to bring him round from his faint.

And what was this motive?

28. At present perhaps it cannot be accurately explained. It is sufficient to be convinced, if what philosophers say be sound, that we are not to seek it somewhere outside ourselves, but that there is universally one and the same cause, which moves us to do or not to do something, to speak or not to speak, to be elated or depressed, to avoid something or pursue it, 29. that very cause which has now moved each of us, you to come and sit and listen to me, and me to speak as I do.

And what is that?

30. Is it anything else than that it seemed right to us to do so?

Nothing else.

And if it had seemed otherwise to us, what else should we have been doing than what we thought right? 31. Surely it was this, and not the death of Patroclus, that caused Achilles to grieve (for not everyone is affected in this way by the death of a friend), that it seemed right to him. 32. This too was the cause of your running away from your child, that it seemed right to you; and again, if you were to stay with her, that would be because it seemed right to you. You are now returning to Rome because it seems right to you; but if you should alter your opinion you will not return. 33. In a word, neither death nor exile, nor pain, nor anything of that kind is the cause of our doing or not doing anything, but rather, our suppositions and judgements. 34. Do I convince you of this, or not?

You do.

Well then, as the causes are in each particular case, so also will be the effects. 35. From this day forward, then, whenever we do anything wrong we will ascribe the blame only to the judgement from which we act; and we will endeavour to remove and extirpate that, with greater care than we would abscesses and tumours from our body. 36. In like manner, we will ascribe what we do rightly to the same cause; 37. and we will blame neither slave, nor neighbour, nor wife, nor children as the causes of any evils that befall us, being persuaded that if we did not think that things were of such a nature, we would not perform the actions that follow from such a judgement. Of these judgements we ourselves, and not externals, are the masters.

Agreed.

38. From this day forth, then, we will not investigate or inquire into the nature or condition of anything, whether our land, or our slaves, or our horses, or our dogs, but this alone, our judgements.

May that be so.

39. You see, then, that it is necessary for you to become a student, that creature which every one laughs at, if you really desire to make an examination of your judgements. 40. But this, as you are quite aware, is not the work of a single hour or day.

## CHAPTER 12

## On Contentment

1. Concerning gods, some affirm that there is no deity: others, that it exists, but is inactive, aloof, and takes no thought for anything; 2. a third group say that it exists, and takes thought, but only for great and heavenly things, and not for anything at

all on earth; a fourth that it takes thought for things on earth and human affairs, but only in a general manner, and takes no thought for individuals on their own account; 3. and there is a fifth group, to which both Socrates and Odysseus belonged, who say, 'Not a move do I make unseen by thee.'

4. It is, before all things, necessary to examine each of these claims, to see which is, and which is not, soundly stated. 5. Now, if there are no gods, how can it be our end to follow them? If there are gods, but they take no care of anything, how will it be right, here again, to follow them? 6. Or, if they both exist, and take care, yet there is no communication from them to men (and, indeed, by Zeus, to myself in particular) how can it be right even in this case? 7. So a wise and good man, after examining all these things, submits his mind to him who administers the universe, as good citizens submit to the laws of the state.

8. He, then, who comes to be instructed, ought to come with this intention: 'How may I follow the gods in everything? How may I live in happiness under the divine governance? And how may I become free?' 9. For he is free for whom all things happen in accordance with his choice, and whom no one can restrain.

10. What! then is freedom madness?

By no means; for madness and freedom are incompatible.

11. But I would have whatever appears to me to be right happen, however it comes to appear so.

12. You are mad: you have lost your senses. Do you not know that freedom is a noble and valuable thing? But for me to desire at random, and for things to happen in accordance with such a desire, may be so far from a noble thing as to be, of all others, the most shameful. For how do we proceed in writing? 13. Do I want to write the name of Dion (for instance) as I will? No; but I am taught to want to write it as it ought to be written. And what is the case in music? The same. 14. And what in every other art or science? The same, or otherwise there would be no purpose in knowing anything, if it were to be adapted to each person's personal wishes. 15. Is it, then, only in the greatest and highest matter, that of freedom, that I am permitted to desire at random? By no means, but true instruction is this: learning to will that things should happen as they do. And how do they happen? As the appointer of them has appointed. 16. He has appointed that there should be summer and winter, abundance

and dearth, virtue and vice, and all such opposites, for the sake of the harmony of the universe, and to each of us he has given a body and its parts, and property and companions. 17. Mindful of what has been appointed, we should enter upon a course of instruction, not so as to change the constitution of things (which is not permitted to us, nor would it be better if it were) but, rather, seeing things are as they are and as they were born to be, so that we may keep our mind in harmony with things as they come to pass. 18. Can we, for instance, flee from mankind? And how is that possible? Can we, by associating with them, change them? Who has given us such a power? 19. What, then, remains to be done, or what method can we find of dealing with them? Such a method that while they will act as they think fit, we will nevertheless remain in accord with nature. 20. But you are wretched and discontented, and if you are alone, you call it desolation, but if you are with men, you call them cheats and robbers and you find fault with even your parents and children and brothers and neighbours. 21. Whereas you ought, when you live alone, to call that peace and freedom, and compare yourself to the gods; and when you are in company, not to call it a crowd and a tumult and a vexation, but a feast and a festival, and thus accept all things with contentment. What, then, is the punishment of those who do not? To be just as they are. 22. Is a person discontented at being alone? Let him be in desolation. Discontented with his parents? Let him be a bad son, and let him grieve. Discontented with his children? Let him be a bad father. 23. 'Throw him into prison.' What kind of prison? Where he already is; for he is there against his will, and wherever any one is against his will, that is to him a prison; just as Socrates was not in prison, for he was willingly there. 24. 'What, then, must my leg be lame?' And is it for one paltry leg, slave, that you accuse the universe? Why will you not give it up to the whole? Why will you not surrender it? Why will you not joyfully yield it up to him who gave it? 25. And will you be angry and discontented with the ordinances of Zeus, which he, with the Fates who spun in his presence the thread of your destiny at the time of your birth, ordained and appointed? 26. Do you not know how very small a part you are compared to the whole? That is, as to the body; for as to reason you are neither worse, nor less, than the gods. For the greatness of reason is not measured by length or height, but by its judgements. 27. Will not you therefore place your good there, where you are equal to the gods? 28. 'How wretched am I to have such a father and mother!' What, then, was it granted you to come beforehand, and make your own selection, and say: 'Let such and such a man have intercourse with such and such a woman, at this hour, to be the authors of my birth?' 29. It was not granted; for it was necessary that your parents should exist before you, and you be born afterwards. Of whom? Of just such as they were. 30. What, then, since they are such, is there no remedy afforded you? Now, surely, if you were ignorant of the purpose for which you possess the faculty of sight, you would be wretched and miserable if you shut your eyes when colours passed before you, so are you not more wretched and miserable at being ignorant that you have the greatness of soul and nobility of spirit to confront everything that may happen to you? 31. Things proportionate to the faculty that you have are brought before you; but you turn that faculty away at the very time when you ought to keep it unclosed and clear-sighted. 32. Why do you not rather, give thanks to the gods that they have made you superior to everything that they did not place in your power, and have rendered you accountable only for that which is in your own power? 33. They have discharged you from all accountability for your parents, and likewise for your brothers, and for your body, and for property, death, life. 34. For what, then, have they made you accountable? For that which alone is in your power, the proper use of your impressions. 35. Why, then, should you draw upon yourself those things for which you are not accountable? You are merely creating trouble for yourself.

## CHAPTER 13

# How Can We Act In Everything In A Manner Acceptable To The Gods?

1. When someone asked him, how one can eat acceptably to the gods, he said, If he eats as he ought and sensibly, and, one might say, with restraint and self-control, will he not also be eating in a manner acceptable to the gods? 2. And when you call for hot

water, and the slave does not obey you, or, if he does, brings it only lukewarm, or is not even to be found in the house: then not to be angry, or lose your temper, is that not acceptable to the gods?

3. But how, then, can one bear with such people?

Slave, will you not bear with your own brother, who has Zeus as his forebear and is born as a son of the same seed as you, and is of the same high descent? 4. But if you chance to be placed in some superior station, will you at once set yourself up as a tyrant? Will you not remember what you are, and what people you are ruling over? That they are by nature your relations, your brothers; that they are the offspring of Zeus?

5. But I have them by right of purchase, and not they me. Do you not see where you are looking to? That it is to the earth, that it is to the pit, that it is to these wretched laws, the laws of the dead, and not to the laws of the gods that you are looking?

## CHAPTER 14

# That The Deity Watches Over Us All

1. When a person asked him how a man might be convinced that each of his actions is observed by god, Epictetus said: Do you not think that all things are bound together in a unity?

I do.

2. Well; and do you not think that things on earth feel the influence of what is in the heavens?

Yes.

3. Else how could it come about so regularly, as if by god's express command, that when he tells plants to flower, they flower, and to bud, they bud, and to bear fruit, they bear it, and to bring their fruit to ripeness, it ripens; and when again, he tells them to shed their fruit and drop their leaves and, gathered in upon themselves, remain at peace and take their rest, they remain at peace and take their rest? 4. And how else could it come about that as the moon waxes and wanes and as the sun approaches and recedes we behold amongst the things on earth so great a transformation and change? 5. But if the plants and

our bodies are so intimately bound to the universe and affected
by its influences, must our souls not be much more so? 6. But if
our souls are thus bound and fastened to god, as being particles
and portions of his being, must he not be aware of their every
motion, as a motion that is akin to and connatural to himself?
7. For you have the power to reflect on the divine governance
and each of its accomplishments, and likewise on human affairs
also, and you have the capacity to be moved by thousands of
things at once both in your senses and in your intelligence,
assenting to some, dissenting from others and sometimes sus-
pending your judgement; 8. and preserve in your mind so many
impressions from so many and various objects, and whenever
you are moved by these impressions, you hit on ideas corresponding to the objects which first impressed you, and from these
thousands of objects, you derive and maintain both arts, one
after another, and memories. 9. If you are capable of all this, is
not god capable of surveying all things, and being present with
all, and having a certain communication with all? 10. Now the
sun is capable of illuminating so great a part of the universe,
and of leaving only that small part of it unilluminated which is
covered by the shadow of the earth; so cannot he who made the
sun (which is but a small part of himself when compared with
the whole) and causes it to revolve, can such a being not perceive
all things?

11. 'But I cannot', say you, 'attend to all these things at once.'
Why, does any one tell you that you possess a power equal to
Zeus? 12. No! but nevertheless he has assigned to each man a
director, his own personal daemon, and committed him to his
guardianship; a director whose vigilance no slumbers interrupt,
and whom no false reasonings can deceive. 13. For to what
better and more careful guardian could he have committed us?
So when you have shut your doors, and darkened your room,
remember never to say that you are alone; 14. for you are not,
but god is within, and your daemon is within, and what need
have they of light to see what you are doing? 15. To this god
you also should swear such allegiance as soldiers do to Caesar.
For they, in order to receive their pay, swear to put the safety of
Caesar before all things, so will you not swear your oath to god,
who have received so many and such great favours, or if you
have sworn, will you not abide by your oath? 16. And what
must you swear? Never to disobey, never to accuse, never to

find fault with anything that god has bestowed, never to do or suffer unwillingly and with a bad grace anything that is inevitable. 17. Is this oath like the former? In the first case, men swear not to honour any other beyond Caesar; but we swear to honour our true selves above all things.

## CHAPTER 15

# What Does Philosophy Promise?

1. When a man consulted Epictetus, as to how he might persuade his brother to be angry with him no longer, he said: 2. Philosophy does not promise to secure anything external for man, otherwise it would be admitting something that lies beyond its proper subject-matter. For as the material of the carpenter is wood, and that of statuary bronze, so the subject-matter of the art of living is each person's own life.

3. What, then, of my brother's life?

That, again, belongs to his own art of living; but with regard to yours it is something external like land, like health, like reputation. Now, philosophy promises none of these. 4. Rather, it says, 'In every circumstance I will preserve the governing part in accord with nature.' Whose governing part? His in whom I exist.

5. But how, then, can I prevent my brother from being angry with me?

Bring him to me, and I will tell him; but to you I have nothing to say about *his* anger.

6. When the man who was consulting him said, 'What I am seeking to know is how I can be in accord with nature, even if he is unwilling to be reconciled with me', Epictetus replied:

7. No great thing comes into being all of a sudden; not even a bunch of grapes or a fig does. If you tell me at this minute, 'I want a fig', I will answer you, 'That requires time.' Let the tree first blossom, then bear fruit, then let the fruit ripen. 8. Now if the fruit of a fig-tree is not brought to perfection suddenly and in a single hour, would you expect to gather the fruit of a man's

mind in so short a time, and so easily? I tell you, expect no such thing.

## CHAPTER 16

# On Providence

1. Do not be surprised if other animals have all things necessary to the body ready provided for them, not only meat and drink but a place to lie down in, and that they are in need neither of shoes, nor of bedding, nor of clothes, while we stand in need of all these things. 2. Since they were not born for themselves, but for service, it would not have been beneficial to create them with these additional needs. 3. For, consider what it would be for us to take thought, not only for ourselves, but for sheep and asses too, as to how they should be clothed, and shod, and how they should find food and drink. 4. But just as soldiers report to their general ready shod, clothed, and armed (for it would be a grievous thing for the commander to have to go round clothing and shoeing the members of his corps), so nature likewise has formed the animals made for service, ready provided, and standing in need of no further care.

5. Thus one little boy, with only a rod, can drive a flock.

6. But now we, instead of giving thanks that we do not have to take as much care of our animals as we do of ourselves, find fault with god on our own account. 7. And yet, by Zeus and the gods, any one thing in creation is sufficient to make a modest and grateful man realize that there is a divine providence. 8. I am not thinking of great things for the moment, but the simple fact that milk is produced from grass, cheese from milk, and wool from skins: who created or contrived these things? No one, somebody says. O what extraordinary stupidity, and shamelessness! 9. But come, let us leave aside the central works of nature. Let us contemplate what she does, as it were, by the way. 10. What is more useless than the hairs which grow on a chin? And yet, has she not made use even of these in the most suitable manner possible? Has she not by these distinguished between male and female? 11. Does not nature in each of us call

out, even at a distance, 'I am a man, approach and address me as such; inquire no farther, see the signs'? 12. On the other hand, with regard to women, as she has mixed something softer in their voice, she has likewise deprived them of a beard. But no, to be sure, the animal should have been left without any distinguishing sign, and each of us obliged to proclaim aloud, 'I am a man!' 13. But how noble this sign is, how becoming and dignified! How much finer than a cock's comb, and more majestic than a lion's mane!

14. Therefore, we ought to preserve the signs conferred by god; we ought not to throw them away, nor, so far as we can, confound the sexes which have been thus distinguished.

15. Are these the only works of providence in us? No, what words are adequate to praise them or set them forth? For if we had any sense, ought we to do anything else, in public and in private, than praise and extol the deity, and rehearse his benefits? 16. Ought we not, as we are digging, or ploughing, or eating, to sing this hymn of praise to god? 'Great is god, that he has supplied us with these instruments to till the earth: 17. great is god, that he has given us hands, and the power to swallow, and a stomach: that he has given us the power to grow insensibly, and to breathe in our sleep.' 18. This is the hymn we should sing on every occasion, and also the greatest and most divine hymn, that he has given us the faculty to understand these things, and use them methodically. 19. Well then: because most of you have become blind, was it not necessary that there should be some one to fill this station, and sing, on everyone else's behalf, the hymn of praise to god? 20. For what else can a lame old man as I am do but sing the praise of god? If, indeed, I were a nightingale, I would act the part of a nightingale: if a swan, the part of a swan. But, since I am a rational creature, it is my duty to praise god. 21. This is my business. I do it. Nor will I ever desert this post as long as it is granted to me; and I invite you to join me in this same song.

## CHAPTER 17

# That Logic Is Indispensable

1. Since it is reason that analyses and brings to completion all other things, reason itself should not be left unanalysed. But by what shall it be analysed?

2. Plainly, either by itself, or by something else.

Well: either that too is reason, or it will be some other thing superior to reason, which is impossible. 3. If it be a form of reason, what, again, shall analyse that? For if it can analyse itself, so could the reason that we began with. If we are going to require another form of reason, the regress will be endless and have no stop.

4. 'Yes, but the more urgent necessity is to cure our judgements', and so forth.

Would you hear about these matters, then? Well, hear. 5. But if you should say to me, 'I cannot tell whether your arguments are true or false', and if I should happen to use some ambiguous expression, and you should say, 'Distinguish', I will bear with you no longer, but reply to you, 'No, there is a more urgent necessity.' 6. That is why, I suppose, the philosophers put logic first, just as, when it comes to measuring grain, we begin by examining the measure. 7. For, unless we first determine what a bushel and what a balance is, how shall we be able to measure or weigh anything? 8. Thus, in the present case, unless we have come to know thoroughly and examined accurately the standard of judgement for all other things, which we use to gain a thorough knowledge of those things, how shall we ever be able to examine everything else accurately and gain a thorough knowledge of it? And how is it possible? 9. 'Yes, but a bushel-measure is just a bit of wood, and bears no fruit.' But it measures grain. 10. 'Logic likewise bears no fruit.' That we will consider hereafter. But if one should concede even this, it is enough that logic has the power to distinguish and examine all other things, and, as one may say, measure and weigh them. 11. Who says this? Is it only Chrysippus and Zeno and Cleanthes? 12. And does not Antisthenes say it? And who is it, then, who wrote that the beginning of education is the examination of terms? Does not Socrates say that? Of whom, then, does Xenophon write, that he began with the examination of terms, to find what each of them signifies?

13. Is this, then, the great and admirable thing, to understand or interpret Chrysippus? Who says that it is? 14. But what, then, is the admirable thing? To understand the will of nature. Well, then, do you understand it on your own account? In that case, what need have you for any one else? For, if it be true, that all men who err do so involuntarily, and you have learned the truth, you must of necessity be acting aright already.

15. But, by Zeus, I do not understand the will of nature. Who, then, interprets that? They say Chrysippus. 16. I go and inquire what this interpreter of nature says. Then I fail to understand what he means, and seek for somebody who can interpret him. The interpreter says 'Come, consider what this means, just as if it were in Latin.' 17. What occasion has he here to be so proud of himself? Nor indeed has Chrysippus himself, if he only interprets the will of nature, but does not follow it himself; how much less his interpreter. 18. For it is not on his own account that we have need of Chrysippus, but to enable us to follow nature; nor do we need a diviner on his own account, but because we think that through him we will be able to understand future events, and the signs sent by the gods; 19. nor do we need the entrails of the victims on their own account, but because it is through them that the signs are sent; neither is it the raven or the crow that we admire, but the god who sends his signs through them. 20. I come, therefore, to this diviner and interpreter, and say, 'Inspect the entrails for me: what is signified for me?' 21. Having taken and laid them open, he thus interprets them: — You have a choice, man, incapable of being restrained or compelled. This is written here in the entrails. 22. I will show you this first in the sphere of assent. Can any one restrain you from assenting to truth? No one. Can any one compel you to admit a falsehood? No one. 23. You see, then, that you have in this area a choice incapable of being restrained or compelled or hindered. 24. Well, is it any otherwise with regard to impulse and desire? What can overpower one impulse but another impulse? What can overpower desire and aversion but another desire and aversion? 25. 'But if a person inflicts the fear of death upon me', someone says, 'he compels me.' No, it is not what is inflicted upon you that compels you, but your own judgement

that it is better to do such and such a thing than to die. 26. Here, again, you see it is your own judgement that compelled you – that is, choice compelled choice. 27. For, if god had created that portion of his own being which he has separated from himself and given to us such that it was capable of being restrained or compelled, either by himself or by any other, he would not have been god, nor have taken care of us in the way he ought.

28. These things, says the diviner, I find in the victims. These are the signs that you have been sent. If you wish it, you are free. If you wish it, you will have no one to blame, no one to accuse. Everything will be in accordance with your own mind, and equally, with the mind of god.

29. It is for this prophecy that I go to the diviner and the philosopher, not to admire the man on account of his interpretation, but to admire the interpretation itself.

## CHAPTER 18

# That We Should Not Be Angry With Those Who Fall Into Error

1. If what the philosophers say be true, that all men's actions proceed from one source, namely feeling, such that in the case of assent, it is the feeling that something is so, and of dissent, the feeling that it is not so, and, by Zeus, in the case of suspended judgement, the feeling that it is uncertain, 2. so also in the case of impulse towards a thing, the feeling that it conduces to my advantage, and that it is impossible to judge one thing advantageous and desire another, and to judge one thing appropriate and be impelled to another – if all this is in fact true, why should we still be angry at the multitude?

3. They are thieves and robbers.

What do you mean by thieves and robbers? They have gone astray in matters of good and evil. Ought we, then, to be angry with them, or to pity them? 4. Do but show them their error, and you will see how they will amend their faults; but, if they do not see it, they have nothing higher than their personal opinion to rely on.

5. What, then, ought not this thief and this adulterer to be put to death?

By no means, but what you should ask instead is, 6. 'Ought not this man to be put to death, who errs and is deceived in things of the greatest importance, and is blinded, not in the sight that distinguishes white from black, but in the judgement that distinguishes good from evil?' 7. By stating your question in this way you see how inhuman what you are saying is, and that it comes to the same as saying, 'Ought not this blind, or that deaf, man to be put to death?' 8. For, if the greatest harm a man can suffer is to be deprived of the most valuable things, and the most valuable thing in each man is a right moral choice, when any one is deprived just this thing, how can one still be angry with him? 9. Man, if you must be affected in this unnatural way at the ills of another, you should pity him rather than hate him; give up this readiness to take offence and inclination to hatred; 10. and do not introduce these expressions that the carping multitude use, 'Away with these accursed and abominable idiots!' 11. So be it; but how have you suddenly become so wise that you are angry at others as though they were mere fools? Why, then, are we angry? Because we admire those things which such people take from us. Do not admire your clothes, and you will not be angry with the man who steals them. Do not admire the beauty of your wife, and you will not be angry with the adulterer. 12. Know that a thief and an adulterer have no place among the things that are properly your own, but only among the things that belong to others, and which are not in your power. If you give up these things, and look upon them as nothing, with whom will you still be angry? But as long as you admire them, be angry with yourself rather than with others. 13. Consider only: You have fine clothes, your neighbour has not. You have a window, you want to air them. He does not know where the good of man lies, but imagines that it lies in having fine clothes, the very thing which you imagine too. 14. Will he not, then, come and take them away? Why, if you show a cake to greedy people, and devour it all yourself, would you not expect them to snatch it from you? Do not provoke them, do not have a window, do not air your clothes. 15. Now I had an iron lamp burning before my household gods, and hearing a noise at the window the other day, I ran downstairs to find that my lamp had been stolen. I

thought to myself that the man who took it had been moved by
a perfectly intelligible feeling. What of it? Tomorrow, I say, you
shall find one of earthenware. 16. For a man can only lose what
he has. I have lost my cloak. Yes, because you had a cloak. I
have a pain in my head. What, can you have a pain in your
horns? Why, then, are you out of humour? For loss and pain
can relate only to what you possess.

17. But the tyrant will chain – what? – Your leg. – He will
cut off – what? – Your head. – What is there, then, that he can
neither chain nor cut off? – Your choice. Hence the advice of
the ancients – Know thyself.

18. What ought to be done, then?

Practise, for heaven's sake, in little things; and thence proceed
to greater. 19. 'I have a pain in my head.' – Do not cry, 'Alas!'
– 'I have a pain in my ear.' – Do not cry, 'Alas!' I do not say
you may not groan, but do not groan within yourself. And if
your servant is a long while in bringing your bandage, do not
cry out and pull a face, and say, 'Everybody hates me.' For who
would not hate such a person? 20. Put your confidence henceforth in these doctrines, and walk upright and free, not trusting
to your bodily bulk like a wrestler: for one should not be
invincible by mere strength of body as an ass is.

21. Who, then, is the invincible man? He whom nothing
outside the sphere of choice can disconcert. So I go on to
consider him in each specific circumstance as one does in the
case of an athlete. He has been victorious in the first encounter:
what will he do in the second? 22. What if the heat should be
excessive? What if he is appearing at Olympia? So I say in this
case. What if you throw a bit of silver in his way? He will
despise it. What, if a girl? What, then, if it is in the dark? What
if he be tested by a touch of fame, or, calumny, praise, death?
He is able to overcome all these things. 23. What then, if it is
burning hot, that is to say, if he is drunk, or depressed, or
asleep? Now that is what I mean by an invincible athlete.

## CHAPTER 19

# How Should We Behave Towards Tyrants?

1. When a person possesses some superiority, or at least thinks he does when in fact he does not, if he be uneducated, he will necessarily be puffed up because of it. 2. A tyrant, for instance, says: 'I am the mightiest of all.' – Well, then, what can you do for me? Can you procure in me desire that is never subject to hindrance? How can you? For do you have it yourself? Or aversion that never falls into what it would avoid? Do you have that yourself? Or impulse that never errs? 3. And what claim could you have to that? Come now, on shipboard, do you trust to yourself, or to the man who knows? In a chariot, to whom but the man who knows? 4. And to whom in all other arts? Just the same. In what then, does your power consist? – 'All men attend to me.' So do I to my writing tablet. I wash it and wipe it; and knock in a peg for my oil flask. – 'Are these things, then, superior to me?' – No: but they are of some use to me, and therefore I attend to them. Why, do I not attend to my ass? 5. Do I not wash his feet? Do I not clean him? Do you not know that every one pays attends to himself, and to you, just as he does to an ass? For who pays attention to you as a man? Show me. 6. Who would wish to be like you? Who would desire to imitate you, as he would Socrates? – 'But I can cut off your head.' – Well said. I had forgotten that one ought to attend to you as to a fever or the cholera, and that there should be an altar erected to you, as there is to the goddess Fever at Rome.

7. What is it, then, that disturbs and confounds the multitude? The tyrant and his guards? By no means. What is by nature free, cannot be disturbed or hindered by anything but itself. 8. But it is a man's own judgements that disturb him. Thus, when the tyrant says to anyone, 'I will chain your leg', he who values his leg, cries out, 'No, have mercy', while he who sets the value on his own will and choice, says: 'If you think it to your greater advantage to do so, chain it.' – 'What! Do you not care?' – No; I do not care. – 'I will show you that I am master.' 9. – You? How could you be? Zeus has set me free. Or do you think that he would suffer his own son to be enslaved? You are master of

my carcase. Take it. 10. – 'Do you mean to say that when you come into my presence, you will not pay due attention to me?' – No; only to myself; but if you want me to say that I pay due attention to you also, I will tell you that I do, in the same way as I do to my water-jug.

11. This is not mere self-love; for every animal is so constituted as to do everything for its own sake. Even the sun does everything for its own sake and, for that matter, so does Zeus himself. 12. But when he wishes to be called 'Rain-giver', and 'Fruit-giver', and 'Father of Gods and Men', you see that he cannot perform these works and gain these titles unless he contributes to the common benefit. 13. And, more generally, he has so constituted the nature of the rational animal, that he is unable to attain any of his own goods unless he makes some contribution to the common good. 14. So ultimately it is not antisocial for a person to do everything for his own sake. 15. For what do you expect? That he will stand completely aside from himself and his personal interest? How, then, can all beings have one and the same original instinct, attachment to themselves? 16.

What follows, then? When people hold absurd opinions about things that lie outside the sphere of choice, regarding them as good and evil, it is quite inevitable that they will pay court to tyrants. 17. And oh that it were tyrants only, and not their lackeys as well! How should a man become wise all of a sudden when Caesar puts him in charge of his chamber-pot? How is it that all at once we are saying, 'With what wisdom has Felicio spoken to me'? 18. I would have him cast off his dung-heap, that you may think him a fool once again! 19. Epaphroditus owned a slave, who was a shoemaker, and sold him because he was useless. Then, as chance would have it, this same man was bought by a member of Caesar's household and became shoemaker to Caesar. If only you could have seen how Epaphroditus honoured him. 20. 'How fares my good Felicio, pray?' 21. Then if someone asked us, 'What is your master doing?', he was told, 'He is consulting Felicio, about some matter.' 22. Yet had he not sold him as being utterly useless? 23. Who, then, has made a wise man of him all of a sudden? This is what it means to honour something other than what lies within the sphere of choice.

24. Someone is raised to the office of tribune. All who meet

him congratulate him. One kisses his eyes, another his neck, and
the slaves his hands. He goes to his house and finds lamps being
lighted. 25. He ascends the Capitol. Offers a sacrifice. Now,
who ever offered a sacrifice for having good desires? Or because
his impulses were in accord with nature? For we thank the gods
for that which we place our good in.

26. A person was talking with me today about the priesthood
of Augustus. I say to him, Let the thing alone, friend: you will
be at great expense for nothing. 27. 'But those who draw up
contracts', says he, 'will write my name there.' Will you stand
by, then, and tell those who read them, 'I am the person whose
name is written there'? 28. But, even if you can always be
present now, what will you do when you die? — 'My name will
remain.' — Write it upon a stone and it will remain just as well.
But, pray, what remembrance will there be of you outside
Nicopolis? 29. — 'But I shall wear a crown of gold.' — If your
heart is quite set upon a crown, take one of roses and put that
on: you will look far prettier in that.

CHAPTER 20

## On How Reason Is Able To Contemplate Itself

1. Every art and every faculty contemplates certain things as its
principal objects. 2. Whenever, therefore, it is of like kind with
the objects of its contemplation, it necessarily contemplates itself
too. But where it is of unlike kind, it cannot contemplate itself.
3. The art of shoemaking, for instance, is exercised upon leather,
but is itself entirely distinct from the materials it works upon;
therefore it does not contemplate itself. 4. Again, grammar is
exercised on written speech. Is the art of grammar itself, then,
written speech? By no means. Therefore it cannot contemplate
itself. 5. For what purpose, then, have we received reason from
nature? To make a proper use of impressions. And what is
reason itself? Something compounded from impressions of a
certain kind: and, thus, by its nature, it becomes contemplative
of itself too. 6. And again, we have been given wisdom to
contemplate what exactly? Things good, and bad, and indiffer-

ent. What, then, is wisdom itself? Good. And what is folly? Evil. You see, then, that it necessarily contemplates both itself and its contrary.

7. Therefore the first and greatest task of a philosopher is to put impressions to the test and distinguish between them, and not admit any that has not been tested. 8. With regard to coinage, where we sense that our interest is affected, you can see what an art we have invented, and how many means an assayer uses to test it, by sight, touch, smell and, lastly, hearing. 9. He throws the denarius down, and attends to the sound, and is not satisfied to hear it only once, but, by frequent attention to it, becomes quite a musician.

10. In the same manner, whenever we think it really makes a difference whether we go wrong or not, we apply the utmost attention to distinguish between those things which may possibly deceive us. 11. But, when it comes to our poor miserable ruling faculty, we yawn and slumber and accept every impression that offers. For here the damage that we suffer does not strike us. 12. When, therefore, you wish to know how careless you are about good and evil, and how eager about things indifferent, consider what your attitude is to blindness on the one hand and delusion of mind on the other, and you will find that you are far from feeling as you ought, in relation to good and evil.

13. 'But this demands a long preparation, and much effort and study.' What of it? Do you expect that the greatest of arts can be acquired with little study? 14. And yet the principal doctrine of the philosophers is in itself very succinct. If you have a mind to know it, read Zeno, and you will see. 15. For it does not take long to say, 'Our end is to follow the gods and the essence of good consists in the proper use of impressions.' 16. Indeed, if you ask, 'What, then, is god, and what is an impression? What is particular, what universal nature?', the argument becomes lengthy. 17. And so if Epicurus should come and say that the good must reside in the flesh, here too it becomes lengthy, and it will be necessary to hear what is the principal part in us, and what is our substantial and what our essential nature. It is unlikely that the good of a snail should reside in its shell: so is it likely that the good of man should? 18. What do you yourself possess, Epicurus, that is superior to that? What is there within you which deliberates, which examines

everything, and which, with regard to the flesh itself, determines that that is the principal part? 19. And why do you light your lamp, and labour for us, and write so many books? That we may not be ignorant of the truth? Who are we? What are we to you? So the argument becomes a long one.

## CHAPTER 21

# To Those Who Wish To Be Admired

1. When a person has his proper station in life, he does not gape after things beyond it. 2. What is it that you wish to have, man?

I for my part am content if my desires and aversions are in accordance with nature, and if I exercise my impulse to act and not to act as I was born to do, and likewise my purpose, design and assent. Why, then, do you walk around as if you had swallowed a spit?

3. 'What I want is that all who meet me should admire me, and as they follow after me cry out, What a great philosopher!'

4. Who are these people, by whom you wish to be admired? Are they not the very people whom you have been in the habit of describing as mad? What, then, do you want to be admired by madmen?

## CHAPTER 22

# On Preconceptions

1. Preconceptions are common to all men; and one preconception does not contradict another. For, who of us does not assume, that the good is advantageous and what we should choose, and, in all circumstances, seek and pursue? And which of us does not assume that justice is fair and becoming? Whence, then, arises the conflict?

2. In applying these preconceptions to particular cases. 3. As

when one person cries: 'He acted well, he is a courageous man'; and another: 'No, he is out of his senses.' Hence arises the conflict of men with one another. 4. This is the conflict between Jews and Syrians and Egyptians and Romans, not whether holiness should be honoured above all else and pursued in all circumstances, but whether eating swine's flesh be consistent with holiness or not. 5. This, too, you will find to have been the conflict between Achilles and Agamemnon. Call on them to step forth. What say you, Agamemnon? Ought not that to be done which is fitting and noble? – Yes, surely. 6. – Achilles, what say you? Is it not agreeable to you, that what is noble should be done? – Yes, beyond every other thing. Apply your preconceptions, then. 7. Here begins the dispute. One says: 'I ought not to restore Chryseis to her father.' The other says: 'Yes, you ought to.' One or the other of them certainly makes a wrong application of the preconception of rightness. 8. Again, one of them says: 'If I ought to give up Chryseis, then I ought to take the prize of one of you.' The other: 'What, do you want to take the woman I love?' 'Yes, your beloved.' 'Must I alone, then, lose my prize?' 'Yes, because I alone have none.' So a conflict arises.

9. What, then, is it to be properly educated? To learn how to apply natural preconceptions to particular cases, in accordance with nature; and, for the future, to distinguish that some things are in our own power, others not. 10. In our own power are choice, and all actions dependent on choice; not in our power, the body, the parts of the body, property, parents, brothers, children, country, and, in short, all with whom we associate. 11. Where, then, shall we place the good? To what class of things shall we apply it? To that of things that are in our own power.

12. What, then, is not health, and an unmutilated body, and life good? And are not children, nor parents, nor country? Who will have patience with you?

13. Let us transfer it, then, to these things. Is it possible, then, for a man who suffers harm and fails to obtain good things to be happy?

It is not.

And can he continue to live in the way that he ought with his fellows? How is it possible that he should? For I naturally incline to my own interest. 14. If, therefore, it is in my interest to have some land, it is in my interest likewise to take it away from my neighbour. If it is in my interest to have a cloak, it is in my interest likewise to steal it from the baths. Hence wars, seditions, tyranny, plots. 15. How shall I, if this be the case, be able any longer to preserve my duty towards Zeus? If I suffer harm and fall into misfortune, he pays no heed to me. And so men say, 'What is Zeus to me if he cannot help me', or again, 'What is he to me if he wishes me to be in the condition I am?' Henceforth I begin to hate him. 16. What, then, do we build temples, do we raise statues to Zeus, in the same way as we do to evil demons, or to Fever? How in that case can he still be Zeus the 'Saviour', and 'Rain-bringer', and 'Fruit-giver'? If we place the essence of good anywhere here, all this will follow. 17. – What, then, are we to do?

This is the inquiry to be made by the man who truly philosophizes and labours to bring forth truth: 'I do not now see what is good and what is evil. Am I not mad?' 18. Yes, but if I should place the good here, amongst things that are within the sphere of choice, everyone will laugh at me. Some grey-headed old fellow will come with his fingers covered with gold rings, and shake his head, and say: 'Listen to me, child, it is right that you should learn philosophy, but it is right too that you should keep your head. This is nonsense. 19. You learn syllogisms from the philosophers, but when it comes to how you should act, you know better than they do.' 20. 'Then, why do you find fault with me, man, if I know?' What can I say to this slave? If I make no answer, he bursts with anger. 21. I must answer thus: 'Forgive me, as you would with lovers. I am not my own master; I am out of my senses.'

## CHAPTER 23

# Against Epicurus

1. Even Epicurus is aware that we are by nature social beings, but once he has placed our good in what is merely our shell, he cannot afterwards say anything other than that. 2. For, again, he strenuously maintains, that we ought not to admire or accept anything that is cut off from the nature of good. And he is in the right to maintain that. 3. But how, then, can we still be

social beings if we have no natural affection towards our offspring? Why do you, Epicurus, dissuade a wise man from bringing up children? Why are you afraid that upon their account he will be caused distress? 4. Is he caused any by a mouse that feeds within his house? What is it to him if a little mouse cries out there? 5. But Epicurus knew that, if once a child is born, it is no longer in our power not to love and care for it. 6. For the same reason, he says, a wise man will not engage in public affairs, for he is well aware what such an engagement would oblige him to do; in truth, if you are going to live amongst men as though amongst flies, what is to prevent you?

7. And does he who knows all this dare to bid us not bring up children? Not even a sheep or a wolf deserts its offspring, so shall a human being? What do you desire? That we should be as silly as sheep? 8. Yet even these do not desert their offspring. Or as savage as wolves? Neither do these desert them. 9. Pray, who would take your advice if he saw his child fallen on the ground and crying? 10. For my part, I am of the opinion that your father and mother, even if they could have foreseen that you would say such things, would not have cast you out.

## CHAPTER 24

# How Should We Struggle Against Difficulties?

1. Difficulties are the things that show what men are. Henceforth, when some difficulty befalls you, remember that god, like a wrestling-master, has matched you with a rough young man.

2. For what end? That you may become an Olympic victor, and that cannot be done without sweat. No man, in my opinion, has a more advantageous difficulty on his hands than you have, if only you will but use it as an athlete uses the young man he is wrestling against. 3. We are now sending you to Rome as a spy; but no one ever sends a coward as a spy, who, if he but hears a noise or sees a shadow somewhere, runs back, frightened out of his wits, and says: 'The enemy is already amongst us.' 4. So now, if you should come and tell us: 'Things are in a fearful way at Rome; death is terrible; banishment, terrible; calumny, ter-

rible; poverty, terrible; run, good people, the enemy is in our midst', 5. we will answer: 'Get you gone, and prophesy to yourself; our only mistake was to send out such a spy.' 6. Diogenes was sent out as a spy before you; but he brought us other tidings. He says that death is not evil, for it is not dishonourable; that defamation is an empty noise made by madmen. 7. And what tidings this spy brought us about pain and pleasure and poverty! He says that to be naked is better than any purple-bordered robe, and that to sleep upon the bare ground is the softest bed, 8. and gives a proof of all he says by his own courage, tranquillity, and freedom; and, moreover, by his gleaming thickset body. 9. There is no enemy near, says he. All is profound peace. – How so, Diogenes? Look at me, says he. Have I been hit? Am I wounded? Have I run away from anyone? 10. That is how a spy should be. But you come and tell us one thing after another. Go back again and examine things more accurately, putting aside your cowardice.

11. What shall I do, then?

What do you do when you get out of a ship? Do you take the rudder or the oars with you? What do you take, then? What is your own, and your oil-flask and knapsack. So, in the present case, if you will but remember what is your own, you will not claim what belongs to others. 12. The emperor says, 'Lay aside your consul's robe!' See, an equestrian robe, 'Lay aside that robe also.' See, a robe and nothing more. 'Put it aside.' See, I am naked. 13. 'But you still arouse my envy.' Then take this poor body of mine, take it all. If I can throw my body to this man, can I still be afraid of him?

14. But So-and-so will not make me his heir. What, then, have I forgotten that one of these things is my own? In what sense, then, do we call them 'my own'? As we do a bed in an inn. If the innkeeper when he dies leaves you the beds, well and good; if he leaves them to another, they will be his, and you will seek one elsewhere; 15. and then, if you do not find one, you will sleep upon the ground; only be of good courage and snore soundly, and remember that tragedies have no other subjects but the rich, and kings, and tyrants; no poor man fills any tragic role except as part of the chorus. 16. Kings there begin, indeed, in prosperity. 'Crown the palace with festive garlands.' – But, then, about the third or fourth act: 'Alas, Cithaeron! why did you receive me?' 17. Slave, where are your crowns, where is

your diadem? Are your guards of no avail? 18. When, therefore, you approach a man like these, keep this in mind, that you are meeting a character from tragedy, not an actor, but Oedipus himself. 19. – But So-and-so is blessed. He walks with a large retinue. Well: I have only to join myself to the crowd, and I too can walk with a large retinue.

20. To summarize: remember that the door is open. Do not be more cowardly than children, but just as they say, when the game no longer pleases them, 'I will play no more', you too, when things seem that way to you, should merely say, 'I will play no more', and so depart; but if you stay, stop moaning.

## CHAPTER 25

# On the Same Subject

1. If these things are true, and we are not stupid or acting a part when we say that good or ill for man lies in choice, and that all else is nothing to us, why are we still troubled? Why are we still afraid? 2. No one else has authority over the things that seriously concern us; and the things over which others have authority are of no concern to us. What is left for us to worry about?

3. But give me some rules.

What rules should I give you? Has Zeus not given you any? Has he not given you what is your own, free from restraint or hindrance; and what is not your own, liable to both? 4. What directions, then, what orders did you bring with you when you came from that world to this? 'Guard by every means what is your own: what belongs to others do not covet. Your good faith is your own; your sense of shame is your own. Who, then, can deprive you of these? Who can restrain you from making use of them but yourself? And how do you do so? When you concern yourself with what is not your own, you lose what is your own.' 5. Having such advice and instructions from Zeus, what further advice do you want from me? Am I greater than he? More worthy of belief? 6. If you observe these, what others do you need? Or are these not his? Produce your preconceptions: produce the demonstrations of the philosophers: produce what you have often heard, and what you have said yourself; what you have read, and what you have practised.

7. How long is it right to observe these rules, and not break up the game?

8. As long as it goes on agreeably. A king is chosen by lot at the Saturnalia (for this is the game they have decided to play): he orders, 'You drink: you mix the wine: you sing: you go: you come.' I obey, to avoid being the one who breaks up the game. 9. 'Suppose now that you are in a bad way.' I do not suppose that, and who shall compel me to suppose that? 10. Again: we agree to play Agamemnon and Achilles. He who is appointed to play Agamemnon, says to me: 'Go to Achilles, and drag away Briseis.' 11. I go. 'Come.' I come.

For we should behave in life as we do with hypothetical arguments. 'I suppose it to be night.' – Well: suppose it. 'Is it day, then?' – No: for I admitted the assumption that it is night. 12. 'Assume that you suppose it to be night.' – So be it. 'Now, suppose that it really is night.' 13. – That does not follow from the hypothesis. Thus, too, in the present case. Suppose you have ill-fortune. – Suppose it. 'Are you, then, unfortunate?' – Yes. 'Are you unhappy?' – Yes. 'But suppose that you really are in a bad way.' – This does not follow from the hypothesis: and there is another who forbids me to think so.

14. How long, then, are we to obey such orders?

As long as it is advantageous: that is, as long as I preserve what is becoming and appropriate.

15. Further, there are some morose and fastidious people who say, I cannot dine with such a fellow, and bear with his daily accounts of how he fought in Mysia. 'I told you, my friend, how I climbed the ridge – I will start again with the siege.' 16. But another says, 'I had rather get a dinner, and hear him prate as much as he pleases.' 17. And it is for you to compare the value of these things, and judge for yourself; but do not do anything as one who is burdened and afflicted and supposes himself to be in a bad way, for no one compels you to that. 18. Has someone made the house smoky? If the smoke is not excessive, stay; if it is, go out. For you must always remember and hold fast to this, that the door is open. 19. 'Do not live at Nicopolis.' – I will not live there. 'Nor at Athens.' – Well, nor at Athens. 'Nor at Rome.' – Nor at Rome either. 20. 'But you shall live at Gyara.' – I will live there. But living at Gyara seems to me like living in

too smoky a house. I will retire where no one can forbid me to live (for that is a dwelling open to all), 21. and put off my last tunic, this paltry body of mine: beyond this no one has any power over me. 22. Thus Demetrius said to Nero: 'You threaten me with death, but nature threatens you with it!' 23. If I place value on my body, I have given myself up for a slave; if on my miserable property, I am a slave likewise; 24. for I immediately show to my own detriment how I may be taken. Just as when a snake pulls in his head, I say, strike that part of him which he guards, so you can be assured, that whatever you wish to guard, there your master will attack you. 25. If you remember this, whom will you flatter or fear again?

26. But I want to sit where the senators do.

Do you not see that you are closing yourself in, that you are crushing yourself? 27. How else, then, shall I get a proper view in the amphitheatre?

Do not try to get a view, man, and you will not get crushed. Why cause trouble for yourself? Or else wait a little while, and when the show is over, go sit in the senators' seats and sun yourself. 28. For remember that this holds universally; we crush ourselves; we close ourselves in: that is, our own principles crush and close us in. What is it to be reviled, for instance? 29. Stand by a stone and revile it; and what effect will you get? If you, therefore, would listen like a stone, what would your reviler gain? But if the reviler has the weakness of the reviled for a vantage-point, then he does achieve something. 30. 'Strip him.' – 'What do you mean by him? Take his cloak and strip it off.' 'I have committed an outrage upon you.' – 'Much good may it do you.'

31. This was what Socrates practised, and that is why he always bore the same expression on his face. But we for our part had rather study and practise anything than how to become unrestrained and free.

32. The philosophers talk in paradoxes.

And are there not paradoxes in the other arts? What is more paradoxical than lancing a person in the eye to make him see? If anyone said this to a person who had no knowledge of the art of medicine, would that person not laugh at the one who said it? 33. Where is the wonder, then, if, in philosophy too, many truths appear paradoxical to the ignorant?

## CHAPTER 26

# What Is The Law Of Life?

1. As someone was reading out hypothetical arguments, Epictetus said it is also a law with regard to hypotheses that we must admit what follows from the hypothesis: but far more important is the law of life, that we must do what follows from nature. 2. For, if we desire in every matter, and in every circumstance, to keep to what is natural, it is clear that in everything we should make it our aim neither to pass over what is in accordance with nature, nor to accept what is in conflict with it. 3. The philosophers, therefore, first exercise us in theory, which is the easier task, and then lead us to the more difficult: for in theory there is nothing to oppose our following what we are taught; but in life there are many things to distract us. 4. It is ridiculous, then, for a person to say that we must begin with the latter, for it is not easy to begin with what is more difficult; 5. and this is the defence that should be offered to those parents who are displeased that their children should be studying philosophy: 'Doubtless I am in error, father, and ignorant of my duty and of what is incumbent on me. Now if this can be neither learned nor taught, what fault can you find with me? If, on the other hand, it can be taught, pray teach me yourself; or, if you cannot do so, give me leave to learn it from those who profess to understand it. 6. Besides: do you think that I fall into evil voluntarily, and miss the good? Heaven forbid! What, then, is the cause of my going wrong? Ignorance. 7. Do you not wish, then, that I should get rid of my ignorance? Who was ever taught the art of music or navigation by anger? Do you expect, then, that your anger should teach me the art of living?' 8. This, however, can only be argued by one who really has that intention. 9. But as for a man who studies these things, and goes to the philosophers, merely for the sake of showing off at an entertainment how he understands hypothetical arguments, what other reason is he doing that for than to court the admiration of some senator who happens to be sitting beside him?

10. For, in truth, it is there at Rome that the great resources

are, and the wealth here in Nicopolis would seem child's play there. That is why it is difficult for a man to be a master of his own impressions there, where the disturbing forces are so great. 11. I once saw a person weeping and embracing the knees of Epaphroditus saying that he was in distress, because he had nothing left but a million and a half sesterces. 12. So how did Epaphroditus react? Did he laugh at him, as we should do? No; but he cried out in astonishment, 'Poor man! How did you keep from mentioning it? How could you endure it?'

13. Once, when he had thrown into confusion the student who was reading out the hypothetical arguments, and the man who had set that student to read laughed, Epictetus said, 'You are laughing at yourself; you did not give the young man any preliminary training, nor find out whether he is capable of following these arguments, but simply used him as a reader. 14. So why is it', he went on, 'that when a mind is incapable of following a judgement on a complex argument, we yet entrust to such a mind the dispensing of praise, and blame, and judgement on what is well or badly done? And if such a person speaks badly of someone, does the man pay any heed; or if he praises someone, is the man elated? When the person in question cannot discover what logically follows even in these small matters?

15. The first step, therefore, towards becoming a philosopher is to become aware of the true state of one's ruling faculty; for, when a person knows it to be in a weak state, he will not immediately employ it in great matters. 16. But as it is, some, who can scarcely swallow a morsel, buy, and set themselves to eat, whole treatises; with the result that they vomit them up again, or suffer indigestion; and then come colics, fluxes and fevers. 17. Such persons ought to consider what they can take. Indeed, it is easy to refute an ignorant person in theoretical matters; but in matters relating to life no one offers himself to be examined; and we hate those who have shown us up. 18. But Socrates used to say that an unexamined life is not worth living.

## CHAPTER 27

# In How Many Ways Do Impressions Arise, And What Should We Have At Hand To Help Us In Dealing With Them?

1. Impressions come to us in four ways. Things are, and appear so to us; or they are not, and do not appear to be: or they are, and do not appear to be: or they are not, and yet appear to be. 2. Thus it is the task of the educated man to form a right judgement in all these cases; whatever the difficulty that afflicts us, we must bring forward, the appropriate aid against it. If the sophisms of Pyrrho and the Academy are what afflict us, let us bring forward what can aid us against them; 3. if it is the plausibilities of circumstances, which make certain things seem good when they are not, let us seek for aid in that area. If it is a habit that afflicts us, we must endeavour to discover aid against that.

4. What aid, then, is it possible to discover against habit? The contrary habit. 5. You hear ignorant people say, 'Poor soul, he is dead; his father died, his mother died, he was cut off before his time and in a foreign land.' 6. Listen to the contrary arguments, draw away from these expressions. Oppose to one habit the contrary habit; to sophistic arguments, the art of reasoning, and the frequent use and exercise of it. Against specious appearances we must have clear preconceptions, polished and ready for use. 7. When death appears an evil, we ought immediately to remember that evils may be avoided, but death is a necessity. 8. For what can I do, or where can I fly from it? Let me imagine myself as Sarpedon the son of Zeus, so I can then speak in the same noble manner. 'I set out on this expedition in the desire either to win glory for myself, or to provide another with the occasion to do so: if I am unable to succeed in something myself, I will not grudge another the honour of performing some noble deed.' Let us concede that this is beyond us, but can we manage these reflections at least? 9. Where shall I go to escape from death? Show me the place, show me the people to whom I may go, whom death does not

overtake. Show me a charm against it. If there be none, what would you have me do? I cannot escape death; 10. but can I not escape the dread of it? Must I die trembling and lamenting? For the origin of the distress is wishing for something that does not come about. 11. In consequence of this, if I can alter externals in accordance with my own inclinations, I do it; if not, I want to tear out the eyes of whoever hinders me. 12. For such is the nature of man, that he cannot bear to be deprived of good, and cannot bear to fall into evil. 13. And so, at last, when I can neither change things, nor tear out the eyes of him who hinders me, I sit down and groan, and revile those whom I can, Zeus, and the rest of the gods. For what are they to me if they take no care of me?

14. Oh! but you will be guilty of impiety.

What then? Can I be in a worse condition than I am now? In general, remember this, that, unless piety and self-interest fall together, piety cannot be preserved in any man.

Do not these arguments seem to have force? 15. Let a Pyrrhomist or an Academic come and oppose them. For my part, I have no leisure for this, nor am I able to stand up as an advocate of the general view. 16. Even if I had a case about a patch of land, I should call in somebody else as my advocate. With what advocate, then, am I content? With that appropriate to the matter in question. 17. I may be at a loss, perhaps, to give a reason as to how sensation is produced, whether through the body as a whole, or from some part of it, because I find difficulties that disturb me in both cases; but, that you and I are not the same person, I know with complete certainty.

18. How so? Why, I never, when I have a mind to swallow anything, carry it to your mouth, but to my own. I never, when I want to take a loaf, take a broom; but go directly to the loaf, as though to a target. 19. And do you yourselves, who deny all evidence of the senses, act in any other way? Who of you, when he intended to go to a bath, ever went to a mill?

20. What, then, must we not defend these points to the best of our ability, and so maintain what is generally accepted, and fortify ourselves against all that would oppose it?

21. Who denies that? But it must be done by one who has the ability, who has the leisure; but he who is fearful and perturbed, and whose heart broken within him, must employ his time on something else.

## CHAPTER 28

# That We Should Not Be Angry With Others; And What Things Are Great, And What Small, Amongst Men?

1. What is the reason that we assent to anything?

Its appearing to be so.

2. It is not possible, therefore, to assent to what appears not to be so?

Why?

Because it is the very nature of the understanding to agree to things that are true, to be dissatisfied with things that are false, and to suspend its belief in doubtful cases.

3. What is the proof of this?

Have the impression, if you can, that it is now night.

Impossible.

Put aside the impression that it is day.

Impossible.

Have, or put aside, the impression that the stars are, or are not, even in number.

Impossible.

4. When any one, then, assents to what is false, be assured that he does not wilfully assent to it as false (for, as Plato affirms, the soul is never voluntarily deprived of truth); 5. but what is false appears to him to be true. Well, then, have we, in actions, anything corresponding to true and false here in the realm of perception?

Duty and what is contrary to duty, the advantageous and disadvantageous, what is appropriate and inappropriate, and the like.

6. A person, then, cannot think a thing advantageous to him, and not choose it.

He cannot. 7. But what of Medea, who says:

> Yes, I understand what evils I propose,
> But passion overwhelms my resolutions?

For it is just this, the gratification of her anger and the taking of vengeance on her husband, that she regards as more advantageous than the saving of her children.

8. Yes; but she is deceived.

Show to her clearly that she is deceived, and she will not do it; but as long as you have not shown it, what else has she to follow but what seems true to her?

Nothing.

9. Why, then, are you angry with her, because, poor woman, she has fallen into error on the most important points, and, instead of being a human being, has become a viper? Why do you not, if anything, pity her instead, and, as we pity the blind and lame, so likewise pity those who are blinded and lamed in their ruling faculties? 10. Whoever, therefore, duly remembers that a person's impressions are the standard for his every action – these impressions may moreover be either right or wrong: and, if right, he is without fault, if wrong, he himself pays the penalty, for it cannot be that one person should be the one who has gone astray, and another person the one who suffers – whoever, then, remembers this, will never be angry with anyone, never be harsh towards anyone, will never revile, or reproach, or hate, or be offended by any one.

11. So, do such great and dreadful deeds have this as their origin, then, sense-impressions? This and no other. 12. The *Iliad* consists of nothing but impressions, and the use of those impressions. An impression prompted Paris to carry off the wife of Menelaus. An impression prompted Helen to follow him. 13. If, then, an impression has caused Menelaus to feel that it was an advantage to be robbed of such a wife, what would have happened? Not only the *Iliad* would have been lost, but the *Odyssey* too.

14. Do these great events, then, depend on so small a cause?

What are these events which you call great?

Wars and seditions, the deaths of many men, and the destruction of cities.

And what is so great about that? Nothing. 15. What is great in the death of many oxen, sheep, or in the burning or pulling-down of many nests of storks or swallows?

16. Are these similar cases, then?

Perfectly similar. The bodies of men are destroyed, and the bodies of sheep and oxen. The houses of men are burned, and the nests of storks. 17. What is there great or dreadful in all this? Pray, show me what difference there is between the house of a man, and the nest of a stork, as a habitation?

18. Is there, then, a similarity between a man and a stork?

How do you mean? As far as the body is concerned, complete similarity; except that men's little houses are built with beams and tiles and bricks, but nests with sticks and clay.

19. Does a man differ in no way, then, from a stork?

Yes, surely; but not in these things.

In what, then?

20. Inquire, and you will find that he differs in something else. See whether it be not in his understanding of what he is doing; in his social sense; in his good faith, sense of shame, his reliability, his intelligence.

21. Where, then, is the great good or evil of man?

Where his difference lies; if that is preserved and remains well fortified, and neither his honour, nor his fidelity, nor his intelligence is destroyed, then he himself is preserved likewise; but when any of these is lost and taken by storm, he himself is lost also. 22. All great things hang on this. Did Paris suffer his great disaster when the Greeks invaded Troy and laid it waste, and his brothers were slain in battle? 23. By no means; for no one is undone by an action not his own. All that was only laying waste the nests of storks. But his true undoing was when he lost his modesty, his good faith, his honouring of the laws of hospitality, and his decency. 24. When was Achilles undone? When Patroclus died? By no means. But when he gave himself up to rage, when he wept over a paltry girl, when he forgot that he came there not to get mistresses, but to make war. 25. These are the ways in which human beings are undone; this is the siege, this the razing of a man's city, when his right judgements are demolished, when they are destroyed.

26. But when wives and children are led away captives, and the men themselves killed, are not these evils?

27. Where do you get this further idea? Pray, inform me in my turn.

No, but how is it that you are saying that they are not evils?

28. Let us have recourse to our standard, produce your preconceptions. For this is the reason why one cannot be sufficiently amazed at how people act in this respect. When we want to judge weights, we do not judge at random; when we

want to judge whether things are straight or crooked, we do not do so at random; 29. and, in general, when it makes any difference to us to know the truth on any matter, not one of us will do anything at random. 30. But where the first and only cause is concerned of either acting rightly or going wrong, of happiness or adversity, or success or failure, there only do we act rashly and at random. Nowhere anything like a balance, nowhere anything like a standard, but some impression strikes me and I instantly act on it. 31. For am I any better than Agamemnon or Achilles, that they, by following their impressions, should do and suffer such evils, while I should be satisfied with the impressions that come to me? 32. And what tragedy has any other origin? The *Atreus* of Euripides, what is it? Impressions. The *Oedipus* of Sophocles? Impressions. The *Phoenix*? Impressions. The *Hippolytus*? Impressions. 33. Who, then, do you think a man is who takes no trouble over this matter? What do we call those who follow every impression that comes to them?

Madmen.

Are we, then, doing anything other than that?

# CHAPTER 29

# On Steadfastness

1. The essence of the good is a certain disposition of our choice, and essence of evil likewise.

2. What are externals, then?

Materials for the faculty of choice, in the management of which it will attain its own good or evil.

3. How, then, will it attain the good?

If it does not admire the materials themselves: for its judgements about the materials, if they are correct, make our choice good, and if they are distorted and perverse, make it bad.

4. This law has god ordained, who says, 'If you want anything good, get it from yourself.' You say, 'No, but from another.' – Rather, you must get it from yourself. 5. So, when a tyrant threatens and sends for me, I say, What does he threaten? If he

says, 'I will chain you', I say, 'He is threatening my hands and my feet.' 6. If he says, 'I will cut off your head', I say, 'He is threatening my neck.' If he says, 'I will throw you into prison', I say, 'He is threatening all of my poor flesh'; and, if he threatens me with exile, I reply the same.

7. Then it is not really you that he is threatening?

If I am persuaded that these things are nothing to me, not at all; 8. but, if I am afraid about any of them, it is me that he threatens. Who is there left for me to fear? The man with power over what? Of things in my own power? Of these no one is the master. Of things not in my power? And what are those to me?

9. What, then! do you philosophers teach us contempt for kings?

Heaven forbid. Who of us teaches any one to contend with them about things of which they have authority? 10. Take my poor body, take my possessions, take my reputation, take those who are about me. If I persuade any one to contend for these things as his own, accuse me with justice. 11. – 'Yes, but I want to control your judgements too.' – And who has given you that authority? How can you conquer another's judgement? 12. – By the application of fear I will conquer it. – You fail to see that it was a person's own judgement that conquered itself, it was not conquered by another. Nothing else can overcome the power of choice but that itself. 13. For that reason too the law of god is most excellent and just, that the better should always prove superior to the worse.

14. 'Ten people are superior to one', you say. In what? In chaining, killing, dragging people away where they please and taking away their property. Thus ten people can overcome one only in that in which they are superior.

15. In what, then, are they worse?

If the one has right judgement and the others have not. For can they conquer him in this? How can they? If we are weighed in a balance, must not the heavier drag down the scales?

16. So that Socrates should suffer in the way that he did at the hands of the Athenians?

Slave! what do you mean by 'Socrates'? State the matter as it really is: that the paltry body of Socrates should be arrested and dragged to prison by those who were stronger than he: that someone should give hemlock to the poor body of Socrates; and that it should expire 17. do these things appear marvellous to you, these things unjust, is it for such things as these that you accuse god? Had Socrates, then, no compensation for them? **18.** In what, then, to him did the essence of good consist? Whom shall we listen to, you or him? And what does he say? 'Anytus and Meletus can kill me, but they cannot harm me.' And again: 'If this is what god wills, so be it.' **19.** But prove to me that one who holds inferior judgements can prevail over a man who is superior in his judgements. You never will prove it, nor anything like it: for the law of nature and of god is this: Let the better always be superior to the worse.

In what?

In that in which it is better. **20.** One body is stronger than another, a number of people are stronger than a single person, and a thief is stronger than one who is not a thief. **21.** Thus I, too, lost my lamp because the thief was better at keeping awake than I. But he bought a lamp at the price of being a thief, a rogue, and a brute. That seemed to him a good bargain.

**22.** Very well; but now someone has seized me by my cloak and drags me to the market-place, and then others shout at me 'Philosopher, what good have your judgements done you? See, you are being dragged off to prison: see, you are going to lose your head!' **23.** – And pray what kind of 'Introduction to Philosophy' could I have studied, that when a stronger man than myself seizes my cloak, I should not be dragged off? Or that when ten men pull me at once and throw me into prison, I should not be thrown there? **24.** But have I learned nothing, then? I have learned to see that whatever happens, if it be outside the sphere of choice, is nothing to me. **25.** So have you gained no benefit in this respect? Why do you seek your benefit in anything other than that in which you have claimed it is to be found? **26.** And so I sit in prison and say: 'The person who shouts at me in this way does not hearken to what is meant, does not follow what is said, and has made no effort at all to know what philosophers say or how they act. Away with him, then.' **27.** 'Come out of prison again.' If you have no further need for me in prison, I will come out; if you need me again, I will return. **28.** For how long? Just as long as reason requires I should continue in this paltry body: when reason does so no longer, take it and good health to you. **29.** Only, let me not abandon it without due reason, or from mere feebleness, or on some casual pretext; for that, again, would be contrary to the will of god: for he has need of such a world and such creatures to live on earth. But if he gives the signal for retreat as he did to Socrates, we should obey his signal as that of our general.

30. Well, should such things to be said to all and sundry?

31. For what purpose? Is it not sufficient to be convinced oneself? When children come to us clapping their hands and saying: 'Today is the good Saturnalia', do we say to them, 'There is no good in that'? By no means; but we clap our hands along with them. 32. Thus, when you are unable to change a person's views, recognize that he is a child, and clap your hands with him; or if you do not wish to do that, merely keep your silence.

33. These things we ought to remember, and when we are called to meet some such difficulty, we should know that the time has come to show whether we have been well educated. 34. For a young man who goes from his studies to confront such a difficulty is like a person who has practised the analysis of syllogisms, and if somebody proposes an easy one, says, 'Give me, rather, a fine intricate one, that I may get some exercise.' So also are wrestlers displeased when matched with lightweight young men. 35. 'He cannot lift me', one says, 'now there is a fine young man.' But no – when the crisis calls, he has to weep and say, 'I wanted to go on learning.' – Learn what? If you did not learn these things to demonstrate them in practice, why did you learn them at all? 36. I imagine there must be someone amongst those who are sitting here that feels secret pangs of impatience, and says: 'When will such a difficulty befall me as has befallen him? Must I sit wasting my life in a corner when I might be crowned at Olympia? When will any one bring me news of such a contest?' Such should be the disposition of you all. 37. Even among the gladiators of Caesar there are some who bear it very ill because no one brings them out or matches them in combat, and they pray to god, and go up to their managers, begging to fight. And will none of you show such spirit? 38. I would willingly sail off just for that purpose, to see how some athlete of mine is acting and how he treats his task. 39. 'I do not want such a task', say you. Is it in your power, then, to take on what task you choose? Such a body is given you; such parents, such brothers, such a country, and such a rank in it; and then you come to me and say: 'Change my task.' Besides, have you not abilities to deal with that which is given you? 40. What you

should say is, 'It is your business to propose; mine to practise it well.' No, but you say instead, 'Do not propose such an argument to me; but such a one: do not offer such an objection to me; but such a one.' 41. – There will come a time, I suppose, when tragic actors will fancy that their masks and buskins and long robes are their real selves. Man, you have these things as your materials and your rule of action. 42. Say something, so that we may know whether you are a tragic actor or a buffoon: for, save their words, these hold everything else in common. 43. If any one, therefore, should take away his buskins and his mask, and bring him on stage like a ghost, is the tragic actor lost or does he hold good? If he has a voice he holds good. 44. So also in life. 'Take this governorship.' I take it; and, taking it, I show how a person who has been properly educated behaves. 45. 'Lay aside your senatorial robe, put on rags, and come on the stage in that character.' – What of it? Is it not in my power to deploy a fine voice? 46. 'In what character do you now appear?' – As a witness called by god. 47. 'Come you, then, and bear witness for me, for you are worthy to be brought forth as my witness. Is anything outside the sphere of choice, either good or evil? Do I harm anyone? Have I placed the advantage of each individual in anyone but in himself? What is the witness that you bear for god?' 48. I am in a miserable condition, lord; I am undone; no mortal cares for me; no mortal gives me anything; all blame me, all speak ill of me. 49. – Is this the evidence you are to give? And will you bring disgrace upon the appeal that he has made to you, who has thus conferred such an honour upon you, and thought you worthy of being produced as a witness in such a cause?

50. But he who has authority has declared, 'I judge you to be impious and unholy.' What has happened to you? – I have been judged to be impious and unholy. 51. Nothing else? – Nothing. Suppose he had passed his judgement upon a hypothetical proposition, and declared 'I judge the proposition, "if it be day, there is light" to be false', what would have happened to the proposition? Who is being judged here? Who has been condemned? The proposition, or he who is utterly mistaken about it? 52. So who on earth is this man who has authority to pass such judgement on you? Does he know what piety or impiety is? Has he made a study of it, or learned it? Where? From whom? 53. A musician would pay no heed to him if he

pronounced the lowest string to be the highest: nor a mathematician, if he passed sentence that lines drawn from the centre of a circle to the circumference are not equal. 54. So shall the truly educated man pay any heed to an uneducated one when he passes judgement on what is holy and unholy, just and unjust?

How wrong of the educated that would be! Is that, then, what you have learned here? 55. Are you not willing to leave quibbles about such things to others, to trivial men of no endurance, so that they can sit in a corner and accept their paltry fees or grumble that nobody gives them anything? You, though, should come forward and practise what you have learned. 56. For it is not quibbles that are wanted now – the books of the Stoics are full of them. What is wanted, then? The man who will properly apply his arguments and bear witness to them in his actions. 57. This is the character I would have you assume, so that we may no longer make use of old examples in the school, but may have some example of our own.

58. Whose concern is it, then, to contemplate these matters? The concern of the man who has leisure. For man is an animal fond of contemplation. 59. But it is shameful to contemplate these things as runaway slaves do. We are to sit free from distractions and listen, sometimes to the tragic actor, and sometimes to the musician, and not to do as runaway slaves do, for at the same time as one of those is paying attention and praising the actor, he is looking around on every side: and then if somebody mentions the word 'master', he is all at once disturbed and alarmed. 60. It is shameful for philosophers thus to contemplate the works of nature. For, what, in fact, is a master? It is not another man who is the master of a man, but death, and life, and pleasure, and hardship: for, without these, bring Caesar to me and you will see how steadfast I shall be. 61. But if he comes in thunder and lightning along with these, and I am frightened of them, what else am I doing but, like the runaway slave, recognizing my master? 62. But so long as I have any respite from these, I too am like the runaway slave watching in the theatre; I bathe, drink, sing; but all in fear and wretchedness. 63. But if I free myself from my masters, that is, from such things as render a master terrible, what trouble, what master do I still have?

64. What, then, are we to proclaim these things to all men? No. We must show indulgence to laymen and say: This man

is advising for me what he thinks good for himself. I excuse him.
65. For Socrates, too, excused the gaoler who wept when he
was about to drink the poison, and said, 'How nobly he has
wept for me.' 66. Was it to him that Socrates said, 'That is why
we sent the women away'? No; but to his friends, to those who
could understand; the gaoler he treated with indulgence as
though he were a child.

CHAPTER 30

## What Should We Have At Hand In
## Difficult Circumstances?

1. When you appear before some man of authority, remember
that there is another who looks down from above on what
passes here, and that it is him whom you must please rather
than this man. 2. He, therefore, asks you:

In your school, what did you call exile, and prison, and
chains, and death, and dishonour?

I called them indifferent things.

3. What, then, do you call them now? Have they changed in
any way?

No.

Have you changed, then?

No.

Tell me, then, what things are indifferent.

Things outside the sphere of choice.

Tell me also what follows.

Things outside the sphere of choice are nothing to me.

4. Tell me too what you considered to be good things.

A right choice and a right use of impressions.

What was the end?

To follow you.

5. And you say the same even now?

Yes. I say the same things now.

Well, go in confidently, remembering all this: and you will see
how it is for a young man who has studied what he ought to
appear amongst men who have not. 6. I for my part, by the

gods, imagine you will have some such thoughts as these: 'So many, such great preparations, why do we make them for nothing? 7. Was this what power amounted to? The ante-chamber, the chamberlains, the armed guards – was this what they meant? Was it for this that I listened to all those discussions? All this never meant anything: yet I was preparing for it as though it was something tremendous.'

# BOOK 2

# CHAPTER I

## That There Is No Conflict Between Confidence And Caution

1. This assertion of the philosophers may appear a paradox to some, but let us nevertheless examine, as well as we can, whether it is the case that we should combine caution with confidence in all that we do. 2. For caution seems in some sense contrary to courage; and contraries are by no means compatible. 3. What strikes many people as paradoxical in this matter seems to me to rest in something like this: if we in fact asserted that a person should exercise both confidence and caution with regard to the same things, they could justly accuse us of trying to unite qualities that cannot be united. 4. But, really, is there anything strange in the statement? For, if what has so often been said and often demonstrated is sound, that both good and evil rest essentially in the proper use of impressions, and that things that lie outside the sphere of choice are not by nature either good or evil, 5. where is the paradox in the contention of the philosophers when they say, 'In the things that lie outside the sphere of choice, be confident; in the things that lie within it, be cautious'? 6. For with regard to the latter only, if evil consists in a bad choice, is caution to be used. And if the things that lie outside the sphere of choice, and are not in our power, are nothing to us, it is with regard to these that we are to make use of courage. 7. So in this way we shall be at once cautious and courageous: and, indeed, courageous on account of this very caution; for by using caution with regard to things really evil, we shall gain courage with regard to those that are not so.

8. Yet we behave like deer: when the hinds are frightened by the feathers and flee from them, where do they turn, where do they withdraw to in their search for safety? To the nets. And so they meet their end by confusing objects of fear with objects of confidence. 9. So it is with us too. For where do we show fear? With regard to things outside the sphere of choice. In what, on the other hand, do we behave with courage, as if there were

nothing to be dreaded? In things that lie within the sphere of choice. 10. To be deceived, then, or to act rashly or imprudently, or to indulge an ignominious desire, is of no importance to us, provided we hit the mark in matters that lie outside the sphere of choice. But where death, or exile, or pain, or ignominy are concerned, there we show an inclination to retreat, there we are thoroughly agitated. 11. Hence, as is likely with those who err in matters of the greatest importance, we turn our natural confidence to rashness, desperation, foolhardiness, shamelessness, and our natural caution and modesty to cowardice and an abject spirit, full of fears and perturbations. 12. For if a person should transfer his caution to the sphere of choice and the actions of choice, then along with the will to be cautious, he will at the same time have it in his power to avoid what he wishes to avoid; but if he transfers it to things that are not in our power, and lie outside the sphere of choice, by fixing his aversion on what is not in our own power but dependent on others, he will necessarily be subject to fear, inconstancy and perturbation. 13. For it is not death or pain that is to be feared, but the fear of pain or death. That is why we commend the man who says: 'Death is no ill, but shamefully to die.'

14. Our confidence, then, ought to be turned towards death, and our caution towards the fear of death: whereas we, on the contrary, flee from death, and in coming to a judgement upon it, we show carelessness and neglect and indifference. 15. Socrates used very properly to call these things bogies: for just as masks seem fearsome and intimidating to children, because of their inexperience, we are affected in a similar manner by events for much the same reason as children are affected by bogies. 16. For what is a child? Ignorance. What is a child? Want of instruction; for in so far as a child has knowledge, he is no worse off than we are. 17. What is death? A bogy. Turn it round and see what it is. See, it does not bite. This poor body must be separated, now or later, from its portion of spirit (as formerly it was). Why, then, are you distressed if it be now? If it is not separated now, it will be later. 18. Why? So that the cycle of change in the universe may be accomplished; for it has need of things that are entering into existence, that will exist, and that have fulfilled their existence. 19. What is pain? A bogy. Turn it round and see. This poor flesh is sometimes affected by harsh impressions, sometimes by smooth. If suffering is not

worth your while, the door is open; if it is worth your while, bear it. 20. For it was fitting that the door should be open against all accidents, and then we have no trouble.

21. What, then, is the fruit of these doctrines? Whatever must be noblest and most becoming for those who are being properly educated – tranquillity, fearlessness, freedom. 22. For on these matters we should not trust the multitude who say that none ought to be educated but the free, but rather to philosophers, who say that the educated alone are free.

23. What do you mean?

This. Now is freedom anything other than the power to live as we wish?

Nothing other.

Well, tell me, then, my fellow-men, do you wish to live in error?

We do not.

For nobody who lives in error can be free. 24. Do you wish to live in fear, in pain, in distress?

By no means.

Nobody, then, who lives in fear, pain, or distress, is free; but whoever is delivered from pains, fears, and distresses, by the same means is delivered likewise from slavery. 25. How then are we to trust you any longer, good legislators? Do we allow none to be educated except those who are free? For the philosophers say, 'We allow none to be free but the educated': that is, god does not allow it.

26. What, then, when somebody turns his slave around before the praetor: has he done nothing?

Yes, he has done something.

What?

He has turned his slave around before the praetor.

Nothing more?

Yes. He has to pay over 20 per cent of the slave's value. 27. Well, the man who has gone through this ceremony, has he not won his freedom?

No more than he has won peace of mind. 28. Pray, have you, who are able to give this freedom to others, no master of your own? Are you not a slave to money? To a girl? To a boy? To a tyrant? To some friend of a tyrant? If not, why do you tremble when any of these is in question? 29. That is why I keep saying to you: what you must study, in readiness for its application, is to know what you should confront with confidence, and what with caution; namely, that you should be confident towards things that lie outside the sphere of choice, and cautious towards those that lie within.

30. But have not I read my exercises to you? Do not you know what I am doing?

31. In what? In paltry phrases. You can keep your paltry phrases! No, show me what state you are in with regard to desire and aversion, whether you do not fail to get what you wish, or fall into what you would avoid: but, as to these wretched periods of yours, if you are wise, you will take them away somewhere and obliterate them.

32. What, did not Socrates write?

Yes, who so much? But how? As he could not always have somebody at hand to examine his judgements, or be examined by him in turn, he used to argue with, and examine himself and was always testing the application of some particular preconception. 33. That is what a philosopher writes, but pretty phrases and 'said he', 'said I' he leaves to others, to the senseless or the blessed, to those who fail to take account of logical consequences because of their stupidity or those who live a life of leisure because of their serenity. 34. And now, when the moment calls, will you go off and give a recitation to display what you have written and boast, 'See how I can put a dialogue together'? 35. That should not be your boast, man, but rather this: 'See how I never fail to attain what I desire. See how I never fall into what I want to avoid. Bring death before me, and you will know. Bring hardships, bring imprisonment, bring dishonour, bring condemnation.' 36. That should be the display of a young man who has just left the schools. Leave the rest to others. Let no one ever hear you utter a word about them, nor put up with it if any one praises you for them, but let it be thought that you are a nobody, and that you know nothing. 37. Show that you know only this, how you may never fail in your desire, nor fall into what you want to avoid. 38. Let others study lawsuits, problems and syllogisms. You should study how to face death, imprisonment, the rack, and exile, 39. and, with confidence in him who has called you to face them, show what the rational governing faculty can do when arrayed against forces that lie outside the sphere of choice. 40. And thus, this paradox becomes neither impossible nor a paradox, that we must be at once cautious and courageous: courageous in what does not depend upon choice, and cautious in what does.

## CHAPTER 2

# On Tranquillity

1. Consider, you who are going into court, what you wish to preserve, and what you wish to succeed in. 2. For if you wish to keep your choice in accord with nature, you are entirely secure, all will go easily, you should have no trouble. 3. For if you wish to preserve what is in your own power, and is naturally free, and are contented with that, what else have you to care about? For who is the master of things like these? Who can take them away from you? 4. If you wish to be a man of honour and trust, who shall prevent you? If you wish not to be hindered or compelled, who shall compel you to desires and aversions contrary to your judgement? 5. The judge, perhaps, will pass a sentence against you which he thinks fearful: but how can he make you react to it with aversion? 6. Since, then, desire and aversion are in your own power, what else have you to care for? 7. Let this be your introduction, this your narrative, this your proof, this your victory, this your peroration, and this your applause. 8. That is why Socrates, when somebody put him in mind to prepare himself for his trial, replied, 'Do you not think, that I have been preparing myself for this with my whole life?' 9. By what kind of preparation? 'I have preserved what was in my own power.' What do you mean? 'I have done nothing unjust, either in public or in private life.'

10. But if you wish to preserve externals too, your paltry body, or property or reputation, I advise you immediately to make every possible preparation, and besides, consider the disposition of your judge, and of your adversary. 11. If it be necessary to clasp his knees, clasp them: if to weep, weep: if to groan, groan. 12. For when you have subjected what is your own to externals, submit to slavery from that time forth, and do not struggle, and at one time be willing to be a slave, and at another not willing, 13. but simply, and wholeheartedly, be one

or the other, free or a slave, cultivated or ignorant, a fighting-cock of the true blood or a pusillanimous one, and either endure being buffeted until you die, or give in at once. May you not be the man to receive many blows and then give in at the last.

15. Why, do you think that if Socrates had wished to preserve externals, that he would have come forward and said, 'Anytus and Meletus are indeed able to kill me, but not to harm me'? 16. Was he so foolish as not to see that this road does not lead to that end, but elsewhere? What, then, is the reason that he not only disregards his judges, but provokes them in addition? 17. Thus my friend Heraclitus, in a trifling suit about a patch of land in Rhodes, after having proved to the judges that his cause was just, said when he came to the peroration of his speech, 'I will not entreat you; nor do I care what judgement you give: for it is you who are being judged, not I.' And thus he lost his suit. 18. What need was there of this? Be content not to make entreaties: do not state in addition that you will not make entreaties, unless it be a proper time to provoke the judges deliberately, as in the case of Socrates. 19. But if you too are preparing a peroration of this kind, why rise to speak, why answer the summons? 20. For if you wish to be crucified, wait and the cross will come. But if reason determines that you should answer the summons and persuade the judge as best you can, you must act accordingly, with due regard, however, to the maintenance of your true character.

21. For this reason moreover it is ridiculous to say, 'Give me some advice.' What advice am I to give you? No, what you ought to say is, 'Enable my mind to adapt itself to whatever comes to pass.' 22. The former is just as if an illiterate person should say: 'Tell me what to write when I am set some name to write': 23. and I direct him to write 'Dion', and then another comes, and sets him not the name 'Dion', but 'Theon': what will be the consequence? What is he to write? 24. Whereas, if you had made writing your study, you would be ready prepared for whatever word might occur: if not, what can I suggest to you? For, if the circumstances should dictate something different, what will you say, or what will you do? 25. Remember, then, this general rule, and you will need no suggestion: but if you gape after externals you must necessarily be tossed up and down, according to the inclination of your master. 26. And who

is your master? He who has authority over any of the things
that you strive to acquire, or want to avoid.

## CHAPTER 3

# To Those Who Recommend People
# To Philosophers

1. It was a good answer that Diogenes made to the man who
asked for letters of recommendation from him: 'At first sight he
will know you to be a man: and whether you are a good or a
bad man, if he has the skill to distinguish between good and
bad, he will know likewise: but if he has not, he will never
discover it, though I should write a thousand times.' 2. It is just
as if you were a coin and desired to be recommended to a person
in order to be tested: if the person is an assayer of silver, you
will recommend yourself.

3. We ought, therefore, in life also, to have something
comparable to this skill with silver so that one may be able to
say, like the assayer, Bring me whatever drachma you will, and
I will find out its value. 4. Now with regard to syllogisms I can
say, 'Bring me whomever you want, and I will distinguish for
you whether he knows how to analyse syllogisms or not.' Why?
Because I know how to analyse syllogisms myself, and have the
ability that a man needs if he is to judge whether people can
deal properly with syllogisms. 5. But how do I act in life? At
some times I call a thing good; at others, bad. What is the cause
of this? The opposite of what was the case with syllogisms, a
lack of knowledge and experience.

## CHAPTER 4

# To A Man Who Had Once Been
# Caught In Adultery

1. As Epictetus was saying that man is born for fidelity and that whoever subverts this subverts the distinctive quality of man, one of those who pass for being scholars happened to come in, a man who had been found guilty of adultery in that city. 2. But, continued Epictetus, if laying aside that fidelity for which we were born, we form designs against the wife of our neighbour, what are we doing? What else but ruining and destroying? Whom? The man of trust, of honour, of piety. 3. Is that all? And are we not destroying neighbourly feeling, friendship, our country? What position are we placing ourselves in? How am I to treat you, sir? As a neighbour? A friend? Of what kind? As a citizen? How shall I trust you? 4. Indeed, if you were a pot that was so cracked that no use could be made of you, you would be thrown out on the dunghill and nobody would trouble to pick you up; 5. but if, being a man, you can fill no place in human society, what can we do with you? For, suppose you cannot hold the place of a friend, can you hold even that of a slave? And who will trust you? Do you not agree, then, that you too should be thrown on a dunghill, as a useless pot, as mere excrement? 6. And then you will doubtless say, 'Nobody pays any heed to me, a man and a scholar'. Naturally, because you are a bad man and a useless one. It is much the same as if wasps should be angry that nobody has any regard for them, but rather, that everyone runs away from them, and if anyone can, he strikes them dead. 7. You have such a sting that whomever you strike with it is cast into trouble and pain. What would you have us do with you? There is no place to put you.

8. What, then, are not women by nature common property?

I admit it; and so is a sucking-pig the common property of those who are invited to the feast. But, once it has been shared out, go, if you think proper, and snatch the share of the person sitting next to you or steal it surreptitiously, or stretch out your hand and taste it; and, if you cannot tear off any of the meat, dip your fingers in the fat and lick them. A fine companion! A fellow-diner worthy of Socrates! 9. Again: is not the theatre common to all the citizens? Therefore come, when all are seated, if you think proper, and turn any one of them out of his seat. 10. Thus, women are by nature common property; but when the legislator, like the host at a dinner, has apportioned them, are you not willing like the others to look for your own portion instead of seizing somebody else's and gobbling it down?

But I am a scholar, and understand Archedemus.

11. With all your understanding of Archedemus, then, be an adulterer and faithless; and, instead of a man, be a wolf or an ape. For what can prevent you?

## CHAPTER 5

# How Is Greatness Of Mind Compatible With Careful Behaviour?

1. The materials of action are indifferent; but the use that we make of them is not indifferent. 2. How, then, shall one preserve constancy and tranquillity of mind, and at the same time the due care that saves us from hasty and thoughtless action? By imitating those who play at dice. 3. The counters are indifferent; the dice are indifferent. How do I know what is going to fall? To use whatever does fall with proper care and skill, that is my business. 4. Thus in life, too, this is the chief business: distinguish things and weigh them one against another, and say, 'Externals are not in my power, choice is. 5. Where shall I seek good and evil? Within; in what is my own.' But in regard to what belongs to others, never use the words good, or evil, or benefit, or injury, or any word of that kind.

6. What, then, are we to use these externals in a careless way?

By no means; for this again is an evil for the faculty of choice and hence unnatural to it. 7. Rather, externals must be used with care, because their usage is not an indifferent matter, yet at the same time, with composure and tranquillity, because the material being used is indifferent. 8. For where a thing is not indifferent, there no one can hinder or compel me. Where I am capable of being hindered or compelled, the acquisition does not depend on me and in neither good nor bad; but the use of it is indeed either good or bad, and that does depend on me. 9. It is difficult, I admit, to blend and combine the carefulness of one who is devoted to material things with the constancy of one who disregards them, but it is not impossible: if it were, it would be impossible to be happy. 10. But we act as though we were on a voyage. What is in my power? To choose the helmsman, the sailors, the day, the moment. 11. Then comes a storm. What do I care? My part is performed. This is now the concern of another – the helmsman. 12. But the ship is sinking: what then have I to do? I do what I can, and that alone. I drown without fear, without crying out, or accusing god, but as one who knows that what is born must likewise die. 13. For I am not eternal, but a man; a part of the whole, as an hour is of the day. Like an hour, I must come and, like an hour, must pass away.

14. So what difference does it make to me how I pass away, whether by drowning or by a fever? For, in some way or other, pass I must. 15. This is what you will see skilful ball players doing as well. None of them considers whether the ball is good or bad, but only how to throw it and catch it. 16. Accordingly, facility lies in that, as do skill, speed and good judgement; so that where I cannot catch it even if I spread out my cloak to do so, the expert will catch it whenever I throw. 17. But if we catch or throw it in fear or perturbation, what kind of play will this be? How shall we keep ourselves steady, or how see the order of the game? One will say, 'Throw'; another, 'Do not throw'; a third, 'You have thrown once already.' This is a mere quarrel, not a game.

18. In that sense, Socrates knew how to play at ball.

What do you mean?

He knew how to play in court. 'Tell me, Anytus', says he, 'how can you say that I do not believe in god? What do you think daemons are? Are they not either the offspring of gods, or the mixed offspring of gods and men?' 19. 'Yes.' 'Do you think, then, that one can believe in the existence of mules, but not of asses?' This was just like a man playing ball. And there in court, what was the ball he had to play with? Imprisonment, exile, a draught of poison, being separated from his wife, and leaving his children behind as orphans. 20. These were what he had to play with; but nonetheless he did play, and threw the ball with dexterity. Thus we also should be careful how we play, but indifferent as to the ball itself. 21. We should do all we can to show our skill with regard to any external material, without, however, accepting it for its own sake, but displaying our skill with regard to it, whatever it may be. Thus a weaver does not make the wool, but employs his skill on what is given to him. 22. It is another who gives you food, and property, and can also take them away, and your paltry body too. You should, then, accept the material you are given and set to work on it. 23. And then, if you come off unharmed, the others who meet you will congratulate you on your escape, but the man who has a clearer insight into such things, if he sees that you have behaved in a becoming manner, will praise and congratulate you, but will do the opposite if you owe your escape to any dishonourable action. For where a man has proper reason to rejoice, his fellow men has proper reason to share in that rejoicing.

24. How is it, then, that some external things are said to be in accordance with nature, and others contrary to it?

Because we consider ourselves in detachment from everything else. I will say that it is natural for the foot, for instance, to be clean. But if you take it as a foot, and not as a detached object, it will be fitting for it to walk in the dirt, and tread upon thorns, and sometimes even to be cut off for the sake of the body as a whole; otherwise it is no longer a foot. 25. We should reason in some such manner concerning ourselves also. What are you? A man. If then, indeed, you consider yourself as a detached being, it is natural for you to live to old age, and be rich and healthy; but if you consider yourself as a man, and as a part of the whole, it will be fitting, on account of that whole, that you should at one time be sick; at another, take a voyage, and be exposed to danger; sometimes be in want; and possibly it may happen, die before your time. 26. Why, then, are you displeased? Do you not know that, just as the foot in detachment is no longer a foot, so you in detachment are no longer a man? For what is a man? A part of a city, first, of that made up by gods and men; and next, of that to which you immediately belong, which is a miniature of the universal city.

27. So must I now be called to trial?

Is another, then, to be ill with a fever, another to be exposed to the sea, another to die; and another to be condemned?

For it is impossible, while we are in such a body, in such a world, and among such companions, that such things should not befall us, some affecting one man, some another. 28. It is thus your task to come forward and say what you ought, and deal with these things as is fitting. If the judge then says, 'I judge you guilty', you can reply, 'I wish you well. 29. I have performed my part. It is for you to see whether you have performed yours; for there is some danger in that too, let me tell you.'

## CHAPTER 6

## On What Is Indifferent

1. A hypothetical proposition is an indifferent thing; but your judgement concerning it is not indifferent, but is either knowledge, or opinion, or delusion. Likewise, life is indifferent; but the use of it not indifferent. 2. When you are told, therefore, that these things also are indifferent, do not, on that account, ever be careless; nor, when somebody urges you to be careful, be abject or in awe of the materials of action. 3. It is also good to know your own qualifications and powers, so that where you are not qualified you may keep quiet, and not be upset if others have the advantage over you in such things. 4. For where syllogisms are involved, you in your turn can expect to have the advantage over them, and if they are upset at this, you can console them by saying, 'I have learned these things, and you have not.' 5. Thus, too, where practical skill is necessary, do not pretend to something that only practice can provide, but leave the matter to those who are practised in it, and be content yourself to maintain your composure.

6. 'Go and pay your compliments to so-and-so.' – 'I do so.' – 'How?' 'Not abjectly.' – 'But you had the door shut on you.' 'Yes, for I have not learned to get in at the window; and, finding the door shut, I must either withdraw, or get in at the window.' 7. 'But do go and speak to him.' – 'I do so.' 'In what manner?' – 'Not abjectly.' 8. 'But you did not get what you wanted.' For this was not your business, but his. Why do you claim what belongs to another? Always remember what is your own, and what is another's, and then you will never be disturbed. 9. Therefore Chrysippus rightly says: 'So long as the consequences

are unclear to me, I always hold to the things best adapted to secure what is in accordance with nature, for god himself created me with the faculty for choosing such things. 10. If I really knew that it was ordained for me to be ill at this moment, I would aspire to be so: for the foot too, if it had a mind, would aspire to be muddied.'

11. Now why are ears of corn produced, if it be not to ripen? and why do they ripen, if not to be reaped? For they are not things apart. 12. If they were capable of sense, ought they to pray that they should never be reaped? It would be a curse upon ears of corn never to be reaped: 13. and likewise you should know that it would be a curse upon man never to die; like that of not ripening, and never being reaped. 14. But since we men are beings who at the same time are fated to be harvested and are aware of the very fact that they are being harvested, we become angry on that account. This is only because we neither know what we are, not have studied what belongs to man, as horsemen do what belongs to horses. 15. Yet Chrysantas, when he was about to strike an enemy, on hearing the trumpet sound a retreat, drew back his hand: for he thought it more important to obey the command of his general than his own inclination. 16. But not one of us, even when necessity calls, is ready and willing to obey it, but we suffer whatever things we do suffer with lamentation and groans, and call them our 'circumstances'. 17. What do you mean by 'circumstances', man? For if you mean by 'circumstances' what surrounds you, everything is a circumstance: but, if you apply this name to hardships, where is the hardship when something that was born is destroyed? 18. The instrument of destruction is either a sword, or a wheel, or the sea, or a tile, or a tyrant. And what does it matter to you by what way you descend to Hades? All roads are equal. 19. But, if you would hear the truth, the one that a tyrant sends you along is the shorter. No tyrant was ever six months in cutting any man's throat: but a fever is often a year in killing. All these things are mere noise, and the pomp of empty names.

20. My life is in danger from Caesar.

And am I not in danger, living in Nicopolis, where there are so many earthquakes? And when you yourself cross the Adriatic, are you not in danger? In danger of your life?

21. Ay; but I am also in danger with respect to opinion.

What, your own? How so? Can any one compel you to have

any opinion contrary to your will? Do you refer to the opinions of others? And what sort of danger is it to you if others have false opinions?

22. But I am in danger of being banished.

What is it to be banished? To be somewhere else than in Rome?

Yes; but what if I should be sent to Gyara?

If it be worth your while, you will go: if not, you have another place to go to instead of Gyara, where he who now sends you to Gyara must go likewise, whether he wants to or not. 23. Why, then, do you go to Rome, as though it were something important? It is actually no great thing when compared to your preparation for it: so that a gifted young man might say, 'It was not worthwhile for this to have listened to so many lectures and written so much and to have sat for so long with an old man of no exceptional worth.' 24. Only, remember the distinction to be drawn between what is yours and what is not yours. Never lay claim to anything that is not your own. 25. A tribunal and a prison is, each of them, a place; one high, the other low: but choice remains the same, and if you have a mind to keep it the same in both places, it can be kept so. 26. And then we shall become emulators of Socrates, when, even in prison, we are able to write hymns of praise: 27. but, as we now are, consider whether we could bear if some other person said to us in prison, 'Would you like me to read you hymns of praise?' – 'Why do you trouble me: do you not know what my plight is?' 'What is it, then?' 'I am going to die.' 'Yes, but are other men to be immortal?'

## CHAPTER 7

# What Use Should We Make Of Diviners?

1. Because we consult diviners when there is no occasion for us to do so, many of us fail to carry out many appropriate actions. 2. For what can the diviner see, besides death, or danger, or sickness, or, in general, things of that kind? 3. If it becomes necessary, then, to risk my life for a friend, or if it is appropriate

for me even to die for him, what occasion have I to consult a diviner? Have I not the diviner within me, who has told me the true nature of good and evil, and has expounded the signs that indicate both? 4. What further need have I, then, of the entrails of victims or the flight of birds? Can I bear with a diviner when he says, 'This is expedient for you'? For does he know what is expedient for me? Does he know what good is? 5. Has he learned the signs that indicate good and evil as he has learned the signs in the entrails? For if he knows the signs of good and evil, he also knows those of things honourable and shameful, and just and unjust. 6. It is up to you to tell me, sir, what is indicated for me – life or death, riches or poverty. But whether these things are expedient or inexpedient, am I going to ask that of you? 7. You don't speak on questions of grammar, do you? And yet you venture to do so here, where all of us go astray and are at variance with one another? 8. It was thus a good answer that the woman made when she wanted to send a boatload of supplies to Gratilla in her exile and someone said, 'Domitian will only take them away again.' 'I would rather he took them away', she replied, 'than that I should fail to send them.'

9. What, then, leads us to consult diviners so constantly? Cowardice, our fear of what will turn out. That is why we flatter the diviners. 'Tell me, sir, shall I inherit my father's property?' 'Let us see; let us offer a sacrifice over this.' 'Yes, sir, as fortune wills.' Then if he says, 'You will inherit the property', we give him thanks as if we had received the inheritance from him. And in consequence, they carry on deceiving us. 10. What should we do, then? We should come to them without desire or aversion, just as a traveller asks somebody he meets which of two roads to take, without having any particular desire to travel on the right-hand road rather than the left; for he does not wish to travel on one of them in particular, but on the one that will lead him to where he wants to go. 11. It is in this way also that we should approach god as a guide, just as we make use of our eyes, not calling on them to show us things of one kind rather than another, but accepting the impressions of whatever they display to us. 12. But now, all of a tremble, we grasp at the reader of bird-flights, calling on him as if he were a god, beseeching him, 'Have mercy on me, allow that I may come off safe.' 13. You slave, do you wish for anything, then, but what is best for you? And is anything better than what seems best to

god? Why do you do all you can to corrupt your judge and mislead your counsellor?

## CHAPTER 8

# What Is The True Nature Of The Good?

1. God brings benefit; but the good also brings benefit. It would seem, then, that where the true nature of god is, there too is the true nature of the good. 2. What, then, is the true nature of god? Flesh? – Heaven forbid! Land? Fame? – Heaven forbid! Intelligence? Knowledge? Right reason? – Certainly. 3. Here, then, without more ado, seek the true nature of the good. For do you seek it in a plant? – No. Or in an irrational creature? – No. If, then, you seek it in what is rational, why do you persist in seeking it elsewhere than in what distinguishes that from the irrational? 4. Plants do not even have the capacity to deal with external impressions, and therefore you do not apply the term good to them. Good requires, then, the capacity to deal with these impressions. 5. And is that the only thing it requires? For if that is all, you may say that other animals also are capable of good things, and of happiness and unhappiness. 6. But this you do not say; and you are right; for even if they are altogether capable of dealing with external impressions, they do not have the power to understand how they deal with those impressions. And with good reason, for they are born to serve others and are not ends in themselves. 7. For an ass, say, is surely not born as an end in itself? No, but because we had need of a back that is able to carry burdens. Also, by Zeus, we required that it should be able to walk around; it has therefore received in addition the capacity to deal with external impressions. Otherwise it would have been incapable of moving about. 8. But there its endowments end; for if the ass itself had been granted in addition the power to understand how it deals with those impressions, it clearly follows that it would no longer have been subject to us; nor would it have performed these services for us, but would have been like and equal to ourselves. 9. Are you not willing, therefore, to seek the true nature of the good in that quality

which, when absent from other living things, makes us unwilling
to apply the word good to them.

10. What, then? Are not these creatures also works of the
gods? They are, but not principal works nor parts of the divine.

11. But you are a principal work: you are a fragment of god;
you contain a part of him in yourself. Why, then, are you so
ignorant of your noble birth? Why do you not know whence
you came? 12. Why do you not remember, when you are eating,
who you are that eat, and whom you are feeding? When you
engage in sexual intercourse, who it is that is doing so? When
you are conversing, when you are exercising, when you are
disputing, do you not know that it is god you feed, god you
exercise? You carry god about with you, wretch, and know
nothing of it. 13. Do you suppose I mean some external god
made of gold or silver? It is within yourself that you carry him,
and profane him, without being sensible of it, by impure
thoughts and unclean actions. 14. If even an image of god were
present, you would not dare to act as you do; but when god
himself is within you, and hears and sees all, are not you
ashamed to think and act thus, you who are ignorant of your
own nature and hateful to god?

15. After all, why are we afraid, when we send a young man
out of school into action, that he should behave improperly, eat
improperly, act improperly in his sexual relations, that he should
feel humbled if dressed in rags, and exalted by fancy clothing?
16. Such a person is ignorant of the god within him, ignorant of
what being it is in whose company he is setting out. Can we
allow him to say, 'Oh that I had you with me!'? 17. Is it not the
case that where you are, you have god with you also? And
having him, do you seek for someone else? 18. Or will he have
something else to tell you than this? Why, if you were a statue
of Pheidias, his Athena or his Zeus, you would have remembered
who you are and who it is that made you; and, if you had any
power of perception, you would have endeavoured to do
nothing unworthy of him who had made you, or of yourself:
and, to make no unbecoming show of yourself before the eyes
of men. 19. But as it is, since Zeus has made you, are you
therefore quite unconcerned as to the manner of person you
show yourself to be? And yet, what comparison is there, either
between the one artist and the other, or between the works that
they have made? 20. What work of any artist contains within

itself those faculties which are displayed in its making? Is it anything more than marble, or brass, or gold, or ivory? And the Athena of Pheidias, once she has stretched out her hand and had the Victory placed in it, remains in that attitude for ever. But the works of god are endowed with movement and breath, and are able to deal with impressions and put them to the test. 21. When you are the workmanship of such an artist, will you dishonour him, especially when he has not only formed you, but has entrusted you to the charge of yourself alone? 22. Will you not only be forgetful of this, but, moreover, dishonour the trust? If god had committed some orphan to your charge, would you have been thus careless of him? 23. Yet he has delivered your own self to your care, and says, 'I had no one fitter to be trusted than you. Preserve this person for me, such as he is by nature: modest, faithful, proud, undaunted, dispassionate, unperturbed.' And after that, will you not keep him so?

24. But it will be said: 'Where did he get this haughty look, and solemn face?' – But not yet as much as the case deserves. As yet I lack confidence in what I have learned, and assented to. I still fear my own weakness. 25. Let me but gain confidence a little, and then you shall see me with the kind of expression and bearing that I ought to have, then I will show you what the statue is like when it is completed and polished. 26. What do you think of that? A haughty look? Heaven forbid! For Zeus at Olympia does not display a haughty look, surely? Heaven forbid! For does Olympian Zeus put on a proud expression? No, but maintains a steady gaze, as becomes him who is about to say, 'My word is irrevocable and never deceives.' 27. Of such a nature will I show myself to you: faithful, modest, noble, unperturbed. 28. – What, and immortal too, and exempt from age and disease? – No. But as one who dies like a god, who bears illness like a god. This is in my power; this I can do. The other is not in my power, nor can I do it. 29. I will show you the sinews of a philosopher.

What sinews are those?

Desire that never fails in its achievement; aversion that never meets with what it would avoid; appropriate impulse; carefully considered purpose; and assent that is never precipitate. That is what you shall see.

## CHAPTER 9

## That We Adopt The Profession Of
## A Philosopher When We Are Unable
## To Fulfil That Of A Man

1. It is no ordinary matter merely to fulfil our profession as a man. 2. For what is a man?

A rational and mortal living creature.

At once the question arises, from what are we distinguished by the rational element in our nature?

From wild beasts.

And from what else?

From sheep and the like.

3. Take care, then, never to act like a wild beast; otherwise you have destroyed the man in you and failed to fulfil your profession as a man. Take care, too, that you do not act like a sheep; for in that way too the man in you is destroyed.

4. When do we act like sheep?

When we act for the sake of our stomach or our genitals, when our actions are haphazard, filthy or unconsidered, to what level have we sunk?

To that of sheep.

What have we destroyed?

Our rational faculty.

5. When we behave contentiously, injuriously, angrily, and aggressively, to what level have we sunk?

To that of wild beasts.

6. And further, some of us are wild beasts of a larger size, others, little evil-natured vermin, with respect to whom we are inclined to say 'I should prefer to be food to a lion.' 7. By all these means our profession as a man is destroyed. 8. For when is a complex proposition preserved?

When it fulfils what it professes.

So that the preservation of such a proposition consists in this, that its component parts are true.

When is a disjunctive proposition preserved?

When it fulfils what it professes.

And when are flutes, a lyre, a horse, a dog preserved?
9. Is it surprising, then, that man should be preserved or destroyed in the same manner? 10. Each man is strengthened and preserved by actions that correspond to his nature, the builder by building, the grammarian by grammatical studies, but if the latter gets into the habit of writing ungrammatically, his art will necessarily be destroyed and perish. 11. Thus modest acts preserve the modest man, and immodest ones destroy him; faithful actions, the faithful man, and acts of the opposite nature destroy him. 12. On the other hand, acts of the opposite nature strengthen men of the opposite character. Shamelessness strengthens the shameless man; dishonesty the dishonest man; slander, the slanderous man; anger, the bad-tempered man; and the disproportion between what he takes in and what he gives out strengthen the miser in his ways.

13. For this reason philosophers exhort us not to be contented with mere learning, but to add practice also, and then training. 14. For we have been long accustomed to do the opposite of what we should, and the opinions that we hold and apply are the opposite of the correct ones. If, therefore, we do not also adopt and apply the correct opinions, we shall be nothing more than interpreters of the judgements of others. 15. For who amongst us is not already able to deliver a systematic discourse on what is good and evil? That some things are good, some evil, and others indifferent: the good are virtue, and whatever partakes of virtue; the evil, the contrary; and the indifferent, riches, health, reputation. 16. Then, if while we are saying all this, we should be disturbed by some greater than ordinary noise, or one of the bystanders should laugh at us, we are flustered. 17. Philosopher, what has become of what you were saying? Where did it come from? Merely from your lips? Why, then, do you defile helpful principles provided by others? Why do you gamble with matters of the greatest importance? 18. It is one thing to hoard up bread and wine in a store-cupboard, and another to eat it. What is eaten is digested, distributed and becomes nerves, flesh, bones, blood, a fine complexion, ease of breathing. Whatever is hoarded up is ready, indeed, whenever you have a mind to show it; but no further use to you than the mere reputation that you have for possessing it. 19. For what difference is there, whether you expound these doctrines, or those of other schools? Sit down now, and deliver a technical

discourse on the principles of Epicurus: and perhaps you will talk more cogently there than he could have done himself. Why, then, do you call yourself a Stoic, why do you deceive the world, why when you are a Hellene do you act the part of a Jew? 20. Do not you see in what sense a person is called a Jew, a Syrian, an Egyptian? And, when we see anyone wavering between two creeds, we are accustomed to say, 'He is no Jew, but is acting the part.' But, when he assumes the attitude of mind of one who has been baptized and made his choice, then he really is a Jew and is called one too. 21. And so we likewise, who make a show of having been baptized, are Jews in name only, but are in practice something else, being out of sympathy with reason and far from applying the principles we talk of, for all that we pride ourselves on them as being men who have knowledge of them. 22. So, unable as we are to fulfil the profession of man, we take on in addition that of the philosopher, such a massive burden besides. It is much as if a man who was incapable of lifting ten pounds aspired to raise the stone of Ajax.

## CHAPTER 10

# How Can The Acts Appropriate To Man Be Discovered From The Names Applied To Him?

1. Examine who you are. In the first place, a man, that is, a being in whom there is nothing more sovereign than his power of choice, but in whom all else is subject to that, whilst choice itself is free from slavery and subjection. 2. Consider, then, what you are separated from by reason. You are separated from wild beasts; you are separated from cattle. 3. Furthermore, you are a citizen of the universe, and a part of it; and no subservient, but a principal part of it.

For you are capable of understanding the divine governance of the universe, and of reasoning on what follows from that. 4. What, then, is the calling of a citizen? To consider nothing in terms of personal advantage, never to deliberate on anything as though detached from the whole, but be like our hand or foot, which, if they had reason, and understood the constitution of nature, would never exercise any impulse or desire, except by reference to the whole. 5. Thus the philosophers are right to say that if a wise and good man had foreknowledge of events, he would work to assist nature even when it comes to sickness and death and mutilation, being aware that these things are allotted in accordance with the ordering of the universe, and that the whole is more sovereign that the part, and the city than the citizen. 6. But, since we cannot know beforehand what will happen, it is our duty to hold fast to things that are naturally more suited to be chosen, because that is what we are born to.

7. Remember, next, that you are a son; and what is a person's calling in his character as a son? To regard everything that is his as his father's; to obey him in all things: not to revile him to another; not to say or do anything injurious to him; to give way and yield to him in everything; and to co-operate with him to the utmost of his power.

8. Next know likewise, that you are a brother. In this character also you must be deferent, obedient, restrained in your language, never claiming against your brother anything that lies outside the sphere of choice, but cheerfully giving these up, so that you may have the larger share of the things that lie within the sphere of choice. 9. For consider what it is, at the cost of a lettuce, for instance, or a chair, to procure for yourself good nature, and how great is the advantage that you have gained.

10. If, furthermore, you are on the council of any city, you should remember that you are a councillor; if a youth, a youth; if an old man, an old man. 11. For each of these names, if rightly considered, always points to the acts appropriate to it. 12. But if you go and revile your brother, I tell you, 'You have forgotten who you are, and what your name is.' 13. For if you were a smith and made bad use of your hammer, you would have forgotten what you were as a smith: and, if you have forgotten the brother in you, and become, instead of a brother, an enemy, do you imagine that you have not exchanged one thing for another? 14. If, instead of a man, a gentle and social creature, you have become a wild beast, dangerous, treacherous and liable to bite, have you lost nothing? What, must you lose a bit of money, in order to suffer damage? And does the loss of nothing else cause damage to a man? 15. If you were to lose your skill in grammar or in music, you would count that loss as damage; and yet if you lose your honour and dignity and

gentleness, you think that a trivial matter? 16. Yet the former
are lost by some external cause beyond the power of our will,
and the latter through our own fault. There is no shame either
in having or in losing the former; but either not to have, or to
lose, the others, is shameful and a cause for reproach and a
disaster. 17. What does the catamite lose? The man in him. And
the man who makes use of him? Many other things besides; but
he too loses the man in him no less than the other does. 18.
What does an adulterer lose? The man of self-respect, self-
control and good behaviour; and his character as a citizen and
neighbour. What does an irascible person lose? Something else.
A coward? Something else. 19. No one is wicked without some
loss or damage. If, to be sure, you seek for loss only when it
comes to money, all these people are not subject to injury or
loss; indeed, they may even benefit and gain by such practices, if
these bring them financial profit. 20. But consider: if you refer
everything to money, you will not regard even the man who
loses his nose as having been injured. Yes, he has been (somebody says) for his body is mutilated. 21. Well; but does a person
who loses all sense of smell lose nothing? And is there, then, no
faculty of the mind which brings benefit to the person who
acquires it and injury to the person who loses it?

22. What faculty do you mean?

Have we not a natural sense of honour?

We have.

Does he who destroys this suffer no damage? Is he deprived
of nothing? Does he part with nothing that belongs to him? 23.
Have we no natural sense of fidelity? Or of affection? No
natural disposition to mutual service, to mutual forbearance? Is
the person, then, who carelessly allows himself to be damaged
in these respects, unharmed and undamaged?

24. What, then, shall not I harm the man who has harmed
me?

Consider first what harm is; and remember what you have
heard from the philosophers. 25. For if both good and evil
consist in choice, see whether what you say does not amount to
this: 26. 'Since he has harmed himself by wronging me, shall not
I harm myself by wronging him?' 27. Why do we not represent
the matter to ourselves in some such way as that? When we
suffer some loss regarding our body or possessions, there we see
the harm: but when we suffer some loss that affects our choice,

is there no harm then? 28. For a person who has been deceived, or has committed some wrong, suffers no pain in his head, nor does he lose his eye, or his hip, or his land; 29. and we are interested in nothing beyond such things as these. But whether our choice is to be honourable and trustworthy or shameless and unfaithful concerns us not a bit, except as regards mere chatter in the lecture-room. 30. Therefore all the progress that we make extends only to words, and apart from those we do not make even the slightest advance.

## CHAPTER 11

# What Is The Beginning Of Philosophy?

1. The beginning of philosophy, at least for those who enter upon it in the proper way and by the front door, is a consciousness of our own weakness, and incapacity with regard to necessary things. 2. For we came into the world without any innate conception of a right-angled triangle, or of a quarter-tone or half-tone; but we learn what each of these is by some kind of systematic instruction, and for that reason those who have no knowledge of them do not imagine that they know what they are. 3. But whoever came into the world without an innate conception of what is good and evil, honourable and base, becoming and unbecoming, and what happiness and misery are, and what is appropriate to us and forms our lot in life, and what we ought to do and ought not to do? 4. Thus all of us make use of these terms, and endeavour to apply our preconceptions to particular cases. 5. 'He acted well, as he ought, as he ought not; was unfortunate, was fortunate; is just, is unjust.' Who of us refrains from using such terms? Who defers the use of them until he is taught them, as do those who are ignorant of geometrical figures or musical notes? 6. The reason is that, in the present matter, we come already instructed in some degree by nature, and beginning from this we go on to add our personal fancies. 7. 'By Zeus, do I not know what is noble and base? Have I no conception of them?' – You have. 'Do I not apply this conception to particulars?' – You do. 'Do I not apply it rightly,

then?' – 8. Here lies the whole question; and here fancy enters in. For, beginning from these acknowledged principles, men proceed to get involved in disputes because of their unsuitable application of them. 9. For, if they possessed the right method of application, what would prevent them from being perfect? 10. Now, since you think that you can make a suitable application of your preconceptions to particular cases, tell me, how do you come to assume this?

Because it seems right to me.

But on the same matter it does not seem so to some other person, and he also supposes that he is making a correct application. Or does he not?

He does.

11. Is it possible, then, that each of you should be applying your preconceptions correctly, on the very matters about which you have contradictory opinions?

It is not.

12. Have you anything to show us, then, beyond your own supposition, which will enable us to apply our preconceptions better? And does a madman do anything other than what seems to him to be right? Is this, then, a sufficient ground of judgement for him too?

It is not.

Come, therefore, let us proceed to something higher than mere opinion.

What is that?

13. The beginning of philosophy is this: the realization that there is a conflict between the opinions of men, and a search for the origin of that conflict, accompanied by a mistrust towards mere opinion, and an investigation of opinion to see if it is correct opinion, and the discovery of a certain standard of judgement, comparable to the balance that we have discovered for determining weights, or the rule, for things straight and crooked.

14. Is this the beginning of philosophy, that all things which seem right to all persons are so?

Why, how is it possible for contradictory opinions to be right? So not all of them can be so.

Well, all that seem right to us?

15. Why what seems right to us, rather than to the Syrians, or Egyptians? Or to me personally or to any other man?

I see no reason why.

16. Therefore the fact that something seems right to each individual is not sufficient to make it so. For even in weights or measures we are not satisfied with the bare appearance; but we have discovered a certain standard for each. And is there in the present case, then, no standard higher than mere opinion? Is it possible that what is most needful in human life should be incapable of determination and discovery?

17. There is, then, some standard.

And why do we not seek and discover it and, when we have discovered it, make use of it without fail ever after, so that we do not even stretch out a finger without it? 18. For this is the standard, I think, which on its discovery relieves from their madness those who make use of no other measure than their own way of thinking; so that thenceforth, beginning from certain known and determinate principles, we may apply properly classified preconceptions to particular cases. 19. What is the subject that falls under our inquiry?

Pleasure.

20. Submit it to the standard. Throw it into the scales. Must the good be something that we can fittingly have confidence in and put our trust in?

Yes.

Is it fitting to have trust in something that is unstable?

No.

21. Is pleasure, then, a stable thing?

No.

Take it, then, and throw it out of the scales, and drive it far away from the region of good things. 22. But, if you are not quick-sighted, and one set of scales is insufficient for you, bring another. Is it fitting to feel elated at the good?

Yes.

Is it fitting, then, to feel elated at a present pleasure? See that you do not say that it is; otherwise I shall not think you so much as worthy to use the scales. 23. Thus are things judged, and weighed, when we have the standards ready. 24. This is the task of philosophy: to examine and establish the standards; 25. and to make use of them when they are known is the business of a wise and good man.

## CHAPTER 12

# On Disputation

1. What things a man must learn if he is to be able to argue correctly the philosophers of our school have accurately determined, but we are altogether unpractised in the proper application of them. 2. Give any of us you please some illiterate person to argue with, and he will not find out how to deal with him. But after he has moved the man a little, if the man should in any way thwart him, he is incapable of dealing with him any further, but thenceforth either reviles him or laughs at him, and says, 'He is just a layman – one can do nothing with him.' 3. Yet a proper guide, when he finds his charge going astray, does not revile and ridicule him and then desert him, but leads him back to the right path. 4. So you for your part should show him the truth, and you will see that he follows. But as long as you fail to show the truth, do not ridicule him, but rather recognize your own incapacity.

5. How, then, did Socrates act? He obliged his interlocutor to bear witness for him, and needed no other witness. And so he was able to say, 'I can do without all the others, and am always satisfied to have my interlocutor for a witness; and I do not take the votes of others, but that of my interlocutor alone.' 6. For he would make the consequences of men's conceptions so clear that everyone realized the contradiction involved and so abandoned it. 7. 'Does an envious man rejoice in his envy?' – 'By no means. Rather, he is pained by it.' Thus he has moved his interlocutor by the contradiction. 'Well, and do you think envy to be a feeling of pain at evils? Yet how can there be envy of evils?' 8. And so he has made his interlocutor say that envy is a feeling of pain at good things. 'Does any one envy things that are nothing to him?' – 'No, surely.' 9. Having thus drawn from his opponent a full and distinct conception, he then departed; and did not say, 'Define for me what envy is', and after the man had defined it, 'You have defined it wrong, for the definition does not correspond to the thing defined.' 10. These terms are technical, and thus burdensome for the layman, and hard for him to follow, and yet, it seems, we cannot do without them.

11. But as for terms which the layman could himself understand, and which would thus allow him, by recourse to his own impressions, to concede something or reject it – by using such terms we are quite unable to move him. 12. And then, from a consciousness of this incapacity, those among us who are at all cautious give the matter up entirely; 13. but the mass of men, rashly entering upon these debates, get confused and confuse others, and at last, after an exchange of abuse, walk off. 14. Whereas it was the principal and most peculiar characteristic of Socrates never to be provoked in a dispute, nor to come out with anything abusive or insolent, but to bear patiently with those who abused him, and to put an end to conflict. 15. If you want to know how great his abilities were in this regard, read Xenophon's *Symposium*, and you will see how many disputes he ended. 16. Hence, even among the poets, this quality is justly mentioned with the highest commendation,

'Skilfully he made a quick end of even a mighty quarrel.'

17. But what then? This activity is not very safe at present, and especially at Rome. For he who pursues it must clearly not do so in a corner, but he must go up to some rich man of consular rank, for instance, and ask him. 'Pray, sir, can you tell me to whom you have entrusted your horses?' 18. – 'Yes, certainly.' 'Is it, then, to the first man who comes along, even if he is ignorant of horsemanship?' – 'By no means.' 'To whom have you entrusted your gold, or your silver, or your clothes?' – 'Not to anyone who comes along.' 19. 'And have you ever considered committing your body to somebody else's care?' – 'Yes, surely.' 'To one with expertise in training, or medicine, I suppose?' – 'Without doubt.' 20. 'Are these your best possessions or do you possess something else that is better than all of them?' – 'What do you mean?' 'Something which makes use of these, and tests them and deliberates about each of them?' – 'What, do you mean the soul?' 21. 'You suppose right; for indeed I do mean that.' – 'By Zeus, I do really think it a much better possession than all the rest.' 22. 'Can you tell us, then, in what manner you have taken care of this soul? For it is not probable that a person of your wisdom, and so highly regarded in the state, should carelessly allow the most excellent thing that belongs to you to be neglected and ruined.' 23. – 'Certainly not.' 'But do you yourself take care of it? 24. And did someone else teach you how to do so, or did you discover that yourself?' Here

arises the danger, that he may first say, 'Pray, good sir, what business is that of yours? Are you my master?' Then, if you persist in bothering him, he may lift up his hand and give you a box on the ear. 25. This was a pursuit that I too was once very keen on, until I met with such troubles.

## CHAPTER 13

# On Anxiety

1. When I see somebody in a state of anxiety, I say, 'What can this man want?' Unless he wanted something or other which is not in his own power, how could he still be anxious? 2. That is why a person who sings to the lyre feels no anxiety while he is singing by himself, but is anxious when he enters the theatre, even if he has a very fine voice and plays his instrument beautifully. For he wants not only to sing well, but to gain applause, and that lies beyond his control. 3. In short, where he has knowledge, there he has confidence. Bring in any layman you please and he pays no regard to him. But in the point which he neither understands, nor has studied, there he feels anxious.

4. What point is that?

He does not understand what a crowd is, or the applause of a crowd. He has learned, indeed, how to strike the lowest and highest strings; but what the applause of the multitude is, and what force it has in life, he neither understands, nor has studied. 5. Hence he must necessarily tremble and turn pale. I cannot, indeed, say that a man is no musician when I see him afraid; but I can say something else about him, and not just one thing but many. 6. And, first of all, I call him a stranger, and say, This man does not know where in the world he is; and, though he has lived here all this time, he is ignorant of the laws and customs of the city, and what is permitted and what is not; nor has he ever consulted any lawyer who might tell him the laws and explain them to him. 7. Yet no man writes a will without knowing how it ought to be written, or consulting some one who does know; nor does he rashly put his seal on a bond or give written security. But he exercises desire and aversion, impulse, intention and purpose, without consulting any lawyer about the matter.

8. How do you mean without a lawyer?

He does not know that he is wishing to have what is not allowed him, and wishing to avoid what he cannot escape; and he does not know what is his own and what is not his own; for if he did know, he would never feel hindered, never feel restrained, never feel anxious.

9. How so?

Why, does any one fear things that are not evils?

No.

Or things that are evils indeed, but which it is in his own power to prevent?

No, surely.

10. If, then, things outside the sphere of choice are neither good nor bad, and all things within the sphere of choice are in our own power, and can neither be taken away from us, nor given to us, unless we please, what room is there left for anxiety? 11. But we are anxious about this paltry body or estate of ours, or about what Caesar will think, and not at all about what is within us. Are we ever anxious not to take up a false opinion? No, for this is in our own power. Or about following an impulse contrary to nature? No, nor this either. 12. When, therefore, you see any one pale with anxiety, just as the physician pronounces from a person's complexion that this patient is affected in his spleen, and that in his liver, so you likewise should say: this man is affected in his desires and aversions, he is out of sorts, he is feverish. 13. For nothing else changes the complexion or makes a man tremble or sets his teeth a-chattering, or 'Shift from leg to leg and squat on one foot then the other.'

14. Therefore Zeno, when he was about to meet Antigonus, felt no anxiety. For over the things that he admired Antigonus had no power, and the things that Antigonus did have power over were of no concern to Zeno. 15. But Antigonus felt anxious when he was about to meet Zeno, and with reason, for he wanted to please him, and that lay beyond his control. But Zeno had no great wish to please Antigonus any more than any other expert cares to please someone who does not share his skill.

16. Do I wish to please you? For what? Do you know the standards according to which one man is judged by another?

Have you studied to understand what a good, and what a bad man is; and how each becomes such? Why, then, are you not yourself a good man?

17. On what account am I not?

Because no good man laments, nor sighs, nor groans; no good man turns pale and trembles and says, 'How will he receive me, what sort of hearing will he give me?' 18. He will do so, slave, as he thinks best. Why do you trouble yourself about things that are not your own? Is it not his fault if he receives you ill?

Yes, surely.

Is it possible for one person to make the mistake, and another to suffer the harm?

No.

Why, then, are you anxious over what concerns another?

19. Well, but I am anxious over how I shall speak to him.

What, then, is it not in your power to speak to him as you please?

But I am afraid I shall lose my composure.

20. If you were going to write the name Dio, would you be afraid of losing your composure?

By no means.

What is the reason? Is it not because you have studied how to write?

Yes.

And if you were going to read, would it not be exactly the same?

Exactly.

What is the reason?

Because every art brings with it a certain strength and confidence in the matters that it controls.

21. Have you not studied, then, how to speak? And what else did you study at school?

Syllogisms and equivocal arguments.

For what purpose? Was it not in order to engage in argument skilfully? And what is that but to do so opportunely, and securely and intelligently and, moreover, without permitting oneself to fall into error or be obstructed, and in addition to all this, with confidence?

Very true.

22. If, then, you are a horseman who is riding on to level

ground against a footsoldier, and you have practised in this respect and he has not, can you be anxious?

Yes, but Caesar has power to kill me.

23. Then speak the truth, you wretch, and do not brag, or claim to be a philosopher. Be aware who your masters are, and as long as you allow them this hold on your body, follow everyone who is stronger than you are. 24. But Socrates had studied how to speak, who talked in the way he did to the Tyrants, to the jurymen, and in prison. Diogenes had studied how to speak, who talked in the way he did to Alexander, to Philip, to the pirates, to the person who bought him. 25. Leave this to those who have studied the matter and are confident; 26. as for you, return to your own affairs, and never stir from them again. Go, sit in your corner, and weave syllogisms, and propound them to others 27. – 'In thee there is no captain of a state.'

## CHAPTER 14

## To Naso

1. When a certain Roman came to him with his son, and was listening to one of his lectures, Epictetus said, 'This is the method of my teaching', and fell silent. 2. When the Roman asked to know what he had to say next, he replied 'Every art when it is being handed on is troublesome to a layman who has no experience of it.' 3. Now the products of the arts show immediately what use they are made for, and most of them have a certain attractiveness and charm. 4. For although it is no pleasure to be present and follow how a shoemaker learns his art, the shoe he makes is useful and by no means unpleasing to look at. 5. And likewise, the process by which a carpenter learns is altogether tedious to the layman who happens to be present, but what he produces demonstrates the use of his art. 6. You will see that this is even more the case with music, for if you are present when somebody is being taught, the process will strike you as the most disagreeable of all, yet the products of the art are pleasing to the layman and a delight for him to hear.

7. Here also, we imagine the work of a philosopher to be something like this, to bring his own will into harmony with whatever comes to pass, so that none of the things which happen may happen against our will, nor those which do not happen be wished for by us. 8. Hence, those who have settled this as being the philosopher's work have it in their power never to be disappointed in their desire, or fall into what they want to avoid; but to lead personal lives free from sorrow, fear and perturbation, and preserve in society all the natural and acquired relationships of a son, a father, a brother, a citizen, a husband, a wife, a neighbour, a fellow-traveller, a ruler, or a subject. 9. Something like this is what we imagine the work of a philosopher to be. Next we should inquire how it can be achieved. 10. Now we see that a carpenter becomes a carpenter by learning certain things; and a pilot becomes a pilot by learning certain things. Probably, then, it is not sufficient in the present case also merely to wish to become wise and good, but in addition it is necessary to learn certain things. So we must seek to discover what these things are. 11. The philosophers say that we must first learn that there is a god, and that his providence directs the whole; and that it is impossible to conceal from him, not only our actions, but even our thoughts and intentions. We must next learn what the gods are like: 12. for in accordance with whatever nature they are discovered to have, the person who is going to please them and obey them must endeavour to resemble them to the utmost of his capacity. 13. If the deity is faithful, he too must be faithful; if free, beneficent and high-minded, he too must be free, beneficent and high-minded; and generally, in all his words and actions, act in imitation of god.

14. Whence, then, are we to begin?

If you are going to attempt this task, I will tell you that in the first place you must understand terms.

15. So, then, I do not understand them now?

No. You do not.

How is it, then, that I use them?

Just as the illiterate use written expressions, and cattle use external impressions. For use is one thing, and understanding another. 16. But if you think you understand them, bring forward any term you please, and let us put ourselves to the test, to see whether we understand it or not.

17. It is galling to be subjected to such a cross-examination when one already is quite an age and has served, as it happens, one's three campaigns.

18. I know it very well, for you have come to me now like a man in need of nothing. And what could one even imagine you to be in need of? You are rich, and perhaps have a wife and children, and a great number of slaves. Caesar knows you; you have many friends at Rome; you perform your duties; you know how to requite a favour and revenge an injury. 19. In what are you deficient? Suppose, then, I should prove to you that you are deficient in what is most necessary and important for happiness, and that hitherto you have devoted care to everything except to appropriate action, and, to cap it all, that you understand neither what god is, nor what man is, nor what good is, nor what evil is? 20. That you are ignorant of all the rest, perhaps, you may bear to be told; but if I prove to you that you are ignorant even of your own self, how will you bear with me, and how will you have patience to endure my questioning and remain with me? 21. Not at all. You are immediately offended and go away. And yet what injury have I done you? None, unless a looking-glass injures an ugly man by showing him what he is like. Or unless a physician can be thought to be insulting his patient when he says to him, 'Do you think, sir, that there is nothing wrong with you? You have a fever. Eat nothing today, and keep to water.' Nobody cries out here, 'What dreadful impertinence!' 22. But if you say to anyone, 'Your desires are feverish, your aversions are low, your intentions inconsistent, your impulses are out of harmony to nature, your opinions random and mistaken', he at once goes away, and says, 'He insulted me.'

23. Our situation can be compared to what happens at a public festival. Cattle and oxen are brought there to be sold, and the greatest number of men come either to buy or sell; but there are a few who come only to look at the fair, and inquire how it is carried on, and why, and who set it up, and for what purpose: 24. thus, in the fair of the world, some, like cattle, trouble themselves about nothing but fodder. For as to all you who busy yourselves about possessions and farms and slaves and public posts, these things are nothing else but mere fodder. 25. Few are the men who attend the fair because they are fond of looking on and considering, 'What, then, is the world? Who

governs it? Has it no governor? 26. Yet how is it possible, when neither a city nor a house can remain ever so short a time without some one to govern and take care of it, that this vast and beautiful structure should be regulated in such an orderly manner without plan and by mere chance? 27. So there is somebody who governs it. What sort of a being is he? And how does he govern? And what are we, who have been created by him, and what task were we created to fulfil? Have we some connection and relation with him; or none? 28. Such are the thoughts aroused in these few; and thenceforth they have leisure for this alone, to investigate the festival of life before they depart. 29. And what is the consequence? They are laughed at by the multitude, just as spectators at the fair are laughed at by the traders – and the cattle too, if they had any understanding, would laugh at those who admire anything other than fodder.

## CHAPTER 15

# To Those Who Cling Stubbornly To Whatever Judgements They Have Formed

1. Some people, when they hear such precepts as these – that we ought to be steadfast, that choice is by nature free and not subject to compulsion, whereas all else is subject to hindrance and compulsion, and in bondage to others and not our own – imagine that they must stand unswervingly by every judgement that they have formed. 2. But it is first necessary that the judgement should be a sound one. I want a certain rigour in the body; but such as appears in a healthy, an athletic body: 3. for if you show me that you have the rigour of a madman and boast about that, I will say to you, 'Find someone to cure you, man: this is not rigour but quite the opposite.'

4. Here is another way in which people's minds can be affected when they misinterpret these precepts, as in the case of a friend of mine, who, for no reason, had determined to starve himself to death. 5. I learned of this when he was in the third day of his fast, and went to ask him what had happened. 6. 'I have decided', he replied. Yes, but even so, what moved you to

make this decision? For if you judged rightly, look, here we are at your side and ready to assist you in your departure; but if your judgement was contrary to reason, you must change it. 7. 'Those who have arrived at decisions should abide by them.' What do you mean, man? Not all decisions, but the ones that are correct. If you are led to imagine at this very moment that it is night, and you should suppose that to be true, do not, then, change your opinion but hold to it, and say that one must abide by one's decisions! 8. Do you not wish to lay a firm foundation at the beginning, by examining whether your decision is sound or unsound, and then build on that your firm-set resolve? 9. For if you lay a rotten and crumbling foundation, you cannot build even a small building, but the greater and heavier the superstructure is, the sooner it will fall. 10. Without any reason you are removing from life our friend and companion, our fellow-citizen in both the greater city and the lesser: 11. and then, while you are committing murder and destroying an innocent person, you say, We must abide by our decisions. 12. Suppose, in some way or other, it should come into your head to kill me, would you have to abide by your decisions then?

13. With difficulty, that man was persuaded to change his mind; but there are some people these days who cannot be persuaded. So that now I think I understand what formerly I did not, the meaning of that common saying, that a fool will neither bend nor break. 14. May it never fall to my lot to have a clever fool for my friend. 'I have decided'! Why, so have madmen; but the more strongly they are determined upon absurdities, the more need they have of hellebore. 15. Why will you not act like a sick person, and call a doctor in? 'Sir, I am sick. Give me your assistance: consider what I am to do. It is my part to follow your directions.' 16. So, in the present case, 'I know not what I ought to do, but I have come to learn.' But what you in fact say is, 'Talk to me about other things; this I have decided.' 17. What other things? What is of greater consequence and more to your advantage than to convince you that it is not sufficient to have arrived at a decision and to refuse to change it? This is the rigour of a madman, and not of a healthy man. 18. 'I will willingly die if you compel me to this.' Why so, man: what is the matter? – 'I have decided.' It is lucky for me that you have not decided to kill me. 19. 'I accept no pay.' Why so? 'I have decided.' Be assured that with that very rigour which you now

apply in refusing it may incline you irrationally one day – for
what is there to prevent that? – to accepting it and then saying
once again, 'I have decided.' 20. Just as in a sickly body suffering
from the flux, the rheum inclines now this way, now that, so it
is with a sick mind, one can never be sure which way it will
tend; but if a rigorous determination is added to this inclination
and flow, the evil is beyond help, beyond remedy.

## CHAPTER 16

# That We Fail To Practise The Application Of Our Judgements About What Is Good And Evil

1. Where lies the good? In choice. Where evil? In choice. Where
lies that which is neither good nor evil? In things that lie outside
the sphere of choice. 2. So, what of it? Does any of us remember
these principles outside the classroom? Does any one of us
practise on his own to respond to facts in the same way as he
responds to these questions? 'Is it day?' – 'Yes.' 'Is it night,
then?' – 'No.' 'Is the number of stars even?' – 'I cannot say.' 3.
When money is displayed to you, have you studied to make the
proper answer, 'It is not a good'? Have you trained yourself in
such answers as that, or merely to respond to sophistries? 4.
Why do you wonder, then, that you surpass yourself in the fields
in which you have practised, but in those in which you have not
practised, there you remain the same? 5. When an orator knows
that he has written a good speech, that he has committed to
memory what he has written, and that he brings an agreeable
voice to its delivery, why is he still anxious? Because he is not
satisfied merely to practise his art. 6. What does he want, then?
To be praised by his audience. Now he has trained himself to be
able to practise his art, but he has not trained himself with
regard to praise and blame. 7. For when did he hear from
anyone what praise is, and what blame is? What the nature of
each is? What kinds of applause are to be pursued, and what
kinds of blame to be avoided? And when did he ever go through
the training that accords with these principles? 8. Why do you
wonder, then, if in what he has learned he surpasses all others,

but where he has not studied, he is just the same as everyone else? 9. He is like somebody who sings to the lyre and who knows how to play, sings well, and has beautiful robes, yet trembles all the same when he comes on stage. For all his knowledge, he does not know what a crowd is, or the shouting of a crowd and its mockery. 10. Nor does he even know what anxiety itself is, whether it be our own responsibility or outside it, or whether it be possible to suppress it or not. Because of this, if he is praised, he leaves the stage puffed up with pride: but if he is laughed at, his poor bubble is pricked and collapses.

11. We too experience something of this kind. What do we admire? Externals. What do we strive for? Externals. Are we then at a loss to know how fear and anxiety overcome us? 12. Why, what else is possible when we regard impending events as evils? We cannot help being fearful we cannot help being anxious. 13. And then we say, 'O lord god, how shall I avoid anxiety? Have you not hands, fool? Has not god made them for you? Sit down now and pray that your nose may not run! Wipe it rather, and do not blame god. Well: and has he given you nothing in the present case? 14. Has he not given you endurance? Has he not given you greatness of soul? Has he not given you fortitude? When you have such hands as these, do you still seek for somebody to wipe your nose? 15. We devote no care or attention to such matters. For can you find me a single man who cares how he does what he does, and is interested, not in what he can get, but in the manner of his own action? Who, when he is walking around, is interested in his own action? Who, when he is deliberating, is interested in the deliberation itself, and not in getting what he is planning to get? 16. And if he happens to succeed, he is elated, and cries, 'Here we deliberated to some effect! Did not I tell you, brother, that it was impossible, if we examined the matter properly, for it to turn out otherwise?' But if it does go differently, the poor wretch is dejected, and knows not what to say about the matter. Who of us ever consulted a diviner on a question like this? 17. Who of us ever slept in a temple to learn the manner in which he should act? I say, who? Give me a single man, that I may see what I have long sought, a man who is truly noble and gifted; whether he be young or old, give me one such man.

18. Why then are we still surprised, if, when we waste all our attention on the materials of action, we are, in the manner in which we act, base, shameful, worthless, cowardly, irresolute,

and all in all complete failures? For we have never been concerned about such matters, nor do we practise them. 19. If we were afraid not of death or exile, but of fear itself, we should have studied not to fall into what appears to us to be evil. 20. But, as the case now stands, we are spirited and fluent in the lecture-room, and when any little question arises about any of these things, we are prepared to trace its logical consequences: but drag us into practice, and you will find us miserably shipwrecked. Let some disturbing impression attack us, and you will perceive what we have been studying, and what we have been training for. 21. And because of this lack of practice, we are always piling up worries and fancying things to be graver than they really are. 22. Whenever I go to sea, as soon as I gaze down into the depths or look at the waters around me and see no land, I am beside myself, and imagine that if I am wrecked I must swallow all that sea; nor does it once enter my head that three pints are enough. What is it then that alarms me? The sea? No, my own judgement. 23. Again, in an earthquake, I imagine the city is going to fall on me; but is not one little stone enough to knock my brains out? 24. What is it, then, that weighs on us and puts us out of our minds? Why, what else but our judgements? For what is it but mere judgement that weighs upon a person when he leaves his country, and is separated from the companions, places, and society that he has been accustomed to? 25. When children cry a little because their nurse has left, give them a cake, and they forget their grief. 26. Is it your wish that we too should resemble these children? No, by Zeus. For it is not by cake that I would have you achieve this, but by right judgements. 27. And what are they?

The things that a man ought to study all day long, so that, unaffected by all that is not his own, whether friend or place or gymnasia or even, indeed, his own body, he remembers the law and has that constantly before his eyes. 28. And what is the divine law? To preserve what is one's own, not to claim what is another's; to use what is given us, and not desire what is not given us; and, when anything is taken away, to give it up readily, and to be thankful for the time you have been permitted the use of it, and not cry after it, like a child for its nurse and its mamma. 29. For what does it matter what a man is enslaved to, or what he is dependent on? And in what are you superior to him who cries for a girl, if you grieve for a paltry gymnasium

and colonnade, and silly young men, and diversions like that?
30. Someone else comes, lamenting that he can no longer drink
the water of Dirce. Why, is not the Marcian water as good? 'But
I was used to the other.' And in time you will be used to this.
31. Then if you become attached to it, you can lament for this
too in its turn, and seek to write a line like that of Euripides:
'The baths of Nero, and the Marcian water.'

See how tragedy arises when trifling accidents befall foolish
men. 32. 'Ah, when shall I see Athens and the Acropolis again!'
Wretch, are not you contented with what you see every day?
Can you see anything better or greater than the sun, the moon,
the stars, the whole earth, the sea? 33. And if you understand
him that governs the universe, and carry him about within you,
do you still long for puny stones and a pleasing rock? What will
you do, then, when you are to leave even the sun and moon?
Will you sit crying like an infant? 34. What did you do, then, at
school? What did you hear? What did you learn? Why did you
put yourself down as a philosopher when you might have put
down the truth, saying, 'I have studied a few elementary works
and read a bit of Chrysippus, but I have never darkened the
door of a philosopher. 35. What claim do I have to the calling
of Socrates, who lived and died in the way he did? Or that of
Diogenes?' 36. Can you imagine either of these crying or out of
humour, because he is not going to see such a man or such a
woman; nor to live any longer at Athens, or at Corinth, but at
Susa, for instance, or at Ecbatana? 37. For if it is possible for
him to leave the banquet when he pleases and play no longer,
does such a man stay here and grieve? Does he not stay as
children do, as long as it amuses him? 38. Such a man could
surely face up to exile, whether his sentence be exile for life or
the exile of death. 39. Why are you not willing to be weaned, as
children are, and take more solid food? Will you never cease to
cry after your mammas and nurses, old women's lamentations?
40. 'But if I go away I shall distress them.' *You* distress them!
No, it will not be you, but that which distresses you too, bad
judgement. What have you to do, then? Cast it out, and, if they
are wise, they will cast theirs out too; or, if not, they will be the
cause of their own lamentations.

41. Make a desperate push, man, as the saying is, to achieve
happiness and freedom, and nobility of mind. Lift up your head
at last, like a man freed from slavery. 42. Dare to look up to

god and say, 'Use me henceforth as you please. I am of one mind with you, I am yours. I refuse nothing which seems good to you. Lead me where you will. Clothe me in whatever dress you will. Is it your will, that I should hold office or be a private citizen, remain here or be banished, be poor or rich? Under all these circumstances I will defend you before men. 43. I will show the true nature of each thing as it is.' 44. No. Rather, sit inside like a girl, and wait till your mamma comes to feed you. If Heracles had sat loitering at home, what would he have been? Eurystheus, and not Heracles. Besides, as he travelled throughout the world, how many acquaintances and how many friends did he have? None dearer than god, for which reason he was believed to be the son of Zeus, and was so. In obedience to him, he went about extirpating injustice and lawlessness. 45. But you are not Heracles, nor able to extirpate the evils of others; nor even Theseus to extirpate the evils of Attica. Extirpate your own, then. Expel, instead of Procrustes and Sciron, grief, fear, desire, envy, malice, avarice, effeminacy, intemperance, from your mind. 46. But these can be expelled in no other way than by looking to god, and attaching yourself to him alone, and consecrating yourself to his commands. 47. If you wish for anything else, you will, with sighs and groans, follow what is stronger than you, always seeking happiness outside yourself, and never being able to find it. For you seek it where it is not, and neglect to seek it where it is.

## CHAPTER 17

# How Should We Apply Our Preconceptions To Particular Instances?

1. What is the first business of one who pursues philosophy? To cast away self-conceit. For it is impossible for any one to begin to learn what he thinks he knows. 2. When we go to the philosophers, we all chatter freely enough on what should be done and what should not be done, and things good and evil, fair and base, and on that basis we praise, blame, accuse, reproach, passing judgement on fine behaviour and foul and

distinguishing the one from the other. 3. But what do we go to the philosophers for? To learn what we think we do not know. And what is this? Principles. Some of us want to hear what the philosophers are saying because they think it will be witty and sharp, others because they hope to gain some advantage from it. 4. Now it is ridiculous to suppose that when a person wants to learn one thing, he will in fact learn another, or generally that a person will progress in what he fails to learn. 5. But the mass of people are deluded in the same way as Theopompus the orator, who goes so far as to reproach Plato for wishing to define each individual term. 6. Now what did he say? 'Did none of us before you came along use the words "good" and "just", or did we utter them as empty and inarticulate sounds, without understanding what each of them meant?' 7. Why, who told you, Theopompus, that we did not have natural ideas and preconceptions of each of these? But it is not possible to adapt preconceptions to the corresponding realities, without having minutely distinguished them, and having examined precisely which reality is to be ranged under each preconception. 8. You could, for instance, make a similar remark to the physicians. For who of us did not use the words 'healthy' and 'unhealthy' before Hippocrates was born? Or did we utter them as empty noises? 9. For we have some preconception of the healthy too; but we are incapable of applying it. That is why one person says, 'Eat no food', and another, 'Give him food'; one says, 'Let him be bled', and another, 'Apply cupping-glasses.' And what is the reason, except an inability to apply the preconception of the healthy to particular cases? 10. Thus, too, in life; who of us does not talk of good and evil, advantageous and disadvantageous: for who of us has not a preconception of each of these? But is it properly classified and complete? Show me that.

11. How shall I show it?

Apply it properly to particular realities. Plato, to go no further, classifies definitions under the preconception of 'the useful'; but you, under that of 'the useless'. 12. Can both of you be right? How is it possible? Again, does not one man apply his preconception of 'good' to riches? Another, not to riches, but to pleasure and health? 13. In general, then, if none of us who use these terms, either utter them without meaning, or need to devote any care to differentiating our preconceptions, why do we differ? Why do we engage in polemics and criticize one another?

14. But what need have I to cite our mutual contentions as evidence and call those to mind? For in your own case, if you apply your preconceptions properly, how is it that you are unhappy, and subject to hindrance? 15. Let us for the present leave aside the second area of study, concerning our impulses and the appropriate regulation of them; let us leave aside the third too, concerning assent. 16. I make you a present of all these. Let us insist only on the first, which affords an almost sensible proof that you do not apply your preconceptions rightly. 17. Do you now desire what is possible, and possible for you in particular? Why then are you hindered? Why are you unhappy? Are you not trying now to evade what is inevitable? Why, then, do you fall into difficulties of any kind? Why are you unfortunate? When you want anything, why does it fail to happen? When you do not want it, why does it happen? 18. For this is the greatest proof of unhappiness and misfortune. I desire something, and it does not happen: and what could be more wretched than I? 19. It was because she was unable to endure this that Medea came to murder her own children, the action of a noble spirit in this regard at least, that she had a proper impression of what it means to be disappointed in one's desire. 20. 'Thus', she says, 'shall I take vengeance on one who has injured and wronged me. Yet what shall I gain from putting him into such a miserable plight? How is this to be achieved? I will murder the children. But that will be punishing myself. And what do I care?' 21. This is the error of a soul endued with great vigour. For she knew not where the power to do what we wish lies; that it is not be acquired from outside ourselves, nor by altering and disarranging things. 22. Do not desire the man for your husband, and nothing which you do desire will fail to happen. Do not desire to keep him to yourself. Do not desire to stay at Corinth, and, in a word, have no will but the will of god; and who shall hinder you, who shall compel you? Nobody could do so, any more than he could for Zeus. 23. When you have such a leader, and conform your will and desires to his, what fear could you still have of failing? 24. Offer up your desire and aversion to riches, and poverty: you will fail to get what you desire, you will fall into what you would avoid. Offer them up to health and you will fall into misfortune, and likewise if you offer them up to position, honours, your country, friends, children, in short, to anything outside the sphere of choice. 25.

But offer them up to Zeus and the other gods. Hand them over to these, for them to govern, let your desire and aversion be ranged on the same side as these; 26. and how thenceforth can you be unhappy? But if, poor wretch, you fall prey to envy, and pity, and are jealous, and timorous, and never cease a single day from bewailing yourself and the gods, why do you continue to prate about your education? 27. What kind of education, man? The fact that you have studied syllogisms and arguments with equivocal premises? Will you not consent to unlearn all this, if at all possible, and make a fresh start, in the realization that hitherto you have not even touched on the principal matter? 28. And, thenceforth, beginning from this foundation, establish the next point, as to how nothing shall be that you do not wish, and that nothing that you do wish shall fail to be. 29. Give me but one young man who has come to the school with this purpose in mind, who has become an athlete in this field of action, and says, 'I for my part yield up all the rest: it suffices me, if I become able to pass my life free from hindrance and distress, and to hold up my head in the face of events like a free man, and to look up to heaven as the friend of god, fearing nothing that can happen.' 30. Let any one of you show himself to be such a person, so that I may say, 'Enter, young man, into what is rightly your own, for you are destined to be an ornament to philosophy. Yours are these possessions, yours these books, yours these discourses.' 31. Then, when he has laboured at this first area of study and thoroughly mastered it, let him come to me again, and say, 'I desire indeed to be free from passion and perturbation, but I desire also, as a reverent, philosophic and carefully attentive man, to know what is my duty to the gods, to my parents, to my brothers, to my country and to strangers.' 32. Progress now to the second area of study, for this likewise is yours. 33. 'But I have now made a sufficient study of this second area too; and I would like to be secure and unshaken, not only while I am awake, but even when asleep, and drunk, and depressed.' 'You are a god, man; how great are your designs!'

34. No, but instead someone says, 'I want to know what Chrysippus means in his work on the 'Liar'. Go hang yourself, you wretch, if that is your design. What good will it do you? You will read the whole work, lamenting all the while, and tremble as you talk of it to others. 35. That is how all of you behave as well. 'Shall I read to you, my friend, and you to me?'

'I am full of admiration, man, for the way you write', and 'You write really well in the style of Xenophon.' 36. 'And you in Plato's.' 'And you in Antisthenes'.' And then, having related your dreams to each other, you return to the same ways as before. Your desires and aversions, your impulses, your designs, your resolutions, your prayers and endeavours, are just what they were. 37. You do not even seek for somebody to advise you, but are offended, when you hear such things as these, and cry, 'An ill-natured old fellow! He never wept over me, when I was setting off, nor said, This is quite a situation you are going out to face, my son; if you come off safe, I will light some lamps.' 38. Is that what a good-natured man would have said? It will surely be a wonderfully good thing for somebody like you to come off safe, and worth lighting lamps for. You doubtless ought to be immortal and immune from disease.

39. We must then, as I say, throw away this self-conceit, by which we fancy that we know something useful, and should come to philosophic reasoning, in the same way as we do to mathematics and music. 40. Otherwise we shall not even come near making any progress, even if we should go through all the introductions and treatises of Chrysippus, and of Antipater and Archedemus too.

## CHAPTER 18

# How Must We Struggle Against Impressions?

1. Every habit and capacity is preserved and strengthened by the corresponding actions, that of walking, by walking, that of running, by running. 2. If you want to be a reader, read; if a writer, write. But if you fail to read for thirty days in succession, and turn to something else, you will see the consequence. 3. So also if you lie down for ten days, get up and attempt to take a fairly long walk, you will see how enfeebled your legs are. 4. In general, then, if you want to do something, make it a habit; and if you want not to do something, abstain from doing it, and acquire the habit of doing something else in its place. 5. This is also the case when it comes to things of the mind. Whenever

you are angry, be assured that this is not only a present evil, but that you have strengthened the habit, and added fuel to the fire. 6. When you yield to sexual desire, do not count it a single defeat, but know that you have fed, that you have strengthened, your incontinence. 7. For habits and faculties must necessarily be affected by the corresponding actions, and become implanted if they were not present previously, or be intensified and strengthened if they were.

8. This is, of course, how philosophers say that sicknesses grow in the mind. When you once desire money, for example, if reason is applied to bring you to an awareness of the evil, the desire is curbed, and the governing faculty of the mind regains its authority: 9. whereas, if you apply no remedy, it no longer returns to its former state, but when it is excited again by a corresponding impression, it is inflamed by desire more quickly than before, and, by frequent repetitions, at last becomes callous: and by this infirmity the love of money becomes fixed. 10. For he who has had a fever, and then recovers, is not in the same state of health as before, unless he was perfectly cured; 11. and something similar happens in sicknesses of the mind too. Certain traces and weals are left behind in it, which, unless the person concerned expunges them utterly, the next time he is flogged in the same place, not weals but wounds are created. 12. If, then, you do not wish to be ill-tempered, do not feed the habit. Give it nothing to promote its growth. Keep quiet to begin with, and count the days on which you have not been angry. 13. I used to be angry every day; now every other day; then every third and fourth day: and, if you avoid it as many as thirty days, offer a sacrifice of thanksgiving to god. For habit is first weakened, and then entirely destroyed. 14. 'I was not distressed today; nor the next day; nor for three or four months after; but took due care when things happened that might have caused me distress.' Be assured that you are in a fine way.

15. Today, when I saw a handsome boy or a beautiful woman, I did not say to myself, O that I could sleep with her! And, How happy is her husband! (for he who says this, says too, How happy is the adulterer!): 16. nor do I go on to picture what follows next, the woman with me, and undressing, and lying down beside me. 17. I pat myself on the head, and say, Well done, Epictetus: you have resolved a pretty sophism, a much prettier one than the one they call the 'Master'. 18. But if the

woman should even happen to be willing, and give me the nod, and send for me, and lay hold of me, and press herself against me, and I still hold off and gain the victory, now that would be the refutation of a sophism beyond even the 'Liar' or the 'Silent One'. On this one could rightly pride oneself, rather than on proposing the 'Master' argument.

19. How, then, is this to be effected? You must wish to satisfy your true self, you must wish to appear beautiful in the sight of god; you must desire to become pure in the presence of your pure self and of god. 20. 'And then, if any such impression strikes you', says Plato, 'go and offer expiatory sacrifices, go as a suppliant to the temples of the deities who avert evils.' 21. It is sufficient even if you withdraw 'to the society of noble and virtuous men', and examine your life by comparison with theirs, whether you choose as your pattern one of the living or one of the dead. 22. Go to Socrates, and see him lying with Alcibiades, and laughing off the young man's beauty. Consider what a victory he was conscious of obtaining, what an Olympic prize, and what rank he held amongst the successors of Heracles. So that, by the gods, one might justly greet that man with the cry, 'Hail, wonderful man!', as against those putrid boxers and pancratiasts, and those who are just like them, the gladiators.

23. If you set these thoughts against your impression, you will overpower it, and not be swept away by it. 24. But, in the first place, do not allow yourself to be carried away by its intensity: but say, 'Impression, wait for me a little. Let me see what you are, and what you represent. Let me test you.' 25. Then, afterwards, do not allow it to draw you on by picturing what may come next, for if you do, it will lead you wherever it pleases. But rather, you should introduce some fair and noble impression to replace it, and banish this base and sordid one. 26. If you become habituated to this kind of exercise, you will see what shoulders, what sinews and what vigour you will come to have. But now you have mere trifling talk, and nothing more.

27. The man who is truly in training is the one who exercises himself to confront such impressions. Stay, wretch, do not be carried away. 28. The struggle is great, the task divine, to win a kingdom, to win freedom, to win happiness, to win serenity of mind. 29. Remember god. Call on him to aid and protect you, as sailors do the Dioscuri in a storm. For what storm is greater than that which arises from powerful impressions, that drive out

reason? Indeed, what is the storm itself, but an impression? 30. For, do but take away the fear of death, and let there be as much thunder and lightning as you please, you will find that, in the ruling faculty, all is serenity and calm: 31. but if you are once defeated, and say you will get the victory another time, and then the same thing over again, you can be sure that you will at last be reduced to so weak and wretched a condition, that you will not so much as know when you are going wrong, but you will even begin to make excuses for your behaviour, and thus confirm the saying of Hesiod: 'With constant ills the dilatory must strive.'

## CHAPTER 19

# To Those Who Take Up The Teachings Of The Philosophers For The Sake Of Talk Alone

1. The 'Master' argument appears to have been proposed on the basis of some such principles as these. Of the following propositions, any two imply a contradiction to the third. They are these. That everything that has happened is necessarily true; that the impossible cannot be a consequence of the possible; and that something is a possibility which neither is nor ever will be true. Diodorus, perceiving this contradiction, made use of the probability of the two first to demonstrate this conclusion: nothing is possible which neither is nor ever will be true. 2. Some again hold the second and third: that something is possible which neither is nor ever will be true, and that the impossible cannot be the consequence of the possible and, consequently, assert that not everything that has happened is necessarily true. This appears to have been the opinion of Cleanthes and his school, which was strongly supported by Antipater. 3. But others maintain the first and third: that something is possible which neither is nor ever will be true, and that every thing that has happened is necessarily true; but say that the impossible can indeed be a consequence of the possible. 4. But all these three propositions cannot be maintained at the same time; because of their mutual contradiction.

5. If any one should ask me, 'Which of these do you maintain?', I would reply to him that I cannot tell. But I have heard it related that Diodorus held one opinion about them, the followers of Panthoides, I think, and Cleanthes, another; and Chrysippus the third.

6. What, then, is your view?

I have none. Nor was I born for this, to test my own impression, compare what is said by others, and then form some judgement of my own upon the matter. For this reason I am no better than the grammarian: 7. 'Who was the father of Hector?', he was asked. 'Priam.' 'Who were his brothers?' 'Paris and Deiphobus.' 'Who was his mother?' 'Hecuba. That is the account I have received.' 'From whom?' 'From Homer. But I believe that Hellanicus has also written on these very questions, as, I expect, have other authors of the kind.' 8. And what better account have I of the 'Master' argument? But, if I was vain enough, I might, especially at a banquet, astonish the company by enumerating all the authors who have written on the subject. 9. Chrysippus has written wonderfully on it, in the first book of *On Possibles*. Cleanthes and Archedemus have each written separately on this subject. So has Antipater, not only in his treatise, *On Possibles*, but also specifically in his discourse on the 'Master' argument. 10. Have you not read the work? 'No.' Read it, then. – And what good will it do him? He will be more trifling and impertinent than he is already. For what else have you gained by reading it? What judgement have you formed upon this subject? Yes, you will tell us about Helen and Priam and the island of Calypso, which never was, nor ever will be. 11. And here, indeed, it is of no great consequence if you retain the story, without forming any judgement of your own. But it is our misfortune to do so much more in questions of morality than in literary matters such as these.

12. Tell me about things good and evil.

Listen. 'The wind has blown me from Ilium to the Ciconian shore.'

13. Of things that exist, some are good, some bad, and some indifferent. Now the good are the virtues and everything that shares in them, and the evil vices and what shares in vice; and everything that lies between these, such as riches, health, life, death, pleasure or pain is indifferent.

14. How did you come to know that?

Hellanicus says so in his *Egyptian History*. For it comes to the same thing to say that as to say that Diogenes says so in his *Ethics*, or Chrysippus, or Cleanthes. Now, have you tested any of these doctrines for yourself, and formed a personal judgement on them? 15. Show me how you are accustomed to behave when you meet with a storm on board ship. Do you remember this distinction between good and bad when the sails are rattling and you cry aloud and some bystander mischievously asks, 'Tell me, by the gods, what was it you were saying just now? Is it a vice to suffer shipwreck? Or something that partakes of vice?' 16. Would you not take up a piece of wood, and throw it at his head? 'What have we to do with you, man? We are perishing, and you come and joke.' 17. Again, if Caesar should summon you to answer an accusation, do you remember the distinction? When you are going in, pale and trembling, what if someone came up to you and said 'Why are you trembling, fellow? What are you so worried about? Surely Caesar doesn't put virtue and vice into the people who appear before him?' 18. 'What, do you too make fun of me, and add to my ills?' 'Nay, but tell me, philosopher, why are you trembling? Do you face any other danger than death, or prison, or bodily pain, or exile, or disgrace. Why, what could it be? Is any of these a vice, or something that partakes of vice? What was it that you used to call such things?' 19. 'What have I to do with you, man? My own evils are enough for me.' And in that, you speak well. Your own evils are indeed enough for you; your baseness, your cowardice, and your bluster when sitting in the lecture-hall. Why did you pride yourself on what was not your own? Why did you call yourself a Stoic?

20. Observe your own behaviour in this way, and you will find out what school you belong to. You will find that most of you are Epicureans, and some few are Peripatetics, but pretty feeble ones at that. 21. For, by what action do you prove that you think virtue equal, and even superior, to all other things? Show me a Stoic if you have one. Where, or how? 22. You can show, indeed, a thousand who can repeat the Stoic quibbles. But do they repeat the Epicurean ones less well? Or the Peripatetic ones any less accurately? 23. Who, then, is a Stoic? As we call a statue 'Pheidian' if it has been formed according to the art of Pheidias, so show me some person who is formed in accordance with the judgements that he professes. 24. Show me someone

who is sick, and yet happy; in danger, and yet happy; dying, and yet happy; exiled, and yet happy; disgraced, and yet happy. Show him to me, for, by the gods, I long to see a Stoic. 25. But (you will say) you have not one perfectly formed. Show me, then, one who is in the process of formation, one who has set out in that direction. Do me this favour. Do not refuse an old man a sight which he has never yet seen. 26. Do you suppose that you are going to show me the Zeus or Athena of Pheidias, a work of ivory or gold? Let any of you show me the soul of a man who desires to be of one mind with god, and never to cast blame on god or man again, who wishes to fail in no desire, to fall into nothing that he wants to avoid, never to be angry, never to be envious, never to be jealous, who thus desires (why beat about the bush?) 27. to become a god instead of a man, and though he is in this body, this corpse, is determined to achieve communion with Zeus. Show him to me. But you cannot. 28. Why, then, do you delude yourselves, and cheat others? Why, then, do you assume a costume that is not your own; and walk about in it, mere thieves and filchers of clothes and properties which do not belong to you?

29. Here I am, your teacher, and you come to be instructed by me. And indeed my design is to secure you from restraint, compulsion and hindrance, to make you free, prosperous, and happy, looking to god in everything, great or small. And you are with me to learn and practise these things. 30. Why then do you not finish the work, if you have the proper resolve, and I, in addition to the resolve, the proper qualifications? What is wanting? 31. When I see a craftsman, with his materials lying at hand, I look out for the final product. Now here is the craftsman; here are the materials; what is it that we lack? 32. Is the matter incapable of being taught? No, it can be taught. Is it outside our power, then? No, this alone of all things is within our power. Neither riches, nor health, nor fame, is in our power, nor, in short, anything other than the right use of impressions. This alone is by nature not subject to restraint, not subject to hindrance. 33. Why, then, do not you finish the work? Tell me the reason. It must lie either in me, or in you, or in the nature of the task. The task itself is practicable, and the only thing completely in our power. The fault then must be either in me, or in you, or, more truly, in both. 34. Well, then, is it your wish that we shall now, at last, begin to carry out such a design? Let

us lay aside all that is past. Only let us make a start and, believe me, you shall see.

## CHAPTER 20

# Against The Epicureans And Academics

1. Propositions that are true and evident are necessarily made use of even by those who contradict them. And it is about the strongest proof one could offer of a proposition being evident, that even he who contradicts it finds himself having to make use of it. 2. If a person, for instance, should deny the proposition 'Some universal statement is true', he will be obliged to assert the contrary, 'There is no universal statement that is true.' Then, slave, this cannot be true either. 3. For what else does his assertion mean than this: 'If a statement is universal, it is false'? 4. Again, if any one should come and say, 'Know that there is nothing to be known, but all things are uncertain'; or another, 'Believe me, and benefit from my advice, no man ought to be believed in anything'; or a third, 'Learn from me, man, that it is impossible to learn anything; 5. I tell you this, and will teach the proof of it, if you wish.' Now what difference is there between these people and – now whom shall I say? – those who call themselves Academics? 'Men, give your assent', they say, 'to the proposition that no man ever assents; believe *us* when we say that nobody believes anybody.' 6. And Epicurus likewise, when he wants to destroy the natural fellowship of men with one another, makes use of the very thing he is destroying. 7. For what does he say? 'Be not deceived, men, nor misled, nor mistaken. There is no natural fellowship of rational beings with one another. Believe me. Those who say otherwise are deceiving you and cheating you with false reasoning.' 8. Why should you care, then? Let us be deceived. Will you fare any the worse if all the rest of us are persuaded that we have a natural fellowship with one another, and that this is to be preserved by every means? No, your position will be much better and more secure. 9. Man, why do you concern yourself on our behalf, why do you stay awake for us, why do you light your lamp, why do you

rise early, why do you write such massive books? Is it so that none of us should be deceived into supposing that the gods take any care of men? Or that we may not suppose that the essence of good consists in anything but pleasure? 10. For if that be the case, lie down and sleep, and lead the worm's life which you have judged yourself to be worthy of. Eat and drink and copulate and defecate and snore. 11. What is it to you what others think about these matters, and whether their views are sound or not? For what have you to do with us? Do you worry about sheep because they hand themselves over to us to be shorn, to be milked, and finally, to be slaughtered? 12. And would it not be a desirable thing, that men might be so lulled and enchanted by the Stoics, as to give themselves up to be milked and shorn by you, and such as you? 13. For these are things that you should have told your fellow-Epicureans: but should you not have concealed these things from other men, persuading them most of all and above all other things, that we have been born with a natural sense of fellowship, and that self-control is a good thing – so that everything can be reserved for you? 14. Or is this fellowship to be preserved towards some, and not towards others? Towards whom, then, is it to be preserved? Towards those who mutually preserve it, or those who violate it? And who violate it more than you, who have drawn up these arguments?

15. What was it, then, that roused Epicurus from his sleep, and compelled him to write what he did? What other than that which is the most powerful of all things in mankind, nature, which draws everyone, though against his will and groaning, to her own purposes? 16. 'For since', says she, 'you hold these unsociable opinions, write them down and bequeath them to others, and stay awake on their account, and become by your own practice the denunciator of your own doctrines.' 17. What, we speak of Orestes being pursued by the Furies and roused from his sleep, but are not the Furies and avenging spirits that pursue Epicurus even more unsparing? They roused him from his sleep and would not let him rest, but compelled him to proclaim his own miseries, as wine and madness do the priests of Cybele. 18. So strong and unconquerable a thing is human nature! For how can a vine be moved to behave, not like a vine, but like an olive tree? Or an olive tree, not like an olive tree, but like a vine? It is impossible. It is inconceivable. 19. Neither,

therefore, is it possible for a human being entirely to lose human affections. And even those who have their male organs cut off cannot cut off their desires as men. 20. And so it was with Epicurus, he cut off all that characterizes a man, and the head of a household, and citizen, and friend, but he could not cut off human desires, for he could not, any more than the indolent Academics can cast aside or blind their own sense-perceptions, though this is what they have striven above all to do. 21. Oh, what a misfortune it is when anyone, after having received from nature measures and standards for discovering the truth, does not strive to add to these, and make up their deficiencies, but does precisely the opposite, and endeavours to take away and destroy whatever faculty he does possess for discovering the truth.

22. What say you, philosopher? What do you think of piety and sanctity? – If you please, I will prove that they are good. – Pray, do prove it, so that our citizens may be converted and honour the divine, and may no longer neglect what is of the highest importance. – Have you the proofs, then? – I have, and am thankful for it. 23. Since you are so well pleased with this, then, hear the contrary: that there are no gods, or, if there are, they take no care of mankind, and we have no communion with them, so this piety and sanctity, which is so much talked of by the crowd, is only a lie told by charlatans and sophists, or (great Zeus!) by law-givers, to frighten and deter wrong-doers. 24. – Well done, philosopher. Our citizens are much the better for you. You have won back our young men, who were already inclining towards a contempt for what is divine. 25. – What! does this not please you, then? Learn next, how justice is nothing, how shame is folly, how to be a father, or a son, means nothing. 26. – Well said, philosopher; persevere, convince the young men, so that we may have more people who believe and talk like you. It was these doctrines that made our well-governed cities grow to greatness! It was upon these doctrines that Sparta was founded! These are the convictions that Lycurgus instilled into the Spartans by his laws and programme of education: that to be slaves is no more shameful than noble, and to be free is no more noble than shameful! Those who died at Thermopylae, died because they held such judgements as these! And from what principles but these did the Athenians abandon their city? 27. And then those who talk in this way marry and produce

children, and engage in public affairs, and get themselves made
priests and prophets (of whom? Of gods that have no existence);
and they themselves consult the Pythian priestess, only to hear
falsehoods, and interpret the oracles to others. What colossal
shamelessness and imposture!

28. What are you doing, man? You contradict yourself every
day, and yet you will not give up these paltry cavils. When you
eat, where do you put your hand? To your mouth, or to your
eye? When you bathe, where do you go? Do you ever call a pot
a dish; or a ladle, a spit? 29. If I were a slave to one of these
gentlemen, even at the risk of being flayed every day, I would
plague him. 'Throw some oil into the bath, boy.' I would take
some fish sauce and pour it over his head. 'What is the meaning
of this?' By your fortune, the impression I had was indistinguish-
able from olive oil, it was just the same. 'Bring me the soup.' 30.
I would bring him a dish full of vinegar. 'Did I not ask for the
soup?' Yes, master, this is the soup. 'Is this not vinegar?' Why
so, any more than soup? 'Take it and smell it; take it and taste
it.' 'How do you know, if our senses deceive us?' 31. If I had
three or four fellow-slaves who were of the same mind as I was,
I would make him burst with anger and hang himself, or else
change his opinions. But as it is they are making sport of us, by
using all the gifts of nature, and yet in mere argument abolishing
them. 32. Grateful and modest men, truly! who, if nothing else,
eat bread every day, and yet dare to say, 'We do not know
whether there is a Demeter, or Kore, or Pluto.' 33. Not to
mention that while they enjoy the night and day, the seasons of
the year, the stars, the earth and sea, and the help that men give
one another, they pay no great heed to any of these things, but
seek only to belch out their wretched problem, and, when they
have cleared their stomachs, to go off to the baths. 34. But they
have never given the least thought to what they will say, nor
about what, nor to whom, nor what may be the consequence of
their talk; whether any noble-spirited young man may not hear
such doctrines and be affected by them, and be affected in such
a way as to lose altogether the germs of his nobility of mind;
35. whether they may not be furnishing an adulterer with
grounds for growing shameless in his behaviour; whether an
embezzler of public funds may not gain some facile argument in
his own defence from these doctrines; whether someone who

neglects his parents may not gain some additional audacity from them.

'What, then, in your opinion, is good or evil, noble or base? Is this, or that?' 36. Why should one argue any further against such people as these, or engage in discourse with them, or try to talk them round? 37. By Zeus, one might have greater hope of converting catamites than those who have become so completely deaf and blind.

## CHAPTER 21

# On Inconsistency

1. There are some faults which men willingly admit, and others they do not. No one will admit, for instance, that he is foolish or unintelligent, but, on the contrary, you will hear everyone say, 'I wish my luck was on a level with my wits.' 2. But they readily admit that they are cowards, and say, 'I am a bit of a coward, I confess, but in other respects you will not find me a fool.' 3. A man will not readily admit that he lacks self-control, or admit at all that he is unjust, envious or a busybody; but most will admit that they give way to pity. 4. What is the reason for all this? The principal reason is confusion and inconsistency regarding questions of good and evil; but otherwise the cause varies according to the person, though as a general rule people are most unwilling to admit anything that strikes them as shameful. 5. Timidity and pity they imagine to be a mark of good sense, but stupidity to be something altogether slavish; and offences against society they are not the least willing to admit. 6. Now as regards most faults, they are brought to a confession chiefly through the fancy that there is something involuntary in them, as in the case of fear and pity. 7. And though a person should in some measure admit that he is intemperate in his desires, he attributes this to love, in the expectation of being forgiven as for an involuntary action. But injustice is not imagined to be by any means involuntary. In jealousy, too, there is something, they suppose, of the involuntary, and this likewise, in some degree, they admit. 8. Dwelling,

therefore, amongst such people, who are so confused and so ignorant of what they are saying, or of what evil they have within them, or whether they have it, or where they got it from, or how they can be freed of it, it is worthwhile, I think, to ask oneself continually, 'Am I, perhaps, also one of these people? 9. What do I imagine myself to be? How do I conduct myself? As a prudent, as a temperate person! Do I ever say that I am sufficiently educated to confront whatever may happen? 10. Have I the awareness that a man who knows nothing ought to have, that I indeed know nothing? Do I go to my teacher, as though to an oracle, prepared to obey; or do I, like others, enter school like a snivelling child only to learn nothing but history, and understand books which I did not understand before, and, perhaps, explain them to others?' 11. You have been fighting at home, man, with your slave, you have turned the house upside-down, and disturbed your neighbours; and are you now going to come to me with all the dignity of a sage, and sit and pass judgement on how I explain a text and how I give vent to any nonsense that comes into my head? 12. Have you come here envious and dejected because nothing is being sent to you from home? And, as the discussion proceeds, do you sit back thinking of nothing but how things are between you and your father or your brother? 13. 'What are they saying about me at home? At present they suppose I am making progress, and are saying, "He will come back knowing everything." 14. At one time, I imagine, I did want to learn everything before returning home, but that demands much labour, and nobody sends me anything. The baths are really awful at Nicopolis, and things are going badly for me, both at home and here at the school.'

15. And then they say, nobody is the better for attending a philosopher's school. Why, who comes there, who, I ask, in order to be cured? Who to submit his own judgements to purification, or to become fully conscious of what he is in need of? 16. Why do you wonder, then, that you bring back from the school precisely what you brought there? For you do not come to lay aside, or correct your judgements, or exchange them for others. 17. Not in the least. Far from it. What you should consider, rather, is this, whether you are getting what you came for. You want to chatter about philosophical precepts. Well; and are not you more impertinently talkative than you were? Do these paltry precepts not furnish you with matter for

ostentation? Are you not able to analyse syllogisms and arguments with equivocal premises? Do you not explore the assumptions in the 'Liar', and in hypothetical arguments? Why, then,
are you still displeased if you have the very things for which you
came? 18. – 'Very true; but if my child or my brother should
die, or if I must die or be tortured myself, what good will such
things do me?' 19. Why, did you come for this? Did you sit
beside me for this? Was it upon any such account that you ever
lit your lamp, or sat up at night? Or did you ever, when you
went for a walk, set before your mind an impression instead of
a syllogism, and scrutinize that with your companions? When
did you ever do that? 20. And then you say the precepts are
useless. To whom? To those who apply them badly. For eye-
salves are not useless to those who apply them when and as they
ought. Poultices are not useless; jumping-weights are not useless,
but merely useless to some, and, on the other hand, useful to
others. 21. If you should ask me now, 'Are syllogisms useful?', I
will reply that they are and, if you want, I will show you how.
'What good have they done me, then?' – Man, you were not
asking, surely, whether they are useful to you, but whether they
are useful in general? 22. Let somebody who is suffering from
dysentery ask me whether vinegar is useful, and I will reply that
it is. 'So is it useful to me?' Then I will say, No – try first to get
the discharge stopped, and the ulceration healed. And you too,
men, should first heal your ulcers, stop your discharges, establish
peace in your mind, and bring it to the school free from all
distraction; and then you will know what the power of reason
can be.

## CHAPTER 22

# On Friendship

1. What a man sets his heart on, that he naturally loves. Do men
set their heart on evils? – By no means. Or on what does not
concern them? – No again. 2. It remains for us to conclude,
then, that good things alone are what they set their heart on: 3.
and if they set their heart on those, they love them too. Whoever,

therefore, has knowledge of good things would also know how
to love them; and he who cannot distinguish good things from
evil, and things that are neither good nor evil from both of
these, how could he still have the power to love? It follows that
the wise man alone has the power to love.

4. How so? (someone says) I am not wise myself, and yet I
love my child.

5. By the gods, it surprises me that you should, in the first
place, admit that you are not wise. For what is it that you lack?
Have you not the use of your senses? Do you not distinguish
between impressions? Do you not supply your body with the
appropriate nourishment, and shelter, and a house to live in? 6.
Why, then, do you admit that you lack wisdom? In truth,
because you are often bewildered and disconcerted by
impressions, and their persuasiveness gets the better of you; and
hence you sometimes suppose the very same things to be good,
then evil, and later on neither good nor evil; and, in a word, you
are subject to pain, fear, envy, disturbance and change. That is
why you confess that you lack wisdom. 7. And are you not
changeable too in your love for things? Riches, pleasure and, to
be short, such outward things, you sometimes regard as good,
and sometimes as evil; and do you not regard the same persons,
too, as alternately good and bad? And at one time are you not
well-disposed towards them, at another ill-disposed, and at one
time do you not praise them, and at another reproach them?

Yes. This too is the case with me.

8. Well, then, can a person who has been utterly deceived
about somebody be his friend? What do you think?

Surely not.

Or can a person who has changed his feelings after choosing
someone as a friend bear him genuine goodwill?

No again.

Or a person who first vilifies someone and later admires him?
Nor he.

9. Do you not often see little dogs fawning on one another
and playing with one another, so that you exclaim, 'Nothing
could be more friendly'? But, to see what this friendship is,
throw a bit of meat between them, and then you will know. 10.
And if you likewise throw a bit of land between yourself and
your son, you will see that he will quickly wish you dead and
buried, and you him: and then you will come to cry, 'What a

son I have raised! He has been longing to see me buried!' 11.
Throw a pretty girl between, and the old fellow and the young
one will both fall in love with her; or a bit of glory. And if you
have to risk your life, you will end up saying the same as the
father of Admetus: 'You hold life dear; does not your father
too?'

12. Do you suppose that he did not love his own child when
he was small? And that he was not in agonies when it had a
fever, and would often say, 'If only it were I who had the fever
instead'? But then when the trial comes and is close upon him,
just see what expressions he uses. 13. Were not Eteocles and
Polyneices born of the same mother and of the same father?
Were they not brought up together, and did they not live and
eat and sleep together? Did they not often kiss one another? So
that anyone who saw them would have laughed at all the
paradoxes which philosophers utter about friendship. 14. And
yet, when a kingdom, like a bit of meat, was thrown between
them, see what they say:

ETEOCLES     Where will you stand before the walls?
POLYNEICES   For what reason do you ask me?
ETEOCLES     I mean to face you and slay you.
POLYNEICES   And such is my desire too.

Such are the prayers that they give voice to. 15. For universally
(and you should not be deceived on this) every living creature is
attached to nothing so strongly as it is to its own interest. So
whatever appears to it to be acting as a hindrance to that interest
– be it a brother, or father, or child, or beloved, or lover – is
hated, abhorred, and execrated by it; 16. for by nature it loves
nothing so much as its own interest. This is father to it, and
brother, and family, and country, and god. 17. Whenever,
therefore, the gods seem to hinder us in this, we vilify even
them, and throw down their statues and burn their temples, as
Alexander ordered the temple of Aesculapius to be burned,
because he had lost the man he loved.

18. Whenever, therefore, anyone puts his interest in the same
scale with sanctity, virtue, his country, parents, and friends, all
these are safe; but if he puts his interest in one scale, and friends,
and country, and family, and justice itself, in the other, these are
all borne down by the weight of self-interest and are lost. 19.
For wherever 'I' and 'mine' are placed, thither must the creature

necessarily incline. If they are in the flesh, the determining power will be there, if in moral choice, it will be there, and if in external things, it will be there. 20. If, therefore, I am where my choice is, then only I shall be a friend, a son, or a father, such as I ought. For in that case it will be my interest to preserve my faithful, modest, patient, abstinent, and co-operative character, and to keep my relationships with others inviolate. 21. But, if I place myself in one scale, and what is noble in another, the doctrine of Epicurus will stand its ground, which argues that the noble is either nothing or, at the most, what people hold in repute.

22. It was this ignorance that led the Athenians and Lacedae-monians to quarrel with each other, and the Thebans with both, and the king of Persia with Greece, and the Macedonians with both of them, and now the Romans with the Getae; and in still remoter times, the Trojan war arose from the same cause. 23. Paris was the guest of Menelaus, and whoever had seen the mutual proofs of goodwill that passed between them would never have believed that they were not friends. But a tempting morsel, a pretty woman, was thrown in between them; and for this they went to war. 24. At present, therefore, when you see friends or brothers who seem to be of a single mind, do not immediately pronounce upon their friendship, even if they swear to it, and even if they say that it is impossible for them to be apart from one another. 25. For the governing faculty of a bad man cannot be trusted; it is unstable, irresolute, now subjugated by one impression, now by another. 26. No, do not inquire, as others do, whether they were born of the same parents, and brought up together, and under the same attendant, but ask this one question alone: In what do they place their interest – in things outside themselves, or in their power of choice? 27. If place it in externals, do not call them friends, any more than you can call them faithful, or constant, or resolute, or free; no, do not even call them human beings, if you are wise. 28. For it is no human judgement that makes them snap at (or vilify) one another, and occupy the public spaces as wild beasts do the mountains and deserts, and convert courts of justice into dens of robbers; nor any human judgement that prompts them to be intemperate, adulterers, seducers; or leads them into other offences that men commit against one another. That follows from one judgement and one only, that they place themselves

and all that belongs to them amongst those things that lie outside the sphere of choice. 29. But if you hear that these men sincerely believe that the good lies where choice does, and where impressions are correctly used, no longer take the trouble to enquire if they are father and son, or brothers, or companions who have associated with one another for a considerable time, but even if this is the only thing that you know about them, confidently declare that they are friends, and likewise, faithful and just. 30. For where else can friendship be found than where there is fidelity and modesty, and a respect for what is honourable, and for nothing besides?

31. Yes, but he has paid attention to me all this while, so did he not love me?

How can you tell, slave, whether he paid attention to you just as he does to his shoes when he cleans them, or his horse when he rubs it down? And how do you know whether, when you have lost your usefulness as his utensil, he may not throw you away, like a broken plate?

32. But she is my wife, and we have lived together all this while.

And how long did Eriphyle live with Amphiaraus, and was the mother of his children, and quite a number too? But a necklace came between them. 33. What was this necklace? Her judgement about things of that kind. This was the brutish factor, this was what cut asunder all love, and would not allow the woman to be a wife, and the mother a mother.

34. Whoever, therefore, amongst you is anxious to be or to gain a friend, let him root out those judgements, despise them, drive them right out of his soul. 35. And then he will, in the first place, be secure from self-reproach and inner conflict, and instability of mind, and self-torment. 36. And, secondly, in his relationships with others, he will be wholly frank and open to one who is like himself, and to one who is unlike, he will be patient, mild, gentle and forgiving as to one who is ignorant or falling into error on matters of the highest importance; he will be harsh to nobody, being fully convinced of Plato's saying, that the soul is never willingly deprived of the truth. 37. Without all this you may, in many respects, live as friends do; and drink and lodge and sail together; and be born of the same parents; and so may snakes also. But they can never be friends, and nor can you, so long as you hold these brutish and despicable judgements.

# CHAPTER 23

# On The Faculty Of Expression

1. A book will always be read with greater pleasure, and ease too, if it be written in clearer characters; so, likewise, everyone would listen with greater ease to discourses that are expressed in graceful and appropriate language. 2. It ought not, then, to be said that there is no such thing as the faculty of expression: for that would be to speak as one who is both impious and cowardly. Impious, because one is dishonouring the gifts of god, just as if one was denying the usefulness of the faculty of vision, or of hearing, or even of speech itself. 3. Has god, then, given you eyes for nothing? Was it for nothing that he has infused into them a spirit of such strength and ingenuity that it can reach far out and model the images of whatever is seen? What messenger is so quick and diligent? 4. Was it for nothing that he made the intervening air so active and elastic that vision penetrates through it as through a taut medium? Was it for nothing that he made light, without which all the rest would be useless? 5. Man, be not ungrateful for these things, nor again forgetful of better things than these; but for sight and hearing, and by Zeus for life itself and whatever supports it, for fruits, and wine, and oil, be thankful to god: 6. but remember, that he has given you another thing, superior to all these things, which makes use of them, tests them, and estimates the value of each. 7. For what is it that pronounces upon the value of each of our faculties? Is it each faculty itself? Now did you ever hear the faculty of sight or hearing say anything concerning itself? No. These things have been appointed as servants and slaves, to obey the faculty that is capable of dealing with impressions. 8. If you ask the value of anything, whom do you ask? Who is it that answers you? How, then, can any other faculty be superior to this, which both uses all the rest as servants, and tests each of them and pronounces judgement upon it? 9. For which of them knows what it is, and what it is worth? Which of them knows when it is to be used, and when not? Which is it that opens and shuts our eyes, and turns them away from the objects that it should turn them away from, and directs them towards others?

Is it the faculty of sight? No; but that of choice. Which is it that opens and shuts our ears? 10. What is it that makes us curious and inquisitive, or, on the contrary, unaffected by what is said? Is it the faculty of hearing? 11. No; but that of choice. Will this, then, when it sees that all the other faculties, are blind and deaf, and are unable to discern anything but those offices for which they have been appointed so as to minister to the faculty of choice and serve it, and that choice alone sees clearly, and distinguishes the value of each of the rest, is it going to pronounce that any other faculty besides itself is the highest? 12. What else does the eye do, when it is opened, than see? But whether we ought to look upon somebody's wife, and in what manner, what tells us that? The faculty of choice. 13. Whether we ought to believe, or to disbelieve, what is said; or whether, if we do believe, we ought to be moved by it or not; what tells us that? Is it not the faculty of choice? 14. Again, the very faculty of expression, and of the embellishment of discourse, if there be any such peculiar faculty, what does it do beyond ornamenting and arranging expressions, as hairdressers do our hair? 15. But whether it be better to speak or to be silent, and better to speak in this or in that manner, and whether this be appropriate or inappropriate, and the proper moment for each manner of speaking and its usefulness, what is it that tells us that, but the faculty of choice? What, would you have it step forth and bear testimony against itself?

16. 'But what', somebody says, 'if the matter is instead like this, and it is in fact possible for that which serves to be superior to what it serves, the horse to the rider, the dog to the hunter, the instrument to the musician, or the servants to the king?' What is it that makes use of everything else? Choice. 17. What is it that takes care of all? Choice. What is it that destroys the whole man, at one time by hunger, at another by a rope or a precipice? Choice. 18. Is there, then, anything stronger in men than this? And how can things that are subject to hindrance be stronger than that which is not? 19. What has a natural power to impede the faculty of vision? Both choice, and things that lie outside the sphere of choice. And with regard to the faculties both of hearing and speech the situation is the same. But what has a natural power to impede the faculty of choice? Nothing that lies outside the sphere of choice, but only choice itself,

when it has been perverted. Therefore choice alone is vice; choice alone is virtue.

20. Since, then, choice is so great a faculty, and placed in authority over all the rest, let it step forth and say to us that the flesh is, of all things, the most excellent. No, even if the flesh itself declared itself the most excellent, one would not have countenanced it. 21. But what in fact is it, Epicurus, that pronounces such a judgement? That wrote those volumes *On the End* and *The Physics* or *The Canon*? That caused you to grow a philosopher's beard? That, as it was dying, wrote that it was then spending its last and happiest day? 22. Was this the flesh, or was it the faculty of choice? And can you, then, without madness, confess anything superior to this? Are you in reality so deaf and blind?

23. Well then, is one to disdain one's other faculties? Heaven forbid! Does one say that there is no use or advancement except in the faculty of choice? Heaven forbid! That would be stupid, impious, and ungrateful to god. Rather, we render to each its due. 24. For there is some use in an ass, though not so much as in an ox; and some also in a dog, though not so much as in a slave; and in a slave, though not so much as in the other citizens; and in the citizens, though not so much as in the magistrates. 25. And, though some things are better than others, the use that the others provide is not to be despised. The faculty of eloquence has its value too, though not as great a value as the faculty of choice. 26. When, therefore, I talk in this way, none of you should suppose that I would have you neglect eloquence, any more than I would have you neglect your eyes or ears or hands or feet or clothes or shoes. 27. But if you ask me what is the most excellent of things, what am I to say? The faculty of eloquence? I cannot. But rather that of choice, whenever it becomes right choice. 28. For it is choice that makes use of the faculty of eloquence and all the other faculties, both great and small. If this be set right, a man becomes good; if it go wrong, a man becomes bad. 29. It is through this that we are unfortunate or fortunate; that we disapprove or approve one another. In a word, it is this that produces unhappiness when neglected, and, when properly tended, happiness.

30. But to do away with the faculty of eloquence, and to say that it is in reality nothing, is not only ungrateful to those who have bestowed it, but cowardly too. 31. For one who would

want to seems to me to be afraid that, if there is any such faculty, we may not be able to scorn it. 32. Such are those, too, who deny any difference between beauty and ugliness. Then would it be possible to be affected in the same way by seeing Thersites as seeing Achilles, or Helen as any commonplace woman? 33. No, these are the crude and foolish notions of those who are ignorant of the specific nature of each thing and afraid that whoever perceives a difference must at once be carried away and overcome. 34. But the great point is to leave each thing to its own proper faculty, and then to see what the value of that faculty is, and to learn what is the highest of things, and upon every occasion to pursue that and to make it the chief object of our attention, considering all else as trifling in comparison with it, and yet, as far as we are able, not neglecting even these. 35. We ought, for instance, to take care of our eyes also, but not as the highest thing, but only on account of the highest; because that will not preserve its own nature unless it uses the eyes with reason and chooses some things rather than others.

36. What is the usual practice, then? People behave like a traveller, who, returning to his own country, comes across a good inn on the road, and because the inn pleases him, remains there. 37. Have you forgotten your intention, man? You were not travelling to this place, but only through it. 'But this is a fine inn.' And how many other fine inns are there, and how many pleasant meadows? But only to be passed through on the way. 38. Your business is, to return to your country, to relieve the anxieties of your family, to perform the duties of a citizen, to marry, to have children, and to hold public office. 39. for you have not, I think, come into the world to pick out the most charming places, but to live and act in the place where you were born, and of which you have been appointed a citizen. 40. Something like this comes to pass in this matter of eloquence also. Because one must progress to perfection through the spoken word and what is passed on to you here in the school, and must purify one's choice, and rectify the faculty that deals with impressions, and because this knowledge must be transmitted by means of certain precepts, and in a particular style, making use of a certain variety and incisiveness in the expression of those precepts, 41. some people are captivated by these very things and remain where they are, one captivated by the style,

another by syllogisms, another by arguments with equivocal premises, and another by some other inn of this kind, and there they remain and moulder away, as though amongst the Sirens.

42. Your business, man, was to prepare yourself to be capable of using impressions as nature demands, and, as regards desire, not to be unsuccessful in attaining it, and, as regards aversion, not to fall into what you would avoid, and never to suffer misfortune or ill-fortune, but to be free, unhindered, unconstrained, conforming to the governance of Zeus, obedient to it, well contented with it, finding fault with nobody, accusing nobody, but able to say from your whole soul the verses which begin: 'Lead me, Zeus; and thou, O Destiny.' 43. When you have this purpose before you, will you be so pleased with some pretty turn of phrase, or a few precepts, as to choose to stay and live with them, forgetful of your home, and say, 'Here are fine things!' Why, who says they are not fine things? But only as a passage way; as an inn. 44. For even if you could speak like Demosthenes, what is to prevent you from being unhappy? If you could analyse syllogisms like Chrysippus, what is to prevent you from being wretched, sorrowful, envious, and, in a word, being distracted and miserable? Not a single thing. 45. You see, then, that these were mere inns of no value, and that your purpose was quite another thing. 46. When I talk in this way to some people, they suppose that I am rejecting all study of rhetoric or general principles. Yet it is not this that I am rejecting, but the way in which people endlessly dwell on such matters, and place their hopes in them. 47. If any man, by maintaining this, causes harm to his audience, place me amongst those harmful people; for when I see that what is highest and most sovereign is one thing, I cannot say that it is another thing just to gratify all of you.

## CHAPTER 24

# To One He Thought Unworthy

1. Someone said to him, 'I have often come to you desiring to hear you, and you have never given me an answer; 2. but now,

if at all possible, I beg you to say something to me.' 'Do you suppose', replied Epictetus, 'that in speaking, as in other things, there is an art which enables the person who possesses it to speak with skill, while the person who lacks it will speak without skill?'

'I do.'

3. He, then, who by speaking benefits himself and is able to benefit others, would be speaking skilfully; whilst, conversely, he who speaks injuriously to others and himself would be unskilled in this art of speaking? Yes, you would find that some speakers are injured and others benefited. 4. And are all listeners benefited by what they hear? Or will you find some benefited, and some injured?

Yes, that is the case with them also.

Here also then, those who listen skilfully are benefited, and those who listen unskilfully, hurt?

Granted.

5. So there is a skill in hearing, then, as well as in listening?

It seems so.

6. If you please, consider the matter in this way also. Whose part do you think it is to play an instrument musically? The musician's.

7. And whose do you suppose it is to make a statue in the proper manner?

The sculptor's.

And to view a statue skilfully, don't you think that requires a certain art as well?

I do.

8. If, therefore, to speak properly demands a skilled person, do not you see that to listen with benefit also demands a person with the requisite skill? 9. As regards what is ultimately beneficial, let us, if you please, put that aside for the present, since both of us are far removed from anything of that kind; 10. but this seems to be universally admitted, that he who would listen to philosophers needs some kind of practice in listening. Is that not so? 11. What, then, shall I speak to you about? Tell me. What are you capable of hearing about? About good and evil. The good and evil of what? Of a horse perhaps?

No.

Of an ox?

No.

12. So of what then? Of a human being?

Yes.

Do we know, then, what a human being is, what his nature is, what the concept of a human being is? And to what extent have we ears to hear in respect of this matter? Nay, do you understand what nature is; or are you able to follow me to any great extent as I speak? 13. Am I to offer you a demonstration? How can I? Have you any understanding at all of what a demonstration is, or how a thing is demonstrated, or by what means? Or what resembles a demonstration, and yet is not a demonstration? 14. Do you know what truth or falsity is? What follows what, or is in contradiction with what, or in disagreement or discord with what? Can I arouse in you an interest in philosophy? 15. How can I show you that the majority of people have contradictory ideas, which makes them disagree about matters of good and evil, benefit and harm, when you do not even know what contradiction is? Show me, then, what I can achieve by holding a discussion with you. Excite my enthusiasm. 16. Just as the sight of appropriate grazing excites a sheep's enthusiasm to eat, whilst if you offer it a stone or a loaf of bread, it will remain unmoved, so likewise are some of us naturally excited to speak, whenever somebody who will be capable of listening appears, and he himself urges us on. But if he simply sits there like a stone or a clump of grass, how can he excite any enthusiasm in a man? 17. Does the vine say to the farmer, 'Take care of me'? No; but it shows by its very appearance that the man who cares for it will profit from it, and so invites him to care for it. 18. Who fails to respond to the invitation of engaging and sprightly children to join in their games and crawl alongside them and talk to them in baby talk? But who was ever taken with a desire to play with, or bray with an ass? For, be it ever so little, it is still a little ass.

19. Why do you say nothing to me, then?

I have only this to say to you: That whoever is ignorant who he is, and what he was born for, and in what kind of a world, and with what companions; who does not know what things are good, and what evil, what noble, and what base; who cannot follow either discourse or demonstration, or what is true or what is false, nor is able to distinguish between them: such a one will neither exercise desire, nor aversion, nor impulse, nor design, in accordance with nature, nor his assent, nor his dissent, nor his witholding of judgement: but will wander up and down entirely deaf and blind, supposing himself to be somebody, while he is in reality nobody. 20. Is there anything new in all this? Is not this ignorance the cause of all the errors and misfortune that have arisen since the origins of mankind? 21. Why did Agememnon and Achilles quarrel? Was it not for want of knowing what is advantageous, what disadvantageous? Does not one of them say, It is advantageous to restore Chryseis to her father, the other, that it is not? Does not one say, that he ought to take away the prize of the other, the other, that he ought not? Did they not, by these means, forget who they were, and for what purpose they had come there? 22. Why, what did you come for, man; to gain a mistress or to fight? – 'To fight.' With whom? With the Trojans or the Greeks? – 'With the Trojans.' Will you, then, let Hector go, and draw your sword against your own king? 23. And as for you, good sir, will you desert your duties as a king, 'With a people to watch over and so many cares', and get involved in a brawl over a paltry girl with the most warlike of your allies, whom you ought by every means to conciliate and keep on your side? And will you show yourself inferior to the refined high-priest, who treats the noble gladiators with all consideration? Do you see the kind of thing that ignorance of what is advantageous brings about? 24. 'But I too am rich.' – What, richer than Agamemnon? 'But I am handsome too.' – What, handsomer than Achilles? 'But I have fine hair too.' – Had not Achilles finer, and golden besides? And did he not comb it and dress it elegantly. 25. 'But I am strong too.' – Can you lift as great a stone, then, as Hector or Ajax? 'But I am of a noble family too.' – Is your mother a goddess, or your father descended from Zeus? And what good did all that do Achilles, when he sat crying for a girl? 26. 'But I am an orator.' – And was Achilles not so? Do you not see how he dealt with the most eloquent of the Greeks, Odysseus and Phoenix? How he struck them dumb? 27. This is all I have to say to you; and even this was against my inclination.

Why so?

28. Because you have given me no encouragement. For what can I see in you to encourage me as thoroughbred horses do their riders? Your poor body? You disfigure it. Your clothing? That too is effeminate. Your air, your mien? Nothing worth looking at there. 29. When you want to hear a philosopher, do

not say to him, 'Have you nothing to say to me?'; but only show yourself capable of hearing him, and you will see how you excite him to speak.

## CHAPTER 25

# How Is Logic Necessary?

1. When one of the company said to him, 'Convince me that logic is useful', he said, Would you like me to demonstrate it to you? 'Yes.' 2. Then I must make use of a demonstrative argument? 'Granted.' 3. And how will you know, then, whether I am deceiving you with a sophism? And when the man remained silent, he said, You see how you yourself admit that logic is necessary, since without it you cannot even determine whether it is necessary or not.

## CHAPTER 26

# What Is The Distinctive Characteristic Of Error?

1. Every error implies a contradiction: for, since the man who errs does not wish to err, but to act rightly, it is evident that he is not doing what he wishes. 2. For what does a thief wish to achieve? His own interest. If, then, thieving is against his interest, he is not doing what he wishes. 3. Now every rational soul is naturally averse to contradiction: but so long as a person fails to understand that he is involved in a contradiction, there is nothing to prevent him from performing contradictory actions, but when he has come to understand it, he must necessarily renounce and avoid the contradiction, just as bitter necessity makes a man renounce what is false as soon as he perceives that it is false, though as long as he does not have that impression, he assents to it as true.

4. So, the man who is skilled in argument, and able both to

encourage and to refute, is the one who can make plain to each individual the contradiction which causes him to err, and make him clearly see how he is not doing what he wishes, and is doing what he does not wish. 5. For if one can make this clear to him, he will withdraw from his error of his own accord; but as long as you fail to make it clear, do not be surprised if he persists in it, for he will do so because he has the impression that he is right. 6. That is why Socrates, relying on this faculty, used to say, 'It is not my custom to call any other witness in support of what I am saying, but I am always contented with my interlocutor, and call for his vote and summon him as a witness, and he alone as a single person is sufficient for me in place of all others.' 7. For Socrates knew how a rational soul is moved; that it is like a balance, and if a weight is thrown in the scale, it will incline whether you wish it or not. Show the rational governing faculty a contradiction, and it will renounce it: but if you fail to do so, blame yourself rather than the person whom you are unable to convince.

# BOOK 3

BOOK 3

## CHAPTER I

# On Personal Adornment

1. When a young student of rhetoric came to him who had his hair arranged in a rather elaborate fashion and was in general richly dressed, Epictetus said: Tell me, do you not think that some dogs are beautiful, and some horses, and likewise with every other animal?

I do.

2. Is not the same true of human beings also, that some are beautiful and others ugly?

Certainly.

Do we, then, call each of these beautiful in its kind, on the same general grounds, or on special grounds in each case? 3. Look at the question in this way. Since we see that a dog is born for one thing, a horse for another, and a nightingale, for instance, for another, in general, it would not be absurd to pronounce each of them beautiful, when it best fulfils its own nature; but, since the nature of each is different, each of them must, I think, be beautiful in a different way. Is that not so?

Agreed.

4. So, what makes a dog beautiful, makes a horse ugly, and what makes a horse beautiful, makes a dog ugly, if their natures are different?

So it seems.

5. For, I imagine, what makes a pancratiast fine does not make a wrestler good, and would be altogether absurd in a runner; and the very same person who appears beautiful as a pentathlete would appear most ugly for wrestling.

Very true.

6. Then what makes a man beautiful is just the same as what makes a dog or a horse beautiful in its kind?

The same.

What is it, then, that makes a dog beautiful?

The presence of a dog's excellence.

What a horse?

The presence of a horse's excellence.

So what makes a human being beautiful? Must it not be the presence of a human being's excellence? 7. If you for your part want to appear beautiful, young man, you should strive for this, the excellence that characterizes a human being.

And what is that?

8. Consider, when you praise people dispassionately, what sort of people you praise: is it the just or the unjust?

The just.

The temperate or the intemperate?

The temperate.

The self-controlled or the dissolute?

The self-controlled.

9. Then, if you make yourself such a person, you can be sure that you will make yourself beautiful; but while you neglect these things, whatever contrivances you employ to appear beautiful, you will necessarily be ugly.

10. Beyond that I do not know what more I can say to you; for if I say what I think, I will offend you, and you will go away and perhaps never return. And if I do not, consider how I will be acting then. You come to me in the hope of gaining some improvement, and I bring you none at all; and you come to me as to a philosopher, and I do not speak to you as a philosopher. 11. Besides, how could it be other than cruel for me to leave you uncorrected? If hereafter you should come to your senses, you will have good reason to accuse me, saying: 12. 'What did Epictetus espy in me, that when he saw me come to him in such a shameful condition, he left me as I was, and never said so much as a word to me? Did he so absolutely despair of me? 13. Was I not young? Was I not able to listen to reason? How many other young men at that age are guilty of many such errors? 14. I am told of one Polemo, who from being a most dissolute youth became totally changed. Suppose he did not think I should become a Polemo, he might however have put my hair right, he might have stripped off my bracelets and rings, he might have prevented me from plucking the hairs from my body. But when he saw me dressed like a – what shall I say? – he was silent.' 15. For what you look like, I for my part will not say; when you come to your senses, you will say it yourself, and will know what manner of adornment this is, and who they are who adopt it.

16. If you should at some future time lay this charge against me, what defence could I make? Yes, but what if I do speak, and he will not obey me. Did Laius obey Apollo? Did he not go away and get drunk, and bid farewell to the oracle? What then? Did that prevent Apollo from telling him the truth? 17. Indeed, I am uncertain whether you will obey me or not, but Apollo positively knew that Laius would not obey him, and yet he spoke. 18. 'And why did he speak?' You may as well ask, Why is he Apollo, why does he deliver oracles, why has he placed himself in such a post as a prophet and fountain of truth, for the inhabitants of the whole civilized world to resort to? Why is 'Know Thyself' inscribed on the front of his temple, even if nobody heeds it?

19. Did Socrates persuade all who came to him, to take proper care of themselves? Not one in a thousand. Nevertheless, since he had been appointed to this post, as he himself says, by the deity, he never deserted it. What does he say even to his judges? 20. 'If you acquit me, on condition that I should no longer act as I do now, I will not accept your offer, nor cease to act in that way, but I will go up to whomever I meet, whether young or old, and ask him the same questions as I presently ask, and I will question you, my fellow-citizens, far more than everyone else, because you are more closely related to me.' 21. 'Are you so prying and meddlesome, Socrates? What is it to you how we act?' – 'What are you saying? You are my companion and kinsman, and yet you neglect yourself, and provide the city with a bad citizen, and your relatives with a bad relative, and your neighbours with a bad neighbour.' 22. 'Why, who are you?' – Here it is no small thing to reply, 'I am he who must care for mankind.' For when a lion comes, it is no ordinary member of the herd that dares to confront him; but if the bull comes forward and confronts him, say to the bull, if that seems right to you, 'Why, who are you?' 'What do you care?' Man, in every species nature produces some exceptional being: 23. in oxen, in dogs, in bees, in horses. Do not say to that exceptional being 'Why, who are you?' If you do, it will, somehow or other, find a voice to tell you, 'I am like the purple in a robe. Do not expect me to be like the rest, or find fault with my nature, which has distinguished me from others.'

24. What then, am I a person of that kind? How could I be? As for you, are you the kind of person who can listen to the

truth? I wish you were. Nevertheless, since I have been condemned somehow to wear a grey beard and rough cloak, and
you come to me as to a philospher, I will not treat you cruelly,
nor as if I despaired of you, but will ask you — Whom is it,
young man, whom you would render beautiful? 25. Know first
who you are, and then adorn yourself accordingly. You are a
human being; that is, a mortal animal capable of making a
rational use of impressions. And what does it mean to use them
rationally? In accordance with nature and perfectly. 26. What is
exceptional in you? Is it the animal part? No. The mortal? No.
That which enables you to deal with impressions? No. What is
exceptional in you is your faculty of reason. Adorn and beautify
that, but leave your hair to him who formed it, as he thought
good. 27. Well, what other names do you bear? Are you a man,
or a woman? A man. Then adorn yourself as a man, not a
woman. A woman is naturally smooth and delicate, and, if very
hairy, is a prodigy, and shown among the prodigies at Rome.
28. It means the same in a man, not to be hairy, and if by nature
he has no hair, he is a prodigy. But if he clips and plucks out his
hairs, what shall we do with him? Where shall we show him,
and how shall we advertise him? 'A man to be seen, who would
rather be a woman.' 29. What a scandalous exhibition! Who
would not wonder at such an advertisement? I believe, indeed,
that even these men who pluck out their hairs do so without
understanding that this is just what they are doing.

30. Man, what complaint have you to make against nature?
That it has made you a man? Why, were all to be born women,
then? In that case, what would have been the use of your finery?
For whom would you be adorning yourself, if all were women?
31. But the whole affair displeases you? — Go to work upon the
whole, then. Remove — what shall I call it? — the cause of these
hairs, and make yourself a woman entirely, that we may be no
longer deceived, nor you be half man, half woman. 32. Whom
to you want to please? The women? Please them as a man.

Yes, but they are pleased with smooth men.

Go hang yourself. Suppose they were pleased with catamites,
would you become one? 33. Is this your business in life? Were
you born to please dissolute women? 34. Shall we make a man
like you a citizen of Corinth, and, perhaps, a city-warden, or
master of the youth, or commander of the army, or director of
the public games? 35. Come, will you pluck your hairs even

when you are married? For whom, and for what? Will you be the father of children, and introduce them into our citizenship plucked just as you are? Oh, what a fine citizen, and senator, and orator! Is it young men like these that we should be praying to have bred and reared for us?

36. No, by the gods, young man, but once you have heard these words, go home, and say to yourself: 'It was not Epictetus who told me all these things (for how should he?), but some propitious god speaking through him: for it would never have entered the head of Epictetus, who is not in the habit of speaking with anyone. 37. Well, let us obey god, then, to avoid incurring his wrath.' No, if a raven gives a sign to you by his croaking, it is not the raven that gives it, but god through him. So if he gives a sign through a human voice, will you pretend that it is simply the man who is saying this to you, so that you fail to recognize the power of the deity, and that he gives a sign to some men in this way, and to others in that, but when it concerns the greatest and most authoritative matters, he gives a sign through his noblest messenger? 38. What else does the poet mean when he says:

> ... since we ourselves warned him,
> By sending keen-sighted Hermes, the slayer of Argus,
> Neither to murder the man, nor make love to his wife.

39. And just as Hermes went down to tell Aegisthus this, so now the gods are telling you the same, 'By sending keen-sighted Hermes, the slayer of Argus', not to overturn what is right and good, nor to meddle with it, but to suffer a man to be a man, and a woman a woman, and the beautiful person beautiful, and the ugly person ugly; 40. for you yourself are not your flesh and hair, but your choice. If you take care to have this beautiful, then you will be beautiful. 41. But all this while, I dare not tell you that you are ugly; for I fancy you would rather hear anything than that. 42. But consider what Socrates says to that most beautiful and attractive of all men, Alcibiades: 'Endeavour to make yourself beautiful.' What is he trying to tell him? 'Curl your locks, and pluck the hairs from your legs'? Heaven forbid! Rather, 'Adorn your choice; throw away your wrong judgements.'

43. How, then, are you to deal with your poor body?

Leave it to nature. Another has taken care of such things. Give them up to him.

44. What! is one's body to be unclean?

By no means, clean yourself in accordance with the nature that you have and were born to, so that a man is clean as a man, a woman as a woman, and a child as a child. 45. If not, let us pluck out the mane of a lion, lest he be unclean; and the comb of a cock, for he ought to be clean too. Yes, but let it be clean as a cock, and the lion as a lion, and the hound as a hound.

## CHAPTER 2

# What A Person Must Train Himself In If He Is To Make Progress; And That We Neglect What Is Most Vital

1. There are three areas of study, in which a person who is going to be good and noble must be trained. That concerning desires and aversions, so that he may neither fail to get what he desires nor fall into what he would avoid. 2. That concerning the impulse to act and not to act, and, in general, appropriate behaviour; so that he may act in an orderly manner and after due consideration, and not carelessly. The third is concerned with freedom from deception and hasty judgement, and, in general, whatever is connected with assent.

3. Of these, the principal, and most urgent, is that which has to do with the passions; for these are produced in no other way than by the disappointment of our desires, and the incurring of our aversions. It is this that introduces disturbances, tumults, misfortunes, and calamities; and causes sorrow, lamentation and envy; and renders us envious and jealous, and thus incapable of listening to reason.

4. The next has to do with appropriate action. For I should not be unfeeling like a statue, but should preserve my natural and acquired relations as a man who honours the gods, as a son, as a brother, as a father, as a citizen.

5. The third falls to those who are already making progress

and is concerned with the achievement of certainty in the matters already covered, so that even in dreams, or drunkenness or melancholy no untested impression may catch us off guard. 'This', someone says, 'is beyond our powers.' 6. But our present philosophers neglect the first two areas of study and busy themselves with the third, studying arguments with equivocal or hypothetical premises, and those that conclude with a question, or that involve fallacies, like the 'Liar'. 7. 'Of course', he says, 'when a man is dealing with these subjects he must take care that he is not liable to be deceived.' Who must? 'The man who is already virtuous and good.' 8. So do you fall short in this? Have you mastered the other subjects? Are you not liable to be deceived when handling money? When you see a pretty girl, do you withstand the impression? If your neighbour receives an inheritance, do you not feel a bite of envy? And is security of judgement now the only thing you lack? 9. Wretch, even whilst you study these very matters you are fearful and anxious lest anyone think ill of you, and ask whether anyone is passing comments on you; 10. and if someone comes and tells you, 'A discussion arose about who was the best philospher, and somebody who was present remarked that you were the one true philosopher', that little soul of yours grows from an inch to a yard; but if another who was present said, 'You are mistaken, he is not worth listening to, for what does he know? He has the first rudiments, but nothing more', you are distraught, you turn pale and cry out at once, 'I will show him what kind of man I am, that I am a great philosopher. 11. But what you are can be seen from this very behaviour; why do you wish to show it in any other way? Do you not know that Diogenes showed up one of the sophists in such a way, by pointing at him with his middle finger, and saying, when the man grew enraged at that, 'That is the man; I have shown him to you.' 12. Now a man is not something that can be shown in the same way as a stone, or a piece of wood, simply by pointing a finger; but when one shows what his judgements are, then one has shown what he is as a man.

13. Let us look at your judgements too. For is it not evident that you place no value on your own choice, but look beyond it to things outside the sphere of choice, as to what, for instance, So-and-so will say, and what people will think of you, whether they regard you as a scholar, a man who has read Chrysippus

or Antipater? Why, if you have read Archedemus too, you have everything you could wish! 14. Why are you still anxious that you may be failing to show us what you are? Will you let me tell you what manner of person you have shown yourself to be? One who has come before us as a querulous, quick-tempered, cowardly fellow, complaining of everything, accusing everybody, never at peace, and a blusterer. This is what you have shown us. 15. Go off now, and read Archedemus, and then, if a mouse falls down and makes a din, you will die of fright. For that is the sort of death that awaits you, just like – who was it? – Crinis, who also prided himself on understanding Archedemus.

16. Wretch, why will you not let alone these things that do not concern you? For such things are suitable only to those who are able to learn them with an undisturbed mind, and can properly say, 'I am not subject to anger, or grief, or envy. I am free from restraint, free from compulsion. What remains for me to do? I am at leisure; I am at ease. 17. Let us see how arguments with equivocal premises should be treated; let us see how one may adopt a hypothesis and never be reduced to an absurd conclusion.' It is to people like that that these things belong. Those who are safe may light a fire, go to dinner and, if they please, even sing and dance; but you are coming to me and hoisting the topsails when your ship is already sinking.

## CHAPTER 3

# What Is The Material The Good Man Works Upon, And What Should Be The Main Object Of Our Training?

1. The specific material that the good and noble man works upon is his own governing faculty, as that of the doctor or masseur is the human body, and that of the farmer, his land; and it is the function of the good man to deal with his impressions in accordance with nature. 2. Now as it is the nature of every soul to assent to what is true and dissent from what is

false, and suspend judgement in matters of uncertainty, it must be its nature likewise to be moved by desire for what is good, aversion from what is evil, and a neutral disposition towards what is neither good nor evil. 3. For just as a money-changer or a greengrocer is not at liberty to reject Caesar's coinage, but when it is shown, is obliged, whether he wants to or not, to hand over what is being sold for it, so do things stand with the soul. 4. Immediately the good appears, it draws the soul towards it; and by evil the soul is repelled. A soul will never reject a clear impression of good, any more than a man will reject Caesar's coinage.

5. On this depends every motion of god and of man; and the good is thus preferred above every form of relationship. My father is nothing to me, only the good. − Are you so hard-hearted? − Such is my nature, and such is the coin which god has given me. 6. If, therefore, the good is different from the noble and just, off go father and brother and country, and everything else of that kind. 7. What! Shall I overlook my own good so that you can have yours, and make way to you? Why should I? 'I am your father.' But not my good. 'I am your brother.' But not my good. 8. But, if we place the good in right choice, then the preservation of such relationships does in itself become a good, and, furthermore, he who yields up some of his external possessions attains the good. 9. 'My father is taking my money away.' But he is causing you no harm. 'My brother will get the greater part of the land.' Let him have as much as he likes. Would he be taking any of your modesty from you, your fidelity, your sense of brotherly love? 10. For who can expel you from possessions like those? Not even Zeus. Nor would he ever wish to; rather, he placed my good nature in my own power, and gave it to me as he has it himself, free from all hindrance, compulsion and restraint.

11. In so far, then, as different people use different coinage, a person offers the coinage he has and buys what can be bought in exchange for it. 12. A thief has come to the province as Proconsul: what coin does he use? Silver. Offer it, and carry off what you please. An adulterer comes: what coin does he use? Young girls. Take the coin, says one, and give me this trifle. 'Give, and buy.' 13. Another is addicted to boys: give him the coin, and take what you please. Another is fond of hunting: give him a fine nag or a puppy; and, though with sighs and groans,

he will sell you whatever you like for it, for he is compelled from within by another, who has established this currency.

14. It is according to this plan of action that a man should chiefly exercise himself. Go out at the break of dawn, examine whomsoever you see or hear, and then answer, as if to a question. What have you seen? A handsome person? Apply the rule. Is this within the sphere of choice or outside it? Outside it. Throw it away. 15. What have you seen? One grieving for the death of his child? Apply the rule. Death is outside the sphere of choice. Throw it aside. A consul met you? Apply the rule. What kind of thing is a consulship? Within the sphere of choice or outside it? Outside it. Throw this aside too. It does not stand the test. Fling it away. It is nothing to you.

16. If we had acted thus, and trained ourselves in this manner from morning till night, then, by the gods, something would have been achieved. 17. Whereas now, we are caught half asleep by every impression, and if we ever do wake up, it is only for a little in the lecture-hall. And then we go out, and if we see anyone in distress, we say, 'He is done for'; if a consul, 'Happy man!'; if an exile, 'What misery!'; if a poor man, 'How wretched for him; he has nothing to buy a meal with!'

18. These vicious principles must be eradicated; and to this our whole strength must be applied. For what is weeping and groaning? A judgement. What is misfortune? A judgement. What is sedition, discord, complaint, accusation, impiety, foolish talk? 19. All these are judgements, and nothing more; and judgements concerning things outside the sphere of choice, taking them to be good or evil. Let anyone transfer these judgements to things within the sphere of choice, and I will guarantee that he will preserve his constancy, whatever be the state of things about him.

20. The soul is like a vessel filled with water; and impressions are like a ray of light that falls upon the water. 21. If the water is disturbed, the ray will seem to be disturbed likewise, though in reality it is not. 22. Whenever, therefore, a man is seized with vertigo, it is not the arts and virtues that are confounded, but the spirit in which they exist; and, if this comes to rest, so will they likewise.

## CHAPTER 4

# To One Who Grew Improperly Excited In The Theatre

1. The Procurator of Epirus had displayed a somewhat unseemly partiality for a certain comic actor, and was abused in public for doing so. When he then reported to Epictetus that he had been abused, and expressed his indignation at those who had abused him, Epictetus asked: Why, what wrong were they doing? They too were displaying their partiality, just as you yourself were.

2. Is that the way, then, in which a man expresses his partiality?

When they saw you, their governor, and the friend and procurator of Caesar, expressing his favour in that way, was it not to be expected that they would do so too? 3. For if it is not right to express such favour, nor should you do so yourself; and, if it is, why are you angry at them for imitating you? For whom have the multitude to imitate, but you, their superiors? Whom are they to look to when they come into the theatre but you? 4. 'Just look how Caesar's Procurator behaves in the theatre. He cries out: Well, I will cry out too. He jumps from his seat: I too will jump from mine. His slaves sit in different parts of the house and shout their applause: Well, I for my part have no slaves – but I will shout as loud as I can, and match them all.' 5. You ought to know, then, that when you enter the theatre, you enter as a pattern and example to others, as to how they should behave there. 6. Why, then, did they abuse you? Because every man hates what stands in his way. They wanted one actor crowned, you another. They stood in your way, and you in theirs. You proved the stronger. They did what they could, by abusing what stood in their way. 7. How would you have it, then? That you should do what you wish, and they should not even say what they wish? Where is the wonder in all this? Do not farmers revile Zeus when he stands in their way? And sailors too? Do men ever stop reviling Caesar? Does Zeus not know of this? 8. Is Caesar not informed of what is being said? What does he do then? He knows that if he were to punish all who abuse him, he would have nobody left to rule.

9. When you enter the theatre, then, ought you to say, 'Come, let Sophron be crowned'? No. But, 'Come, let me ensure that my faculty of choice with regard to this subject-matter remains in accord with nature.' 10. For no one is dearer to me than myself; it would be absurd, therefore, that I be harmed so another can win the crown as a comic actor. 11. Whom, then, do I want to see win? The man who does: and in that way, the man I want will always win. – But I would have Sophron crowned. Why, hold as many contests as you want in your own house, and proclaim him a Nemean, Pythian, Isthmian and Olympic victor; but in public, do not claim more than your due, nor seize for yourself what is public property: 12. otherwise, you must put up with abuse, for if you act as the masses do, you put yourself on their level.

## CHAPTER 5

# To Those Who Leave Because Of Illness

1. I am ill here, says one of the students, and want to go back home. 2. Were you never ill at home, then? Do you give no thought to whether you are doing anything here that contributes to the improvement of your choice, for if you are not achieving anything, it was pointless for you even to have come? 3. Go home. Take care of your domestic affairs. For, if your ruling faculty cannot be brought into conformity with nature, your little patch of land may. You may add to your loose change, support your father in his old age, hang around in the market-place, hold office, and not being a good man yourself, perform badly whatever you happen to do next. 4. But if you are conscious in your own mind that you are ridding yourself of some of your bad judgements, and taking up different ones in their place; and that you have changed your position, from a reliance on things outside the sphere of choice to a reliance on those within it; and that, if you do sometimes cry Alas, it is not upon the account of your father or your brother, but yourself –

in that case, why take any further account of illness? 5. Do you not know that disease and death will necessarily overtake us whatever we are doing? They overtake the farmer at his plough and the sailor at sea. 6. What would you like to be doing when you are overtaken by them? For you surely will be, whatever you are doing. If you think you could be doing something better than this when you are overtaken, go and do it. 7. For my own part, may death overtake me while I am engaged in nothing other than the care of my own faculty of choice, so that it may be unhindered, unrestrained, serene, and free. 8. I would wish to be found attending to this, so that I could say to god, 'Have I in any way transgressed your commands? Have I used the resources you gave me for other purposes than what you gave them for, or misused my senses or my preconceptions? Have I ever had any accusation to bring against you, or ever found fault with your governance? 9. I fell sick, when it was your will, and so did others, but I fell sick willingly. I became poor, because it was your wish, but rejoiced in it. I never held office, because that was not your wish, and I never yearned for it. Have you ever seen me dejected on that account? Have I not always approached you with a cheerful countenance, prepared to execute whatever you might command, or indicate as being your will? 10. Now it is your pleasure that I should depart from this festival, and I depart, in all gratitude that you should have condescended to let me share in this festival with you, and behold your works and understand your governance.' 11. Let these be my thoughts, and my writing or reading, when death overtakes me.

12. But I shall not have my mother to hold my head when I am sick.

Go home then to your mother, for you deserve to be ill and have someone hold your head.

13. But at home I had a nice bed to lie on.

Get to this bed of yours, for you are fit to lie on such a bed, even when healthy; so do not, by being here, miss out on what you could be doing there. 14. But what does Socrates say? 'As one man rejoices in the improvement of his land, and another in that of his horse, so I rejoice day by day in following my own improvement.'

15. In what, in mere phrases?

Hush, man!

In trifling theories, then?

How do you mean?

16. Well, I cannot see what else it is that philosophers busy themselves about.

Does it strike you as nothing never to accuse anyone, never to blame anyone, whether god or man? And always to go out and come in again with the same expression on one's face? 17. These are the things that Socrates knew, and yet he never professed to know or teach anything; but if anyone asked for pretty phrases or theories, he took him off to Protagoras or Hippias; for, likewise, if somebody had come looking for vegetables, he would have taken him off to a market-gardener. Who of you, then, makes this his enterprise? 18. Why, if you did, you would willingly suffer sickness and hunger, and death. 19. If any of you has been in love with a pretty young girl, he will know that I am telling the truth.

## CHAPTER 6

# Some Scattered Sayings

1. When somebody asked how it is that although more effort is devoted at present to the art of reasoning, more progress was made in earlier times, 2. Epictetus replied, On what is the effort spent now, and in what was the progress greater then? For in that on which effort has been spent at present, progress will also be found at present. 3. People at present have been devoting their effort to the study of syllogisms, and in that there is progress. But formerly they devoted their efforts to keeping their governing faculty in conformity with nature; and progress was made in that. 4. Therefore, do not confuse different things, nor when you devote effort to one thing, expect to make progress in another. But see whether any one of us who devotes his efforts to keeping in accord with nature and living his life so, fails to make progress. For you will find nobody of whom that could be said.

5. The good man is invincible; for he engages in no contest where he is not superior. 6. 'If you want my land, take it, and take my servants, take my public post, take my poor body. But

you will not cause my desire to fail to attain its end, or my aversion to fall into what it would avoid.' 7. This is the only contest he enters into: how can he fail, then, to be invincible?

8. When someone asked Epictetus what 'general perception' is, he replied, Just as one might call the faculty which distinguishes between sounds 'general hearing', but that which distinguishes between musical notes is no longer general, but rather, technical, so there are certain things that people who are not altogether perverted can see by virtue of their general faculties. Such a condition of the mind is called 'general perception'.

9. It is not easy to gain the attention of young men who are soft, for you cannot get hold of soft cheese with a hook; but the naturally gifted, even if you try to turn them away, hold all the more firmly to reason. 10. So Rufus, for the most part, tried to turn them away, using that as a test to distinguish the gifted from the ungifted. For he used to say, 'Just as a stone, even if you throw it upwards, will fall to the earth by virtue of its own nature, so is it with a gifted person, the more one tries to beat him off, the more he inclines towards his natural object.'

## CHAPTER 7

# A Discourse With The Commissioner Of The Free Cities, Who Was An Epicurean

1. When the commissioner, who was an Epicurean, came to him, Epictetus said, It is proper that we laymen should inquire of you philosophers what is the best thing in the world, just as those who come to a strange city do of the citizens, who know the area; so that, when we have heard what it is we may seek it out, as visitors to cities do, and have a look at it.

2. Now, scarcely any one denies that there are three things that belong to man: soul, body, and externals. It remains for you to answer which is the best. What shall we tell mankind? The flesh? 3. And was it for this that Maximus sailed in winter all the way to Cassiope to accompany his son? Was it for pleasure in the flesh?

4. No, surely.

Is it not proper, then, to pay most concern to what is best in us?

Yes, beyond all other things.

What have we, then, better than the flesh?

The soul.

Are the goods of the best thing better, or those of the inferior?

5. Those of the best.

Are the goods of the soul things within or things outside the sphere of choice?

Things within it.

Is the pleasure of the soul, then, within the sphere of choice?

It is.

At what, then, does this pleasure arise? At itself? 6. No, that is inconceivable. For there must exist some essence of the good, by hitting upon which we shall enjoy this pleasure of the soul.

This too I grant.

7. At what, then, does this pleasure of the soul arise? For if it be at goods of the soul, the essence of the good is found. For it is impossible that the good should be one thing and that at which we reasonably feel delight should be another; or that, if the cause is not good, the effect should be good. For to make the effect reasonable, the cause must be good. 8. But this, if you are in your senses, you will not allow; for it would be inconsistent with both Epicurus and the other doctrines of your school. 9. All that remains for you to say, then, is that the pleasure of the soul is pleasure in bodily things; and these now come to be of primary value and what is essentially good. 10. Maximus therefore acted foolishly, if he took a voyage for the sake of anything but the flesh; that is, for the sake of what is best. 11. He acts foolishly, too, if he refrains from taking what is another's when he is a judge, and able to take it. But let us consider only this, if you please, how it may be done secretly and safely, and so that no one may know it. 12. For Epicurus himself does not declare stealing to be evil, but only being found out, and says, 'Do not steal', simply because it is impossible to be confident that one will escape detection. 13. But I say to you, that if it be done dexterously and cautiously, we shall escape detection. Besides, we have powerful friends at Rome and women friends too and the Greeks are feeble, and none will dare to go up to Rome on such an affair. 14. Why do you refrain

from your own proper good? It is madness; it is folly. But if you were to tell me that you do refrain, I would not believe you. 15. For, as it is impossible to assent to an apparent falsehood, or to deny an apparent truth, so it is impossible to abstain from an apparent good. Now, riches are a good; and, indeed, the chief means of procuring pleasures. 16. Why do you not acquire them? And why do we not corrupt the wife of our neighbour, if it can be done secretly? And, if the husband should talk nonsense, why not break his neck in addition? 17. That is what you should do, if you have a mind to be a philosopher of the kind you ought to be, a perfect one, and to be consistent with your own doctrines. Otherwise you will not differ from us, who are called Stoics; for we too say one thing and do another. 18. We talk well and act shamefully; but you will be perverse in a contrary fashion, by teaching shameful doctrines, and performing noble acts.

19. In god's name, I ask you, can you conceive of a city of Epicureans. 'I shall not marry.' 'Nor I. For we ought not to marry.' No, and we ought not to have children either, or engage in public affairs. What will be the consequence of this? Where are the citizens to come from? Who will educate them? Who will be overseer of the youth? Who will supervise their athletic training? And what will they be taught? What the Spartans were taught or what the Athenians were taught? 20. Take a young man; bring him up according to your doctrines. These doctrines are wicked, subversive of the state, pernicious to families, and not fitting even for women. 21. Give them up, man. You live in an imperial city. You must exercise your office and judge uprightly, and keep your hands off things that belong to others; no woman but your own wife should seem beautiful to you, nor should any boy seem beautiful, nor plate of silver or gold. 22. You should seek for doctrines which are in harmony with such behaviour, and will enable you to refrain gladly from things so persuasive to attract and overpower you. 23. But if to the persuasiveness of these things we add some such philosophy as the one we have just discovered, to help push us towards them and encourage us in this, what will be the consequence?

24. In a piece of plate, what is best, the silver or the workmanship? The substance of a hand is flesh, but its operations are the principal thing. 25. Now appropriate actions are of three kinds, those relating to mere existence, those relating to

existence of a specific kind, and thirdly, those that are themselves
principal duties. And thus with man, it is not his material
substance that we should honour, his scraps of flesh, but his
principal duties. What are these? 26. Engagement in public
affairs; marriage; the procreation of children; the worship of
god; the care of our parents; and, in general, having desire and
aversion, and impulse to act and withhold from action, such as
each of them ought to be, in accordance with our nature. What
is our nature? 27. To be free, noble-spirited, self-respecting. (For
what other animal blushes? What other has the idea of shame?)
28. But pleasure must be subjected to these, as an attendant and
handmaid, to excite our will to act and to keep us acting in
accordance with nature.

29. But I am rich and need nothing.

Then why do you pretend to be a philosopher? Your gold and
silver plate are enough for you. What need have you of
judgements?

30. I am, furthermore, judge of the Greeks.

Do you know how to judge? Who has imparted this knowledge to you?

Caesar wrote me a commission.

Let him write that you are to be a judge of music; and what
good will it do you? 31. All the same, how did you come to be
made a judge? Whose hand did you kiss? That of Symphorus,
or Numenius? In front of whose bed-chamber did you sleep? To
whom did you send presents? After all, do you not realize that
the office of judge is worth precisely what Numenius is worth?

But I can throw whom ever I please into prison.

As you may a stone.

32. But I can club to death whomever I will.

As you may an ass. This is not the governance of men. 33.
Govern us like reasonable creatures. Show us what is to our
interest, and we will pursue it; show us what is against our
interest, and we will avoid it. 34. Like Socrates, make us
imitators of yourself. He was properly a governor of men, who
caused men to subject to him their desires and aversions, and
their impulses to act and not to act. 35. 'Do this; do not do that,
or I will throw you into prison.' This is not the way to govern
men as rational creatures. 36. No, but what you should be
saying is, 'Do as Zeus has ordained, or you will be punished,
you will be harmed.' Harmed in what way? In this alone, in not

doing what you ought; you will destroy in yourself the man of
good faith, the man of honour, the man of moderation. Look
for no greater harm than that.

## CHAPTER 8

# How Should We Exercise Ourselves
# To Deal With Impressions?

1. In the same way as we exercise ourselves to deal with
sophistical questioning, we should exercise ourselves daily to
deal with impressions; 2. for these too put questions to us. 'So-
and-so's son is dead. What do you think of that?' It lies outside
the sphere of choice, it is not an evil. – 'So-and-so has been
disinherited by his father. What do you think of that?' It lies
outside the sphere of choice, it is not an evil. – 'Caesar has
condemned him.' – This lies outside the sphere of choice, it is
not an evil. 3. – He has been distressed by all this. – This is
within the sphere of choice, it is an evil. – He has borne it nobly.
– This is within the sphere of choice, it is a good.

4. And if we make this our habit we shall make progress, for
we shall never assent to anything unless we get a convincing
impression. 5. His son is dead. – What happened? – His son is
dead. – Nothing more? – Nothing. – The ship is lost. – What
has happened? – The ship is lost. – He was carried off to prison.
– What happened? – He was carried off to prison. The remark
'He has fared ill', is an addition that each man must make for
himself. – 6. 'All the same', you say, 'Zeus is not acting rightly
in all this.' – Why so? Because he has made you patient? Because
he has made you noble-minded? Because he has prevented these
things from being evils, because he has made it possible for you
to suffer and still be happy, because he has left the door open
for you, whenever they do not suit you? Go out, man, and do
not complain.

7. If you want to know what the Romans think of philosophers,
listen to this. Italicus, who had the greatest reputation amongst
them as a philosopher, once grew angry with his friends in my

presence, claiming that his situation was desperate. 'I cannot bear it!' he exclaimed. 'You are the death of me, you will make me just like him' – and he pointed to me!

CHAPTER 9

## To A Rhetorician Who Was Going To Rome On A Lawsuit

1. A person came to him who was going to Rome on a lawsuit about an honorific post for himself, and, after telling him the occasion of his journey, asked him what he thought of the matter. 2 If you are asking me, said Epictetus, what you will do at Rome, and whether you will win or lose your case, I have no guidance to offer you. But if you are asking me how you will fare, I can answer, If your judgements are right, you will fare well, and if they are wrong, ill; for, in every case, how a man fares is determined by his judgement. 3. For what made you desire to be elected patron of the Cnossians? Your judgement. And what prompts you now to go to Rome? Your judgement. And in wintry weather, too, and at some risk and expense? Why, because it is necessary. 4. What tells you so? Your judgement. If, then, judgements are the causes of all our actions, whenever any one has bad judgements, the outcome will correspond to the cause. 5. Well, then, are all our judgements sound? Are both yours and your opponent's? How is it, then, that you disagree? Or is it that you are right and he is wrong? Why? Because you think so; and so does he, and so do madmen. This is a bad criterion. 6. But show me that you have made some examination of your judgements and taken some care over them. As you are now sailing to Rome with a view to becoming patron of the Cnossians, and are not contented to stay at home with the honours you enjoyed before, but desire something greater and more illustrious, tell me, have you ever embarked on such a journey in order to examine your own judgements and reject any that may be unsound? 7. Whom have you ever approached with such a purpose in view? What time have you set aside for this, what period of your life? Go through those periods (in your

own mind, if you are ashamed to do so in my presence). 8. Did you examine your judgements when you were a child? Did you not do what you did then just as you do everything now? When you were a youth, and attended the teachers of rhetoric and wrote declamations yourself, did you ever imagine that you were deficient in anything? 9. And when you became a man, and began to take part in public affairs, and plead causes, and acquire a reputation, did you think anyone was still your equal? How would you have borne that anyone should examine whether your judgements were bad? 10. What, then, would you have me say to you?

Assist me in this affair.

For that, I have no precepts to offer. And if you have visited me on that account, you have done so not as one should a philosopher, but as one might visit a greengrocer or shoemaker.

11. To what purpose, then, do philosophers have precepts to offer?

To this purpose, that whatever happens, we keep and continue to keep our ruling faculty in accord with nature. Do you think this a small thing?

No, but the greatest.

Well, and does it take only a short time and a brief visit to acquire this? If you can acquire it in this manner, do so!

12. And then you will say, 'I met Epictetus, and it was just like meeting a stone or a statue.' Yes, for you simply saw me, and nothing more than that. A person meets a man as a man only when he comes to understand his judgements and exposes his own in return. 13. Discover my judgements, and show me your own, and, then say that you have met me. Let us cross-examine one another; if any of my judgements is bad, take it away, if you have any that you value, put it forward. That is what meeting a philosopher is all about. 14. No, instead you say, 'We are passing through, and while we are chartering our ship, we can see Epictetus as well; Let us see what on earth he can be saying.' And then when you leave, 'Epictetus was nothing, he murdered the language, spoke utter gibberish.' What else could you be judges of, coming here like that?

15. 'But if I turn to such matters, I shall no more be a landowner than you are; I shall not possess silver goblets any more than you do, or fine cattle any more than you do.' 16. To this, perhaps, it is sufficient to reply, 'But I have no need of

them; and even if you for your part come to acquire much property, you need still more, and whether you wish it or not, are even poorer than I am.'

17. What, then, am I in need of?

What at present you do not have: constancy, a mind in accord with nature, and freedom from perturbation. 18. Patron or no patron, what do I care? But *you* care. I am richer than you. I am not anxious about what Caesar will think of me. I flatter no one on that account. This I have, instead of your silver and gold plate. You have your vessels of gold; but your reasoning, your judgements and assent, your impulses and desires, are of earthenware. 19. When I have all these in accord with nature, why should I not bestow some study upon my reasoning too? I am at leisure. My mind is not distracted. What shall I do, now there is nothing to distract me? What could be more fitting for a human being than this? You, when you have nothing to do, are restless. 20. You go to the theatre, or drift around. Why should not the philosopher cultivate his reason? 21. You have fine crystal vases, I the argument of the 'Liar'; you have murrhine ware, I the argument of the 'Denyer'. To you, all you have appears little; to me, all I have appears great. Your desire is unsatiable; mine has been satisfied. 22. When children thrust their hands into a narrow-necked jar and try to get nuts and figs out, the same thing happens: if a child fills his hand, he cannot get it out, and then breaks into tears. Drop a few of them and you will get it out. You too should drop your desire; do not covet many things, and you will get what you want.

## CHAPTER 10

# How We Should Bear Illnesses

1. We should have each of our judgements ready for when we need it. At dinner, such as relate to dinner; in the bath, such as relate to a bath; and in bed, such as relate to bed.

2. 'Let not sleep approach thy weary eyes,
    Ere every action of the former day

Strictly thou dost and righteously survey:
What have I done? In what have I transgressed?
What good or ill has this day's life expressed?

3. Where have I failed, in what I ought to do?
If evil were thy deeds, repent and mourn,
If good, rejoice . . .'

4. We should keep these verses at hand, so as to apply them practically, not merely to declaim them, like a shout of 'Paean Apollo!'

5. Again, in a fever, we should have our judgements ready with regard to that; and not, as soon as we fall into a fever, abandon and forget them all, saying, 'If I ever study philosophy again, let things turn out as they will. I shall have to go off somewhere and care for my poor body.' As if the fever will not go along with you too! 6. But what is it to study philosophy? Is it not to prepare yourself for future events? Do you not understand, then, that what you are saying comes to something like this, 'If ever again I prepare myself to bear what may befall me with equanimity, let things turn out as they will'? It is as if a man should give up the pancration because he has suffered blows! 7. But there it is possible to give up, and escape a beating; in the present case, however, if we were to give up philosophy, what good would it do us? What, then, should each of us say as each hardship befalls us? 'It was for this that I was exercising, it was for this that I was training.' 8. God says to you, 'Give me a proof, whether you have competed according to the rules, whether you have followed a proper diet, and exercised, and obeyed your trainer.' After that, do you weaken when the time for action comes? Now is the time for your fever, bear it well; for thirst, bear it well; for hunger, bear it well. 9. Is it not in your power? Who shall hinder you? A physician may hinder you from drinking, but he cannot hinder you from bearing your thirst aright. He may hinder you from eating, but he cannot hinder you from bearing hunger aright. 10. – But am I not a scholar? – And to what end do you pursue your studies? Slave, is it not so that you may be happy? That you may be constant? That you may think and act in conformity with nature? 11. What hinders you, when you have a fever, from keeping your ruling faculty in accord with nature? Here is the proof of the matter. Here is the trial of the philosopher; for a fever is a part of life, just as a walk, a voyage, or a journey is. 12. You do not

read when you are walking, do you? — No. — Nor do you read when you have a fever. But when you walk aright, you are fulfilling your part as a walker: and if you bear your fever aright, you are fulfilling your part as a man with a fever. 13. What is it to bear a fever aright? Not to blame either God or man, not to be distressed at what happens; to await death in a right and becoming manner, and to do what you are bidden. When the physician enters, not to be afraid of what he may say; nor, if he should tell you that you are in a fair way, to rejoice overmuch, for what good is there to you in what he has told you? 14. For when you were well, what good did it do you? Not to be dejected either when he tells you that you are in a bad way; for what does being in a bad way signify? That you are near the separation of soul and body. What is so terrible about that, then? If you are not coming near to it now, will you not come near to it later? What, will the world be turned upside down when you die? 15. Why, then, do you flatter your physician? Why do you say, 'Master, if you wish it, I shall get well'? Why do you give him occasion to display his vanity? Why do you not simply give him his due, as you do to the cobbler in regard to your foot, or to the builder in regard to your house, and thus, likewise to the physician in regard to your poor body, which is not your own, and is by nature a corpse? These are the things required of somebody who is suffering from a fever. If he fulfils these requirements, he has what belongs to him. 16. For it is not the business of a philosopher to take care of these mere externals, of his paltry wine, his paltry oil, or his paltry body; but of his ruling faculty. And how concerned should he be about externals? Only so far as not to trouble himself about them unreasonably. 17. What occasion, then, is there for fear? What occasion for anger, about things that are not our own and are of no value? 18. For there are two rules we should always have at hand: That nothing is good or evil, but choice; and, That we are not to lead events, but to follow them. 19. 'My brother ought not to have treated me so.' Very true, but it is for him to see to that. However he treats me, I am to act rightly with regard to him. For this is my concern, the other is somebody else's; this no one can hinder, the other is open to hindrance.

# CHAPTER II

# Some Scattered Sayings

1. There are certain punishments laid down, as though by law, for those who disobey the divine governance. 2. Whoever shall regard anything as good except what falls within the sphere of choice, let him envy, let him covet, let him flatter, let him be full of perturbation. Whoever shall regard anything else as evil, let him grieve, let him mourn, let him lament, let him be wretched. 3. And yet, despite these cruel punishments, we cannot desist.

4. Remember what the poet says of the stranger:

> A worse than thou might enter here secure;
> No rude affront shall drive him from my door;
> For strangers come from Zeus . . .

5. You should keep this at hand to apply to your father too: It is not lawful for me to dishonour you, father, even if a worse than you should come; for all come from Zeus, Protector of Parents. 6. And to apply to a brother: for all are from Zeus God of Kindred. And likewise, in all our other relationships, we shall find Zeus to be the overseer of them all.

# CHAPTER 12

# On Training

1. We should not train ourselves by resorting to unnatural or abnormal practices, for otherwise we, who call ourselves philosophers, will be no better than mountebanks. 2. For it is difficult, too, to walk on a tightrope, and not only difficult, but dangerous. Should we also, for that reason, practise walking on a tightrope, or setting up a palm, or embracing statues? By no means. 3. For not everything difficult or dangerous is suitable for training, but only that which is conducive to our achieving the task we set for ourselves. 4. And what have we set ourselves

to achieve? To have our desires and aversions free from hindrance. And what does that mean? Neither to fail to get what we aim at, nor to fall into what we would avoid. It is to this, therefore, that our training too should be directed. 5. For, without severe and constant training, it is not possible to ensure that our desire should not fail or our aversion should not fall into what it would avoid: so you should know that if you allow your training to be directed towards external things that lie outside the sphere of choice, your desire will neither gain its object, nor your aversion avoid it.

6. And because habit has a powerful influence, when we have become habituated to apply our desire and aversion to externals only, we must oppose one habit to another, and where impressions are most liable to make us slip, there resort to training to counter the risk. 7. I am inclined to pleasure. I will move to the opposite side of the deck to a greater extent than usual for the sake of training. I have an aversion to suffering. I will train and exercise my impressions to ensure that my aversion is withdrawn from everything of this kind. 8. For who is the man under training? The man who practises not exercising his desire, and directing his aversion only to things that lie within the sphere of choice, and who practises the hardest in the things most difficult to achieve. So different people will have to practise harder in different respects 9. How can it be to the purpose here to set up a palm, or carry about a tent or skins or a pestle and mortar? 10. If you are quick-tempered, man, train yourself to bear abuse with patience, and when you are insulted, not to get angry. Then you will make such progress that even if somebody strikes you, you can say to yourself, 'Imagine that you are embracing a statue.' 11. Next, train yourself to make a decent use of wine, not in order to drink the more, for there are some so foolish as to train themselves even for that, but to be able to abstain, first, from wine, and then from pretty girls and sweet-cakes. Afterwards you will venture into the lists at some proper season, by way of trial, if at all, to see whether your impressions get the better of you as much as they used to do. 12. But at first, remove yourself a good distance from what is stronger than you. A contest between a fine girl and a young man just initiated into philosophy is unequal. 'Pot and Stone', the saying goes, 'do not belong together.'

13. After the desire and aversion, the second area of study has

to do with your impulse to act and not to act, so that they should be obedient to reason, and not be exercised at the wrong time, or in the wrong place, or wrongly in any other respect. 14. The third area of study has to do with assent, and what is plausible and attractive. 15. For, just as Socrates used to say that we are not to lead an unexamined life, so neither are we to accept an unexamined impression, but to say, 'Stop, let me see what you are, and where you come from', just as the night-watch say, 'Show me your token.' 'Have you that token from nature, which every impression must have if it is to be accepted?'

16. In conclusion, whatever means are applied to the body by those who are exercising it, may also be valuable for training, if in some way they aim towards desire and aversion; but if their aim is mere display, these are the traits of a man who has turned to externals, and is hunting after something other, and is seeking for spectators to exclaim, 'What a great man!' And thus Apollonius was right when he used to say, 'If you have a mind to train for your own benefit, take a little cold water in your mouth when you are thirsty in hot weather, and spit it out again, and tell nobody.'

## CHAPTER 13

# What Desolation Means, And The Nature Of A Person Who Is Desolate

1. Desolation is the condition of a person who is bereft of help. For a man is not desolate simply because he is alone, any more than a man in a crowd is secure from desolation. 2. When, therefore, we lose a son, or a brother, or a friend whom we have relied upon, we say that we have been left desolate, though often we are in Rome, with such a crowd continually meeting us, and so many people in the house, and when we have, perhaps, a mass of slaves. For the term desolate means, according to the general conception, a person who is bereft of help and exposed to those who want to injure him. 3. That is why, when we are travelling, we call ourselves desolate above all when we fall among robbers; for it is not the sight of a man that removes our

desolation, but of a man who can be trusted, a man of honour and a helpful companion. 4. If merely being alone was sufficient to make one desolate, why, even Zeus would be desolate at the conflagration of the universe, and lament to himself, 'I have neither Hera, nor Athena, nor Apollo, nor, in a word, brother or son or grandson or relative.' 5. There are even those who say that he does behave in this way when he is left alone at the conflagration. People such as these, setting out from a natural principle – the fact that human beings are sociable by nature, and are fond of their kind, and enjoy associating with one another – cannot, then, conceive of the manner of life of one who lives completely alone. 6. We ought, nevertheless, to prepare ourselves for this also, to be capable of being self-sufficient and bearing our own company. 7. For just as Zeus converses with himself, is at peace with himself, and contemplates the nature of his own governance, and occupies himself with thoughts worthy of himself, so should we too be able to talk with ourselves, and not to need others, nor be at a loss for some way to occupy ourselves; 8. to consider the divine governance, and our relationship to other things; to look to how we used to react to events, and how we react now; and what are the things that still afflict us, and how these too may be cured, how removed. If any of these things needs perfecting, we must perfect it in accordance with reason. 9. You see that Caesar seems to provide us with a profound peace; there are no wars any longer, nor battles, nor hosts of brigands and pirates, but we may travel at all hours, and sail from sunrise to sunset. 10. But can Caesar procure us peace from fever too? From shipwreck? From fire? From earthquake? From lightning? Nay, even from love? He cannot. From grief? From envy? No, not from any one of these. 11. But the doctrine of philosophers promises to procure us peace from these too. And what does it say? 'If you will attend to me, O mortals, wherever you are, and whatever you are doing, you shall neither grieve nor be angry, nor be compelled nor restrained; but you shall live your lives in peace and free from all such things.' 12. When a person has this peace proclaimed to him, not by Caesar (for how should he have it to proclaim?) but by god through the voice of reason, 13. is he not contented when he is alone, reflecting and considering: 'Now no evil can befall me. For me no robber, no earthquake can exist. All is full of peace, all full of tranquillity;

every road, city, fellow-traveller, neighbour, associate, unable to harm me.' Another, whose care it is, provides you with food and clothing, another has given you senses and preconceptions. 14. When he no longer provides what is necessary, he sounds the recall, he opens the door, and says to you, 'Come.' Where to? To nothing fearful, but to that from which you came, to what is friendly and akin to you, the elements. 15. Whatever in you was of fire, departs into fire; what was of earth, into earth; what of air, into air; what of water, into water. There is neither Hades, nor Acheron, nor Cocytus, nor Pyriphlegethon; but all is full of gods and divinities. 16. He who has this to reflect upon, and can look upon the sun, moon, and stars, and enjoy the earth and sea, is no more desolate than he is helpless. 17. – Well, but suppose any one should come and murder me, when I am alone. – Fool, not you, but that poor body of yours.

18. What desolation is left, then? What helplessness? Why do we make ourselves worse than little children? What do they do when they are left alone? They gather up potsherds and dirt, build houses, then pull them down, then build something else, and thus are never short of amusement. 19. Suppose you were all to sail away, am I to sit and cry because I am left alone and desolate? Shall I not have my scraps of pottery, my dirt? When children act thus in their foolishness, must we in our wisdom be miserable?

20. Any great capacity is dangerous for a beginner. We should, therefore, bear such things according to our capacity, and, to be sure, in accordance with nature . . . [there is a gap in the text here] . . . but not for a consumptive.

21. Practise living as an invalid at one time, so that you may live like a healthy man at another. Abstain from food. Keep to water. Abstain from desire altogether for the present, to exercise it later, in accordance with reason. And if you do so in accordance with reason, whenever you have some good in you, you will direct your desire aright. 22. 'No, we want to live as wise men at this moment, and bring benefit to mankind.' What kind of benefit? What do you mean? Why, have you brought any benefit to yourself? But you want to exhort other men. Exhort yourself first! Do you want to be of benefit to them? 23. Show them, by your own example, what kind of men philosophy produces, and refrain from empty talk. When you eat, be of

benefit to those who eat with you, when you drink, to those who drink with you. Be of benefit to them, by giving way to all, yielding to them, bearing with them; and not by voiding your phlegm upon them.

## CHAPTER 14

# Some Scattered Sayings

1. Just as bad tragic singers are unable to sing on their own, but only with many others, so some people cannot walk around on their own. 2. Man, if you are anybody, walk around on your own, talk to yourself, and do not hide away in the chorus. 3. Put up with being laughed at on occasion, look around you, give yourself a shaking, so that you may learn who you are.

4. When a person drinks water only, or does anything else for the sake of training, on every possible occasion he tells everyone he meets, 'I drink nothing but water.' 5. Why, do you drink water merely for the sake of drinking it? Man, if it is good for you to drink it, drink it; if not, your behaviour is ridiculous. 6. But if you are drinking it for the benefit it brings you, say nothing about it to people who are irritated by those who follow such a course. So why do you? Are these the very people you wish to please?

7. Of actions some are performed on their own account; others occasioned by circumstances; some proceed from motives of good organization; some from complaisance to others; and some are done in pursuance of a manner of life which we have taken up.

8. Two things must be rooted out of men: conceit and diffidence. Conceit lies in thinking that there is nothing more you can need; and diffidence in supposing it impossible that, under such adverse circumstances, you should ever live a happy life. 9. Now, conceit is removed by the cross-questioning that Socrates was the first to employ ... [there is a gap in the text here] ... that the undertaking is not impossible, you must seek to find by your own enquiry: such an enquiry will do you no harm. 10. Indeed, the practice of philosophy virtually is just

that, seeking to discover how it is possible to employ desire and aversion without hindrance.

11. 'I am better than you, for my father is of consular rank.' 12. 'I have been a tribune', says another, 'and you have not.' If we were horses, would you say, 'My father was swifter than yours', or 'I have abundance of barley and fodder', or, 'I have exquisite trappings'? What if you were to say such things and I replied, 'Be that as it may, Let us run a race.' 13. Is there nothing in man comparable to a race in horses, by which it may be known which is better or worse? Is there no honour, fidelity, justice? 14. Show yourself the better in these, that you may be the better, as a man. But if you tell me, 'I have a powerful kick', I will answer, 'It is the quality of an ass that you take such pride in.'

## CHAPTER 15

# That We Must Approach Everything With Circumspection

1. In everything you undertake consider what comes first and what follows after, and only in this way proceed to the matter itself. Otherwise you will show eagerness in the beginning, but since you have not given any thought to the consequences, when some of them appear you will give up in a shameful manner. 2. 'I wish to win at the Olympic games.' But consider what comes first and what follows, and then, if it be for your advantage, set to work. 3. You must conform to the discipline, submit to a diet, refrain from pastries; train under orders, at an appointed hour in heat or cold; you must not drink cold water, nor even wine as you like. In a word, you must give yourself up to your trainer as you would to a doctor. 4. Then, when it comes to the contest, you have to compete in digging, and sometimes dislocate your wrist, twist your ankle, swallow an abundance of dust, get whipped, and even after all that you are sometimes defeated. 5. Reflect on these things, and then, if you still wish to, go on to become a competitor. Otherwise, take notice, you will be behaving like children, who sometimes play wrestlers, some-

times gladiators, sometimes blow a trumpet, and then make a drama of whatever they see and admire. 6. Thus you too will be at one time a wrestler, at another a gladiator, now a philosopher, then an orator; but with your whole soul, nothing at all. Like an ape, you imitate whatever you see, and one thing after another is sure to please you, but no longer to please you as soon as it becomes familiar. 7. For you have never entered upon anything with due consideration, nor after examining the whole matter carefully and systematically, but always approach things in a random and poorly motivated manner. 8. Thus some people, when they have seen a philosopher and heard a man speaking like Euphrates (after all, who can speak like him?), have a mind to be philosophers too. 9. Consider first, man, what you are embarking upon, and then your own nature, and what you can endure. If you wanted to be a wrestler, you would have to look to your shoulders, your back, your thighs; 10. for different persons are made for different things. Do you think that you can behave as you do, yet be a philosopher? That you can eat and drink, and give vent to your anger and displeasure as you do now? 11. You must stay up at night, you must toil, you must get the better of certain desires, must abandon your familiars, be scorned by a slave, be laughed at by those you meet; come off worse than others in everything, in office, in honour, in the courts. 12. When you have considered all these things with care, then, if you think fit, approach philosophy, and be willing to give up all of this in exchange for serenity, freedom and an undisturbed mind. Otherwise, do not come near; do not, like children, be at one time a philosopher, later a tax-collector, then a rhetorician, and then one of Caesar's procurators. 13. These things are not compatible. You must be one man, either good or bad. You must cultivate either your own ruling faculty or externals, and apply yourself either to things within or those outside you; that is, you must assume either the attitude of a philosopher or that of a layman.

14. When Galba was assassinated, somebody said to Rufus, 'And is providence governing the universe now?' But he replied, 'Did I ever, even incidentally, found my argument that providence governs the universe by pointing to Galba?'

## CHAPTER 16

# That We Should Enter Into Social Relationships With Caution

1. He who frequently associates with others, for talk or parties, or simple sociability, must necessarily either become like them himself, or bring them over to his own way of behaving. 2. For, if a dead coal be placed by a live one, either the dead will put out the live, or the live set fire to the dead. 3. Since, then, the danger is so great, caution must be used in entering into these familiarities with laymen; remembering that it is impossible to rub up against a person who is covered with soot without getting some of the soot on oneself. 4. For what will you do, if he talks about gladiators, horses, athletes, and, what is still worse, about individuals? 'So-and-so is bad, so-and-so good; this was well, that ill done.' Or further, if he should jeer or ridicule, or be ill-natured? 5. Has any of you a skill like that of the lyre-player, when he takes up his lyre and recognizes the moment he touches the strings which of them are out of tune, and so can tune the instrument? Or such a capacity as Socrates had, who, in every conversation, could bring his companions over to his own side? 6. How could you? Rather, it is you who are sure to be talked over by the laymen. 7. So why are they stronger here than you are? Because their corrupt chatter is founded on judgements, while your smart talk comes only from your lips. And so it has no vigour or life; and it would turn one's stomach to hear your exhortations and the miserable 'virtue' that you keep going on about, up hill and down. 8. Thus it is that the laymen get the better of you; for judgement is all-powerful, judgement is invincible. 9. Therefore, until these clever ideas are firmly fixed in you, and you have acquired the capacity you need to ensure your safety, I advise you to be cautious about going into the ring with laymen; otherwise, if you write anything down in the lecture-room, it will melt away each day like wax in the sun. 10. You should withdraw, then, to some place far away from the sun, as long as your opinions are merely of wax.

11. It is for this reason that the philosophers even advise us to leave our country, because old habits distract us, and prevent us

from beginning to develop new ones. We cannot bear to have those who meet us say, 'Look, So-and-so has turned philosopher, who was like this or that.' 12. Thus physicians send patients with chronic disorders to a different place and a different climate; and rightly so. 13. And you also should adopt different habits. Fix your opinions, and exercise yourself in them. 14. No, but from here you go to the theatre, to the gladiators, to the walks, to the circus, and then back here again, and then back there, remaining just the same people all the while. 15. No sign of any good habit, no attention or regard to yourselves. You do not watch yourself closely, and ask, 'How do I deal with the impressions that befall me? In accordance with nature or contrary to nature? As I ought, or as I ought not to? Do I say to the things that lie outside the sphere of choice that they are nothing to me?' 16. If you are not yet in this state, fly from your former habits, fly from all laymen, if you ever want to make a start on becoming somebody.

## CHAPTER 17

# On Providence

1. Whenever you find fault with providence, do but reflect on the matter, and you will find that what came to pass was in accordance with reason.

2. Yes, but the dishonest man is better off. In what? In money. For in that regard he has the advantage over you, because he flatters, he throws away shame, he lies awake at night. Why be surprised? 3. But look to see whether he has the advantage over you in fidelity or self-respect. You will find he has not; but where you are superior to him, there you will find that you are better off than he is. 4. I once said to a man who was indignant at the prosperity of Philostorgus, 'Why, would you be willing to sleep with Suras?' Heaven forbid, said he, that such a day should ever come! 5. Why, then, are you angry that he is paid for what he sells; or how can you count him blessed, for possessions he acquires by means which you detest? Or what harm does providence do, in giving the better things to the better men? Is it

not better to have a sense of shame, than to be rich? – Granted.
6. Why, then, are you angry, man, if you have the better part?
Always remember, then, and keep this reflection at hand that it
is a law of nature that the superior man has the advantage over
the worse in the respect in which he is superior – and then you
will never have cause for indignation.

7. But my wife behaves badly to me.

Well, if you are asked what is the matter, answer, 'My wife
behaves badly to me.'

Nothing more?

Nothing.

8. My father gives me nothing . . . [there is a gap in the text
here] . . . but need you add further in your own mind the
judgement that this is an evil, and thus add on a falsehood? 9.
For that reason, it is not poverty that we should reject, but our
judgement regarding it, and then we shall be at peace.

## CHAPTER 18

# That We Must Not Allow News To Disturb Us

1. Whenever disturbing news is brought to you, be ready with
this reflection, that news can never affect anything that lies
within the sphere of choice. 2. Can any one bring you news that
you have been wrong in a supposition or a desire? By no means;
but he can bring news that somebody is dead. What is that to
you, then? Or that somebody is speaking ill of you. And what is
that to you, then? 3. That your father is making preparations of
some kind. Against what? Against your choice? How can he?
Well, against your poor body or possessions? You are safe; this
is not against yourself. 4. But the judge has pronounced you
guilty of impiety. And did not the judges pass the same judgement on Socrates? Is his pronouncing a sentence any business of
yours? No. Then why trouble yourself about it any longer? 5.
Your father has a certain function, which he must fulfil, or else
lose his character as a father, and a man who loves his offspring
and is tender towards them. Do not try to make him lose
anything else on that account. For it is never the case that a man

goes wrong in one thing, but is injured in another. 6. As for you, it is your business to conduct your defence firmly, respectfully, and without anger; otherwise you lose your character as a son, and one who is both respectful and noble-minded. 7. Well, and is your judge free from danger? No. He runs an equal risk. Why, then, are you still afraid of his decision? What have you to do with somebody else's evil? 8. Making a bad defence would be your own evil. Let it be your only care to avoid that; but whether you are condemned or not condemned, that is another man's business, and thus also another man's evil. 9. 'So-and-so is threatening you.' – Me myself? No. 'He is casting blame on you.' – It is for him to look to how he does his own business. 'He is going to condemn you unjustly.' – Poor wretch!

### CHAPTER 19

# What Is The Position Of The Layman, And What That Of The Philosopher?

1. The first difference between a layman and a philosopher is this: the one says, 'Woe is me for my child, for my brother, woe is me for my father'; but the other, if he can ever be compelled to say 'Woe is me' reflects, and adds, 'for myself'. 2. For choice cannot be hindered or hurt by anything outside the sphere of choice, but only by itself. 3. If, therefore, we too are inclining in this direction, and whenever we go astray lay the blame on ourselves, and remember that nothing besides our own judgement is responsible for disturbance and inconsistency of mind, I swear to you by all the gods that we have been making some progress. 4. But in point of fact, we have followed a different path from the beginning. Already when we were still children, if we were ever wandering along absent-mindedly and bumped into something, our nurse did not tell us off, but struck the stone. Why, what has the stone done? Should it have moved out of its place because of a little child's foolishness? 5. Again, when we are children, if we do not find something to eat when we come out of our bath, our attendant does not try to moderate our appetite, but beats the cook. Why, did we appoint you

attendant of the cook, man? No, but of our child. It is he whom you are to correct and improve. 6. Thus even when we are grown up, we resemble children. For it is being a child to be uncultivated in artistic matters, unlettered in literary matters, uneducated in the art of living.

## CHAPTER 20

# That Some Advantage May Be Gained From Every External Circumstance

1. Almost everyone allows that with regard to our intellectual impressions good and evil are in ourselves, and not in externals. 2. No one calls the proposition, 'It is day', good, or, 'It is night', bad, or 'Three makes four' the greatest of evils. 3. What do they say, then? That knowledge is good and error evil, so that even with regard to what is false a good can arise, namely, the knowledge that it actually is false. 4. So the same should be true in life also. Is health a good, and sickness an evil? No, man. What, then? Health is good when used well, and bad when used ill.

So that it is possible to benefit even from disease?

In god's name is it not possible to benefit even from death? And from lameness too? 5. Do you suppose it was only a small benefit that Menoeceus gained when he died?

May the person who says such things gain the same kind of benefit as he did!

Why, pray, sir, did not he preserve his patriotism, his magnanimity, his fidelity, his noble spirit? And, if he had lived on, would he not have lost all these? And would he not have gained the very opposite? 6. Would not cowardice, mean-spiritedness, and hatred of his country, and a wretched love of life, have been his portion? Well, now, do you think he gained only a small benefit from his death? No? 7. Well, did the father of Admetus gain any great benefit by living on in such a wretched and ignoble fashion? And later did he not die anyhow? 8. You must, I adjure you by the gods, cease to admire material things, cease to make yourselves slaves, first of things, and then, on their account, of the men who have the power either to bestow them or take them away. 9. 'Then is there any advantage to be gained from these things?' Yes, from all of them. 'Even from a man who reviles me?' What advantage does a wrestler gain from his training-partner? The greatest. Well, the man who reviles me serves as my training-partner; he trains me in patience, in freedom from anger, in gentleness. 10. You disagree? But the man who grips my neck and gets my loins and shoulders into shape brings me some benefit, and the trainer does well to tell me, 'Raise the pestle with both hands', and the harsher he is, the more I benefit; and yet you mean to say that if somebody trains me to be free of anger, he is bringing me no benefit? 11. This simply means that you do not know how to derive benefit from other people. Is my neighbour a bad one? He is so to himself; but a good one to me. He trains me to be good-tempered and fair-minded. Is my father bad? To himself, but good to me. 12. 'This is the magic wand of Hermes. Touch with it whatever you please, and it will turn to gold.' No; but bring whatever you please, and I will turn it into something good. Bring sickness, death, poverty, reproach, a trial for one's very life. All these, through the wand of Hermes, shall become beneficial. 13. 'What will you make of death?' — Why, what else but an adornment to you; what but a means of your showing in action what kind of person a man is who follows the will of nature. 14. 'What will you make of sickness?' — I will show its nature, I will excel in it, I will be serene and happy. I will not flatter my physician. I will not pray to die. 15. What need you ask further? Whatever you give me, I will make it something blessed, and a source of happiness, something imposing and admirable. 16. Not you; you say 'Take care not to get sick.' Just as if one should say, 'Take care not to get the impression that three is four, it is an evil.' How is it an evil, man? If I think about it as I ought, how can it harm me any longer? Will it not rather bring me benefit, even? 17. If then, I think as I ought about poverty, sickness, lack of office, is not that enough for me? Will they not be beneficial to me? Why, then, should I any longer seek good or evil in externals? 18. But how do things stand? These things are agreed to as far as the door of this room, but nobody carries them home, but immediately every one is in a state of war with his slave-boy, his neighbours, with those who sneer and laugh at him. 19. Good luck to you, Lesbius, for proving every day that I know nothing.

## CHAPTER 21

# To Those Who Set Out To Become Lecturers

1. Those who have learned precepts as mere theory want to vomit them up immediately, just as people with weak stomachs do with their food. 2. Digest your precepts first, and you will not vomit them up in this way; otherwise they really do turn to vomit, tainted matter unfit to eat. 3. Then show us some change that results from those precepts in your own ruling faculty, just as athletes can show their shoulders as the results of their training and diet, or those who have learned various arts can show the result of their learning. 4. A builder does not come up and say, 'Listen to me lecturing on the builder's art', but acquires a contract to build a house and shows by building it that he knows the art. 5. And you should do likewise: eat as a man, drink as a man, adorn yourself, marry, sire children, play your part as a citizen; put up with abuse, bear with an inconsiderate brother, bear with a father, bear with a son, neighbour, fellow-traveller. 6. Show us these things so we can see that you have in truth learnt something from the philosophers. No; but, 'Come and listen to me reading out my commentaries.' Away with you! Look for someone else to vomit over. 7. 'Yes, but I will expound the doctrines of Chrysippus to you as no one else can, and analyse his language in the clearest manner, and add in, I hope, some of the brio of Antipater and Archedemus.' 8. And is it for this, then, that young men are to leave their countries and their parents, that they may come and hear you explaining little points of language? 9. Ought they not to return forbearing and helpful towards others, with free and undisturbed minds, and furnished with some such provision for life that, setting out with it, they will be able to bear all events well, and draw distinction from them? 10. But how can you impart what you do not possess yourself? For have you done anything else from the beginning than spend your time in solving syllogisms and

equivocal arguments and those that are developed by questioning? 'But So-and-so do lectures – why should I not do so?' 11. – Slave, these things are not to be done in a careless and haphazard manner. One must be of the right age, and lead the right life, and have god as one's guide. 12. You disagree? But no one sails from a harbour without sacrificing to the gods, and imploring their assistance; nor do men sow without first invoking Demeter. And shall any one who has undertaken so great a work undertake it safely without the aid of the gods? 13. And shall those who approach such a teacher be fortunate in doing so? Are you doing anything other, man, than profaning the Mysteries? You are saying, 'There is a temple at Eleusis, and, look, there is one here too. There is a hierophant there, and I will make a hierophant too; there is a herald there, and I will appoint a herald too; there is a torch-bearer there, and I will have a torch-bearer too; there are torches there, and there will be torches here too. 14. The words are the same. What is the difference between what goes on here and what goes on there?' Most impious man! is there no difference? Are the same proceedings beneficial if they are conducted in the wrong place, and at the wrong time? No, a man should come with sacrifices and prayers, after being purified, and with his mind predisposed to the thought that he will be approaching sacred and ancient rites. 15. It is in this way that the Mysteries become beneficial; it is in this way that we arrive at the consciousness that all these things were appointed by the ancients for the education and amendment of our lives. 16. But you are divulging and publishing them without regard to time and place, without sacrifices, without purity; you neither have the robes that the hierophant should have, nor the right hair, nor the proper head-band, nor the voice; you are not of the right age, nor have you lived a life of holy purity as he has, but you have taken up his words and nothing more, and now you repeat them. Have these words, then, a holy power in themselves?

17. Such things are to be approached in quite another way. This is a great undertaking, a solemn mystery, not granted at random to all who come. 18. Indeed, it may well be that not even wisdom is a sufficient qualification for the care of the young; one should also have a particular predisposition, by Zeus, and aptitude for this, and the right bodily build, and, above all, the recommendation from god that one should occupy

this office, 19. as he recommended to Socrates that he should undertake that of cross-examining people, and to Diogenes that of rebuking people in kingly tones, and to Zeno that of instructing people and establishing doctrines. 20. But you open up as a physician, with nothing but your medicines, and without knowing, or having studied, when or how they are to be applied. 21. 'Look, that man has these eye-salves, and I have too.' Have you also, then, the capacity to make use of them? Have you the least knowledge of when and how they will be of benefit, and to whom? 22. Why, then, do you gamble over matters of the greatest importance? Why do you act so recklessly? Why do you attempt something that is wholly inappropriate to you? Leave it to those who are able to do it, and can do it with distinction. You should not bring disgrace on philosophy by your own action, nor become one of those who disparage the calling. 23. But if you find a charm in philosophical precepts, seat yourself down and go over them in your mind; but do not ever call yourself a philosopher, and do not allow anyone else to call you one, but say, 'He is mistaken; for my desires are not different from what they were, nor are my impulses otherwise directed, nor is my assent otherwise given, nor, in a word, have I altered in the least from my former condition in the way I make use of impressions.' 24. This is what you should think and say of yourself if you want to think aright. If not, keep on gambling and doing as you are now: for such things suit you.

## CHAPTER 22

## On The Cynic Calling

1. When one of his pupils, who seemed inclined to the Cynic philosophy, asked him what sort of man a Cynic should be, and what was the basic conception of the Cynic endeavour, Epictetus replied: 'Let us examine this at our leisure. 2. But this much I can tell you now, that the man who attempts so great an endeavour without the aid of god is subject to the wrath of god, and is desiring nothing other than to disgrace himself in public. 3. For, in a well-regulated household no man comes along and

says to himself, 'I ought to be the manager here', or if he does, and the master returns and sees him insolently ordering people around, he drags him out and gives him a beating. 4. Such is the case also in this great city of the universe. For here, too, there is a master of the household who appoints everything to its place. 5. 'You are the sun, and by your revolutions you have the power to give rise to the year and the seasons, and give increase and nourishment to the fruits of the earth, and raise and calm the winds, and give a fitting warmth to the bodies of men. Go; set out on your circuit, and so impart motion to all things, from the greatest to the least. 6. As for you, you are a calf: when a lion appears, do what is appropriate to you, or you will have cause to lament. You, though, are a bull: come forward and fight, for that is your part, and you are fit and able to do so. 7. As for you, you can lead the army against Troy: be Agamemnon. And you can fight Hector in single combat: be Achilles.' 8. But if Thersites had come forward and claimed the command, he would not have got it, or, if he had, he would have disgraced himself before a multitude of witnesses.

9. So you also should deliberate with care upon this matter; it is not what you think it is. 10. 'I wear a coarse cloak now, and I shall have one then. I sleep on a hard surface now, and I shall do so then. I will, furthermore, take a wallet and a staff and begin to go about begging from the people I meet, and abusing them; and if I see anyone ridding himself of hair by using pitch-plasters, or with finely dressed curls, or walking in purple, I will rebuke him.' 11. If you imagine the Cynic calling to be something like that, keep well away; you should not come near it, for it is not your concern. 12. But, if you imagine it as it really is, and do not think yourself unworthy of it, consider what a great enterprise you are undertaking.

13. First, with regard to yourself: you must no longer, in any instance, show yourself to be behaving in the same way as you do now. You must accuse neither god nor man. You must totally suppress desire, and must turn your aversion to such things only as are within the sphere of choice. You must harbour neither anger, nor malice, nor envy, nor pity. Neither pretty boy, nor young girl, nor your paltry reputation, nor sweet-cakes must have charms for you. 14. For you must recognize this, that other men are protected by walls and houses and darkness when they do anything of this kind, and have much to conceal them. A

man shuts his door, stations somebody outside his bedroom, and says, 'If anyone comes, say, "He is out, he is busy".' 15. But the Cynic, instead of all this, must have his sense of shame as his protection; otherwise he will be acting indecently when he himself is naked and in the open air. His sense of shame is his house; and this is his door, his door-keeper and his darkness. 16. He must not wish to conceal anything relating to himself; for, if he does, he is lost; he has lost the Cynic in him, the free and outdoor character; he has begun to fear something external; he has begun to have need of concealment. Nor has he the ability to find concealment when he wants it. For where shall he conceal himself, or how? 17. And if by any chance this educator, this pedagogue of the public, happens to get caught, what must he suffer? 18. So can a man who is afraid of all this still have the confidence to be able to devote himself wholeheartedly to supervising the behaviour of the rest of mankind? It is not practicable, not possible.

19. In the first place, then, you must purify your own ruling faculty, and hold to this plan of life. 20. 'From this time forth, the material I must work upon is my own mind, as wood is the material of a carpenter or leather that of a shoemaker; for my business is to make a right use of my impressions. 21. My wretched body is nothing to me; its parts are nothing to me. Let death come when it will, either to the whole or a part. 22. Exile? And where can anyone banish me to? Not beyond the universe. But wherever I go, there will be the sun, the moon, the stars, dreams, auguries, communication with the gods.' 23. And even this preparation is by no means sufficient for a true Cynic: he must know that he has been sent as a messenger from Zeus to men concerning what is good and evil; to show them that they have gone astray, and are seeking the true nature of good and evil where it is not, without ever considering where it really is; 24. and that he is a spy, like Diogenes, when he was brought to Philip after the battle of Chaeronea. For a Cynic is indeed a spy, to discover what things are friendly, and what hostile, to man; 25. and he must, after making accurate observations come back and report the truth; and not be so struck with fear that he points to enemies where there are none, nor in any other way be troubled or confounded by his impressions.

26. He must then, if the chance arises, be able to lift up his voice, climb on to the tragic stage, and say what Socrates said:

'Tell me, men, where are you hurrying to? What are you doing, poor miserable creatures? Like blind men, staggering this way and that, you have strayed from the proper path and are going off on another; you are seeking fulfilment and happiness in the wrong place, where they are not to be found, and are unwilling to believe another when he points out the way. 27. Why do you look for it in external things? It is not to be found in the body: if you do not believe me, look at Myro, look at Ophellius. It does not lie in property: if you do not believe me, look at Croesus, look at the rich of the present age, how full of lamentation their life is. It does not lie in office; for otherwise, those who have twice and thrice been consul ought to be happy, but they are not. 28. Whom are we to believe on this matter? Those of you who view the condition of such men from the outside and are dazzled by appearances, or the men themselves? 29. For what do they say? Listen to them when they lament, when they groan, when they think themselves to be all the more wretched and in greater danger just because of these very consulships, and their own glory and celebrity. 30. Happiness does not lie in kingship; otherwise Nero and Sardanapalus would have been happy. But not even Agamemnon was happy, though a better man than Sardanapalus or Nero. But when the rest were snoring, what did he do?

Many hairs did he tear by their roots from his head.

And what did he himself say? 'Thus do I wander', he says,

. . . and in my anguish, my heart
leaps from my breast.

31. Why, what is it that is going badly for you, poor wretch? Your possessions? No; for you have 'copious gold and bronze'. Your body? Nor that either; What, then, is wrong with you? I tell you, it is this, that you have neglected and corrupted that part of you, whatever it may be, with which we feel desire or aversion, and the impulse to act or not to act. 32. Neglected in what way? By letting it remain ignorant of the true nature of the good, to which it was born, and of the nature of evil, and of what it has as its own and what is not its own. And when something that is not its own goes badly, it says, 'I am undone, the Greeks are in danger!' 33. Poor ruling faculty! which alone is neglected and has no care taken of it. 'They will die by the

sword of the Trojans!' – And, if the Trojans should not kill them, will they not die anyway? – 'Yes, but not all at once.' – Why, where is the difference? For, if it be an evil to die, it is equally an evil whether they die together or singly. Will anything else come about than the separation of soul and body? – 'Nothing.' – 34. And, if the Greeks perish, is the door closed for you? Is it not in your own power to die? – 'It is.' – Why, then, do you lament, while you are a king and hold the sceptre of Zeus? A king cannot become unfortunate any more than a god can. 35. What are you, then? You are a shepherd, and rightly called so; for you weep, just as shepherds do when the wolf seizes one of their sheep; and those who are governed by you are mere sheep. 36. But why did you come to Troy? Was your desire in any danger? Your aversion? Your impulses to act or not to act? 'No', says he, 'but my brother's poor wife was abducted.' 37. – Is it not a great gain then to be rid of a poor adulterous wife? – 'But must we be held in contempt by the Trojans?' What are they? Wise men or fools? If wise, why do you go to war with them? If fools, what does it matter to you what they think?

38. Where, then, does our good lie, since it does not lie in these things? Tell us, sir, you who are our messenger and spy. It is neither where you suppose, nor where you are willing to seek for it. For, if you had wished, you would have found it within yourselves; and you would not have been wandering outside, nor seeking after what is not your own as though it were. 39. Direct your thoughts towards yourselves, discover what preconceptions you have. What kind of thing do you imagine the good to be? – What is tranquil, happy, unhindered. – Well, and do you not imagine it to be something naturally great? Do you not imagine it to be invulnerable to harm? 40. In what kind of material, then, must you seek tranquillity and freedom from hindrance? In that which is enslaved, or that which is free? – In the free. – Is your poor body, then, enslaved or free? – We do not know. – Do you not know that it is a slave to fever, gout, eye-disease, dysentery; to a tyrant; of fire, and steel; to everything that is stronger than itself? – Yes, it is a slave. 41. – How, then, can anything belonging to the body be unhindered? And how can something be great, or valuable, which is by nature lifeless, and mere earth or clay? What then, have you nothing in you that is free? 42. – Perhaps nothing. – Why, who can compel you to assent to what seems to you to be false? – No one. – Or

not to assent to what appears true? – No one. Here, then, you see that there is something in you that is by nature free. 43. Now who of you can desire or be averse, or exercise his impulse to act or not to act, or make preparations, or set something for yourself to do, unless he has conceived an impression of what is to his advantage or appropriate to him? – No one. – You have, then, in these too, something unrestrained and free. 44. Cultivate this, you wretches, devote your pains to this and seek your good here.

45. – 'But how is it possible for a man who has nothing, who is naked, who is without a house, or a hearth, or cleanliness, or a slave, or a city, to lead a happy life?' 46. – See, god has sent us somebody to show that it is indeed possible. 47. 'Look at me, I am without a country, without a home, without possessions, without a slave; I sleep out on the ground; I have no wife, no children, no fine residence, but only earth and heaven and one sorry cloak. 48. And what do I lack? Am I not without sorrow, without fear? Am I not free? Did any of you ever see me disappointed in my desires, or falling into what I would avoid? Have I ever blamed god or man? Have I ever accused any one? Has any of you seen me with a sullen face? 49. How do I treat those whom you fear and stand in awe of? Do I not treat them like slaves? Who, when he sees me, does not think that he is seeing his own king and master?' 50. This is the language of a Cynic, this his character and his endeavour. No, you say, you can tell a Cynic by his wallet and staff and massive jaws, and the way he swallows or stores away whatever is given to him, and reviles whomever he meets, and displays a fine shoulder. 51. Do you see the manner in which you are proposing to set out on so great an endeavour? First take a mirror. View your shoulders, examine your back, your thighs. You are going to be enrolled as a competitor at the Olympic games, man, not in some poor, second-rate contest. 52. At the Olympic games it is not possible for a man just to be defeated and leave, but you must, in the first place, be disgraced in the view of the whole world, not only of the Athenians or Spartans or Nicopolitans; and then, the man who simply leaves when he fancies, is subject to a flogging, and, before that, must suffer thirst and heat, and swallow an abundance of dust.

53. Consider the matter more carefully, know yourself, consult the divinity, attempt nothing without god; for, if god advises

you, be assured that it is his will that you should be a great man, or suffer many a blow. 54. For this is a pretty strand woven into the Cynic's destiny, that he must be beaten like an ass, and, when he is beaten, must love those who beat him as though he were the father or the brother of them all. 55. No, that is not how you would react; but, if someone beats you, you stand out in public and shout, 'O Caesar, am I to suffer such things in breach of your peace? Let us go before the proconsul.' 56. – But what is Caesar to a Cynic, or what is the proconsul or anyone else, except Zeus, who despatched him on his mission, and whom he serves? Does he call upon anyone except him? And is he not persuaded, that whatever of those things he suffers, is imposed by Zeus to train him? 57. Now, Heracles, when he was being trained by Eurystheus, did not think himself miserable, but fulfilled without hesitation all his appointed tasks. And shall he who is contending and being trained under the orders of Zeus, cry out and take offence? A worthy person, truly, to bear the sceptre of Diogenes! 58. Hear what Diogenes said, when he had a fever, to those who were passing by. 'Wretches, will you not stay? To watch the battles or downfall of athletes you go all the way to Olympia: have you no wish to watch a battle between a fever and a man?' 59. Such a man, who took a pride in difficult circumstances, and thought himself worthy to be a spectacle to those who passed by, was a likely person, indeed, to accuse god, who had sent him into the world, of treating him unworthily! What cause for accusation could he find? That he is living a decent life? What charge can he bring? That he is displaying his virtue in a clearer light? 60. – Well, and what does Diogenes say of poverty? of death? of pain? How did he compare his happiness with that of the Persian king? Or, rather, he thought there was no comparison. 61. For, where there are perturbations and griefs and fears, and disappointed desires, and aversions that fall into what they would avoid, how can happiness find an entrance? And, where there are corrupt judgements, there all those things must necessarily be.

62. The same young man asked him whether, when he fell sick and a friend invited him to his house so that he could be nursed, it would be right to comply. And where, replied Epictetus, will you find for me the friend of a Cynic? 63. For to be worthy of being numbered amongst his friends, a person must be another Cynic like himself; he must share the sceptre with

him and the kingdom, and be a worthy minister, if he is to be honoured with his friendship, as Diogenes became the friend of Antisthenes, and Crates of Diogenes. 64. Or do you think that if a person merely comes up to him and salutes him he will be the Cynic's friend, 65. and the Cynic will think the man worthy to receive him into his house? If such a thought comes into your head, it would be better to look round for some pretty dunghill to shelter you from the north wind whilst you have your fever, so that you may not catch a chill. 66. But, it seems to me, all that you want is to get into somebody's house and be well fed there for a while. What business have you, then, even to attempt so great an endeavour as this?

67. But (said the young man) will the Cynic engage in marriage, and the production of children, as preferred actions?

If you grant me a city of sages, replied Epictetus, it is quite possible that nobody there will readily embark on the Cynic life. For on whose account should he embrace that mode of life? 68. However, supposing he does, there will be nothing to prevent him from marrying and having children. For his wife will be another person like himself, his father-in-law another person like himself, and his children will be brought up in the same manner. 69. But as things are ordered at present, as though for a battle, is it not necessary that a Cynic should be free from distraction, wholly dedicated to the service of god, at liberty to walk about among mankind, not tied down to private duties, nor entangled in relationships which cannot be violated if he is to maintain his character as a wise and good man, relationships which, if he remains faithful to them, will destroy him in his nature as a messenger and spy and herald of the gods? 70. For, consider, there are some services due to his father-in-law, some to the other relations of his wife, some to his wife herself; so that henceforth he is excluded from his calling, to become a sick-nurse and provider for his family. 71. Not to mention other things, he must have a vessel to warm water for his baby, so that the child can be washed in a tub; and wool for his wife when she has a child, and oil, and a bed, and a cup (see how the gear is mounting up); 72. and there will be much else to occupy and distract him. Where, I ask you, after all this, will that king be whom we were speaking of, whose time is devoted to the public good, 'Who has his people to watch over and many a care'? That king who must supervise others, those who have married, and are fathers of children, to see who is treating his wife well, and who badly, and to see who is quarrelling, and which household is well ordered, and which not: just like a physician, who travels on his rounds feeling the pulses of his patients; 73. 'You have a fever. You have a headache. You have the gout. You should abstain from food, you should eat, you should go without baths, you need an operation, and you need to be cauterized.' 74. 'Where shall a man have leisure for all this, if he is tied down by private duties? Must he not provide clothes for his children, and send them to a schoolmaster with their writing-tablets, great and small, and implements. Must he not provide a bed for them? (For they cannot be Cynics from their mother's womb.) If he fails to make proper provision for them, it would have been better to expose them as soon as they were born than kill them off in such a way. 75. Do you see to what level we are reducing our Cynic? And how we are depriving him of his kingdom? 76. – 'Yes, but Crates was married.' – The case you are speaking of was a peculiar one, because the marriage resulted from a love-affair, and you are reckoning on a wife who is herself another Crates. But we are inquiring about ordinary marriages, which are not affected by these special considerations, and we do not find that marriage, in normal circumstances, is a preferred action for a Cynic.

77. How, then, will he keep society going?

For heaven's sake, do those who leave two or three snivelling children to replace them confer a greater benefit upon the world than those who, in so far as they can, watch over all mankind, examining what men do, and how they live, and what they take due care over, what they improperly neglect? 78. And from whom did the Thebans derive the greater benefit: from all those who left them children, or from Epaminondas, who died childless? And did Priam, who was the father of fifty sons, all utterly worthless, or Danaus, or Aeolus, contribute more to society than Homer? 79. Shall a military command or the writing of a book, then, exempt a man from marrying and becoming a father, so that he shall be thought to have made sufficient amends for the want of children, and yet the kingship of a Cynic not be thought a proper compensation for it? 80. Perhaps we do not understand the greatness of Diogenes, or rightly estimate his character, but consider Cynics as they are now, dogs 'fed at the table and guarding the door', who imitate the founders in nothing, except perhaps in breaking wind in front of others, but in nothing besides. 81. Otherwise, the things you were saying would not move us, nor should we be astonished that a Cynic will not marry or have children. Consider, man, that he is the father of humankind, that all men are his sons, and all women his daughters. It is in this character that he approaches them all, and takes care of them all. 82. Or, in your opinion, is it out of mere officiousness that he rails at the people he meets? No, he does it as a father, as a brother, as a servant of our common parent, Zeus.

83. Ask me too, if you like, whether a Cynic will engage in public affairs. 84. Tell me, you fool, what higher public business are you looking for, than that which he is engaged in already? Or should he step forward and address the Athenians about revenues and taxes, whose business it is to speak to all mankind, Athenians, Corinthians and Romans equally, not about taxes and revenues, or peace and war, but about happiness and misery, good fortune and bad, slavery and freedom? 85. Do you ask me whether a man engages in public affairs who is engaged in public business of such importance as this? Ask me, too, whether he will accept any public office? I will answer you again, what office, fool, could be greater than the one that he holds?

86. A Cynic, however, has need of the proper kind of body, for if he should come forward with the body of a consumptive, thin and pale, his testimony no longer carries the same authority. 87. For he must not only prove to laymen, through the constancy of his mind, that it is possible to be a good and noble man without the things that they set such value on, but he must show too, by his body, that a plain and simple life in the open air has no harmful effect even on his body. 88. 'See, both I and my body are witnesses to this.' That was the case with Diogenes; for he walked about radiant with health, and would draw the attention of the crowd by the very nature of his body. 89. But a Cynic who arouses pity seems a mere beggar; all avoid him, all are offended at him. Nor ought he to appear dirty, lest he scare people away for that reason also, but even his rough negligence should be neat and engaging.

90. Great natural charm and sharpness of mind are likewise necessary in a Cynic (otherwise he becomes a mere driveller, and nothing else), so that he will be able to respond readily and

appropriately on every occasion. 91. Thus Diogenes, when somebody asked him: 'Are you the Diogenes who does not believe there are any gods?' replied, 'How could I be, when I think you odious to them?' 92. Again, when Alexander surprised him sleeping, and repeated:

> To sleep the whole night through Ill befits a man of counsel,

Diogenes answered before he was fully awake,

> Who has his people to watch over, and many a care.

93. But above all, the ruling faculty of a Cynic must be purer than the sun, otherwise he must necessarily be a gambler, and a rascal, if, while being guilty of some vice himself, he reproaches everyone else. 94. For, consider how the case stands. Common kings and tyrants have their arms and bodyguards, which give them the power to reprove and punish those who do wrong, even though they themselves may be wicked; but to a Cynic, it is conscience that gives him this power and takes the place of arms and bodyguards. 95. When he knows that he has watched over men and laboured on their behalf; that his sleep has been pure, and has left him still purer than he was before; and that whatever he has thought, he has thought as a friend and servant to the gods, and one who shares in the governance of Zeus, and who is ready to say upon all occasions,

> Lead me, Zeus; and thou, O Destiny

and 'If this is what pleases the gods, so be it', why, then, when he is such a person, should he not dare to speak boldly to his own brothers, to his children; in a word, to his kindred? 97. Therefore the man who is thus disposed is neither meddlesome nor a busybody, for he is not busied about the affairs of others, but his own, when he oversees the transactions of men. Otherwise say that a general is a busybody when he oversees, reviews, and keeps watch on his soldiers, and punishes the disorderly. 98. But if you reprove others at the very time that you have a cake under your own arm, I will ask you: Had you not better go into a corner and eat up what you have stolen? 99. But what have you to do with the concerns of others? For who are you? Are you the bull of the herd? Are you the queen of the bees? Show me such tokens of authority as she has from nature. But, if you are a drone, and lay claim to the kingship of the bees, do

you not think that your fellow-citizens will drive you out, just
as the bees do the drones?

100. Furthermore, a Cynic must have so much patience as to
seem insensible to the multitude, and like a stone. No one
reviles, no one beats, no one insults him; but he has surrendered
his body to any one who wishes, to deal with as he pleases. 101.
For he remembers that what is inferior, in whatever respect it
may be so, must be overcome by what is superior to it, and that
his body is inferior to the multitude, as something that is weaker
to those who are stronger. 102. So he never enters into this
contest in which he can be defeated, but immediately gives up
what is not his own, and lays no claim to what is slavish. 103.
But, where choice and the use of impressions are concerned, you
will see that he has so many eyes, that you would say Argos was
blind by comparison. 104. Is his assent ever precipitate? His
impulse ever rash? His desire ever disappointed? His aversion
ever incurred? His purpose ever unfulfilled? Is he ever querulous,
ever abject, ever envious? 105. It is to these matters that he
directs all his attention and effort. When it comes to other
things, he lies back and snores, and is wholly at peace. Nobody
can rob him of his choice or be master of it. – But of his body?
– Yes. 106. Of his property? – Yes. Of his offices and honours?
– Yes. And what does he care for these? So when anyone
therefore tries to frighten him with them, he says, 'Go, look for
children; to them masks are frightening; but I for my part know
that they are made of clay, and have nothing inside them.'

107. The enterprise that you are contemplating is nothing
other than that. So I ask you, in the name of god, to defer it if
you will, and look first to your resources. 108. For see what
Hector says to Andromache: 'Go rather into the house', he says,
'and weave:

> But war shall be the concern of men,
> All men, and mine most of all.'

109. Such was his awareness of his own resources, and of her
incapacity.

CHAPTER 23

# To Those Who Read And Dispute
# For Mere Display

1. First tell yourself what sort of man you want to be; then act
accordingly in all you do. For in almost everything else we see
this to be the practice. 2. Athletes first determine what kind of
athlete they want to be, and then act accordingly. For a long-
distance runner there is a particular diet, a particular way of
walking, of massage, of exercising; for a runner in the stadium
these are all somewhat different; for a pentathlete more different
still. 3. You will find the same in the arts. If you are a carpenter,
you will have these procedures, if a blacksmith, those. For, if we
do not refer each of our actions to some standard, we shall be
acting at random; if to an improper standard, we shall fail
utterly. 4. There is, besides, a general and a particular standard.
First, for acting as a man. What is included in this? Not to be,
though gentle, like a sheep; nor noxious like a wild beast. 5. But
the particular end relates to the occupation and choice of each
individual. A lyre-player must act as a lyre-player; a carpenter,
as a carpenter; a philosopher, as a philosopher; an orator, as an
orator. 6. When, therefore, you say, 'Come and hear me lecture',
see first that you are not acting in an arbitrary manner. Then, if
you find that you are referring your actions to a standard, see if
it is the right one. 7. Do you wish to do good, or be praised? At
once you get the answer, 'What do I care for praise from the
crowd?' And here he speaks well. For neither does a musician in
his capacity as a musician, nor does a geometrician. 8. You want
to benefit others, do you not? In what? Tell us, so that we too
may run to your lecture-hall. Now, is it possible for anyone to
benefit others who has received no benefit himself? No; for
neither can the man who is not a carpenter do so when it comes
to carpentry, nor the man who is not a cobbler when it comes
to cobbling. 9. Do you want to know, then, whether you have
received any benefit? Produce your judgements, philosopher.
What does desire promise? Not to fail in getting. And aversion?
Not to fall into what we would avoid. 10. Come, do we fulfil
their promise? Tell me the truth; but, if you should lie, I will tell

you: 'The other day, when the audience that gathered for you was somewhat cool and did not cry out in applause, you went away dejected. 11. On another such occasion, when you did receive applause, you went about asking everybody, "What do you think of me?" – "Upon my life, sir, it was prodigious." – "But how did I express myself upon that subject?" – "Which?" – "Where I gave a description of Pan and the nymphs." – "Most excellently."' 12. And do you mean to tell me, after this, that with regard to desire and aversion your behaviour is in conformity with nature? Off with you. Persuade somebody else. 13. The other day, did you not praise a man contrary to your own opinion? Did you not flatter a certain senator? Would you wish your own children to resemble that man? – 'Heaven forbid!' – 14. 'Why, then, did you praise and cajole him?' – 'He is a gifted young man, and enjoys listening to discourses.' – 'How do you know?' – 'He admires me.' – Now, indeed, you have produced your proof. What do you suppose, then? Is it not the case that these very people secretly despise you. 15. So when a man who is conscious of never having done, or considered doing, a single good thing finds some philosopher who tells him, 'You are wonderfully gifted and honest and unspoilt', what do you think he says but, 'This man wants to make use of me in some way'? 16. Pray tell me what action of genius he has displayed. You see, he has associated with you all this time, has heard your discussions, has heard your lectures. Has he acquired self-restraint? Has he paid regard to himself? Has he realized what a bad state he is in? Has he thrown off his conceit? 17. Is he looking for the man who can teach him? – 'Yes, he is.' – The man who can teach him how he ought to live? No, fool, but how he should talk; for it is upon this account that he admires you. Listen to him now, hear what he says. 'This man writes with very great art, in a far finer style than Dio's.' 18. That is quite another thing. For he is not saying, 'This man has respect for himself, and is trustworthy, and imperturbable?' And even if he did say that, I would ask him, 'Since this man is trustworthy, what precisely does it mean to be a trustworthy man?' And, if he could not say, I would add, 'First learn the meaning of what you are saying, and then speak.' 19. While you are in this sorry state, then, and gaping after people to applaud you, and counting your audience, do you wish to be of benefit to others? 'Today I had a much greater audience.' – 'Yes, huge; we think

there were five hundred.' – That's nonsense; make it a thousand.
– 'Dio never had so great an audience.' – 'How could he?' –
'And they have a fine understanding of argument.' – 'Beauty,
sir, can move even a stone.' 20. Here is the language of a
philosopher! Here is the disposition of a man who wants to be
of benefit to mankind! This is a man who has listened to reason,
who has read the Socratic literature in true Socratic fashion, and
not as though it were something that came from Lysias or
Isocrates! 'I have often wondered by what arguments' – no, he
should have said, 'by what argument'; that would read more
smoothly. 21. For have you really read this literature otherwise
than you read mere songs? If you had read it as you ought, you
would not have dwelt on such trifles, but would instead have
considered such a passage as this: 'Anytus and Meletus can kill
me, but they cannot harm me.' And 'I have always been of such
a nature that I pay no attention to my personal affairs, but only
to the argument which appears to me on examination to be the
best.' 22. And thus, who ever heard Socrates say, 'I have
knowledge, and teach'? But he used to send different people to
different instructors; and so it was that people came to him
asking to be introduced by him to philosophers, and he would
take them off and introduce them. 23. No, you suppose; but as
he went along with them, he would say, 'Come and listen to me
when I lecture today at the house of Quadratus'! – Why should
I listen to you? Have you a mind to show me how finely you put
words together? You do put them together neatly, sir; and what
good does that do you? 'But praise me.' 24. – What do you
mean by praise? – 'Shout "bravo" or "wonderful!"' – Well, I
will say it. But if praise is one of the things that philosophers
include in the category of the good, what praise can I offer you?
If it is a good thing to speak well, show me that, and I will
praise you. 25. – 'What, should one listen to fine words without
pleasure?' – By no means. I do not even listen to a harper
without pleasure; but should I on that account stand up and
play the harp? Hear what Socrates says to his judges. 26. 'It
would not be fitting for me to appear before you at my age and
weave fine words like a schoolboy.' 'Like a schoolboy', he says.
For it is, without doubt, a pretty knack to choose out words and
put them together, and then to read or recite them gracefully in
public; and, in the midst of the discourse, to declare 'I vow by
all that is good, there are not many who understand these

things.' 27. But does a philosopher invite people to a lecture? Is it not the case that just as the sun draws nourishment to itself, so the philosopher draws those to whom he can do good? What physician invites anybody to be cured by him? (Though now, indeed, I hear that the physicians at Rome invite patients; but in my time it was they who were invited in.) 28. 'I invite you to come and hear that you are in a bad way; and that you take care of everything but what you ought; that you are ignorant of what is good or evil, and are unfortunate and unhappy.' A charming invitation! And yet, unless the discourse of a philosopher has this effect, both the discourse and its speaker are empty of life. 29. Rufus used to say, If you find leisure to praise me, I am speaking to no purpose. And indeed he used to speak in such a manner that each of us who heard him supposed that some person had once informed on him; such was his grasp of how men behave, and his sureness in placing each man's personal faults before his eyes.

30. The school of a philosopher is a surgery. You should not depart from it in pleasure, but in pain, for you are not healthy when you come in, but one of you has a dislocated shoulder, another an abscess, another a fistula, another a headache. 31. And am I to come up with pretty thoughts and reflections, so that each of you will go away praising me, but with the same dislocated shoulder, the same aching head, the same fistula, and the same abscess that you brought in? 32. And is it for this that young men are to travel abroad and leave their parents, their friends, their relations and their property, so that they can say, 'Splendid!' when you come up with fine reflections? Was that what Socrates used to do? Or Zeno? Or Cleanthes?

33. 'What! is there not a suitable style for exhortation and conversion?' – Who denies it? Just as there is a style for refutation or instruction. But who ever added a fourth, a style for display? 34. So what is the style for exhortation? The one that enables you to show to an individual or a crowd the contradictions that they are involved in, and that they care for everything rather than what they mean to care for; for they want the things conducive to happiness, but they seek them where they are not to be found. 35. To achieve this is it necessary that a thousand benches be set out, and an audience invited, and you, in a fine robe or cloak, ascend the rostrum and describe the death of Achilles? I beg you, by the gods, to cease

from doing all that is in your power to bring noble words and actions into disrepute. 36. Nothing, to be sure, gives more force to exhortation than when the speaker shows that he has need of the audience. 37. But tell me, who, when he hears you reading or speaking, is anxious about himself, or turns his attention upon himself? Or says when he departs, 'That philosopher has well and truly grabbed hold of me: I must no longer behave as I do'? 38. No, instead of this, for all that you are in high fashion, one man says to another 'That bit about Xerxes was neatly expressed', to which the other replies, 'No, I thought the bit about Thermopylae was better.' Is this what it means to listen to a philosopher?

## CHAPTER 24

# That We Should Not Become Attached To Things That Are Not In Our Own Power

1. Let not what is contrary to nature in another be an evil to you; for you were not born to share in the humiliation or bad fortune of others, but to share in their good fortune. 2. And if any one is unhappy, remember that he himself is responsible, for god made all mankind to be happy, to enjoy peace of mind. 3. He has furnished them with the resources to achieve this, having given each man some things for his own, and some not for his own. Whatever is subject to hindrance, compulsion or deprivation is not his own; whatever is not subject to hindrance is his own. And the true nature of good and evil he has placed amongst the things which are our own, as was befitting in one who cares for us and protects us with paternal care.

4. But I have just parted from somebody, and he is disconsolate.

And why did he consider what was not his own to be his own? Why did he not reflect, while he was pleased at seeing you, that you are mortal, that you are liable to change your home? Thus he is simply paying the penalty for his own foolishness. 5. But to what purpose or for what cause are you yourself lamenting? Have you too failed to study these things?

But, like women of a worthless kind, did you rejoice in the things you delighted in, the places, the persons, the conversations, as if they were to last for ever? And now you sit crying because you do not see the same people, nor live in the same place. 6. Indeed, you deserve to be so affected, and thus to become more wretched than ravens or crows, which, without groaning or longing for their former home, can fly where they will, build their nests in another place, and cross the seas.

7. Yes, but they react in that way because of their want of reason.

Was reason then given us by the gods to bring us unhappiness and misery, to make us live our lives in wretchedness and lamentation? 8. Or should all men be wholly unchanging, and never leave their homes but remain rooted to a spot like plants? And, if any one of our friends should leave his home, should we sit and cry, and when he comes back, should we dance and clap our hands like children? 9. Shall we never wean ourselves, and remember what we have heard from the philosophers 10. (unless we listened to them simply as weavers of tales): that the world is one great city, and the substance out of which it is formed is single, and there must necessarily be a cycle of change, in which one thing gives way to another, and some things are destroyed and others come into being, and some things remain where they were and others are moved. 11. And the world is full of friends, first the gods, then also men, who are by nature endeared to each other; and some must remain with one another and others depart, and we should rejoice in those who are with us, and not be grieved at those who depart; 12. and that man, besides possessing a natural greatness of mind and contempt for things outside the sphere of choice, is formed not to be rooted or attached to the earth, but to go at different times to different places, sometimes on urgent business, and sometimes merely to look around. 13. Such was the case with Odysseus: 'Cities of men he saw, and learned their ways.' And earlier still, it was the lot of Heracles, to travel over the whole inhabited world, 'Observing the effrontery of men and their lawful behaviour', to expel and clear away the one, and, in its stead, introduce the other. 14. Yet how many friends do you think he had at Thebes, how many at Argos, how many at Athens, and how many did he acquire on his travels, considering that he married too when he thought fit, and sired children, and then deserted his children, without lamenting and longing for them, or considering that he was leaving them to be orphans. 15. For he knew that no human creature is an orphan, but that there is a father who constantly and continually cares for them all. 16. For to him it was not simply hearsay that Zeus is the father of mankind, but he always thought of him as his own father, and called him so, and looked to him in all that he did. And so he was able to live happily wherever he was. 17. But it is never possible to be happy and at the same time yearn for what is not present. For that which is happy must possess in full all that it wants, must resemble a person who has achieved his fill – neither hunger nor thirst can come near it.

18. But Odysseus longed for his wife, and sat crying on a rock.

Why, do you refer to Homer and his tales for everything? If Odysseus really did cry, what was he but an unhappy man? But what wise and good man is unhappy? 19. The universe is surely but ill governed if Zeus does not take care that his subjects may be happy like himself. But these are unlawful and unholy thoughts; 20. and Odysseus, if he did indeed weep and lament, was not a good man. For who can be a good man when he does not know what he is? And who can know that, if he has forgotten that all things that come into being are perishable, and that it is not possible for one human being and another always to live together? 21. What then? To desire impossibilities is slavish and foolish: it is the behaviour of a stranger in the world and of one who is fighting against god in the only way that is possible – with his judgements.

22. But my mother grieves when she does not see me.

So why has she not learnt these doctrines? I am not saying that it is wrong to take care that she should not lament; but that we are not to wish absolutely what is not in our own power. 23. Now, the grief of another is not in my power; but my own grief is. I will, therefore, absolutely suppress my own grief, for that is in my power; and I will endeavour to suppress another's grief as far as I am able: but not absolutely. 24. otherwise I shall be fighting against god, I shall be opposing Zeus, and ranging myself against him with regard to his governance of the universe. And not only 'my children's children' will bear the punishment of this warfare against god and this disobedience, but I myself too, both during the day and at night when I start from my dreams, and when I am uneasy in my mind, and tremble at every message, and my peace of mind hangs upon letters from others. 25. Somebody has arrived from Rome. 'I only hope there is no bad news.' Why, what harm can happen to you when you are not there? — Somebody has arrived from Greece. 'I only hope there is no bad news.' Why, at this rate, every place can be the cause of misfortune to you. 26. Is it not enough for you to be unfortunate where you are, but must you be unhappy on the other side of the sea also, and by letter? Such is the security of your condition!

27. But what if my friends there should die?

What else could that signify except that men who are mortal have died? Do you at once wish to live to be old, and yet not to see the death of any one you love? 28. Do you not know that, in a long course of time, many and various events must necessarily happen? That a fever must get the better of one person, a highwayman of another, a tyrant of a third? 29. For such is the world we live in; such are those who live in it with us. Heat and cold, improper diet, journeys by land, voyages by sea, winds, and all kinds of accidents destroy some, banish others, and send one on an embassy, another on campaign. 30. Sit down, then, and get distraught at all of these things, lamenting, disappointed, wretched, dependent on something other than yourself, and distrought not at one thing or two, but thousands and thousands.

31. Is this what you used to hear from the philosophers? Is this what you have learnt? Do you not know that this life is like a campaign? One man must keep guard, another go out to reconnoitre, and another to fight. It is neither possible, nor, indeed, better that all should stay in the same place: 32. but you, neglecting to fulfil the orders of your general, complain whenever you are given a somewhat harsh order, and do not understand what, so far as you can, you are doing to the army. For, if all should imitate you, nobody will dig a trench, or raise a palisade, or keep watch at night, or expose himself to danger; but everyone will appear useless as a soldier. 33. Again, if you go as a sailor on a voyage, fix upon one place, and there remain. If it should be necessary to climb the mast, refuse to do it; if to run to the bow of the ship, refuse to do it. And what captain will put up with you? Would not he throw you overboard as a useless bit of tackle and mere obstruction, and a bad example to

the other sailors? 34. Thus, also, in the present case, every one's life is a kind of campaign, and a long and changeable one. You must observe the duty of a soldier, and perform everything at the bidding of your general, 35. and even, if possible, divine what he wishes. For there is no comparison between this general and an ordinary one, either in power or excellence of character. 36. You are stationed in an imperial city, and not some wretched little place, and are a senator not for the year but for life. Do you not know that such a man must spend but little time on his household affairs, and most of it away, either commanding or being commanded, or as subordinate to some official, or serving in the field, or sitting as a judge? And then you tell me you want to be fixed and rooted to the same spot, like a plant?

37. Why, it is pleasant.

Who denies it? So is a sauce pleasant; and a beautiful woman gives pleasure. Do those who make pleasure their end say anything different? 38. Do you not see what kind of man it is whose language you have been using? That this is the talk of Epicureans and catamites? And while you follow their practices and hold their principles, do you quote to us of the words of Zeno and Socrates? 39. Why do you not throw aside, and as far from you as possible, these ornaments which belong to others and are wholly unfitting to you? What else do the Epicureans desire than to sleep without hindrance or compulsion, and, when they have got up, to yawn at their leisure, and wash their faces; then to write and read what they please; then to prate about some trifle or other, and be applauded by their friends, whatever they happen to say; then go out for a walk, and, after they have taken a turn, have a bath; and then eat, and then go to bed: as to what kind of bed such people would most likely go to sleep in, why should one say? For it is easily guessed. 40. Come, now, you must also tell me what way of life you yearn for, you who are a zealot for the truth and an admirer of Diogenes and Socrates. What do you want to do in Athens?

41. These very same things? Not something different? Why, then, do you call yourself a Stoic? Those who falsely pretend to the Roman citizenship are punished severely; so are those who falsely claim something as great as this and so venerable a title to be dismissed with impunity? 42. Or is that impossible, and is there not a divine and powerful and inescapable law which exacts the greatest punishments from those who are guilty of

the greatest offences? 43. For what says this law? Let him who pretends to things that have nothing to do with him be a braggart, be vain-glorious; let him who disobeys the divine governance be base, be a slave, let him grieve, let him envy, let him pity, and, in a word, let him be unhappy, let him lament.

44. Well then, would you have me pay my court to So-and-so? Would you have me go to his door?

If reason requires it, for your country, for your relations, for mankind, why should you not go? You are not ashamed to go to the door of a shoemaker when you want shoes, nor a gardener when you want lettuce. Yet you are ashamed to go to the rich when money is what you need?

45. Yes; but I am not in awe of a shoemaker.

Don't be so of a rich man either.

I need not flatter a gardener.

Nor a rich man either.

46. How then shall I get what I want?

But am I telling you 'Go as someone who will get what he wants'? And not this alone: so that you will do what is appropriate to you?

47. Then why after all, should I go?

So as to have gone there and discharged your duties as a citizen, as a brother, as a friend. 48. Moreover, you should remember that you have come to see a shoemaker, a gardener, a man who has no authority over anything great or significant, whatever the price he sells it at. You are going, so to speak, to buy lettuces. They are sold for an obol, not for a talent. 49. So in the present case, too, the matter is worth going to a man's door about. Very well, I will go. It is worth an interview. Well, I will have one with him. Yes, but one must kiss his hand, too, and flatter him by singing his praises. Away with you. That is worth a talent. It is not to the benefit of myself, nor my country, nor my fellow-citizens, nor my friends, to destroy the good citizen and friend in me.

50. But if you fail people will think that you did not put your heart into it.

What, have you forgotten again why you went? Do you not know that a wise and good man never acts for the sake of appearance, but only for the sake of having acted well?

51. So what benefit does it bring him to have acted well?

What benefit does it bring to the person who writes the name 'Dio' as he ought to write it? Simply that of writing it correctly.

Is there no further reward, then?

Why, do you seek a further reward for a good man that is greater than doing what is admirable and right? 52. And yet at Olympia nobody wants anything additional, but you think it enough to have won an Olympic crown. Does it appear to you so small and worthless a thing to be good, noble, and happy? 53. Since, therefore, you have been introduced by the gods into this great city of the world, and are now under an obligation to discharge the duties of a man, do you still hanker after nurses and the breast, and do the tears of poor foolish women soften you and make you effeminate? And will you thus never cease to be a little child? Do you not know that he who acts like a child is the more ridiculous the older he is?

54. Did you never go to see any one at Athens, at his own house? Yes, the man I wanted to see. Here again, decide to see this man, and you will see him; only, do so without humbling yourself, and without desire or aversion, and then things will go well for you; 55. but their going well or not does not depend on going to the house or standing at the door, but on the judgements that lie within you. 56. When you have acquired a contempt for things that are external and lie outside the sphere of choice, and have come to regard none of them as your own, but only this as your own, to judge and think aright, and exercise your impulses, desires and aversions aright, what further room is there after that for flattery, what room for an abject mind? 57. Why do you still long for the quiet you enjoyed there, for places familiar to you? Stay a little and these places will become familiar to you in their turn; and then, if you are so mean-spirited, weep and lament again when you depart from these also.

58. How, then, shall I be affectionate?

As becomes a noble-spirited and happy person. For reason will never tell you to be abject and broken-hearted, or to depend on another, or to reproach either god or man. 59. Be affectionate in such a manner as to observe all this. But if from affection, as you call it, you are to be a slave and a wretch, it is not worth your while to be affectionate. 60. And what restrains you from loving a person as one who is mortal, as one who may be obliged to leave you? Pray, did not Socrates love his own children? But as a free man, and one who was mindful that his first duty was to be a friend to the gods. 61. Thus he violated no part of the character of a good man, either in making his defence, or in proposing a penalty for himself. Nor did he previously, when he was a member of the council or a soldier. 62. But we make use of every excuse to be mean-spirited; some on account of a child, some of a mother, and some of a brother. 63. But it is not fitting for us to be unhappy on anybody's account, but rather, we should be happy for all, and chiefly for god, who has made us for this purpose. 64. What! did Diogenes love nobody, who was so gentle and benevolent that he cheerfully underwent so many pains and miseries of body for the common good of mankind? Yes, he did love them; but how? 65. As became a servant of Zeus; at once taking care of men and submitting himself to god. 66. That is why the whole earth, not any particular place, was his country. And, when he was taken captive, he did not long for Athens and his friends and acquaintance there, but got to know the pirates, and tried to reform them; and later, when he was sold, he lived at Corinth just as he had previously lived at Athens: and, if he had gone off to the Perrhaebians, he would have done exactly the same. 67. In such a way is freedom achieved. That is why he used to say, 'Ever since Antisthenes set me free, I have ceased to be a slave.' 68. Set free in what manner? Listen to what Diogenes has to say: 'He taught me what was my own, and what was not my own. Property is not my own. Kindred, relations, friends, reputation, familiar places, association with others, all these are not my own.'

69. 'What is your own, then?'

'The proper use of impressions. He showed me that this is in my power, to be free from all compulsion; no one can hinder or force me to use them any otherwise than I please. 70. Who after this has any power over me? Philip, or Alexander, or Perdiccas, or the Persian king? How should they have it? For he that can be subjected by man must, long before, let himself be subjected by things. 71. He, therefore, whom neither pleasure nor pain, nor fame nor riches, can get the better of, and who is able, whenever he thinks fit, to spit his whole body into his tormentor's face and depart from life, whose slave can he ever be? To whom is he subject?' 72. But if Diogenes had taken pleasure in living at Athens, and had been subjected by that way of life, his affairs would have been at every one's disposal, and whoever was stronger would have had the power to cause him distress. 73. How would he have flattered the pirates, do you imagine, to make them sell him to some Athenian, so that he might see the beautiful Piraeus again, the long walls, and the Acropolis? 74. And what sort of man would you be when you saw them, you wretch? An abject slave. 75. And what good would that do you? – 'No; a free man.' – Show me in what way you are free. See, somebody lays hold on you; somebody, whoever he may be, takes you away from your usual manner of life and says, 'You are my slave; for it is in my power to prevent you from living as you wish. It is in my power to raise you up or to humble you. Whenever I please, you may be cheerful again, and set out in exhilaration for Athens.' 76. What do you say to this man who enslaves you? What sort of emancipator can you offer to him? Or do you not even dare to look him in the face, but, without further argument, do you beseech him to release you? 77. Man, you ought to go happily to prison, hurrying off and getting there before those who arrest you. Instead of this, are you reluctant to live at Rome, and do you long for Greece? And, when you must die, will you then too come crying to us that you are never going to see Athens again nor walk in the Lyceum? 78. Is it for this that you travelled abroad? Is it for this that you have been seeking for somebody to do you good? What good? To be able to analyse syllogisms more easily, or manage hypothetical arguments? And was it for this reason that you left your brother, your country, your friends, your family – to be able to return after learning things like that? 79. So you did not travel abroad to achieve constancy of mind, nor tranquillity; nor to become secure from harm and never blame or accuse others again; nor to make it impossible for another to injure you, and so keep yourself free from hindrance in your social relationships. 80. This is fine bit of trade that you have managed, to carry home syllogisms, and hypothetical arguments, and arguments with equivocal premises! Yes, you should sit in the market-place if you think fit, and put up a sign, as the medicine-sellers do. 81. Really you ought to deny that you know even what you have learned, lest you bring down on philosophical precepts the accusation of being useless. What harm has philosophy done you? In what has Chrysippus injured you, that you should try to prove by your actions that his labours are of no value? Did you not have sufficient ills at home to cause you sorrow and distress, even if you had not travelled abroad, that you then have to acquire still more?

82. And if you gain other friends and acquaintances, you will find fresh reasons to lament; and likewise, if you become attached to another land. To what purpose, therefore, do you live? To heap sorrow upon sorrow to make yourself wretched? 83. And then do you tell me that this is affection? What kind of affection, man? If affection is good, it cannot be the cause of any evil; if an evil, I will have nothing to do with it. I am born for what is good for me, not for what is evil.

84. What, then, is the proper training for this? Firstly, the highest and principal form of training, and one that stands, so to speak, right at the entrance way to the enterprise, is, that when you become attached to something, let it not be as though it were to something that cannot be taken away, but rather, as though it were to something like an earthenware pot or crystal goblet, so that if it happens to be broken, you may remember what kind of thing it was and not be distressed. 85. So in this, too, when you kiss your child, or your brother, or your friend, never entirely give way to your imagination, nor allow your elation to progress as far as it will; but curb it in, restrain it, like those who stand behind generals when they ride in triumph and remind them that they are men. 86. In a similar way, you too should remind yourself that what you love is mortal, that what you love is not your own. It is granted to you for the present while, and not irrevocably, nor for ever, but like a fig or a bunch of grapes in the appointed season; and if you long for it in the winter, you are a fool. 87. So, if you long for your son or your friend when he is not granted to you, know that you are longing for a fig in winter. For as winter is to a fig, so is every state of affairs that arises from the order of things in relation to what is destroyed in accordance with that state of affairs. 88. Henceforth, when you take delight in anything, bring to mind the contrary impression. What harm is there while you are kissing your child to say softly, 'Tomorrow you will die'; and likewise to your friend, 'Tomorrow either you or I will go away, and we shall see each other no more'?

89. But these are words of ill omen.

And so are certain incantations, but because they are beneficial, I do not mind, if only they do good. But do you call

anything ill-omened, except what signifies some ill? Cowardice
is ill-omened; 90. mean-spiritedness is ill-omened; lamentation,
grief, want of shame. These are words of ill omen; and yet we
ought not to shrink from using them, so as to guard against the
things themselves. 91. But do you tell me that any word is ill-
omened which signifies something that is in accordance with
nature? Say, too, that it is ill-omened for ears of corn to be
reaped, for this signifies the destruction of the corn (though not
of the world). Say, too, that the falling of the leaves is ill-
omened, and for a fresh fig to change into a dried one, and a
bunch of grapes into raisins. 92. For all these are changes from
a preceding state into a new and different state; and thus not
destruction, but an ordered management and governance of
things. 93. Travelling abroad is like that, a small change; and so
is death, a greater change, from what presently is into – but here
I must not say, into what is not, but rather: into what *presently*
is not.

94. What, then, shall I cease to be?

*You* will not be; but something else, of which the universe
then has need, will be; for indeed, you come into being, not
when you wished it, but when the universe had need of you. 95.
Thus a wise and good man, mindful who he is and whence he
came, and by whom he was created, is attentive to this alone,
namely, to how he may fill his place in a disciplined manner and
in obedience to god. 96. 'Is it your will that I continue to
remain? I will do so as a free man, as a man of noble spirit, as
was your desire; for you made me free from hindrance in the
things that are my own. 97. But have you no further need of
me? May all be well with you. I have remained here until now
because of you and none other; now I obey you and depart.' 98.
'How do you depart?' 'Again, in accordance with your will, as
a free man, as your servant, as one sensible of your commands
and your prohibitions. 99. But while I am employed in your
service, what would you have me be? An official or a private
man, a senator or a common man, a soldier or a general, a
teacher or the master of a household? Whatever post or rank
you assign me, as Socrates said, I will die a thousand times
rather than desert it. 100. Where would you have me be? At
Rome or at Athens, at Thebes or at Gyara? Only remember me
there. 101. If you send me to a place where men cannot live in
accordance with nature, I shall depart from this life, not out of

disobedience to you, but in the belief that you are sounding the signal for my retreat. I do not desert you; heaven forbid! but I perceive that you no longer have need of me. 102. If a life in accordance with nature be granted, I will seek no other place but that in which I am, nor any other company but those with whom I am.'

103. Have these reflections at hand by night and day. Write them down, read them, talk about them, both to yourself, and to somebody else when you say, 'Is there any help that you can give me in this?' And then approach another man and then another. 104. Then, if any of those things that are called undesirable should happen, it will, in the first place, be an immediate relief to you that it was not unexpected. 105. For it is no small thing to say on every such occasion, 'I knew that I had begotten a mortal.' For that is what you will say, and, furthermore, 'I knew that I was liable to die', 'I knew that I was liable to leave home', 'I knew that I was liable to be exiled', 'I knew that I was liable to be imprisoned.' 106. If afterwards you reflect within yourself and inquire from what region the happening has come, you will immediately remember: 'It is from things outside the sphere of choice, not from what is my own. What, then, is it to me?' 107. And next (which is the principal question): 'Who sent it?' The emperor, the general, the city, the law of the city? 'Grant it to me, then, for I must always obey the law in all things.' 108. Furthermore, when your imagination gnaws at you (for that is something outside your control), strive against it with your reason, subjugate it, do not allow it to gain strength, nor to advance to the next stage of picturing what it wants as it wants. 109. If you are in Gyara, do not imagine your way of life in Rome, and all the pleasures that you enjoyed when you were living there and how many you could expect on your return; but since that is where you have been stationed, you should live manfully in Gyara, as is right for a man who lives in Gyara. And if you are in Rome, do not imagine the way of life in Athens, but consider only how you ought to live in the place where you are. 110. Lastly, to all other pleasures oppose that of being conscious that you are obeying god, and performing, not in word, but in deed, the duty of a wise and good man. 111. For how great a thing it is to be able to say to yourself, 'What others solemnly speak of in the schools, things thought to be paradoxical, I am now accomplishing in practice. They are sitting there

expatiating upon my virtues, and enquiring into myself and singing my praises. 112. And Zeus wished me to receive a proof of this from myself, and, indeed, he himself wished to know whether he has a soldier, whether he was a citizen, such as each should be, and to present me as a witness to other men, concerning things that lie outside the sphere of choice. See that your fears were vain, your desires vain. Seek not good from without; seek it in yourselves, or you will never find it. 113. For this reason he now brings me here, and then sends me there; shows me to mankind, poor, without office, sick; sends me to Gyara, puts me in prison: not that he hates me; heaven forbid! For who hates the best of his servants? Nor that he neglects me, for he does not neglect even the least of his beings; but because he is exercising me, and making use of me as a witness to others. 114. Appointed to such a service, do I still care where I am, or with whom, or what is said of me, instead of being wholly attentive to god, and to his orders and commands?'

115. Having these thoughts always at hand, and engrossing yourself in them when you are by yourself, and making them ready for use, you will never need any one to comfort and strengthen you. 116. For dishonour does not consist in not having anything to eat, but in not having reason enough to exempt you from fear or sorrow. 117. But, if once you acquire that exemption, will a tyrant, or his guards or members of Caesar's household be anything to you? Or will imperial appointments nettle you, or the position of those who offer sacrifices on the Capitol, and take the auspices, you who have received so great an office from Zeus? 118. Only, do not make a parade of it, or boast about it, but demonstrate it in your actions; and, even if no one perceives it, be content in yourself to live a healthy and happy life.

## CHAPTER 25

# To Those Who Fail To
# Achieve Their Purposes

1. Consider which of the things that you initially proposed you have managed to achieve, and which you have not, and how it gives you pleasure to remember some of them, and pain to remember others, and, if possible recover the things that have slipped away from your grasp. 2. For those who are engaged in this greatest of contests must not shrink back, but must be prepared to endure the blows. 3. For the contest that lies before us is not in wrestling or the pancration, in which, whether a man succeeds or fails, he may be a man of great worth or of little (and by Zeus, may be very fortunate or very miserable); no, it is a contest for good fortune and happiness itself. 4. What follows, then? In this, even if we falter for a time, no one prevents us from renewing the contest, nor need we wait another four years for the next Olympic games to come, but as soon as a man has got a hold on himself and recovered himself, and shows the same zeal as before, he is allowed to take part in the contest; and even if you should falter again, you may begin again, and, if you once become the victor, you are as one who has never faltered. 5. Only, do not begin out of habit to do the same thing willingly again, and then, in the manner of a bad athlete, go round being beaten in the whole cycle of the games, like quails that run away. 6. 'I am overwhelmed by the impression of a pretty girl. What of it? Was I not overwhelmed in the same manner the other day.?' 'The desire comes upon me to disparage somebody. Did I not do so the other day?' 7. You talk to us just as if you had got off unpunished. It is as though a man should say to his physician, who had forbidden him to bathe, 'Why, did I not bathe the other day?' Suppose the physician should answer him, 'Well, and what was the consequence of your bathing? Were you not feverish? Did you not suffer a headache?' 8. So, when you disparaged somebody the other day, did you not act like an ill-natured person? Was it not foolish nonsense that you spoke? And did you not feed this habit of yours by setting before it the example of other actions

akin to it? And when you were overcome by the pretty girl, did
you get off unpunished? 9. Why, then, do you talk of what you
were doing just recently? You ought to remember it, I think, as
slaves do their whippings, so as to refrain from the same faults
again. 10. But the case is not the same, for with slaves it is the
pain that brings back the memory, but what pain, what punishment, follows on your offences? And when did you ever acquire
the habit of shunnng evil actions?

## CHAPTER 26

# To Those Who Are Afraid Of Want

1. Are you not ashamed to be more cowardly and mean-spirited
than runaway slaves? What lands and servants do they trust to,
when they run away and leave their masters? Do they not steal
just a little to suffice for the first few days, and then make their
way by land or sea, contriving first one means, and then another,
to sustain themselves? 2. And what runaway slave ever died of
hunger? But you tremble, and lie awake at night, for fear you
may lack the necessities of life. 3. Wretch! are you so blind? Do
you not see what road such a lack of necessities leads to? Why,
where does it lead? Where a fever, where a stone falling down
on you, leads — to death. Have you not, then, often said this
very thing to your companions? Have you not read, have you
not written, many things of this kind? And how often have you
arrogantly boasted that you are fairly confident with regard to
death at least?

4. Yes, but my family too will starve.

What of it? Does their hunger lead in any other direction than
yours? Is not the road that leads below the same? And the world
below the same? 5. Are you not willing to look, then, with a
courage equal to every necessity and want, on that place to
which even the wealthiest men and holders of the highest offices
must descend, yes, even kings and tyrants themselves? Though
it could well be that you would go down hungry, and they fit to
burst with indigestion and over-drinking. 6. I fancy you have
hardly ever seen a beggar who was not an old man? Who was

not an extremely old man? But although they are cold by night and by day, and lie outside on the ground, and have only the bare necessities for food, they have arrived at a state where it is hardly possible for them to die; 7. and yet you, a man still sound in all your limbs, are so afraid of starving? Can you not draw water, or write, or guide children to school, or be a watchman at somebody's door?

But it is shameful to be reduced to this necessity.

You should begin by learning what really is shameful, and then come to us calling yourself a philosopher; as it is, even if somebody else calls you one, you should not allow it. 8. Can something be shameful to you which is not your own action, which you are not responsible for, which has come upon you by accident, like a fever, or a headache? If your parents were poor, or if they were rich and left others as their heirs, or, whilst still alive give you no assistance, are these things shameful for you? 9. Is this what you have learned from the philosophers? Have you never heard, that what is shameful is blameworthy; and what is blameworthy is what deserves to be blamed? Do you ever blame a man for something that is not his own work, for something that he himself did not bring about? 10. Well then, did you make your father what he is? Or is it in your power to put him right? Is that granted to you? And then, ought you to desire what is not granted to you; and, when you fail to get it, be ashamed? 11. Is this the habit that you acquired while you were studying philosophy – of looking to others and hoping for nothing from yourself? 12. Lament, then, and groan, and eat in fear of having no food tomorrow. Tremble for your slaves lest they should rob you, or run away from you, or die. 13. Live in such a way and never cease to live thus, you, who never entered upon philosophy, save in name alone, and so far as you could have disgraced its principles by showing them as useless and unprofitable to those who take them up. You have never desired to achieve serenity, constancy and peace of mind; you have never approached a single teacher with this as your aim, but a great many for the sake of syllogisms. You have never put any of these impressions to the test, asking yourself, 14. 'Can I bear this, or can I not? What have I still to face?', but as if all was safe and well with you, you have dwelt upon the final area of study, which has to do with unchangeability, so that you can make yourself unchangeable – in what? Your cowardice, mean-spiritedness, admiration for the rich, your failure to achieve what you desire, and your lack of success in avoiding what you want to avoid. These are the things that you have been labouring to secure. 15. Ought you not first to have acquired something by the use of reason, and then to have made that secure? Whom did you ever see building a cornice without having a wall to build it around? And what door-keeper is ever placed where there is no door? 16. But you are studying to be able to prove things in argument. Prove what, though? You are studying so as not to be shaken by fallacious arguments. Shaken from what? 17. Show me first what you are watching over, what you are measuring, or what you are weighing; and then, accordingly, show me your balance or bushel-measure. 18. Or how long will you be measuring mere dust and ashes? Should you not be showing what makes men happy, what makes their affairs proceed as they wish, and enables them never to blame any one, never accuse any one, and to acquiesce in the governance of the universe? Show me these. 19. 'See, I do show them,' he says, 'I will analyse syllogisms for you.' – This is what we measure with, slave, and not the thing measured. 20. That is why you are now paying the penalty for what you neglected. You tremble, you lie awake, you confer with everybody; and if it seems unlikely that your plans will please everybody, you think that you have been ill advised. 21. And then you are afraid of going hungry, as you fancy; but it is not hunger that you fear, but you are afraid that you may not have a man to cook for you, and another to do the shopping, and another to put on your shoes, and a fourth to dress you, and others to give you a massage, 22. and others to troop after you, so that when you have undressed in the baths, and stretched yourself out like those who have been crucified, you can be massaged on this side and that, and then the masseur can stand over you and say, 'Shift along; give me his side; take hold of his head; let me have his shoulder', and then, when you are returned home from the bath, you may bawl out, 'Will nobody bring me something to eat?' And then, 'Take the tables out, and wipe them down.' 23. This is your dread, that you may not be able to lead the life of an invalid. You should learn how the healthy live by looking to how slaves live, how labourers, how those who are genuine philosophers, how Socrates lived, even with a wife and children; how Diogenes, how Cleanthes, at once studying and drawing water. 24. If these are the things you want to have, you will have them everywhere, and can live with confidence. In what? In the only thing that a man can have confidence in; what is trustworthy, what is free from hindrance and cannot be taken away — your own choice.

25. But why have you contrived to make yourself so useless and good for nothing, that nobody is willing to take you into his house, and take care of you? When an unbroken and serviceable pot has been thrown out, whoever finds it will pick it up, and count it as a gain, yet nobody will pick you up, but everybody count you a loss? 26. And thus you are unable even to perform the office of a dog, or a cock. Why, then, do you wish to live any longer, if that is the kind of person you are? 27. Does any good man fear that food may fail him? It does not fail the blind, it does not fail the lame. Shall it fail a good man? A good soldier will not be short of somebody to pay him, or a labourer, or a shoemaker, so shall a good man find none? 28. Is god so negligent of his own creatures, of his servants, of his witnesses, whom alone he makes use of as examples to the uninstructed, both that he is, and that he governs the universe well, and does not neglect human affairs, and that no evil happens to a good man, either living or dead? 29. What, then, if he no longer provides food? Surely that could only mean that, like a good general, he has given me the signal to withdraw? I obey, I follow, speaking well of my leader, praising his works. 30. For I came when it seemed good to him, and again, when it seems good to him, I depart; and in life it was my business to sing the praises of god, both by myself, to each particular person, and to the world. 31. It is not much that he gives me, no abundance, it is not his will that I should lead a life of luxury; for he did not grant that even to Heracles, his own son, but another reigned over Argos and Mycenae, while Heracles lived subject to command, and laboured, and was exercised. 32. Yet Eurystheus was just what he was, neither king of Argos nor of Mycenae, who was not even king over himself; but Heracles was governor of the entire earth and sea, the expeller of lawlessness and injustice, the introducer of justice and sanctity. And this he achieved naked and alone. 33. Again, when Odysseus was shipwrecked and cast ashore, did his helpless condition make him dejected? Did it break his spirit? No. But how did he approach Nausicaa and her attendants, to ask them for the

necessities of life, which people think most shameful to beg from another? 'Like a mountain-bred lion.'

34. What did he trust in? Not in reputation, or riches, or office, but in his own strength, that is to say, in his judgements about what things are in our power and what are not. 35. For these judgements alone are what make us free, make us immune from hindrance, raise the head of the humiliated, and make them look into the faces of the rich with unaverted eyes, and into the faces of tyrants. 36. And this was what the philosopher could give; but you will not be departing with confidence, will you, but trembling about such trifles as clothes and silver plate? Wretch! Is that how you have wasted your time up until now?

37. But what if I should fall ill?

You will face illness as you ought.

Who will take care of me?

God, and your friends.

I shall have a hard bed to lie on.

But you will do so like a man.

I shall not have a suitable room.

You will be sick in an unsuitable one, then.

Who will prepare my food?

Those who prepare it for others too; you will be like Manes in your illness.

And what will be the conclusion of my illness? Any other than death?

38. Why, do you not reflect, then, that the source of all human evils, and of mean-spiritedness and cowardice, is not death, but rather the fear of death? Discipline yourself, therefore, against this. 39. To this let all your discourses, readings, exercises, tend. And then you will know that in this way alone are men made free.

# BOOK 4

## CHAPTER I

# On Freedom

1. That man is free who lives as he wishes; who can be neither compelled, nor hindered, nor constrained; whose impulses are unimpeded, who attains his desires and does not fall into what he wants to avoid. Who, then, wishes to live in error? – 'Nobody.' 2. Who wishes to live deceived, headstrong, unjust, dissolute, querulous, abject? – 'Nobody.' 3. No bad man, then, lives as he likes; therefore neither is he free. 4. And who wishes to live in sorrow, fear, envy, pity; desiring and failing in his desires, seeking to avoid things and then falling into them? – 'Nobody.' 5. Do we, then, find any bad man who is free from sorrow and fear, and does not fail in his desires and fall into what he wants to avoid? – 'None.' So we find none that is free.

6. If a person who has been twice consul should hear this, he will forgive you provided you add, 'But you are a wise man; this does not apply to you.' But if you tell him the truth 7. – that in point of slavery he does not differ from those who have been sold three times over – what can you expect but a beating? 8. 'For how', says he, 'am I a slave? My father was free, my mother free. Besides, I am a senator, too, and a friend of Caesar, and have been twice consul, and have many slaves.' 9. In the first place, most excellent senator, it could well be that your father too was a slave in the same way as you are, and your mother, and your grandfather, and all your ancestors in turn. 10. But even if they were ever so free, how does that affect you? For what if they were noble and you mean-spirited, if they were fearless and you a coward, if they were self-controlled and you licentious?

11. 'And what', someone asks, 'has this to do with being a slave?' – Does it strike you as having nothing to do with being a slave, if a person acts against his will, under compulsion, and groaning? 12. 'Agreed. But who can compel me except the master of all, Caesar?' 13. – By your own admission, then, you have one master. And you should not draw comfort from the

fact that he is, as you say, the common master of all: no, you must realize that you are a slave in a great household. 14. Thus the Nicopolitans, too, are accustomed to cry, 'By the fortune of Caesar we are free men!'

15. All the same, if you please, let us put Caesar aside for the moment. Now tell me this. Have you never been in love with any one, with some nice young girl or boy, either slave or free? 16. – 'Why, what has that to do with being either slave or free?' 17. Were you never commanded by your beloved to do something that you did not wish to do? Have you never flattered your little slave? Have you never kissed his feet? And yet, if you were compelled to kiss Caesar's feet, you would think it an outrage, and the height of tyranny. 18. Have you never gone out by night to where you did not wish? What else besides is slavery? Have you never spent more than you wished? Have you never spoken with groans and lamentations, endured derision, had the door closed in your face? 19. But, if you are ashamed to confess your own follies, see what Thrasonides says and does, who, after having fought more campaigns perhaps than you, went out by night when Geta would not dare to go; nay, had he been compelled to it by him, would have gone crying aloud and lamenting his bitter servitude. 20. What, then, does he say?

> A sorry girl has enslaved me,
> Whom no enemy ever enslaved.

21. Wretch! to be the slave of a girl, and a cheap girl too! Why, then, do you still call yourself free? Why do you boast of your campaigns? 22. Then he calls for a sword, and is angry with the person who, out of kindness, refuses to give it; and sends presents to the girl who hates him; and begs, and weeps, and then again is elated at every slight success. 23. But even then, when he has not learned to repudiate desire and fear, how could he be free?

24. Now consider how we apply the concept of freedom with regard to animals. 25. Men rear lions as tame creatures in cages, and feed them, and some even take them around with them; and who will say that any such lion is free? Nay, does he not live the more slavishly the more he lives at ease? And what lion, if he acquired sense and reason, would wish to be one of those lions? 26. Come, think of birds and what, when they are captured and reared in cages, they are willing to suffer as they struggle to

escape. Some of them starve themselves to death rather than endure such a life; 27. while even those that survive pine away on the brink of death, and sally forth the moment they find any opening. Such a desire do they have for natural freedom, and to be independent and free of restraint. 28. – 'And what harm does this confinement do you?' – 'What a thing to ask. I was born to fly where I please, to live in the open air, to sing when I please. You deprive me of all this, and ask, "What harm does that do you?".'

29. Therefore we shall call free only those creatures that are unwilling to put up with captivity, but, as soon as they are taken, escape by dying. 30. Thus Diogenes says somewhere that the one sure means to freedom is to die cheerfully. And he writes to the Persian king, 'You can no more enslave the city of the Athenians than you can enslave fishes.' 31. – 'How is that? Shall not I capture them?' – 'If you do capture them', says he, 'they will leave you, and be gone like fish. For take a fish, and it dies. And, if the Athenians die likewise as soon as you have taken them, what is the use of your military force?' 32. This is the voice of a free man, who had examined the matter in earnest, and, as might be expected, had found the truth. But if you seek it elsewhere than where it is, what wonder if you never find it?

33. A slave prays to be set free at once. Why? Do you think it is because he is eager to pay his money to those who collect the manumission duty? No; but because he fancies that up until now as a result of not having acquired his freedom, he has lived under restraint and in misery. 34. 'If I am set free', he says, 'it will be happiness all the way, I will defer to nobody, I will speak to all men as their equal and a man of equivalent rank. I will go where I please, and come whence and where, I please. 35. Then he is in fact freed, and all at once, having nowhere to eat, he looks for someone he can flatter and go to dine with. Then he makes his living through his body and undergoes the most frightful things, and even if he does get a manger to feed at he has fallen into a slavery far harsher than the first; 36. or if he does perhaps make his fortune, being a man of little taste he falls for some worthless girl, and in his misery sheds tears for himself and yearns to be a slave again. 37. 'What harm did it do me? Someone else clothed me, and shod me, and fed me, and took care of me when I was sick, while I did little enough in his service. But now, miserable wretch that I am,

what things I suffer in being a slave to many instead of to one! 38. Yet, if I can get the rings of office on my fingers, then I shall live in the greatest prosperity and happiness.' In order to obtain them he first suffers what he deserves, and, as soon as he has obtained them, things are the same all over again. 39. 'But, then', says he, 'if I serve in the army, I shall be delivered from all my troubles.' He goes off on campaign. He suffers as much as any convict, and, nevertheless, he asks for a second campaign, and a third; 40. and, when he adds the finishing touch and is made a senator, then he becomes a slave indeed, as he goes to the senate and embarks on the finest and most luxurious slavery of all.

41. Let him not be a fool, but, rather, let him learn, as Socrates used to say, 'the true nature of each reality', and not apply his preconceptions indiscriminately to particular cases; 42. for this is the cause of all human ills, that people are incapable of applying their general preconceptions to particular cases. 43. Rather, some of us think one thing, and some another. One man thinks that he is ill. By no means; rather, he is failing to apply his preconceptions rightly. Another, that he is poor; another, that he has a harsh father or mother; another, that he is not in the good graces of Caesar. But really this means one thing only, none of them know how to apply their preconceptions. 44. For who does not have a preconception of evil, that it is harmful, that it is to be avoided, that it is something we must rid ourselves of by every means? One preconception does not conflict with another 45. – except when it comes to be applied. So what exactly is this evil, this thing that is harmful and to be avoided? 'Not to be the friend of Caesar', someone says. He has left the path, he has failed to make a proper application, he is in distress, he is seeking for something that is nothing to the purpose. For, if he gets to be Caesar's friend, he has nevertheless failed to achieve what he was seeking. 46. For what is it that every man seeks? To be secure, to be happy, to do what he pleases without hindrance or compulsion. When he becomes the friend of Caesar, then, is he absolved from hindrance or compulsion, does he live in tranquillity and happiness? Whom shall we ask? Whom can we better trust than this very man, who has become Caesar's friend? 47. Come forth and tell us when it was that you slept more peacefully, at the present time, or before you were the friend of Caesar? At once you get the

answer, 'Leave off, for heaven's sake, stop making fun of my fortune. You do not know the miseries I suffer, wretch that I am; there is no sleep for me; but one person comes in, followed by another, saying: Caesar is now awake, is now coming out. Then come troubles, and anxieties.' 48. Well, when did you dine more pleasantly, formerly, or now? Hear what he says about this too. When he is not invited, he is upset; and if he is, he dines like a slave with his master, anxious all the while not to say or do anything foolish. And what do you suppose he is afraid of? Being whipped like a slave? How can he hope to escape so well? No; but as becomes so great a man, a friend of Caesar, he is frightened of losing his head. 49. And when did you bathe more in greater tranquillity; when did you perform your exercises at greater leisure; in short, which life would you prefer to live, your present one, or the former? 50. I could swear, there is no one so wanting in sense and so incurable as not to lament his fortune the more grievously the more he is Caesar's friend.

51. Since, therefore, neither those who are called kings, nor the friends of kings live as they wish, who, in the end, can be free? Seek, and you will find; for you are furnished by nature with resources for discovering the truth. But if you are unable to discover for yourself what follows next by recourse to these resources alone, 52. listen to those who have searched before you. What do they say? Do you consider freedom to be a good? – 'The greatest.' – Can anyone, then, who attains this greatest good be unhappy or fare badly? – 'No.' – Whoever, therefore, you see to be unhappy, woebegone, mournful, you should confidently declare not to be free. – 'I do!' – 53. Henceforth, then, we have done with buying and selling and such means to acquisition. For if you are right in conceding the points you have, whether it be the Great King who is unhappy, or a minor king, whether it be a man of consular rank or one who has been consul twice over, he could not be free. – 'Agreed.'

54. Further, then, answer me this: Do you think freedom to be something great and noble and valuable? – 'How should I not?' Is it possible, then, that he who acquires anything so great and valuable and noble should be mean-spirited? – 'It is not.' 55. Whenever, therefore, you see a man grovelling to another, or flattering him contrary to his own opinion, confidently say that he too is not free; and not only if he is doing so for the sake

of a wretched dinner, but even if it be for a governorship or indeed a consulship; you should call those who are acting in this way for the sake of little things, petty slaves, and the rest, as they deserve, slaves in the grand manner. 56. – 'This too I grant.' Well, do you think that freedom is something independent and self-determining? – 'How can it be otherwise?' So whenever a man is subject to hindrance and compulsion at the hands of another, say confidently that he is not free. 57. And do not look to his grandfathers, or great-grandfathers, and inquire whether he was ever bought or sold; but if you hear him say from his heart, and with true feeling, 'Master', though twelve fasces go before him, call him a slave. And if you should hear him say, 'Woe is me, what things I suffer!' call him a slave. In short, if you see him wailing, complaining, miserable, call him a slave in a purple-bordered robe. 58. Supposing, however, he does none of these things? Do not yet say that he is free, but examine his judgements to discover whether they are subject in any way to compulsion and hindrance or affected by unhappiness; and if you find that to be the case, call him a slave on holiday at the Saturnalia. Say that his master is away: he will presently return, and you will know what state he is in. 59. 'Who will return?' – Whoever has authority over the things that a man desires, to get them for him or to take them away. 'Have we so many masters, then?' – We have. For, prior to all human masters, circumstances are our masters – and they are many. It necessarily follows, then, that those who have power over any of these circumstances are also our masters; 60. for it is not Caesar himself that anyone fears, but death, banishment, prison, loss of property, deprival of civic rights. Nor does anyone love Caesar himself, unless he happens to be a man of great worth; but we love riches, a tribunate, a praetorship, a consulship. When we love and hate and fear these things, those who have the disposal of them must necessarily be our masters. That is why we even bow down to such people as gods. 61. For we consider that whoever has the disposal of the greatest advantage is divine; and if we then lay down the false minor premise, 'This man has the disposal of the greatest advantage', the particular conclusion from these premises will necessarily be false as well.

62. What is it, then, that makes a man free from hindrance and his own master? For neither riches, nor a consulship, nor a province, nor a kingdom, make him so; 63. but something else

must be found. Now what is it that preserves him from being
hindered and restrained in writing? – 'The knowledge of how to
write.' In playing the harp? 'Knowledge of harp-playing.' Therefore, in life, too, it is knowledge of how to live. 64. You have
heard this as a general principle; consider now its particular
applications. Is it possible for the man who desires any of those
things that are in the power of others to be free from hindrance?
'No.' Is it possible for him to be free from restraint? 'No.' 65.
Therefore neither can he be free. Consider then, have we nothing
that is wholly in our power, or is everything thus, or are some
things in our power and some in the power of others? 66. –
'What do you mean?' When you wish your body to be sound, is
it in your own power, or is it not? – 'It is not.' When you wish
it to be healthy? – 'Nor this.' When you wish it to be handsome?
– 'Nor this.' And to live, or die? – 'Nor this.' Our body, then, is
not our own, but subject to everything stronger than itself. –
'Agreed.' 67. Well, is it in your own power to have land when
you please, and as long as you please, and of the kind you
please? – 'No.' Slaves? – 'No.' Clothes? – 'No.' A house? – 'No.'
Horses? – 'Indeed none of these.' Well, if you wish ever so much
for your children to live, or your wife, or your brother, or your
friends, is it in your own power? – 'No, nor this.' 68. Have you,
then, nothing that is subject to your authority and under your
control alone, or do you in fact have something of that kind? –
'I do not know.' 69. Well, look at the question in this way, and
examine it. Can anyone make you assent to what is false? – 'No
one.' In the area of assent, then, you are unrestrained and
unhindered. – 'Agreed.' 70. Again, can anyone force you to
direct your impulses towards what you do not wish? – 'Indeed
he can. For when he threatens me with death or chains, he forces
me to do so.' If, however, you were to despise dying or being
chained, would you still pay any heed to him? – 'No.' 71. Is
despising death, then, your own action, or not your own action?
– 'My own action.' And is the directing of your impulses your
own action, or not? – 'I concede that it is.' And the impulse not
to do something? That is your own action also. – 72. 'Yes, but
what if my impulse is to walk freely and another person hinders
me?' What part of you can he hinder? Not your assent, surely?
– 'No, but my poor body.' Yes, as he could a stone. – 'So be it;
but I can no longer go for my walk.' 73. And who told you that
walking was an action of your own that cannot be hindered?

For I said only that your impulse to do so was not subject to hindrance; but when it comes to the use of our body, and cooperation from it, you have heard long ago that nothing is your own. – 'Let that be agreed too.' 74. And can anyone compel you to desire what you do not wish? – 'No one.' Or to propose an aim or to plan, or, in general, to deal with the impressions that fall to you? – 'Not that either. 75. But when I desire something, somebody can hinder me from getting what I desire.' If you desire something that is your own and not subject to hindrance, how will he hinder you? – 'In no way.' Who, then, tells you that the person who desires what is not his own is not subject to hindrance? 76. – 'May I not desire health, then?' By no means, nor anything else that is not your own; 77. for what is not in your own power either to procure or to keep when you wish is not your own. You should keep not only your hands far away from it, but, first and foremost, your desire; otherwise, you are handing yourself over to be a slave, and putting your head under the yoke, if you admire anything that is not your own, and hunger for anything that is subject to others and mortal. 78. – 'Is not my hand my own?' It is a part of you, but it is by nature clay, and subject to hindrance and to compulsion, a slave to everything stronger than itself. 79. And why do I speak of your hand? You ought to treat your entire body like a poor overburdened ass, as long as it is possible, as long as it is allowed you; but if it is pressed into public service and a soldier should lay hold of it, let it go. Do not resist or mutter, otherwise you will get a beating, and lose your poor ass just the same. 80. When this is the way in which you should conduct yourself with regard to your body, consider what is left for you to do about the things that are procured for the sake of the body. If the body be a little ass, those other things become bridles, pack-saddles, shoes, barley, fodder for the ass. Let these go too; dismiss them more quickly and more cheerfully than the little ass itself. 81. And when you are thus prepared and thus trained to distinguish what is not your own from your own, what is subject to hindrance from what is not, to regard the latter as your concern and the former as not, and carefully keep your desire directed toward the latter and your aversion directed towards the former, will there any longer be anyone for you to fear? 'No one.' 82. For what is there for you to be afraid about? About the things that are your own, in which your true good and evil lie? And who has any authority over these, who can take them away, who can hinder them? Nobody can, any more than he could hinder god. 83. Or is it your body and possessions that you are afraid for? Things that are not your own, that are nothing to you? And what have you been studying all this while, but to distinguish what is your own from what is not your own, what is in your power from what is not in your power, what is subject to hindrance from what is not? And for what purpose did you approach the philosophers? That you might be no less miserable and unfortunate than you were before? 84. So, surely you will then be free from fear and perturbation? And what is pain to you? (For fear of things expected turns to pain when they are present.) And what will you desire any longer? For you have a measured and composed desire for things that are within the sphere of choice, as being good and within your grasp; and you have no desire for things outside the sphere of choice, and thus leave no room for that irrational and impetuous desire that impels you beyond all measure. 85. When this is your attitude to things, what man can inspire fear in you any longer? For how can one man cause fear in another, by his appearance, or speech, or his society in general, any more than one horse can in another, one dog in another, one bee in another? No, the cause of fear in men is things; and whenever any person can either confer or take away these from another, then he becomes a cause of fear too. 86. 'How, then, is the tyrant's citadel to be destroyed?' – Not by sword or fire, but by judgements. For if we should demolish the citadel in the city, shall we have demolished also the citadel of fever, or of pretty girls, in short, the citadel within ourselves; and turned out the tyrants within ourselves, to whom each one of us is subject day by day, sometimes the same tyrants, sometimes others? 87. No, it is from here that we must begin, and thence that we must destroy the citadel, and expel the tyrants; we must give up our poor body, and every part of it, and our influence, property, reputation, offices, honours, children, brothers, friends, and regard all these as not our own. 88. And if the tyrants are expelled, what further need have I to raze the walls of the citadel, at least on my own account? For what harm does it do me by standing? Why should I go on to expel the guards? For where am I aware of them? It is against others that they direct their rods, their spears, and their swords. 89. But I have never been hindered in anything I wished, or compelled to anything against my wish. Indeed, how is this possible? I have submitted my impulses to god. Is it his will that I should have a fever? It is my will too. Is it his will that I should set out to get something? It is my will too. Is it his will that I should desire something? It is my will too. Is it his will that I should get something? It is mine too. That is not his will. It is not mine. 90. And so, if he wills it, it is my will to die; and likewise my will to be stretched on the rack. Who can hinder me any longer, contrary to my opinion, or compel me? I am as immune to hindrance or compulsion as Zeus. 91. This is also the way in which cautious travellers act. One of them has heard that the road is beset with robbers; he does not venture to set out alone, but waits for the retinue of an ambassador or quaestor or proconsul, and, attaching himself to their company, goes along in safety. 92. A prudent man acts likewise in this world. Many are the gangs of robbers, and tyrants, storms, tribulations, and occasions to lose the things we most value. 93. Where can a man find refuge? (he asks) How can he escape unrobbed? What retinue shall he wait for to make his way through safely? To what company shall he attach himself? 94. To some rich man, or man of consular rank? And what good will that do him? The man himself is stripped and groans and laments. And what if my fellow-traveller himself should turn against me, and rob me? What shall I do? 95. I will be a friend of Caesar. While I am a companion of his, no one will injure me. But firstly, to become his friend, how many things must I endure and submit to, how often must I be robbed and by how many! 96. And then, if I do become his friend, he too is mortal; and, if by any accident he should become my enemy, where would I do best to withdraw to? To a desert? Well, and does not a fever come there? 97. What is to become of me, then? Is it not possible to find a fellow-traveller who is trustworthy, strong, and incapable of treachery? 98. He thinks things over in this way, and reflects that, if he attaches himself to god, he will complete his life's journey in safety. 99. – 'How do you mean, attach himself?' So that whatever god wills, he wills too, and what god does not will, he does not will either. 100. 'How, then, can this be achieved?' – Why, how otherwise than by considering god's purposes and his governance? What has he given to me to be my own and subject to my own authority? What has he reserved for himself? He has given to me whatever

lies within the sphere of choice, and made that over to me free
from all hindrance and restraint. This body formed of clay, how
could he make that free from hindrance? And so he has made
subject to the circulation of the universe my property, my
furnishings, my house, my children, my wife. 101. Why, then,
shall I fight against god? Why do I will what is outside the reach
of my will, to possess absolutely what is not granted to me
absolutely? So how shall I possess them? As they were granted
to me, and for as long as is possible. But he who gave takes
away again. Why, then, do I resist? Not to say that I shall be a
fool in contending with one stronger than myself; but prior to
that, I shall be doing wrong. 102. For where did I get things
when I came into the world? My father gave them to me. And
who gave them to him? And who made the sun, who the fruits,
who the seasons, and who the fellowship and intercommunion
between men? 103. And then, when you have received everything, even your very self, from another, are you angry with the
giver and do you reproach him if he takes anything away from
you? 104. Who are you, and for what purpose have you come?
Was it not he who brought you here? Was it not he who showed
you the light? Has he not given you fellow-workers? Has he not
given you senses? Has he not given you reason? And as what
did he bring you here? Was it not as a mortal? Was it not as one
who would live, with a little portion of flesh, upon this earth,
and behold his governance and take part with him, for a short
time, in his pageant and his festival? 105. Are you not willing,
then, for the time that is granted to you, to behold his pageant
and his solemn assembly, and then, when he leads you out, will
you not pass on your way, after paying him obeisance and
offering him thanksgiving for what you have heard and what
you have seen? 'No, but I wanted to enjoy the festival still
longer.' 106. So would initiates into the Mysteries like to be
longer in their initiation, so perhaps would the spectators at
Olympia like to see more athletes. But the festival is over. Leave
it and depart like a grateful and modest person; make room for
others. Others too must be born, as you were, and when they
are born must have land and houses and the necessities of life.
But if those who come first do not withdraw, what room is there
left? Why are you insatiable? Why are you never satisfied? Why
do you crowd the world? 107. — 'Yes, but I want my wife and
children to be with me.' Why, are they yours? Are they not the

property of the one who gave them? Of the one who made you also? Will you not give up what is not your own, then? Will you not yield to your superior? 108. – 'Why, then, did he bring me into the world on these conditions?' If it is not worth your while, depart. He has no need of a censorious spectator. He needs people who join in the festival and the dance, so that, on the contrary, they may applaud it, and view it with reverence, and sing its praises. 109. But the sluggish and cowardly he will not be sorry to see dismissed from it. For when they were present, they did not behave as though they were at a festival, nor filled their proper place, but were dispirited and found fault with the deity, and with their fortune and their companions; and they were thus insensible to the nature of their fortune and their own powers, which they had received for quite the opposite purpose, for greatness of soul, nobility of mind, courage, and the very freedom that we are now investigating. 110. – 'For what purpose then have I received these things?' – To use them. 'For how long?' – For as long as he who lent them pleases. 'But what if they are essential to me?' Do not hanker after them, and they will not be. Do not tell yourself that they are essential, and they are not.

111. This is what you should practise from morning till evening, beginning with the meanest and frailest things, with an earthen vessel or a cup. Afterwards, proceed to a tunic, a dog, a horse, a piece of land, and thence to yourself, your body and its parts, and your children, wife, brothers. 112. Look around you in every direction, and hurl these things away from you. Purify your judgements. See that nothing is attached to you or cleaves to you that is not your own and may give you pain when it is torn away. 113. And say while you are training yourself day after day, as you do here, not that you are pursuing philosophy (to claim that title would surely be pretentious), but that you are providing for your emancipation. For this is true freedom. 114. This is the freedom that Diogenes gained from Antisthenes, and then he said that it was impossible that he could ever be enslaved again by any one. 115. So how did he behave when he was captured, how did he treat the pirates? Did he call any of them master? (I do not mean the name, for I am not afraid of a word, but the state of mind from whence the word proceeds.) 116. How did he rebuke them for feeding their prisoners badly? How did he behave when he was sold? Did he seek a master? No, but

a slave. And when he was sold, how did he behave towards his master? He immediately began to talk with him, saying that he ought not to be dressed nor shaved in the way that he was, and telling him how his sons ought to live their lives. 117. And is that so strange? For if the same master had bought a trainer, would he have used him as a servant or a master in the exercises of the wrestling-school? And likewise, if he had bought a physician or an architect? In every subject the man who possesses a skill must necessarily be superior to the man who lacks it. 118. So in general, the man who possesses knowledge of how to live, how can he be anything other than the master? For who is master in a ship? The helmsman. Why? Because whoever disobeys him suffers the penalty. 119. – 'But my master can flog me.' Can he do it, then, with impunity? – 'So I, like others, used to think.' But because he cannot do so with impunity, for that very reason it is not in his power; for no one can act unjustly with impunity. 120. – 'And what punishment does a man suffer who puts his own slave in chains, when he so wishes?' The very act of putting him in chains. This you yourself must grant if you want to hold to the principle that man is not a wild beast but a civilized animal. 121. For when does a vine do badly? 'When it is acting against its own nature.' When a cock? – 'Likewise.' 122. So also with man. What, then, is his nature? To bite and kick and throw people into prison and behead them? No; but to do good, to cooperate with others and pray for their good. Whether you will or no, then, he is faring badly whenever he acts unreasonably. – 123.'Did not Socrates, then, fare badly?' No; but his judges and accusers. – 'Nor Helvidius at Rome?' No; but his murderer. 124. 'How do you mean?' Just as you too do not say that the winning cock, even if wounded, has fared badly, but the one that is beaten without a scratch. Nor do you call a dog happy when he is neither hunting nor toiling, but when you see him sweating and in pain and panting with the chase. 125. Where is the paradox if we say that what is evil for everything is what is contrary to its nature? Do you not say it yourself with regard to everything else? Why, therefore, in the case of man alone do you take a different course? 126. But when we say that man is by nature gentle and affectionate and trustworthy, is that a paradox? 'That is no paradox either.' 127. So next, how is it that a person suffers no harm if he is flogged, or imprisoned, or beheaded? Is it not the case, that if he endures such things nobly, he goes away with added profit and the greater benefit, while the person who is truly harmed is the one who suffers the most pitiful and shameful fate, that of becoming a wolf or a serpent or a wasp instead of a human being?

128. Come, then, let us recapitulate what has been agreed. The man who is not subject to hindrance and has things ready at hand as he wants them is free; but the man who can be hindered or compelled or propelled into anything against his will is a slave. 129. And who can never be hindered? The man who sets his desire on nothing that is not his own. And what are those things that are not our own? Those that are not in our own power, either to have or not to have, or to have them of a particular nature, or under specific conditions. 130. Our body, therefore, is not our own, its parts are not our own, and our property is not our own. So if you become attached to any of these as your own, you will be punished, as he deserves to be who sets his desire on what is not his own. 131. This is the road that leads to freedom, this the only deliverance from slavery, to be able to say at any time from the bottom of one's soul:

> Lead me, Zeus, and thou, O Destiny,
> To wheresoever your decrees have ordained.

132. But what say you, philosopher? A tyrant calls on you to say something that does not become you. Do you say it, or do you not? — 'Stay, let me consider the matter.' Consider it now? And what did you spend your time considering when you were in the lecture-hall? Did you not study what things are good and evil and what indifferent? — 'I did.' 133. So what conclusions did you and the others agree to? 'That right and noble actions were good, wrong and shameful ones evil.' Is living a good? — 'No.' Dying an evil? — 'No.' And prison? — 'No.' Ignoble and faithless speech, the betraying of a friend, or the flattering of a tyrant, what did these strike you as being? 'Evils.' 134. Why, you are not considering the question, nor have you ever considered it or devoted any thought to it. For what sort of a consideration is this, to ask whether it is fitting, when it is in my power, to procure for myself the greatest goods instead of procuring the greatest evils? A fine and necessary consideration, truly, and requiring considerable thought! Why do you trifle with us, man? Never was any such point considered. 135. Nor, if you really imagined that shameful things were bad and all

other things indifferent, would you ever have arrived at this position, or anything near it, but you would be able to decide the matter at this very moment as if by direct vision, by recourse to your own understanding. 136. For do you ever stop to consider whether black is white, or light heavy? Do you not follow the plain evidence of your senses? Why, then, do you say that you are now considering whether things indifferent are to be avoided rather than evils? 137. In fact these are not your judgements – imprisonment and death do not seem indifferent to you, but rather the greatest evils; nor the other things evil, but matters of no concern to us. 138. For that is the habit you have acquired from the beginning. 'Where am I? In the lecture-hall? And who is listening to me? I am talking amongst philosophers. But now I have left the lecture-hall. Away with this talk that befits only pedants and fools.' That is how a philosopher bears witness against a friend, that is how a philosopher turns parasite, 139. that is how he hires himself out for pay, that is how in the Senate a man does not say what he truly thinks, though within him his judgement is crying aloud 140. – and no half-hearted and miserable leftover suspended from empty discussions as though by a thread, but a robust and serviceable judgement, which has received its initiation by having been trained in action. 141. Observe yourself carefully, and see how you take the news, not, I say, that your child is dead (for how could you endure it?) but that your oil is spilled, your wine drunk up. You react in such a way 142. that somebody standing by, as you fall into a passion, might say just this: 'Philosopher, you talk otherwise in the lecture-hall. Why are you deceiving us? Why, when you are a worm, do you call yourself a man?' 143. I should like to be near one of these philosophers when he is fornicating, that I might see how he exerts himself, and what sayings he utters, whether he remembers his name and the discourses that he hears or delivers or reads.

144. 'And what has this to do with freedom?' – Truly nothing at all besides this has anything to do with it, whether you rich people wish so or not. 145. 'And who is your witness to this?' – Who but yourselves, who have this powerful master, and live at his beck and call, and faint away if he merely looks at you with knotted brows; who pay your court to old men and old women, and say, 'I cannot do this, I am not allowed to.' 146. Why are

you not allowed to? Were you not arguing with me just now and claiming that you were free? 'But Aprulla has forbidden me.' Speak the truth, then, slave, and do not run away from your masters, nor deny them, nor dare to claim your freedom when you have so many proofs of your slavery. 147. One might indeed find some excuse for a person compelled by love to do something contrary to his opinion, even when at the same time he sees what is best and yet has not resolution enough to follow it, because he has become possessed by a power that is violent and, in a certain sense, divine. 148. But who can put up with you, whose love is for old men and women, as you wipe their noses, and wash them, and bribe them with gifts, and wait upon them like a slave when they are sick, at the same time praying for them to die, and inquiring of the physicians whether they are at last fatally ill? Or again, when for these great and venerable offices and honours you kiss the hands of other people's slaves, so that you are the slave of those who are not free themselves! 149. And then you walk about in state as a praetor, or a consul. Do I not know how you came to be a praetor, where you obtained your consulship, who gave it you? 150. For my own part, I would not even wish to live, if I had to live by Felicio's favour, and bear his pride and slavish arrogance. For I know what a slave is who considers himself prosperous and is puffed up with pride.

151. Are you free yourself, then? (someone says). By the gods, I wish and pray to be. But I cannot yet face my masters. I still value my poor body, and am greatly concerned to keep it sound (though it is not sound anyhow). 152. But I can show you one who was free, that you may no longer have to seek for an example. Diogenes was free. — 'How so?' Not because he was born of free parents, for he was not, but because he was free himself, because he had cast away all that gives slavery a hold on a person, so that there was no way that anybody could come up to him or seize hold of him to enslave him. 153. Everything he had could be easily loosed, was loosely fastened. If you had seized hold of his property, he would have let it go rather than have followed you to recover it; if you had seized his leg, he would have let his leg go, and if you had seized his whole poor body, his whole body, and relatives, friends, country, just the same. For he knew whence he had them, and from whom and upon what conditions he had received them. 154. But he would

never have forsaken his true ancestors the gods, and his real country, nor have suffered any one else to be more dutiful and obedient to them than himself; nor would any one have died more cheerfully for his country than he. 155. For it was not the mere reputation of acting for the universe that he sought, but he remembered that everything that comes into being has that as its source, and is done on behalf of that country, and is consigned to us by its governor. Accordingly, see what he himself says and writes. 156. 'For this reason, Diogenes', he says, 'you have the power to converse as you will with the king of the Persians, and with Archidamus, king of the Lacedaemonians.' 157. – Was it because he was born of free parents? Or was it because they were descended from slaves that all the Athenians and all the Lacedaemonians and Corinthians could not converse with kings as they wanted, but feared and paid court to them? 158. So why, somebody asks, has Diogenes the power to do so? 'Because I do not regard this sorry body as my own. Because I need nothing. Because the law and nothing else is everything to me.' These were the things that permitted him to be free.

159. And to prevent you getting the impression that I am offering you as an example a man free of encumbrances, without a wife or children, or country or friends, or relatives to bend or divert him, take Socrates, and consider him, who had a wife and children, but deemed them not his own, who had a country (to the extent and in the manner in which duty demanded) and friends and relatives, all subject to the law and obedience to the law. 160. For that reason, when duty demanded that he serve as a soldier he was the first to go out, and exposed himself to danger without the least reserve. But when he was sent by the Thirty Tyrants to arrest Leon, because he considered it a shameful thing to do, he never even contemplated it, though he knew that he would have to die if that was how things turned out. 161. But what difference did that make to him? For it was something else that he wanted to preserve, not his paltry flesh, but his fidelity, his honour. These are things that cannot be put in the hands of another, cannot be made subject to another. 162. And afterwards, when he was on trial for his life and had to defend himself, did he behave like a man who had children? Or a wife? No; but like a single man. And how did he behave when he had to drink the poison? 163. When he might have

escaped, and Crito said to him, 'You must escape for the sake of your children', what did he answer? Did he consider this a godsend? Out of the question; he considered what was fitting, and as for everything else, he neither looked at it nor gave any thought to it. For he did not wish, he said, to save his paltry body, but that which is increased and preserved by right action, and diminished and destroyed by wrong. 164. Socrates did not save his life by acting shamefully, he who refused to put the proposal to the vote when the Athenians were demanding it, who held the Tyrants in contempt, who used to talk in the way that he did about excellence and goodness. 165. Such a man is not to be saved by any shameful means; he is saved by dying, and not by running away. For a good actor too is preserved by leaving off when he ought, and not acting beyond the proper time. 166. 'What, then, will become of your children?' – 'If I had gone away to Thessaly you would have taken care of them; and will there be no one to take care of them when I have gone down to Hades?' See how he scoffs at death and calls it by fair names. 167. But, if it had been you or I, we would have proceeded to prove, by philosophical arguments, that those who act unjustly are to be repaid in kind; and would have added, 'If I escape, I shall be of use to many; if I die, to none.' Nay, if it had been necessary to creep through a mouse-hole to escape, we would have done so. 168. But how should we have been of use to anyone? For how could we have been, if the others stayed behind in Athens? Or if we were useful when alive, should we not have been even more useful to mankind by dying when we ought, and as we ought? 169. And now that Socrates is dead, the memory of him is of no less benefit to mankind (and perhaps of even greater benefit) than what he did or said while still alive. 170. Study these points, these judgements, these arguments, contemplate these examples, if you wish to be free, if you desire freedom in accordance with its true value. 171. And where is the wonder that you should purchase so great a thing at the price of other things, so many, and so great? Some hang themselves, others hurl themselves down precipices, and sometimes even whole cities have been destroyed, for the sake of what is commonly called freedom; 172. so will you not, for the sake of the true and secure and inviolable freedom, restore to god that which he has given you when he demands it back? Will you not practise, not only as Plato says, dying, but also being tortured on the rack and going into exile and being flogged, and in short, giving up all that is not your own? 173. If not, you will be a slave among slaves, even if you are consul a thousand times over and even if you ascend to the Palace, you will be a slave none the less. And you will perceive the truth of what Cleanthes used to say, that 'Philosophers do, perhaps, say what is contrary to common opinion, but not what is contrary to reason.' 174. For you will find that it is in reality true, that these things which are eagerly pursued and admired are of no use to those who have gained them; while those who have not yet gained them imagine that, once these things are theirs, they will possess all that is good, and then, when they are theirs, there is the same scorching heat, the same agitation, the same nausea and the same desire of what they do not have. 175. For freedom is not secured by the fulfilment of people's desires, but by the suppression of desire. 176. And, so that you may learn the truth of this, just as you have toiled for those other things, apply that same toil to these instead: sit up at night to acquire a judgement that will make you free. 177. Instead of attending on a rich old man, attend a philosopher, and be seen about his doors. You will not get any disgrace by being seen there, and you will not return empty, or without profit, if you approach him as you ought. At any rate, try it at least. There is no shame in trying.

## CHAPTER 2

# On Association With Others

1. This is a point you must attend to before all others: not to be so attached to any one of your former acquaintances or friends as to descend to the same ways as his, otherwise you will destroy yourself. 2. But, if the thought steals into your mind, 'I shall appear awkward to him, and he will not treat me as before', remember that nothing can be had for nothing, and that it is impossible for a person to remain the same as he used to be, if he is not acting in the same way. 3. Choose, then, which you prefer, to be loved as you used to be by those who loved you

formerly by remaining like your former self, or to be better and not meet with that same affection. 4. For if this latter course is preferable, direct yourself at once to that, and do not let the other considerations draw you away from it; for no one can make progress while facing two ways. If, then, you have chosen this course before all others, if you want to hold to this alone, and work hard at it, give up everything else. 5. Otherwise by facing in two ways you will incur a double penalty – you will neither make progress as you ought, nor continue to get what you used to get previously. 6. For before, by setting your heart entirely on things of no value, you were agreeable to your companions. 7. But you cannot excel in both courses, but in so far as you follow one course you must necessarily fall short in the other. If you do not drink with the people whom you drank with before, you cannot appear equally pleasing. Choose, then, whether you want to be a drunkard and pleasing to those people, or sober and unpleasing to them. If you do not sing with the people with whom you used to sing, you cannot be equally dear to them. Here too you must choose which you prefer. 8. For if it is better to be modest and well-behaved than have someone to say of you, 'What an agreeable fellow!', you must be done with these other considerations, renounce them, turn away from them, have nothing more to do with them. 9. But, if that does not please you, turn wholeheartedly in the opposite direction. Be one of those catamites, one of those adulterers, and act in the corresponding manner, and you will obtain what you want. Jump up in the theatre, too, and roar out your applause for the dancer. 10. But characters so opposite cannot be mixed. You cannot act as Thersites and Agamemnon too. If you want to be Thersites, you must be humpbacked and bald: if Agamemnon, you must be tall and handsome, and love the people who have been assigned to your care.

## CHAPTER 3

# What Should Be Exchanged For What?

1. This is the reflection you should keep in hand for when you lose any external thing: what have you got in exchange for it? And if that be of more value, never say, 'I have been the loser'; 2. whether it be a horse for an ass, an ox for a sheep, a good action for a small piece of money, a properly settled mind for foolish talk, or a sense of shame for indecent talk. 3. If you remember this, you will invariably maintain your character as it ought to be. If not, consider that you are spending your time in vain, and that the troubles you are now taking on your own behalf will all be upset and flow to waste. 4. It takes but a little to destroy and overturn everything, just a slight deviation from reason. 5. To overturn his ship, a helmsman does not need the same proficiency as he does to keep it safe, but, if he turns it a little too far into the wind, he is lost: and even if he does not do so deliberately, but simply loses his concentration for a moment, he is lost. 6. Such is the case here too. If you nod off for just a moment, all that you have acquired up till then is gone. 7. Attend, then, to your impressions, watch over them unsleepingly. For it is no small thing that you are guarding, but modesty, fidelity, constancy, a tranquil mind undisturbed by fear, pain or disorder; in short, freedom. 8. What will you sell all these for? Consider what your purchase is worth. – 'But I shall not get the like in exchange.' – Consider, if you do get it, what you are accepting in exchange. 9. 'I have virtuous conduct, he has a tribuneship; he has a praetorship, I have self-respect. But I do not shout out where it is unseemly: I shall not rise up from my seat where I ought not; for I am a free man, and a friend of god, so as to obey him of my own free will; 10. but I must not lay claim to anything else, neither body, nor possessions, nor office nor fame; in short, nothing. For it is not his will that I should lay claim to them. For if this had been his desire, he would have made them my good, which in fact he has not done; therefore I cannot transgress his commands.' 11. In everything guard your own proper good, and as for the rest, guard them also to the extent that they are granted to you and you can use them

rationally. Otherwise you will be unfortunate, disappointed, restrained, hindered. 12. These are the laws, these the ordinances, transmitted to you from above; these are the laws you should interpret and offer your obedience to, not to those of Masurius and Cassius.

CHAPTER 4

# To Those Who Have Set Their Hearts On A Quiet Life

1. Remember that it is not only a desire for riches and power that makes you abject and subservient to others, but also a desire for quiet and leisure, and travel and learning. For the value you place on an external object, whatever it may be, makes you subservient to another. 2. What difference does it make, then, whether you desire to be a senator or not to be a senator? Or whether you desire to hold office or not to hold office? What difference does it make to say, 'I am in a wretched way; I have nothing to do, but am tied to my books as though I were a corpse'; – 'I am in a wretched way; I have no leisure to read'? 3. For as acknowledgements and the holding of office belong amongst things that are external and outside your control, so likewise does a book. 4. For what purpose do you wish to read? Tell me. If you turn to it merely for amusement's sake or to learn some novelty, you are frivolous and indolent. But if you judge it by the proper standard, what else is that but peace of mind? And if reading does not procure you peace of mind, what is the good of it? 5. 'But it does procure me peace of mind', someone says, 'and that is why it distresses me to be deprived of it.' – And what sort of serenity is that, which anything, not to mention Caesar or a friend of Caesar, but a mere crow, or a flute-player, or ten thousand other things can hinder? But nothing so characterizes peace of mind as being continuous and unhindered. 6. I am now called to do something. I now go, therefore, and will be attentive to the bounds and measures which ought to be observed, that I may act modestly, steadily, and without desire or aversion with regard to externals.

7. Furthermore, I am attentive to other people, to what they say and how they move, and this not from ill-nature, or to acquire the opportunity for censure or ridicule; but to enable me to turn to myself, to see if I too am committing the same errors. 'How, then, can I cease to do so?' Once I too was at fault; but, god be thanked, no longer. 8. Well, if you have acted like this and made this your concern, have you done anything worse than reading a thousand lines, or writing as many? For when you eat, are you aggravated that you are not reading? Are you not satisfied to be eating in conformity with the principles that you have read about? And likewise when you wash and take exercise? 9. Why, then, do you not maintain an even balance in everything, both in approaching Caesar, and in approaching whomsoever. If you are preserving your character as a man free from passion, who is not easily daunted or disturbed, 10. if you are more an observer of what goes on than yourself observed, if you do not envy those who are preferred to you, if the materials of action do not confound you, what do you lack? 11. Books? How, or to what end? For is not reading a kind of preparation for living, but living itself made up of things other than books? It is as if an athlete, when he enters the stadium, should break down and weep because he is not exercising outside. 12. This is what you were exercising for; this is what the jumping-weights, and the sand and your young partners were all for. So are you now seeking for these, when it is the time for action? 13. That is just as if, in the sphere of assent, when we are presented with impressions, some of which are evidently true and others not, instead of distinguishing between them, we should want to read a treatise *On Direct Apprehension*. 14. What, then, is the reason for this? It is because we have neither read nor written with this in view, to be able to treat in accordance with nature, in our actual behaviour, the impressions that befall us. Rather, we stop at learning what is said and being able to explain it to another, and at analysing syllogisms and examining hypothetical arguments. 15. And thus, where our enthusiasm lies, there also lies our impediment. Do you desire absolutely what is not in your power? Be hindered, then, be impeded, fail. 16. If we read a treatise *On Impulse*, not in order to see what is said about impulse, but so that we can direct our own impulses well; or a treatise *On Desire and Aversion*, so that we should never fail in our desires or fall into what we would avoid; or a treatise *On*

*Appropriate Action*, so that we may remember that in our social relationships we should do nothing irrational or contrary to what is appropriate 17. – if we read with this in view, we should not be aggravated at being hindered in our reading, but should be contented with the performance of actions suitable to us, and should not calculate as we have hitherto been accustomed to calculate. 'Today I have read so many lines; I have written so many'; 18. but, 'Today I have controlled my impulse as the philosophers direct. I have restrained my desires absolutely; I have applied my aversion only to things that are within the sphere of choice. I was not terrified by this person, nor put out of countenance by that. I have exercised my patience, my abstinence, my cooperation.' And thus we should be thanking god for what we ought to thank him.

19. But as it is we resemble the multitude in another way also, and are not aware of it. Another man is afraid that he shall not hold office; you, that you shall. You really ought not to be afraid of it, man; 20. but just as you laugh at him, laugh also at yourself. For it makes no difference whether a person thirsts for water in a fever or is afraid of water as a result of rabies. 21. Else how can you say, like Socrates, 'If god so pleases, so be it.' Do you think that if Socrates had set his desire on leisure in the Lyceum or the Academy, and daily conversation with the young men there, he would have gone out on so many campaigns, so often and so willingly? Would he not have lamented and groaned, 'How wretched I am to be here now in misery and affliction when I might be sunning myself in the Lyceum'? 22. Was that your task in life, then, to sun yourself? Was it not to be happy, to be free from hindrance and restraint? And how would he still have been Socrates, if he had lamented in such a manner? How could he, after that, have written paeans in prison?

23. In short, then, remember this, that if you attach value to anything outside the sphere of choice, you destroy that choice. And not only is office external to it, but freedom from office too; not only business, but leisure too. 24. – 'So must I now spend my life in the midst of this uproar?' – What do you mean by 'uproar'? Being amongst many people? – And where is the hardship in that? Imagine you are at the games in Olympia, think of this as a festival. There too one man shouts out this, another that, one man does this, another that, and one man

shoves against another; and the baths are overcrowded. But which of us fails to enjoy such a festival, and who is not sorry to leave? 25. Do not be hard to please, and squeamish at what happens. 'Vinegar is foul, for it is sour.' 'Honey is foul, for it upsets my constitution.' 'I do not like vegetables.' And in the same way, people say, 'I do not like leisure, it is a desert.' 'I do not like a crowd, it is an uproar.' 26. Why, if things turn out in such a way that you live alone or with a few other people, call this tranquillity and make use of it as you ought. Converse with yourself, work at your impressions, perfect your preconceptions. But if you fall in with a crowd, call it the games, a grand assembly, a festival. 27. Endeavour to share in the festival with the rest of the world. For what sight is more pleasant to a lover of mankind than a great number of men? We see companies of oxen, or horses, with pleasure. We are delighted to see a great many ships. Is one to be sorry at seeing a great many men? 28. – 'But they deafen me with their shouting.' – Then your hearing is hindered, and what is that to you? Is your faculty of dealing with impressions hindered too? Or who can restrain you from using in accordance with nature your desire and aversion, your impulse to act or not to act? What uproar is sufficient to do that?

29. Do but remember these general principles: 'What is mine? What not mine? What is allotted me? What does god will that I should do now? What does he not will?' 30. A little while ago it was his will that you should be at leisure, should converse with yourself, write about these things, read, hear, prepare yourself. You have had sufficient time for that. At present he says to you, 'Come now to the contest. Show us what you have learned, how you have trained. How long are you going to exercise by yourself? It is now time for you to learn whether you are one of those who are worthy of victory, or one of those who go about the world being constantly defeated.' 31. Why, then, are you vexed? There can be no contest without an uproar. There must be many trainers, many to cry out in applause, many officials to supervise, many spectators. 32. – 'But I wanted to live in tranquillity.' Why, lament then, and groan, as you deserve. For what greater punishment is there to those who are uninstructed, and disobedient to the orders of God, than to grieve, to mourn, to envy; in short, to be disappointed and unhappy? Do you not wish to deliver yourself from all this? – 33. 'And how shall I

deliver myself?' – Have you not heard many times that you must completely eradicate desire, and apply aversion to such things only as are within the sphere of choice? That you must give up your everything, body, reputation, fame, books, tumult, office, exemption from office. For the moment you stray from this course, you have become a slave, you have subjected yourself, you are made liable to hindrance, to compulsion; you are altogether the property of others. 34. But the saying of Cleanthes is always at hand: 'Lead me, Zeus; and thou, O Destiny.' Is it your will that I should go to Rome? Off to Rome. To Gyara? Off to Gyara. To Athens? Off to Athens. To prison? Off to prison. 35. If you once say, 'When can one get to Athens?', you are undone. This desire, if it be unfulfilled, must necessarily render you disappointed, and if fulfilled, vain about something that should not elate you: then again, if you are hindered, you incur misfortune, by falling into something that you do not wish. 36. So be done with all these things. – 'Athens is a fine place.' – But it is a much finer thing to be happy, to have a peaceful and undisturbed mind, to have what concerns you dependent on nobody but yourself. 37. – 'There are noisy crowds in Rome and people hailing one another.' – But a happy life is worth all the aggravations. If, then, it be a proper time for these things, why do you not withdraw your aversion from them? What need have you to carry your burden to the accompaniment of blows, like an ass? 38. Otherwise, consider that you must always be a slave to the man who has the power to procure your release or can hinder you in anything, and him you must serve as your evil genius.

39. The only way to a happy life (keep this rule at hand morning, noon, and night) is to stand aloof from things that lie outside the sphere of choice, to regard nothing as your own, to surrender everything to the deity and fortune, to appoint those to watch over things whom Zeus himself has appointed, 40. and to devote yourself to one thing only, that which is your own and free from all hindrance, and when you read, to refer your reading to this, and likewise when you write or listen to another.

41. Therefore I cannot call any one industrious if I hear merely that he reads or writes, and even if someone adds that he does so the whole night through, I cannot yet call him industrious, until I know what his aim is in doing so. For neither would you call a man industrious who sits up for the sake of a

girl, and neither do I. **42.** But if he does it for fame, I call him ambitious, if for money, avaricious; but not industrious. **43.** If, however, he refers his labour to his ruling faculty, in order to keep it (and thus live his life) in accordance with nature, then only do I call him industrious. **44.** For you should never praise or blame a person for things that can be either good or bad, but solely for his judgements. These are the peculiar property of each individual, and the things which make his actions good or bad.

**45.** Mindful of this, rejoice in what you have, and be contented with what the moment brings. **46.** If you see any of those things which you have learned and studied coming to pass for you in action, rejoice in them. If you have laid aside ill-nature and reviling; if you have lessened your impetuosity, indecent language, recklessness, laziness; if you are not moved by the same things as formerly, or at least not in the same manner as formerly, every day becomes a festival for you to keep; today, because you have behaved well in one action, tomorrow, because you have done so in another. **47.** How much better a reason for sacrifice is this, than obtaining a consulship or a governorship! These things come to you from your own self and from the gods. Remember who it is that gave them, and to whom and for what purpose. **48.** If you are brought up to reason in such a way, how can you enquire any longer as to where you will be happy, and where you will please god? Are men not equally far from god wherever they are? And wherever they are, do they not equally behold what comes to pass?

## CHAPTER 5

# Against Those Who Are Contentious And Brutal

**1.** A good and noble man neither quarrels with any one himself, nor, so far as he can, does he allow others to. **2.** The life of Socrates affords us an example of this too, as well as so much else, who not only always avoided quarrelling himself, but also tried to prevent others from doing so. **3.** See in Xenophon's *Symposium*, how many quarrels he ended; and, again, how he bore with Thrasymachus, with Polus, with Callicles; how with his wife; how with his son, when he was accused by him of using sophistical arguments. 4. For he well remembered, that no one is master over the ruling faculty of another, and therefore he desired nothing that was not his own. 5. – 'And what is that?' – Not that this or that person should be caused to act in conformity with nature, for that is not his business; but that while others carry out their own actions, as they think best, he himself should nevertheless be and live in conformity with nature, pursuing only his own business, in such a way that others also may be in accord with nature. 6. For it is this that the good and noble man always has in view. To become praetor? No; but if this be given him, to preserve the right conduct of his own ruling faculty. To marry? No; but if a marriage be given him, to keep himself in this matter too in accordance with nature. 7. But if he wishes that his wife or his child should never commit a fault, he is wishing that something which is not his own should be his own. And to become educated means just this, to learn what things are our own, and what are not.

8. What room is there, then, for contention if a person is thus disposed? For does he wonder at anything that happens? Does anything appear strange to him? Does he not expect worse and more grievous harm from bad people than does in fact come to him? Does he not reckon it as so much gained, as they fall short of the extreme? That man reviled you. 9. – I am much obliged to him for not striking me. – But he struck you too. – I am much obliged to him for not wounding me. – But he wounded you too. – I am much obliged to him for not killing me. 10. For when did the man ever learn, or at whose school, that he is a tame, that he is a social animal, that injustice is in itself of great harm to the man who inflicts it? As, then, he has not learned these things, nor been convinced of them, why should he not follow what appears to him to be his advantage? 11. 'My neighbour has thrown stones.' Have you on that account done any wrong? 'No, but things in my house have been broken.' Are you a piece of crockery, then? 12. No, but a man with the capacity for choice. What, then, has been given you to counter all this? If you consider yourself as a wolf – to bite back, to throw more stones. But if you ask the question as a man, examine what treasure you possess; see what faculties you have brought into the world with you. Surely no faculty for acting

like a brute, or for bearing malice? 13. When is a horse miserable? When he is deprived of his natural faculties. Not when he cannot crow, but when he cannot run. 14. And a dog? Not when he cannot fly, but when he cannot hunt. Is not a man too, then, unhappy in accordance with the same principle? Not when he is unable to strangle lions, or embrace statues (for he has received no faculties for this purpose from nature), but when he has lost his trustworthiness and beneficence. 15. This is the man for whom 'men should meet together and mourn, because he has fallen into such evils'; not, by Zeus, 'the man who is born', or 'the one who dies', but the man whose lot it has been while still alive to lose what is properly his own; not his patrimony, his paltry land or his house, his lodging or his slaves – for none of these are a man's own, but all belong to others, and all are in bond to, and answerable to, the gods their masters, who grant them now to one man, now to another – but his personal qualities as a man, the imprints which he brought into the world stamped upon his mind, 16. such as we seek in money, and, if we find them, allow it to be good, if not, throw it away. 'Whose imprint is on this sestertius?' 17. – 'Trajan's.' 'Give it me.' – Nero's. 'Throw it away. It will not pass, it is good for nothing.' So in the other case. 'What is the imprint on his judgements?' – 'He is gentle, sociable, patient, affectionate.' Bring him to me, I accept him, I make this man a citizen, I accept him as a neighbour and fellow-traveller. 18. Only, see that he does not carry the imprint of Nero. Is he prone to anger, is he malicious, does he like to find fault? 19. If the fancy takes him, he strikes at the heads of the people he meets. Why, then, did you call him a man? For surely the nature of a thing is not to be judged merely from its outward form? For then you would have to say likewise that a cobbler's apple is an apple. 20. No, it must also have the smell and taste of an apple; the outward appearance is not enough; nor, consequently, is the possession of a nose and eyes sufficient to prove somebody a human being, if he lacks the judgements that are proper to a human being. 21. Here is a person who does not listen to reason, and does not understand when he is refuted. He is an ass. Another is dead to any sense of shame. He is a worthless creature, a sheep; anything rather than a man. Here is another who is looking for somebody to kick or bite; so this one is neither a sheep nor an ass, but some kind of wild beast.

22. 'Well, would you have me despised, then?' – By whom? By those who have knowledge? And how can those who have knowledge despise a person who is gentle and modest? But, perhaps by those who lack it? And what is that to you? For no other craftsman cares about those who lack his skill. 23. – 'But people will be much the readier to attack me.' – What do you mean by *me*? Can any one hurt your choice, or prevent you from dealing according to nature with the impressions that are presented to you? – 'No.' – 24. Why, then, are you still disturbed, and why do you want to show yourself to be a man who is prey to fear? Why do you not make a public proclamation that you are at peace with all mankind, however they may act, and that you laugh most strongly at those who suppose that they are hurting you? 'These slaves neither know who I am, nor where my good and evil lies; and they have no access to what is really mine.' 25. Thus also do the inhabitants of a fortified city laugh at the besiegers. 'Why are these people giving themselves this trouble now to no purpose? Our wall is secure, we have provisions for a very long time, and supplies of every kind.' 26. These are what render a city secure and impregnable, but nothing but its judgements make the human soul so. For what kind of wall is so strong or what kind of body so impenetrable, or what possession so secure against robbery, or what reputation so unassailable? 27. For all things everywhere are mortal, and easily captured, and whoever in any way sets his mind on any of them, must necessarily be subject to perturbation, bad expectations, fears, and lamentations, and will necessarily be disappointed in his desires, and fall into what he wants to avoid. 28. Are we not willing, then, to strengthen the only means of security that is granted to us, and, standing aside from what is mortal and slavish, to direct our labours to what is immortal and by nature free? Do we not remember that no man either harms or benefits another, but that his judgement about each of these things is what harms him, and overturns him; and that this is contention, and inner conflict, and war? 29. What made Eteocles and Polyneices enemies was nothing else than this – their judgement concerning kingship and their judgement concerning exile; that the one was the greatest of evils, the other the greatest of goods. 30. Now, it is the nature of everyone to pursue good, and avoid evil, and to regard that man as an enemy and betrayer who deprives us of the one, and involves us

in the other, even though he be a brother, or a son, or a father. For nothing is more closely related to us than good. 31. It follows that if good and evil lie in externals, there is no affection between father and son, brother and brother; but all the world everywhere is full of enemies, betrayers, informers. 32. But if a right choice be the only good, and a wrong one the only evil, what further room is there for quarrelling, for reviling? About what? About what is nothing to us? Against whom? Against the ignorant, against the wretched, against those who are deceived in things of the greatest importance?

33. Mindful of this, Socrates lived in his own house, patiently bearing with an ill-tempered wife, and an unfeeling son. For what were the effects of her ill-temper? Throwing as much water as she pleased over his head, trampling his cake under her feet. And what is that to me, if I consider that these things are nothing to me? 34. But this, the right exercise of choice, is my task, and neither tyrant nor master shall hinder me against my will, nor multitudes the single person, nor the stronger man the weaker. For this is given by god to every one, free from restraint.

35. These are the judgements that bring about friendship in families, concord in cities, peace among nations. They make a person grateful to god, and confident in all his outward dealings, as having to do with things that are not his own, things of no inherent value. 36. But we, alas! are able indeed to write and read these thoughts, and to praise them when they are read to us; but we are very far from being convinced by them. 37. So what is said of the Lacedaemonians, 'Lions at home, foxes at Ephesus', applies to us too: lions in the lecture-hall, but foxes outside.

## CHAPTER 6

# To Those Who Are Distressed At Being Pitied

1. It pains me, he says, to be pitied. Is this your doing, then, or theirs who pity you? And further: is it in your power to prevent it? – 'It is, if I show them that I do not deserve their pity.' 2. But is this something within or something outside your power, not

to deserve pity? – 'I think it is within my powers. But these people do not pity me for what, if anything, would deserve pity, that is to say, my faults, but for poverty and lack of office, and diseases, and death, and other things of that kind.' 3. Are you, then, prepared to convince the world that none of these things is in reality an evil, but that it is possible for a person to be happy, even when he is poor and without honours and power? Or do you make a show in their presence of being a man of wealth and authority? 4. This latter course is the part of a braggart, and a mediocre, worthless fellow. Observe, too, by what means this pretence must be effected. You must borrow some paltry slaves, and possess a few pieces of silver plate and often show them off in public, and, if you can, show off the same pieces many times over, trying not to let people know that they are the same; you must have garish clothes and other finery, and make a show of being honoured by the most prominent people, and endeavour to dine with them, or be thought to dine with them; and use ignoble arts on your person, to appear better-looking and more distinguished than you really are. 5. All this you must contrive, if you would take the second course to avoid being pitied. But the first is impracticable, as well as tedious, to undertake the very thing that Zeus himself could not do: to convince all mankind what things are good and what are evil. 6. For has this been granted to you? Surely not. This alone has been granted to you, to convince yourself, and you have not yet done that. And yet you are now attempting to convince everyone else? 7. Why, who has lived as long with you as you have with yourself? Who could persuade you so convincingly as you could yourself? Who is better disposed or closer to you, than you are to yourself? 8. How is it, then, that you have not yet persuaded yourself to learn? Surely everything at present is upside down? Is this what you have been so concerned about? And not learning how to be free of pain, and disturbance, and humiliation, and accordingly, free? 9. Have you not heard, then, that there is only a single path that leads to this, namely, to give up the things that lie outside the sphere of choice, to relinquish them, and to admit that they are not your own? 10. What kind of thing, then, is another's opinion about you? – 'Something that lies outside the sphere of choice.' Is it nothing, then, to you? – 'Nothing.' While you are still nettled and disturbed by it, then, do you suppose that you are convinced as to what is good and evil?

11. Will you not, then, let others be, and become your own pupil and teacher? It is for others to consider whether it is to their advantage to be and live in an unnatural state; but no one is nearer to me than myself. 12. What, then, is the meaning of this? I have heard the arguments of philosophers, and assented to them; yet, in fact, my burden has become none the lighter. Am I so short of ability? Yet all the same, in whatever I have chosen to do, I was not found to be unusually dull, but learned my letters quickly, and wrestling and geometry likewise, and how to analyse syllogisms. 13. Can it be, then, that reason has failed to convince me? Why, there is nothing else that I have so approved or preferred from the very beginning, and at the present time this is what I read about, listen to, and write about. Up to this day we have not found a stronger argument than this. 14. What is it, then, that I lack? Is it that the contrary judgements have not been removed from my mind? Is it that I have not strengthened my convictions by exercise, nor accustomed them to come to grips with the facts, and like old armour that has been laid aside, they have grown rusty and can no longer be fitted to me? 15. Yet neither in wrestling, nor writing, nor reading, am I contented with mere learning: but whatever arguments are presented to me I twist in every direction, and I construct new arguments, and do likewise with arguments based on equivocal premises. 16. But the necessary principles, by which I might escape from fear, grief, passion and hindrance, and be free, these I neither exercise myself in nor devote the appropriate care to. 17. And then I trouble myself what others will say of me; whether I shall appear to them worthy of regard; whether I shall appear happy. 18. – Will you not see, wretch, what it is that you are saying about yourself? What sort of person you strike yourself as being? What kind of person in your thoughts, in your desires, in your aversions; in your impulse, preparation, intention, in the other works proper to man? Yet you are worried whether other people pity you? 19. 'Yes, but they pity me when I do not deserve to be pitied.' So that is what distresses you? But a man who is distressed, is he not worthy of pity? 'Yes.' How, then, can it still be said that you are pitied without deserving it? By these very feelings that you have about pity you make yourself worthy of pity.

20. What does Antisthenes have to say, then? Have you never heard? 'It is a king's lot, Cyrus, to do well, and to be ill spoken

of.' 21. My head is well and all around me think I have a headache. What is that to me? I have no fever and people sympathize with me as if I had one. 'Poor soul, what a long time you have had this fever!' I assume a lugubrious expression and say, 'Yes, it is really quite a time now that I have been far from well.' – 'What will come of it then?' 'As god pleases.' And at the same time I secretly laugh at those who are pitying me. 22. What prevents me, then, from doing the same in the present case? I am poor, but I hold the right judgement on poverty. What is it to me, then, if people pity me for my poverty? I am not in office, and others are; but I have the opinions that I ought to have concerning office and the want of it. 23. Let those who pity me look to their own, but I for my part am neither hungry nor thirsty, nor cold, yet because they are hungry and thirsty, they suppose me to be so too. What can I do for them, then? Am I to go about making a proclamation, saying, 'Do not deceive yourselves, good people, all is well with me. I pay no attention to poverty, or lack of office or, in a word, anything other than right judgements. These I possess free from all hindrance; I have given no thought to anything further.' 24. And what nonsense is this? How can I still have right judgements when I am not satisfied with being the man I am, but distraught about how I appear to others? 25. But others will get more than I do and be held in greater honour. – Why, what is more reasonable than that they who take pains for anything should have the advantage in that on which they have taken pains? They have taken pains to win public office; you, to acquire right judgements: they, concerning riches; you, concerning the proper use of impressions. 26. See whether they have the advantage over you in the things which you have taken pains over, but they neglect; whether their assent is more in conformity with natural standards; whether their desires are more unerring in their aim or their aversions fall less often into what they would avoid; whether in design, purpose and impulse they are better at hitting the mark; whether they abide by what is fitting as men, as sons, as parents, and then successively in other relationships according to their respective designations. 27. But if they are in office, and you not, why will you not tell yourself the truth – that you do nothing for the sake of office, but that they do everything, and it is most unreasonable, that he who takes pains over something should be less successful than he who neglects it. 28. – 'No; but because I take trouble over right judgements, it is more reasonable that I should rule.' – Yes, in what you take trouble over, your judgements. But in anything that others have taken more trouble over than you, you must give way. Otherwise it is just as if, because you have right judgements, you should expect when you shoot an arrow to hit the mark better than an archer, or to forge better than a smith. 29. So stop taking your judgements so seriously – the things you should concern yourself with are the things that you wish to acquire. And then lament if you fail to get them; in that case you have a right to. 30. But, as it is, you say that you are engaged on other things and devote your attention to these, and the popular saying that 'one business has nothing to do with another' is a good one. 31. One man gets up at dawn, and looks for somebody from Caesar's household to salute, somebody to address pleasing words to, somebody to send a present to, and thinks how he can please the dancer, and how he can gratify one man by reviling another. 32. Whenever he prays, he prays for things like these; whenever he sacrifices, he sacrifices for things like these. To these he transfers the Pythagorean precept 'Let not sleep approach thy weary eyes . . .'. 33. 'Where did I transgress: in matters of flattery? What did I do? Could it be that I acted as a free man, as a noble-spirited man?' If he discovers any such action, he rebukes and accuses himself. 'What business did you have to say that? For could you not have lied? Even the philosophers say there is nothing to stop one telling a lie.'

34. But if you have in reality given thought to nothing other than the proper use of impressions, then as soon as you get up in the morning ask yourself, 'What do I lack in order to be free from passion? What, to enjoy tranquillity? What am I? Am I a mere worthless body? Am I property? Am I reputation? None of these. What, then? I am a rational creature.' 35. What, then, is required of you? Go over your actions. 'Where did I transgress: in relation to peace of mind? What did I do that was unfriendly, or unsociable, or inconsiderate? What have I failed to do that I ought to have done with regard to these matters?'

36. Since there is so much difference, then, in men's desires, and actions, and prayers, would you yet have an equal share with others in those things about which you have not taken pains and they have? 37. And do you wonder, after all, and are

you annoyed, if they pity you? But they are not annoyed if you pity them. Why? Because they are convinced that they are in possession of their proper good; but you are not convinced that you are. 38. And thus you are not satisfied with what you have, but covet what they have; whereas they are satisfied with what they have and do not covet what you have. For, if you were really convinced that it is you who are in possession of what is good, and that they are mistaken, you would not even have given a thought to what they say about you.

## CHAPTER 7

# On Freedom From Fear

1. What makes a tyrant frightening? His guards, someone says, and their swords; the chamberlains, and those who shut the door on people who would enter. 2. What is the reason, then, that, if you bring a child to him when he is surrounded by his guards, it is not afraid. Is it because the child is unaware of the guards? 3. Suppose, then, that someone is indeed aware of them, and the fact that they have swords, and has come for that very reason, because he wishes, as the result of some misfortune, to die, and is seeking to die easily by the hand of another; does such a man fear the guards? – No; for he wants the very thing that renders them an object of fear. 4. Well, then, if someone who has no absolute desire to live or die, but is satisfied with what he is granted, comes before the tyrant, what prevents him from approaching him without fear? – Nothing. 5. – If, then, another should feel in the same way about his property or wife or children as the other does about his body, and, in short, from some madness or desperation, should be of such a disposition as not to care whether he has them or not; but, as children playing with potsherds contend with one another in the game, but are not concerned about the potsherds as such, this man likewise has come to count material things as nothing, but enjoys the game that is played with them and moving them back and forth, what tyrant, what guards, what swords are still capable of inspiring fear in such a man?

6. Then is it possible that a person can arrive at such an attitude towards these things through madness, or, as in the case of the Galileans, through mere habit, and yet that nobody should be capable of learning, through reason and demonstration, that god has made all things in the universe, and the whole universe itself, to be free from hindrance and perfect in itself, and all its parts to serve the needs of the whole? 7. All other creatures have indeed been excluded from being able to understand the divine governance, but the rational creature possesses faculties that enable him to reason about all these things, both that he is a part of them (and what kind of a part) and that it is well that the parts must yield to the whole. 8. And further, being by nature noble, great of soul, and free, he sees that, of the things around him, he has some that are free from hindrance and under his own control, whilst others are subject to hindrance and under the control of others; free from hindrance are those which lie within the sphere of choice, subject to hindrance are those which lie outside it. 9. And therefore, if he decides that his own good and advantage lies in the former alone, the things that are free from hindrance and under his control, he will be free, happy, self-fulfilled, safe from harm, high-minded, reverent, thankful to god for all things, never finding fault with anything that comes to be, nor accusing anything. 10. But if he regards his good and advantage as lying in externals and things outside the sphere of choice, he must necessarily be restrained, and hindered, and enslaved to those who have power over the things that he has admired and fears. 11. He must necessarily be irreverent, because he supposes that god is injuring him, and inequitable, because he is always claiming more than his share; he must necessarily be abject, too, and mean-spirited.

12. What is to prevent a man who has grasped these things from living with a light and easy heart, gently awaiting whatever may befall him, and bearing contentedly what has already befallen him. 13. Would you have me poor? Bring that on, and you will learn what poverty is when a good actor is playing the part. Would you have me hold office? Bring it. Would you have me out of office? Bring it. Would you have me suffer hardships? Bring hardships too. 14. And exile? Wherever I go it will be well with me, for it was well with me here, not on account of the place, but of my judgements which I shall carry away with me, for no one can deprive me of these; on the contrary, they alone

are my property, and cannot be taken away, and to possess them suffices me wherever I am or whatever I do. 15. 'But it is now time to die.' – What do you mean by 'die'? Do not talk of the matter in a tragic strain, but state the simple truth of it: 'It is now time for the material from which you were composed to be restored again to whence it came.' And what is so terrible about that? Is any part of the universe going to be lost? Will anything new or unreasonable be coming to pass? 16. Is it for this that a tyrant causes fear? Is it on this account that the swords of his guards seem so long and sharp? Try these things upon others. For my part I have considered everything, and no one has authority over me. 17. God has set me free; I know his commands; after this no one can enslave me. I have the proper emancipator; the proper judges. 18. 'Am I not master of your body?' What is that to me, then? 'Am I not master of your wretched property?' What is that to me, then? 'Am I not master of exile and imprisonment?' Why, all these, again, and my whole body I give up to you: whenever you please, test out your power, and you will find how far it extends.

19. Whom, then, can I be afraid of any longer? The chamberlains? Lest they should do – what? Shut me out? If they find me wanting to enter, let them shut me out. 'Why do you come to the palace gates, then?' – Because I think it fitting for me to take part in the game while it lasts. 20. 'How does it come about, then, that you are not shut out?' – Because if I am not admitted I do not wish to go in, but rather, my wish is always for what actually comes to pass; for I regard whatever god wills as being better than what I myself will. I shall attach myself to him as his servant and follower; I share the same impulses, share the same desires, in a word, I will what he wills. 21. Being shut out is not something that can happen to me, but only to those who push to get in. Why, then, do I not push in? Because I know that nothing good is handed over within to those who have entered. But when I hear anyone praised as happy because he is honoured by Caesar, I say, What has he gained? – 'A province or a procuratorship.' – Then has he gained also the judgement needed for governing a province? Or to employ when serving as a procurator? When, then, should I still try to thrust my way in? Someone is scattering nuts and figs. 22. Children scramble and quarrel for them, but not men, for they think it a trivial matter. But if anyone should scatter potsherds, not even children would

scramble for those. 23. Provinces are being distributed. Let children look to them. Money. Let children look to it. A praetorship, a consulship. Let children scramble for them. Let these be shut out, be beaten, kiss the hands of the giver, and of his slaves. 24. But to me they are but mere figs and nuts. But what if by chance while he is throwing them, a fig should fall into my lap? Pick it up and eat it; for one can value even a fig as far as that. But if I am to stoop for it, and upset somebody else or be upset by him, and flatter those who come into the palace, a fig is not worth this, nor any other of the things which are not really good, and which the philosophers have persuaded me not to regard as good.

25. Show me the swords of the guards. — 'See how big and how sharp they are.' So what do these swords do, big and sharp as they are? — 'They kill.' 26. And what does a fever do? — 'Nothing different.' And a tile? — 'Nothing different.' Would you have me, then, be struck with awe at all these things, and pay obeisance to them, and go about as the slave of them all? Heaven forbid! 27. But, having once learned that everything that is born must likewise die (so that the world is not brought to a standstill, or the course of it hindered), it no longer makes any difference to me whether this be brought about by a fever, or a tile, or a soldier; but, if a comparison has to be made, I know that the soldier will bring it about with less pain and more speedily. 28. Since, then, I neither fear any of the things that he can inflict upon me, nor desire any of the things that he can bestow, why am I any longer in awe of a tyrant? Why am I struck with astonishment? Why do I fear his guards? Why do I rejoice if he speaks kindly to me and receives me graciously, and tell others how he spoke to me? 29. For he is surely not Socrates or Diogenes, that his praise should be a proof of what I am? 30. Or have I set my heart on imitating his character? Rather, it is to keep up the game that I come to him and serve him, as long as he commands nothing stupid or improper. But if he should say to me, 'Go to Salamis and fetch Leon', I reply, 'Look for someone else — I am no longer willing to play.' 31. — 'Take him into custody.' I follow, as part of the game. — 'But you will lose your head.' And will he keep his own for ever, and will you who obey him? — 'But you will be thrown out unburied.' If the corpse is myself, I shall be thrown out; but if I am something other than the corpse, you should speak with greater subtlety, in

accordance with the facts of the matter, and not seek to frighten me. 32. Such things are frightening to children and fools. But if a man who has once entered into the school of a philosopher does not know what he himself is, he deserves to be afraid, and to flatter those whom he flattered previously; if he has not yet learnt that he is neither flesh nor bones nor sinews, but that which makes use of these, and governs impressions and understands them.

33. 'Yes, but such arguments make men despise the laws.' — What arguments are better suited to make the men who follow them more obedient to the laws? 34. Law is not within the reach of any fool. And yet, see how these arguments cause us to behave properly, even towards these fools, since they teach us not to claim in opposition to them anything in which they can surpass us. 35. They teach us to give way with regard to our poor body, to give way with regard to our property, with regard to our children, parents, brothers, to concede everything, to let everything go; only with regard to our judgements, which in accordance with the will of Zeus are each person's special property, do they make an exception. 36. What unreasonableness, what breach of the laws, is there in this? Where you are superior and stronger, there I give way to you. 37. Where, on the contrary, I am superior, you make way for me; for this has been my concern, and not yours. What you concern yourself with is how to live with marbled walls, how to be served by slaves and freedmen, how to wear fine clothes, how to have a great number of huntsmen, harpists, and tragic actors. 38. Do I lay any claim to these? But, on the other hand, have you concerned yourself with judgements, or even your own rational faculty? Do you know what its component parts are, and how they are connected and arranged, and what capacities it has, and their nature? 39. Why, then, do you take it amiss, if another who has studied these matters has the advantage of you here? — 'But these are of all things the greatest.' — Well, and who prevents you from busying yourself with them, and devoting your attention to them? Or who is better provided with books, with leisure, with assistants? 40. You have only to turn your thoughts to these matters some day, and bestow even a little time on your own ruling faculty. Consider what this is that you possess, and where it has come from, this faculty that uses all other things, that puts them to the test, and chooses, and rejects.

41. But as long as you occupy yourself with externals, you will have those, indeed, to an extent that no one else can match, but you will have this ruling faculty just as you want it, squalid and neglected.

## CHAPTER 8

# To Those Who Hastily Adopt The Outward Appearance Of Philosophers

1. Never praise or blame any one for things that can be either good or bad, nor ascribe to him either skill or lack of skill on that account, and then you will escape from both rashness and ill-nature. 2. 'This man washes hurriedly.' Is he therefore acting badly? Not at all. 'Well, what is it that he does?' Washes hurriedly. 3. – 'Does it follow that all things are well done?' – By no means. But what is done on the basis of right judgements is well done; and what is done on the basis of bad judgements is badly done. But until you know what judgement a person is acting upon in each case, neither praise his action nor blame it. 4. But a judgement is not easily discerned from externals. This man is a carpenter. Why? He uses an adze. So what does that signify? This man is a musician; for he sings. And what does that signify? He is a philosopher. Why? Because he wears a coarse cloak and long hair. 5. What, then, do beggar-priests wear? And because of that, when a person sees one of these behaving improperly, he immediately says, 'Look what the philosopher is doing.' But he should rather have said, on the evidence of his misbehaviour, that the man was not a philosopher at all. 6. For, if indeed the preconception which we have of a philosopher and his profession is to wear a cloak and long hair, they would be right; but, if it be rather to keep himself free from error, why do they not deprive him of the name of philosopher, because he does not fulfil that profession? 7. For that is what we do with regard to other arts. When we see any one shaping wood badly with an axe, we do not say, 'What is the use of this art? See how badly carpenters work.' But we say quite the contrary, 'This man is no carpenter, for he handles an

axe badly. 8. Likewise, if we hear anyone singing badly, we do not say, 'Observe how musicians sing', but rather, 'This man is no musician.' 9. It is with regard to philosophy alone that people take such an attitude. When they see any one acting contrary to the profession of a philosopher, they do not deprive him of the title, but assume that he is a philosopher, and then, finding from the facts of the case that he behaves badly, they conclude that being a philosopher brings no benefit.

10. 'What, then, is the reason for this?' The reason is that we pay some regard to the preconceptions which we have of the carpenter and the musician and likewise of other artists, but not to that of the philosopher, but because it is vague and confused in our minds we judge it by externals only. 11. And what other art is acquired from the manner of one's dress or hair, and has no principles, and subject-matter, and end? 12. What, then, is the subject-matter for a philosopher? Is it a cloak? – No; but reason. What his end? To wear a cloak? – No; but to keep his reason right. What are his principles? They have nothing to do, surely, with how one can grow a long beard or thick hair? – No; but rather, as Zeno says, to know the elements of reason, the nature of each one, and how they are adapted to one another, and what follows from all this. 13. Why, then, will you not first see whether by acting in an improper manner he fulfils his profession, and only then accuse the occupation itself? But as it is, when you yourself are behaving in a befitting manner, you say in reaction to the way in which he seems to you to be behaving badly, 'Look at the philosopher!' As if it was fitting to call a person who acts in that way a philosopher! And again, you say, 'Is that what being a philosopher means?' But you do not say, 'Look at the carpenter', or, 'Look at the musician', when you learn that one of them is an adulterer, or see one eating like a glutton. 14. So, in some small degree, even you perceive what the profession of a philosopher is, but you slip up and fall into confusion through your own carelessness. 15. But even those who are called philosophers pursue their profession by means that can sometimes be good and sometimes bad. As soon as they have put on a rough cloak and let their beard grow they cry, 'I am a philosopher.' 16. Yet no one says, 'I am a musician' because he has bought a lyre and a plectrum; nor, 'I am a smith' because he has put on a felt cap and an apron. But they take their name from their art, not from their gear.

17. For this reason Euphrates was right to say, 'I tried for a long while not to be recognized as a philosopher, and this was of benefit to me. For, in the first place, I knew that what I did rightly I did for my own sake and not for the spectators. I ate in a proper manner for myself. I was composed in my mien and my gait, and this was all for myself and for god. 18. And, furthermore, the contest was mine alone, so also was the danger. Philosophy was in no danger, if I did anything shameful or unbecoming; nor did I harm the rest of the world by committing faults as a philosopher. 19. For this reason, those who were ignorant of my intention used to wonder that, while I conversed and lived entirely with philosophers, I never assumed the part of a philosopher myself. 20. And where was the harm, that I should be discovered to be a philosopher by my actions and not by the outward signs?'

See how I eat, how I drink, how I sleep, how I bear and forbear, how I assist others, how I make use of my desires and aversions, how I preserve my relationships, natural or acquired, without confusion and without hindrance. Judge me by this, if you can. 21. But, if you are so deaf and blind that you would not suppose Hephaestus himself to be a good smith unless you saw the felt cap on his head, where is the harm of not being recognized by so foolish a judge?

22. It was in this way too that most people failed to recognize Socrates for what he was, and would come to him and ask him to introduce them to philosophers. 23. Did he become annoyed then, as we should, and say, What! do you not take *me* for a philosopher? No; he would take them off and introduce them, contented simply to be a philosopher, and rejoicing in not being annoyed that he was not taken for one. For he remembered his own business; 24. and what is the business of a wise and good man? To have many pupils? By no means. Let those who have made that their aim look to that. Well, then, is it to express difficult theories with precision? Let others see to that too. 25. In what then was he, and did he desire to be, somebody? Where his harm and his benefit lay. 'If', says he, 'anyone can hurt me, I am achieving nothing. If I wait for someone else to benefit me, I am myself nothing. I wish for something, and it does not come to be: accordingly, I am miserable.' 26. To such a field of combat he invited every one, and in my opinion, yielded there to no one. But in what fashion, do you suppose? Was it by

proclaiming, and saying, 'I am a man of such a kind'? Far from it; it was by actually being a man of such a kind. 27. For, again, it is the part of a fool and a braggart to say: 'I am free from passion and undisturbed. Be it known to you, men, that while you are agitated and confused over things of no value, I alone am free from every perturbation.' 28. Are you, then, so far from being contented with having no pain yourself, that you must needs announce: 'Come hither, all you who are suffering from gout, or headache, or fever, or are lame, or blind, and observe how I am free from every affliction.' 29. This is vain and vulgar, unless you could show, like Asclepius, by what treatment they may presently become as free from disease as yourself, and are bringing forward your own health as a proof of it.

30. Such is the Cynic, who is deemed worthy of the sceptre and diadem bestowed by Zeus, and says, 'In order that you may see, O mankind, that you are seeking happiness and tranquillity not where it is, but where it is not, 31. behold, I have been sent to you as an example by god, having neither property nor house, nor wife nor children, nor even a bed, or tunic, or furniture. And see how healthy I am. Test me out, and, if you see me free from perturbation, hear the remedies, and by what means I was cured.' 32. Now this truly is benevolent and noble-minded. But consider whose work it is: that of Zeus or the person he deems worthy of this office, such that he may never lay bare before the world anything by which he himself may invalidate his own testimony, which he gives in favour of virtue, and against externals.

> His fair features never paled, nor from his cheeks
> Ever wiped he a tear.

33. And not only this, but he must neither yearn nor seek for anything, whether it be man, or place, or pastime, as boys do for the vintage-time, or holidays; and he must be adorned on all sides by virtuous shame, as others are by walls, and doors and doorkeepers.

34. But, as it is, those who are only inclined towards philosophy, as dyspeptics are towards certain kinds of food (which they will soon come to loathe) immediately lay claim to the sceptre and the kingdom. Such a man lets his hair grow, assumes the rough cloak, bares his shoulder, contends with all he meets; and if he sees anyone in a thick, warm cloak, picks a quarrel

with him. 35. First, man, you must undertake hard winter training; see how you are with regard to appetition, that yours is not that of a dyspeptic, or of a woman with the cravings of pregnancy. First study to conceal what you are; 36. keep your philosophy to yourself for a while. For this is the way in which plants produce their fruits: the seed must be buried, and lie hidden for a while, and grow little by little, to bring the fruit to perfection. But, if it produces the ear before the stalk is properly jointed, the fruit is never perfected, as with the plants in a garden of Adonis. 37. Now, you are a plant of this kind. You have blossomed too soon, the winter will shrivel you. 38. See what farmers say about seeds, when the hot weather comes too early. They are in great anxiety, for fear that the seeds should grow with impertinent haste, and then, a single frost taking them, reveal their deficiency. You, man, should beware also. 39. You have developed with impertinent haste, you have sprung forward to win a petty reputation, before the proper season. You think that you are somebody, as a fool may among fools. You will be bitten by the frost; or rather, you are already frost-bitten down at the root; although you still blossom a little at the top, and thus you think you are still alive and flourishing. 40. Allow us, at least, to ripen naturally. Why do you lay us open to the elements? Why do you force us? We cannot yet bear the open air. Allow the root to grow; and allow the first, and then the second, and then the third, joint of the stalk to spring from it; and then, in like manner, the fruit will force its way out in accordance with nature, whether I wish it or not. 41. For who that has become pregnant and full with such judgements does not become aware of his own resources, and hurry on to the corresponding actions? 42. Why, a bull is not ignorant of his own nature and resources, when any wild beast approaches, nor does he wait for somebody to encourage him; nor does a dog, when he sees some wild animal. 43. And if I for my part have the qualifications of a good man, shall I wait for you to equip me for my own proper work? But take my word for it, I do not have them yet. Why, then, would you have me wither away before my time, as you yourself have withered away?

## CHAPTER 9

# To One Who Had Become Shameless

1. When you see another in power, set against that the fact that you have the advantage of not wanting power. When you see another rich, see what you have instead of riches. 2. For if you have nothing in their stead, you are miserable; but if you have the advantage of not needing riches, know that you have something more than he has, and of far greater value. 3. Another has a beautiful wife; you, the happiness of not desiring a beautiful wife. Do you think these are small matters? And what would those very persons, who are rich and powerful and have beautiful wives, give to be able to despise riches and power, and those very women whom they love and win? 4. Do you not know what the thirst of a man in fever is like? It has no resemblance to that of a person in health. A healthy man drinks, and his thirst is gone. But the other, after a brief gratification, feels nauseous, turns the water into bile, vomits, suffers colic pains, and is far thirstier than before. 5. It is much the same to have wealth and yet covet it, have power and yet covet it, sleep with a fine woman and yet covet her: jealousy will be there, and fear of being deprived, and shameful words, shameful thoughts, shameless deeds.

6. 'And what', someone says, 'do I lose?' – You were modest, man, and are so no longer. Have you lost nothing? Instead of Chrysippus and Zeno, you read the smut of Aristides and Euenus. Have you lost nothing, then? Instead of Socrates and Diogenes, you admire the man who can corrupt and seduce the most women. 7. You want to look fine and set yourself out to be what you are not, and parade in garish clothing to catch the attention of women, and, if you come across a good perfume anywhere, you count yourself blessed. 8. But formerly you did not so much as think of any of these things, but only where you might find a decent discourse, a worthy person, a noble thought. For this reason, you used to sleep like a man; to appear in public like a man; to wear manly dress; to hold discourses worthy of a good man. And after this, do you say to me, 'I have lost nothing'? 9. What, is cash the only thing that men can lose? Can

self-respect not be lost? Or decency? Or does the loss of these things carry no penalty? 10. You, indeed, no longer think, perhaps, that the loss of any of these brings any penalty; but there was once a time when you accounted this the only penalty and harm, and you were most anxious that nobody should drive you from these thoughts and actions. 11. See, you have indeed been driven from them, and not by another, but by yourself. Fight against yourself, recover yourself to decency, to self-respect, to freedom. 12. If, at one time, anyone had told you this about me, that somebody was compelling me to commit adultery, to wear such clothing as yours, to put perfume on, would not you have gone and murdered the man who was ill-treating me in such a fashion? 13. So now, are you not willing to help yourself? And how much easier such assistance is! You need not kill, imprison, or assault a man; you need not come into the market-place, you have merely to talk with yourself, the man who will be most readily persuaded, and to whom no one can be more persuasive than yourself. 14. So, in the first place, pass judgement on your actions; but when you have condemned them, do not give up on yourself, nor be like those mean-spirited people who, when they have once given way, abandon themselves entirely, and are, so to speak, swept off by the flood. 15. Rather, learn from the wrestling-masters. Has the boy fallen down? 'Get up', they say, 'and wrestle again, until you have gained strength.' 16. You too should think in some such way as that; for you should know this, there is nothing more tractable than the human mind. You have only to will a thing, and it comes to pass, and all is put right; and yet, on the other hand, you have only to doze off, and all is ruined. For both ruin and recovery come from within.

17. 'What good will I gain, then?' – And what good do you seek? Where once you were shameless, you will become self-respecting; where once you were disorderly, well-behaved; where once you were faithless, trustworthy; where once you were dissolute, self-controlled. 18. If you seek any greater things than these, go on acting as you do now. It is no longer in the power of even a god to save you.

## CHAPTER 10

# What Should We Despise, And What Should Be Important To Us?

1. All the difficulties and perplexities of men arise in connection with externals. 'What shall I do?' 'How will it come about?' 'How will it turn out?' 'I am afraid that this, or that, may befall me.' 2. All this is the talk of people who are occupied with things outside the sphere of choice. For who says, 'How can I save myself from assenting to what is false? or turning aside from what is true?' 3. If any one is so naturally gifted as to be anxious about these things, I will remind him: Why are you anxious? It is in your own power. Be assured. Do not rush to give your assent before you have applied the rule of nature. 4. Again, if somebody is anxious about his desire, fearing that it may fail to accomplish its end or hit its mark, 5. or about his aversion, fearing that it may fall into what it would avoid, I will start by giving him a kiss, because he has put aside the things that excite other men, and their fears, and has devoted his thoughts to his own business in the area where his true self lies; 6. then I will say to him, 'If you wish to desire and always hit your mark, and, with regard to your aversions, never fall into what you would avoid, then never desire anything that is not your own, nor direct your aversion towards anything that is not under your control. Otherwise you must necessarily fail in your desires and fall into what you would avoid.' 7. Where is the difficulty here? Where the room for, 'How will it be?' 'How will it turn out', 'May not this befall me, or that?'.

8. Now, as to how things will turn out, does that not lie outside the sphere of choice? – 'Yes.' – And does not the essence of good and evil lie within the sphere of choice? – 'Yes.' – Is it in your power, then, to make use of whatever turns out in accordance with nature? Can anyone prevent you? – 'No one.' 9. Then no longer say to me, 'How will it come to pass?' For, however it comes to pass, you will turn it to good use, and the outcome will be fortunate to you.

10. Pray, what would Heracles have been if he had said, 'What can be done to prevent a huge lion or a huge boar or

savage men from coming my way?' Why, what is that to you? If a huge boar should come your way, your contest will be the greater; if wicked men, you will rid the world of wicked men. 11. – 'Yes, but if I should die in doing so?' – You will die a good man, in the performance of a noble action. For since you must die in any case, you must necessarily be found doing something or other, whether it be farming, or digging, or trading, or holding a consulship, or suffering from indigestion or an attack of dysentery. 12. What would you wish to be doing, then, when death finds you? For my part, I would wish it to be something that befits a human being, some beneficent, public-spirited, noble action. 13. But if I cannot be found doing such great things as these, I should like at least to be doing that which cannot be impeded and is given me to do, namely, correcting myself, improving the faculty that deals with impressions, toiling to achieve tranquillity, and rendering to the several relationships of life their due; and, if I am so fortunate, advancing to the third area of study, that which deals with the attainment of secure judgements. 14. If death overtakes me when I am engaged in such things, it suffices me if I can lift up my hands to god and say, 'The faculties I have received from you to enable me to understand and follow your governance I have not neglected. As far as it lay in my power, I have not dishonoured you. 15. See how I have made use of my perceptions, how I have made use of my preconceptions. Have I ever found fault with you? Have I ever been discontented at any of your dispensations, or wished them otherwise? Have I transgressed in my relationships with others? 16. I am thankful that you brought me into being. I am thankful for the things that you have given me; I am content with the time for which I had the use of what belongs to you. Receive them back again, and assign them to whatever place you will; for all of them were yours and you gave them to me.'

17. Is it not enough to make one's exit in this state of mind? And what life is better and more becoming than that of such a person? Or what conclusion happier? 18. But, to attain these advantages, a man must accept some not inconsiderable difficulties and some not inconsiderable losses. You cannot wish for a consulship and these also, nor be eager to acquire acres and these also, or give thought both to your wretched slaves and yourself too. 19. But, if you wish for anything at all that is not your own, what really is your own is lost. That is the nature of

the matter: nothing is to be had for nothing. 20. And what is surprising in that? If you wish to be consul, you must stay up at night, run back and forth, kiss hands, pine away at other people's doors, say and do many slavish things, send many people gifts and daily presents to some. And what is the outcome? 21. Twelve bundles of rods, to sit three or four times on the tribunal, to give the games in the Circus and suppers in baskets to all the world; or let any one show me what more there is in it than this. 22. Will you then be at no expense and take no pains to secure freedom from passion and perturbation, to sleep sound while you do sleep, to be thoroughly awake while you are awake, to fear nothing, to be anxious for nothing? 23. But if anything belonging to you be lost or money be wanted while you are thus engaged, or another gets what you ought to have had, will you immediately begin fretting at what has happened? 24. Will you not compare what you have got in exchange for what? How much for how much? But you would have such great things for nothing, I suppose. And how can you? 'One business has nothing to do with another.' 25. You cannot devote your attention both to externals and to your own governing part. But, if you want the former, let the latter go, or you will succeed in neither, while being drawn both ways. 26. On the other hand, if you want the latter, you must be done with outward things. The oil will be spilled, the furniture will be spoiled, but still I shall be free from passion. There will be a fire when I am not there, and my books will be destroyed, but I shall deal with my impressions in accordance with nature. But I shall have nothing to eat. 27. If I am so wretched, death is my haven. That is every man's haven, death, and that his refuge; and, for that reason, nothing that falls to us in life is difficult. You can leave the house whenever you wish, and no longer be troubled by the smoke.

28. Why, then, are you anxious? Why do you lie awake at night? Why do you not calculate where your good and evil lie, and say, 'Both are in my own power; nobody can deprive me of the one, or involve me, against my will, in the other. 29. Why, then, do I not throw myself down and snore? What is my own is safe. As for what is not my own, let that be the care of the person who gets it, when it is given to him by the one who has the authority to give it. 30. Who am I to wish that what is not my own should be this way or that? For is the option given to

me? Has any one appointed me to administer such things? I am content with the things that are under my own authority. I must make the best I can of these, but other things must be as the master of them pleases.'

31. Does anyone who has these things before his eyes lie awake at night, and toss from side to side? What does he wish for, or what does he yearn for? For Patroclus, or Antilochus, or Protesilaus? Why, did he ever consider any of his friends to be immortal? Why, when did he not have before his eyes the fact that tomorrow or the day after he or his friend must die? 32. – 'Yes, very true', he says, 'but I reckoned that he would survive me, and bring up my son.' – Because you were a fool, and reckoned on uncertainties. Why, then, do you not blame yourself, rather than sit crying as little girls do? 33. – 'But he used to put out food for me.' – Because he was alive, fool; but now he cannot. But Automedon will put it out for you; and, if he too should die, you will find somebody else. 34. If the pot in which your meat used to be cooked should happen to be broken, must you die with hunger because you no longer have your usual pot? Do you not send out and buy a new one? He says, 35. 'For no greater evil could afflict me.' Is this what you call an evil, then? And instead of removing it, do you blame your mother for not predicting it to you, so that you could spend your whole life lamenting from that time forth?

36. What do you suppose? Did not Homer compose all this on purpose to show us that the noblest, the strongest, the richest, the handsomest of men may nevertheless be the most unfortunate and wretched, if they do not hold the judgements that they ought to hold?

## CHAPTER II

## On Cleanliness

1. Some dispute whether sociability is comprised in the nature of man, and yet these very people do not seem to me to dispute that cleanliness is undoubtedly comprised in it, and that by this, if anything, man is distinguished from other animals. 2. When,

therefore, we see one of the other animals cleaning itself, we are apt to exclaim in wonder that it is 'just like a human being'. And again, if someone accuses an animal of being dirty, we are at once apt to say, by way of excuse, that it 'is of course not human'. 3. Thus we regard this as a distinctively human quality, which we first received from the gods. For since the gods are by their very nature pure and undefiled, in so far as human beings have drawn close to them by virtue of reason they too cleave to purity and cleanliness. 4. But since it is impossible for the nature of human beings to be altogether pure, being composed of such material as it is, the reason which they have received from the gods strives to make it as clean as possible.

5. The first and highest purity, or impurity, then, is that which develops in the soul. But you would not find the impurity of the soul and body to be alike. For what other kind of impurity could you find in the soul than that which renders it unclean with regard to its own functions? 6. Now the functions of the soul are its impulse to act or not to act, its desires and aversions, preparations, intentions, assents. 7. What can it be, then, that renders it unclean and impure in these functions? Nothing other than its fallacious judgements. 8. So the impurity of the soul consists accordingly in bad judgements, and its purification in the production within itself of judgements of the kind that it ought to have; and a pure soul is one that has judgements of the right kind, for this alone is free from confusion and defilement in its own functions.

9. Now we should, as far as possible, endeavour to achieve something like this with regard to the body too. The composition of man is of such a nature that it is impossible that there should not be some mucous discharge. For this reason, nature has made hands, and the nostrils themselves as channels to let out the humours. If any one therefore sniffs them up again, I say that he is performing an action that does not befit a human being. 10. It was impossible that our feet should not get muddy and dirty when they pass through things of that nature. Therefore nature has provided water and hands. 11. It was impossible that some dirt from eating should not remain on our teeth. Therefore, nature says, wash your teeth. Why? That you may be a man, and not a wild beast or a pig. 12. It was impossible that, as a result of perspiration and the pressure of our clothes, something dirty which needs to be cleaned off should fail to be

left on our body. For this there is water, oil, our hands, a towel, a strigil, soap, and other apparatus required for cleaning the body. 13. You disagree? Yet a smith will remove the rust off his iron, and have proper instruments for that purpose, and you yourself will have your plates washed before you eat, unless you are thoroughly dirty and slovenly; but still, you will not wash nor purify your body. — 'Why should I?' (say you). 14. — I will tell you again. In the first place, so as to act like a human being; and, in the second, so as not to cause distress to those you meet. 15. You are doing something of the kind even here, without being aware of it. You think you deserve to have your own smell? So be it. But do you think those who sit by you deserve it too, and those who recline by you, and those who kiss you? 16. Go away, then, to some wilderness or other, where you deserve to be, and spend your life alone, smelling yourself; for it is right that you should enjoy your uncleanness alone. But since you are in a city, what sort of person do you suppose you are showing yourself to be, to behave in such a thoughtless and inconsiderate manner? 17. If nature had trusted a horse to your care, would you have overlooked and neglected him? Now, consider that your body has been committed to you like a horse. Wash it, rub it down, make it such that nobody will turn away from it or seek to avoid it. 18. But who does not avoid a man who is dirty, and smells and looks unwholesome, even more than a man who is befouled with dung? The stench of the latter is external and adventitious, but that which arises from want of care comes from within, as though from a kind of inward putrefaction. 19. — 'But Socrates rarely bathed.' — Yet his body looked radiant, and was so agreeable and pleasing, that the most handsome and noble were in love with him, and desired to sit by him rather than by those who had the finest features. He might have never washed or bathed if he had pleased, yet even the few baths he did take had their effect. 20. — But Aristophanes says: 'I mean the pallid men who go unshod' — Why, he says too that he 'trod the air', and stole clothes from the wrestling-school. 21. Besides, all who have written about Socrates affirm quite the contrary, that he was not only agreeable in his conversation but in his person too. And, again, they write the same of Diogenes. 22. For we ought not to frighten the world away from philosophy by our bodily appearance, but to show ourselves cheerful and untroubled, in our body as in everything else. 23. 'See, all of you, that I have nothing, that I need nothing. Without house, without city, and an exile (if that should come about), and without a hearth, I live a more happy and untroubled life than the nobly born and rich; and you can see that even my poor body is not injured by plain living.' 24. – But, if someone tells me this, who has the figure and visage of a condemned man, which of the gods will ever persuade me to come near philosophy, if those are the sort of people it produces. Heaven forbid! I would not do it, even if I was sure to become a wise man for my pains. 25. For my own part, by the gods, I would prefer that a young man, on feeling his first inclinations towards philosophy, should come to me with his hair finely dressed, than with it dishevelled and dirty. For that shows that there is in him a certain sense of beauty, and impulsion towards what is seemly; and where he imagines it to be, there he applies his endeavours. 26. All one has to do, then, is show him the way and say, 'You are seeking for beauty, young man, and in that you act well. You should know, then, that it springs from the part of you where your reason lies. Seek for it there, where you have your impulses to act and not to act, where you have your desires and aversions. 27. This is what is exceptional in you, whilst your paltry body is by nature merely clay. Why do you trouble yourself to no purpose about it? You will be convinced by time, if nothing else, that it is nothing. 28. 'But if he should come to me befouled, dirty, with whiskers down to his knees, what can I say to him, what sort of comparison can I use to draw him on? For what has he ever concerned himself with that bears any resemblance to beauty, 29. such that I can redirect his attention, and say, 'Beauty is not there, but here'? Would you have me say to him, 'Beauty lies not in being befouled, but in reason'? For does he in fact aspire to beauty? Does he show any sign of it? Go and argue with a pig, that he should not roll in the mud. 30. It was for this reason that the discourses of Xenocrates gripped even a Polemo, for he was a young man who loved beauty; he had come to Xenocrates with the first glimmers of an enthusiasm for the beautiful, though he was seeking it in quite another place.

31. Indeed, nature has not made dirty even the animals which associate with man. Does a horse wallow in the mud? Or a finely bred dog? No, but swine, and filthy geese, and worms, and spiders, which are banished to the greatest distance from

human society. 32. So do you, who are a man, not wish to belong even amongst the animals that associate with man, but to be instead a worm or a spider? Will you not take a bath on occasion, in whatever manner you please? Will you never wash yourself (in cold water, if you do not wish to use hot)? Will you not be clean when you come to us, to give pleasure to those who share your company? What, do you even enter our temples in such a state, where it is not lawful to spit or blow one's nose, when you yourself are nothing more than spit and rheum?

33. What, then, is anyone asking you to prettify yourself? By no means, except in those things where our nature requires it; in reason, judgements, actions; but as regards our body, only as far as cleanliness demands, and the avoidance of offence. 34. But if you hear that one should not wear purple, you must go, I suppose, and smear your cloak with dung or tear it to pieces. 35. Look, here is a young man worthy to be loved, here an old man worthy to love and be loved in return, to whom a man will entrust his son to be educated, and to whom daughters, to whom young men will come, if it so happens – so that he can address them from a midden! Heaven forbid! 36. Every deviation springs from something in human nature, but this comes close to not being human at all.

## CHAPTER 12

# On Attention

1. When you relax your attention for a while, do not fancy you will recover it whenever you please; but remember this, that because of your fault of today your affairs must necessarily be in a worse condition on future occasions. 2. First, and this is the gravest matter of all, a habit arises in you of not paying attention, and next a habit of deferring attention: and so you get into the habit of putting off from one time to another the happy and befitting life, that would enable you to live, and continue to live, in conformity with nature. 3. Now, if to defer things is advantageous, it is still more so to give them up altogether; but if it is not advantageous, why do you not

maintain your attention continuously? – 'I want to play today.' – What is to stop you, then, provided you attend? – 'I want to sing.' 4. What is to stop you then, provided you attend. For surely there is no part of life to which attention does not extend? For will you do a thing worse by attending, and better by not attending? And is there anything in life 5. which is best performed by inattentive people? Does a carpenter by not attending do his work more accurately? Does a helmsman by not attending steer more safely? Or is any other, even of the less important functions, performed better by inattention? 6. Do you not perceive, that when you have let your mind stray, it is no longer in your power to call it back, either to propriety or self-respect or moderation? But you do everything that occurs to you; you follow your inclinations.

7. To what, then, must I attend?

Why, in the first place, to those universal principles which you must always have at hand, so that you do not sleep, or get up, or drink, or eat, or approach other men without them: that no one is master of another's choice, and it is in choice alone that good and evil lie. 8. No one, therefore, has the power either to procure me good or to involve me in evil; but I alone have authority over myself with regard to these things. 9. Since these, then, are secure for me, what need have I to be troubled about externals? What tyrant can intimidate me? What disease? What poverty? What obstacle? – 'But I have not pleased So-and-so.' 10. – Is he my action, then? Is he my judgement? – 'No.' – Why do I trouble myself any further about him, then? – 'But he is thought to be a man of some consequence.' – Let him look to that, and they who think him so; 11. but I have one whom I must please, to whom I must submit, whom I must obey: god, and after him, myself. 12. He has entrusted me to myself, and made my choice subject to myself alone, having given me rules for the right use of it. If I follow these according to rigorous reasoning, I pay no regard to any one who says anything different, and give no thought to anyone who argues from equivocal premises. 13. Why, then, am I irritated by those who criticize me in the more serious matters? What is the reason for this perturbation? Nothing else than the fact that I have no training in this area. 14. For every science has the right to despise ignorance and ignorant people; and not only the sciences, but arts and crafts also. Take any shoemaker, take any smith you will, and he laughs at the rest of the world with regard to his own business. Take any carpenter too.

15. In the first place, then, these are the principles we must have at hand, and we must do nothing without them, but direct our soul to this mark, to pursue nothing external, nothing that is not our own, but rather to pursue – as he who has the authority ordained – things that lie within the sphere of choice, without reservation, and other things in so far as they are granted to us. 16. In addition to this, we must remember who we are, and what name we bear, and endeavour to direct our appropriate actions according to the rightful demands of our social relationships. 17. We must remember what is the proper time to sing, and to play, and in what company, and what will be out of place, lest our companions despise us, and we despise ourselves; when to joke, and whom to laugh at, and when to associate with others, and with whom; and when we do associate with others, how to preserve our own character. Wherever you deviate from any of these rules the damage is immediate; 18. not from anything external, but from the very action itself.

19. So is it possible to be altogether faultless? No, that is impracticable; but it is possible to strive continuously not to commit faults. For we shall have cause to be satisfied if, by never relaxing our attention, we shall escape at least a few faults. 20. But as it is, when you say, 'I will begin to pay attention tomorrow', you should know that what you are really saying is this: 'I will be shameless, inopportune, abject today; it will be in the power of others to cause me distress; I will get angry, I will be envious today.' 21. See how many evils you are permitting yourself. But if it is well for you to pay attention tomorrow, how much better would it be today? If it is to your advantage tomorrow, it is much more so today, so that you may be able to do the same again tomorrow, and not put it off once more, to the day after tomorrow.

## CHAPTER 13

# To Those Who Casually
# Divulge Their Personal Affairs

1. When we think that somebody has talked frankly to us about his personal affairs, we, too, are drawn in some way to reveal our own secrets to him, and suppose that this is frankness. 2. First, because it seems unfair that, when we have heard the affairs of our neighbour, we should not, in return, allow him a share in ours; and, next, because we think that we shall not give such people the impression of being frank if we keep silent about our personal affairs. 3. Indeed, people are often in the habit of saying, 'I have told you all my affairs; and will you for your part tell me none of yours? Now what is the reason for that?' 4. It is supposed, moreover, that we may safely trust a person who has already trusted us, for we imagine that he will never betray our affairs for fear that we, in our turn, should betray his. 5. It is in this way that reckless people are caught out by the soldiers at Rome. A soldier sits by you, in civilian dress, and begins to speak ill of Caesar. Then you, as if you had received a pledge of his good faith by his first beginning the abuse, say in your turn what you think; and so you are arrested and put in prison. 6. We experience something similar in ordinary life also. But even though this man has safely entrusted his secrets to me, shall I do so likewise to anyone who comes along? 7. No, I listen and keep silent (if I am that sort of person) but he goes off and tells everybody and then, when I find out what has happened, if I too am like him, out of desire of revenge I tell people his secrets, and so besmirch him and am besmirched. 8. But, if I remember that one man does not harm another, but that every one is hurt and benefited by his own actions, I come off better in this at least, that I do not act like the other man, but all the same, because of my own chattering I have suffered what I have.

9. 'Yes, but it is unfair, when you have heard the secrets of your neighbour, not to give him a share of your own in return.' 10. — 'Man, did I invite you to talk in such a way? Did you tell me your affairs upon condition that I should tell you mine in return? 11. If you are a babbler, and believe that everyone you

meet is a friend, do you wish that I too should become like you? And why, if you did well in trusting your affairs to me, but it is not well to trust you, do you want me to rush into doing so? 12. This is just as if I had a sound barrel and you a leaky one, and you should come and deposit your wine with me for me to put it into my barrel, and then should take it ill that I in my turn did not entrust my wine to you.' No; for your barrel has a hole in it.

13. How, then, are we still on equal terms? You deposited your property with a trustworthy man, and a man of honour, one who regards his own actions alone as being either harmful or beneficial, and nothing that is external. 14. Would you have me deposit mine with you, a man who has dishonoured his own faculty of choice, and who wants to get a little money, or a public post, or advancement at court, even if that meant killing his own children, like Medea? 15. Where is the equality in that? But show me that you are trustworthy, a man of honour, a man who can be relied on; show me that your judgements are those of a friend; show me that your vessel is not leaky, and you shall see that I will not wait for you to entrust your affairs to me, but I wil come and entreat you to hear an account of mine. 16. For who would not make use of a good vessel? Who despises a benevolent and faithful adviser? Who will not gladly welcome somebody to share the burden of his difficulties, and, by sharing it, to make them lighter? 17. – 'Yes, but I trust you, and you do not trust me.' – In the first place, you do not really trust me; but you are simply a babbler, who, by virtue of that, cannot keep anything back. For if what you say is true, entrust these things to me alone. 18. But as it is, whenever you see somebody at leisure, you sit down by him and say, 'Brother, there is not a man in the world who is better disposed or more of a friend to me than you; I invite you to listen to my affairs.' And you do this with people whom you have not known even for a short while. 19. But even if you do trust me, it is plainly because you think me a man of fidelity and honour, and not because I have told you my affairs. 20. Allow me, then, to form the same opinion about you. Show me that if a person has told his affairs to any one it is a proof of his being a man of fidelity and honour. For, if this was the case, I would go about and tell my affairs to the whole world, if, as a result, I was going to become a man of fidelity and honour. But that is not the case, and to be such, a

man needs no ordinary judgement. 21. If, then, you see any one taking pains about things that lie outside the sphere of choice and subordinating his own choice to them, be assured that this man has a thousand things to compel or hinder him. 22. There is no need of burning pitch or the rack to make him tell what is in his mind, but a little nod from a girl, if it so happens, is enough to shake him, a favour from somebody at Caesar's palace, desire for public office, or an inheritance, and a thousand and one other things of the sort. 23. So you must remember in general, that confidences demand good faith and judgements that accord with that. 24. And where, nowadays, can these easily be found? Pray, let somebody show me a person who is in such a good way that he can say, 'I concern myself only with what is my own, with what is free from hindrance, and is by nature free. This is what is truly good, and this I have. But let all else be as god may grant; it makes no difference to me.'

# THE HANDBOOK OF EPICTETUS

## I

Some things are up to us and others are not. Up to us are opinion, impulse, desire, aversion, and, in a word, whatever is our own action. Not up to us are body, property, reputation, office, and, in a word, whatever is not our own action. The things that are up to us are by nature free, unhindered and unimpeded; but those that are not up to us are weak, servile, subject to hindrance, and not our own. Remember, then, that if you suppose what is naturally enslaved to be free, and what is not your own to be your own, you will be hampered, you will lament, you will be disturbed, and you will find fault with both gods and men. But if you suppose only what is your own to be your own, and what is not your own not to be your own (as is indeed the case), no one will ever coerce you, no one will hinder you, you will find fault with no one, you will accuse no one, you will not do a single thing against your will, you will have no enemy, and no one will harm you because no harm can affect you.

Since you aim, then, at such great things, remember that it is not sufficient for you to be just moderately motivated to gain them, but that you must give up some things entirely and postpone others for the time being. But if you want to have both these and public office and riches too, you will perhaps not gain even the latter, because you are aiming also at the former, but you will certainly fail to get the former, by which alone happiness and freedom are obtained.

Practise, then, from the start to say to every harsh impression, 'You are an impression, and not at all the thing you appear to be.' Then examine it and test it by these rules which you have, and firstly, and chiefly, by this: whether the impression has to do with the things which are up to us, or those which are not; and, if it has to do with the things that are not up to us, be ready to reply, 'It is nothing to me.'

## 2

Remember that desire promises the attainment of what you desire, and aversion promises the avoidance of that to which you are averse, and that he who fails to gain what he desires is unfortunate, while he who incurs the object of his aversion experiences misfortune. If, then, you confine your aversion to those objects which are both unnatural and up to you, you will never incur anything to which you are averse. But if you are averse to sickness, or death, or poverty, you will experience misfortune. Remove aversion, then, from all things that are not up to us, and transfer it to things which are both unnatural and up to us. But, for the present, totally suppress desire: for, if you desire any of the things that are not up to us, you must necessarily be unfortunate; and none of the things which are up to us, and which it would be right to desire, is yet within your reach. Use only impulse and rejection; and even these lightly, with reservations and without straining.

## 3

In the case of everything that delights the mind, or is useful, or is loved with fond affection, remember to tell yourself what sort of things it is, beginning with the least of things. If you are fond of a jug, say, 'It is a jug that I am fond of'; then, if it is broken, you will not be disturbed. If you kiss your child, or your wife, say to yourself that it is a human being that you are kissing; and then you will not be disturbed if either of them dies.

## 4

When you are about to undertake some action, remind yourself what sort of action it is. If you are going out for a bath, put before your mind what commonly happens at the baths: some people splashing you, some people jostling, others being abusive, and others stealing. So you will undertake this action more securely if you say to yourself, 'I want to have a bath and also to keep my choice in harmony with nature.' And do likewise in everything you undertake. So, if anything gets in your way when you are having your bath, you will be ready to say, 'I wanted not only to have a bath but also to keep my choice in harmony with nature; and I shall not keep it so if I get angry at what happens.'

## 5

It is not the things themselves that disturb people but their judgements about those things. Death, for instance, is nothing terrible, or else it would have appeared so to Socrates too. But the terror lies in our own judgement about death, that death is terrible. So, whenever we are frustrated, or disturbed, or upset, let us never blame others, but only ourselves, that is, our own judgements. It is the action of an uneducated person to lay the blame for his own bad condition upon others; of one who has made a start on his education to lay the blame on himself; and of one who is fully educated, to blame neither others nor himself.

## 6

Do not be elated at any excellence which is not your own. If a horse in its elation should say, 'I am beautiful', it would be bearable. But when you are elated, and say, 'I have a beautiful horse', know that you are elated about what is, in fact, only the good of the horse. What, then, is your own good? The use of impressions. So that when you behave consistently with nature in the use of these impressions, you should be elated; for you will be elated about some good of your own.

## 7

When you are on a voyage, and the ship is at anchor, if you go ashore to get water you may pick up some small shellfish or vegetable on your way, but your thoughts should be fixed on the ship, and you should look back constantly in case the captain should call; and, if he calls, you must cast all these things aside, if you want to avoid being thrown into the vessel with your legs bound like the sheep. This is the case in life also: if, instead of a vegetable or a shellfish, a wife or a child is granted you, this need not hinder you; but if the captain calls, leave all these things and run to the ship without even looking back. And if you are old, never wander far from the ship, so that when the call comes, you will not be left behind.

## 8

Do not ask things to happen as you wish, but wish them to happen as they do happen, and your life will go smoothly.

## 9

Sickness is an impediment to the body, but not to the faculty of choice, unless that faculty itself wishes it to be one. Lameness is an impediment to one's leg, but not to the faculty of choice. And say the same to yourself with regard to everything that befalls you; for you will find it to be an impediment to something else, but not to yourself.

## 10

With regard to everything that befalls you, remember to turn towards yourself and ask what capacity you have for making a proper use of it. If you see a beautiful boy or woman, you will find self-control the capacity to use against this: if you are subject to pain, you will find endurance: if abuse, you will find patience. If you become used to this, impressions will not carry you away.

## 11

Never say about anything, 'I have lost it'; but rather 'I have given it back.' Is your child dead? It is given back. Is your wife dead? She is given back. Is your farm taken away? Well, that also is given back. 'But the person who took it was bad.' And does it matter to you through what means the giver demanded it back? For so long as he gives it to you, take care of it; but as something that is not your own, as travellers treat an inn.

## 12

If you want to make progress, give up such reasonings as these: 'If I neglect my affairs, I shall not have the means to live; if I do not punish my slave-boy, he will be bad.' It is better to die of hunger, but free from grief and fear, than to live in affluence with a disturbed mind; and it is better that your servant should be bad, than that you should be unhappy.

Begin therefore with little things. Is a little oil spilled? A little wine stolen? Say to yourself, 'This is the price paid for peace of mind, for freedom from disturbance, and nothing is to be had for nothing.' When you call your slave-boy, be aware that he is capable of not taking notice; or, if he does, of not doing what you want. But he is by no means of such importance that it should be up to him whether or not you are disturbed.

## 13

If you want to make progress, put up with being thought foolish and stupid with regards to externals, and do not want to be thought knowledgeable about them; and if some people think you a person who counts for something, distrust yourself. For you should know that it is not easy to keep your choice in accord with nature, and, at the same time, to keep external things; but while you devote your attention to the one, you must necessarily neglect the other.

## 14

If you want your children, and your wife, and your friends to live for ever, you are stupid; since you are wanting things that are not up to you to be up to you, and what belongs to others to be your own. In the same way, if you want your slave-boy to be without fault, you are a fool; you are wanting badness not to be badness, but something else. But if you want not to fail in getting what you desire, that is within your power. Exercise yourself, then, in what is within your power. Each person's master is the one who has power over what that person wants or does not want, so as to secure it or take it away. Whoever, then, wants to be free, let him neither want anything, nor avoid anything, that depends on others; otherwise, he must necessarily be a slave.

## 15

Remember that you must behave in life as you do at a symposium. Something is being passed round and comes to you: put out your hand and take your share politely. It goes by: do not detain it. It has not yet come: do not stretch your desire out towards it, but wait till it comes to you. Do this with regard to your children, to your wife, to public offices, to wealth, and the time will come when you are worthy to share the symposia of the gods. And if you do not even take the things which are set before you, but despise them, then you will not only share the symposia of the gods but also share their rule. For by so doing Diogenes and Heraclitus, and others like them, were deservedly divine and deservedly called so.

## 16

When you see someone weeping in sorrow at the departure of his child or the loss of his property, take care not to be carried away by the impression that he is involved in externals that are bad, but at once be ready to say, 'It is not what has happened that afflicts this person (for it does not afflict another), but his judgement concerning it.' As far as words go, however, do not shrink from sympathizing with him, and even, if the opportunity arises, from groaning with him; but be careful not to groan inwardly too.

## 17

Remember that you are an actor in a play, which is as the author wants it to be: short, if he wants it to be short; long, if he wants it to be long. If he wants you to act a poor man, a cripple, a public official, or a private person, see that you act it with skill. For it is your job to act well the part that is assigned to you; but to choose it is another's.

## 18

When a raven croaks inauspiciously, do not let the impression carry you away, but immediately draw a distinction in your own mind, and say, 'None of these omens applies to me, but either to my poor body or my poor property or my poor reputation or my children or wife. But to me all omens are favourable, if I want them to be. For whichever of these things happens, it is up to me to gain benefit from it.'

## 19

You can be invincible if you do not enter any contest in which victory is not up to you. When, therefore, you see someone honoured above you or holding great power or enjoying a good reputation in any other respect; take care that you are not carried away by the impression and call him happy; for if what is essentially of good lies in things that are up to us, there is no place for either envy or jealousy, and you, for your part, will not want to be a general, or a magistrate or a consul, but to be free. And the only way to freedom is to despise things that are not up to us.

## 20

Remember that what is insulting is not the person who abuses or hits you, but the judgement that these things are insulting. So when someone irritates you, realize that it is your own opinion that has irritated you. Try, therefore, in the first place, not to be carried away by the impression; for if you once gain time and respite, you will find it easier to control yourself.

## 21

Day by day you must keep before your eyes death and exile, and everything that seems terrible, but death above all; and then you will never have any abject thought, or desire anything beyond due measure.

## 22

If you set your desire on philosophy, prepare from the very first to be ridiculed and laughed at, to be jeered at by many people, and to hear them say, "Look, he has come back to us, a philosopher all of a sudden', and 'Where did he get that supercilious look?' You for your part should not put on a supercilious look, but hold fast to the things that seem best to you, as one who has been appointed by god to this position. Remember that if you remain true to the same principles, the very same people who laughed at you will afterwards admire you. But if you give way to them, you will be laughed at twice over.

## 23

If it ever happens that you turn to external things in the desire to please some other person, realize that you have ruined your scheme of life. Be content, then, with being a philosopher in everything; and if you wish also to be seen as one, show yourself that your are one, and you will be able to achieve it.

## 24

Do not allow these considerations to afflict you: 'I shall live without honour, and be nobody anywhere'; for if lack of honour is a bad thing, you can no more be involved in anything bad through someone else than you can in anything shameful. It is not your business, surely, to gain public office or to be invited to a dinner-party? Certainly not. How, then, can there still be dishonour here? And how will you be a nobody anywhere, when you only need to be somebody in those things that are up to you, in which you can be a man of the greatest worth? 'But my friends will be without help.' – What do you mean, without help? They will not be getting ready money from you, nor will you make them Roman citizens. Who told you, then, that these are among the things that are up to us, and not the business of someone else? Who can give to another what he does not have himself? 'Well, but get some money, then, so we too may have some.' If I can get it while keeping my sense of shame, trustworthiness, and high-mindedness, show me the way and I will get it; but if you require me to lose the good things that are mine so that you may acquire what is not good, consider how unfair and inconsiderate you are. Besides, which would you rather have, money or a friend who has a sense of shame and is trustworthy? So help me, rather, to gain this character, and do not require me to do things which will cause me to lose it. 'But my country', he says, 'so far as that depends on me, will be without help.' Here again, what kind of help do you mean? It will not have porticoes or baths provided by your efforts. And what does that matter? For it does not have shoes provided by the blacksmith or arms provided by the shoemaker. It is enough if everyone does his own job fully. If you supplied it with one more citizen who is trustworthy and has a sense of shame, would you be bringing it no benefit? 'Yes.' Well, then, you would not be useless to it. 'What place, then, shall I hold in the city?' Whatever place you can hold while maintaining your trustworthiness and sense of shame. But if, by wanting to be useful to the city, you lose these qualities, what use would you be to it, when you have become shameless and untrustworthy?

## 25

Has somebody been preferred before you at a banquet, or in being greeted, or in being called in to give advice? If these things are good, you ought to rejoice that he got them; and if they are bad, do not be grieved that you have not got them. And remember that you cannot, if you do not act in the same way as others do in order to acquire things which are not up to us, expect to be thought worthy of an equal share of them. How can someone who does not hang around a person's door, who does not accompany him as he walks around, who does not praise him, have an equal share with someone who does these things? You are unjust, then, and greedy, if you are unwilling to pay the price for which these things are sold, and would have them for nothing. At what price are lettuces sold? An obol, perhaps. If somebody, then, paying an obol, takes the lettuces, and you, not paying, go without them, do not imagine that he has gained any advantage over you. As he has the lettuces, so you have the obol which you did not give. So, in the present case, you have not been invited to such a person's banquet, because you have not paid him the price for which a meal is sold. It is sold for praise; it is sold for attention. Make up the price, then, if that is for your advantage. But if you would at the same time not pay the one and yet receive the other, you are greedy and stupid. Have you nothing, then, in place of the meal? Yes, indeed, you have: that of not praising someone you did not want to praise, and of not putting up with the people around his door.

## 26

The will of nature may be learned from those things in which we do not differ from one another. For instance, when our neighbour's little slave-boy has broken a cup, we are at once ready to say, 'Such things do happen.' Realize, then, that when your own cup is broken, you should be just the same as you were when another's cup was broken. Transfer the same principle to greater things. Is the child or wife of another dead? There is no one who would not say, 'Such is the human lot.' But when one's own child dies, it is all at once 'Alas! how wretched am I!' But we should have remembered how we react when we hear of this happening to others.

## 27

Just as a target is not set up to be missed, so what is bad by nature does not occur in the universe.

## 28

If someone handed over your body to any one he met along the way, you would be angry. But are you not ashamed that you hand over your judgement to anyone who happens to come along, so that, if he abuses you, it is disturbed and confused?

## 29

See *Discourse* 3.15.1-13.

## 30

Appropriate actions are generally measured by our social relationships. He is a father. This implies, taking care of him, giving way to him in everything, putting up with him if he abuses you, or hits you. 'But he is a bad father.' Is your natural tie, then, to a good father? No; but to a father. 'My brother is wronging me.' Well, maintain the status you have towards him. Do not examine what he is doing, but what you must do to keep your capacity for choice consistent with nature. No one will hurt you, unless you want that. You will be hurt when you think you are hurt. In this way, then, you will discover the appropriate actions to expect from a neighbour, a citizen, a general, if you acquire the habit of observing relationships.

## 31

Realize that the most important factor in piety towards the gods is to form right opinions about them as beings that exist and govern the universe well and justly, and to have set yourself to obey them, and to submit to all that happens, and willingly follow it, as something that is being brought to pass by the most perfect intelligence. For in that way you will never find fault with the gods, nor accuse them of neglecting you. And it is not possible for this to be achieved in any other way than by withdrawing your conception of good and evil from things that are not up to us, and placing it only in those that are. For if you suppose any of the things that are not up to us to be either good or evil, then, when you fail to get what you want and fall into what you do not want, you must necessarily blame and despise those who are responsible for this. For every animal is naturally formed to flee and abhor things that appear harmful, and the causes of them; and to pursue and admire those that appear beneficial, and the causes of them. It is impossible, then, that one who supposes himself to be harmed should rejoice in what he thinks is harming him, just as it is impossible to rejoice in the harm itself. And so it comes that even a father is reviled by his son, when the father fails to give him a share of the things that he takes to be good; and it was the thought that a throne is a good thing that made Polyneices and Eteocles enemies to one another. That is why the farmer, the sailor, the merchant, and those who lose wives and children, revile the gods. For where a person's interest lies, there also lies his piety. It follows that whoever is careful to regulate his desires and aversions as he ought, is at the same time careful about piety also. But it is also fitting on each occasion to offer libations and sacrifices and first fruits, according to the custom of our fathers, with purity, and not in a slovenly manner, nor negligently, nor indeed stingily, nor yet beyond one's means.

## 32

When you have recourse to divination, remember that you do not know what the outcome will be, and you have come to learn it from the diviner; but you do know beforehand what kind of thing it must be, if you are really a philosopher. For if it is amongst the things that are not up to us, it can by no means be either good or evil. Do not, therefore, bring either desire or aversion with you to the diviner, and do not approach him with trembling, but after first being clear in your mind that every outcome is indifferent and nothing to you and that, whatever its nature may be, it will be in your power to make good use of it, and this no one can hinder. So go with confidence to the gods, as your counsellors, and afterwards, when some counsel has been granted to you, remember whom you have taken as your counsellors, and whom you will be disregarding if you disobey. Resort to divination, as Socrates thought right, in cases of which the whole inquiry turns upon the outcome, and in which no opportunities are afforded by reason, or any other art, to discover what lies before one. When, therefore, it is your duty to share the danger of a friend or of your country, you should not resort to divination to ask whether you should share it with them or not. For, if the diviner should forewarn you that the omens are unfavourable, this means no more than that either death or injury to some part of your body, or exile, is portended; but reason proves that even if you are confronted by these, you must stand by your friend and share the danger with your country. Pay heed, therefore, to that greater diviner, the Pythian Apollo, who cast out of his temple the man who gave no assistance to his friend when he was being murdered.

## 33

Lay down from this moment a certain character and pattern of behaviour for yourself, which you will preserve when you are alone and also when you are in company.

Be for the most part silent, or speak merely what is necessary, and in few words. Speak but rarely, when the occasion calls for it, but not about anything that happens to come up; do not talk about gladiators, or horse races, or athletes, or food and drink, the topics that arise on every occasion, but above all, do not talk about individuals, either to praise, or to blame, or to compare them. If you are able, then, you should by your own conversation bring over that of your companions also to what is fitting; but, if you happen to be left on your own among strangers, be silent.

Do not laugh much, nor at many things, nor without restraint.

Avoid oaths, if possible, altogether; if not, as far as you are able.

Avoid entertainments given by outsiders who are ignorant of philosophy; but, if ever an occasion calls you to them, keep your attention strained, lest you slip back into a layman's state. For be assured that if a person be ever so clean himself, yet, if his companion be dirty, he who converses with him will become dirty likewise.

In things relating to the body take just so much as bare need requires, that is to say, in things such as meat, drink, clothing, housing, and household slaves. But cut out everything that is for show and luxury.

As regards sexual matters, you should remain pure, so far as you can, before marriage, and, if you indulge, let it be lawfully. But do not therefore become aggravating or censorious to those who do indulge, nor frequently boast that you yourself do not.

If someone tells you that So-and-so is speaking ill of you, do not defend yourself against what has been said, but answer: 'He did not know my other faults, for otherwise he would not have mentioned only these.'

There is no need for the most part to go to public shows; but if there ever be occasion for you to go, show that your primary concern is for none other than yourself; that is, wish things to happen precisely as they do, and wish only the winner to win, for in that way you will meet with no hindrance. But refrain entirely from shouting or laughing at anyone or in general getting too excited. And when you come away, do not talk a great deal about what took place, except in so far as it tends to your own improvement; for it would appear from such talk that you were impressed by the show.

Do not go casually or readily to people's public readings; but if you do go, preserve your dignity and composure, and at the same time take care not to cause offence.

When you are going to meet with any one, and particularly somebody who is held in very high regard, put the question to yourself, 'What would Socrates or Zeno have done in this situation?', and you will not be at a loss to make a proper use of the occasion.

When you are going to see some man of great power, put the thought to yourself that you will not find him at home, that you will be shut out, that the doors will be slammed on you, that he will take no notice of you. If, in spite of all this, it be your duty to go, go, and put up with what happens, and never say to yourself, 'It was not worth all that.' For this is the mark of a layman, a man disconcerted by externals.

In your conversation, avoid frequent and excessive mention of your own actions and the dangers you have faced. For, however pleasurable it may be to yourself to mention the risks you have run, it is not equally so to others to hear about what has befallen you. Avoid, likewise, any attempt to excite laughter, for this is a habit that tends to slip into vulgarity, and, at the same time, may be apt to lessen your neighbours' respect for you. Lapses into foul language are likewise dangerous. When, therefore, anything of this sort happens, if there be a proper opportunity, you should rebuke the person who lapses in this way; or, if there is not, show by your silence and blushing and frowning that you are displeased by such talk.

## 34

When you are struck by the impression of some pleasure, guard yourself, as with impressions generally, against being carried away by it; rather, let the matter await your leisure, and allow yourself a measure of delay. Then bring to mind both of these moments in time: that in which you will enjoy the pleasure, and that in which you will repent and reproach yourself after you have enjoyed it; and set against these, how you will rejoice and praise yourself if you abstain. But if you feel that it is the right moment to embark upon the action, take heed that you are not overcome by its enticement and its seductions and attractions; but set against this how much better it is to be conscious of having gained a victory over it.

## 35

When you do anything from a clear judgement that it ought to be done, never try not to be seen doing it, even though most people are going to think anything but favourably of it; for, if you are not acting rightly, avoid the action itself; but, if you are, why be afraid of those who will reproach you wrongly?

## 36

Just as the propositions 'It is day' and 'It is night' are of consider-able value when taken separately, but valueless when joined into one, so, at a feast, to choose the largest share may be of value to your body, but is of no value at all when it comes to maintaining good fellowship. When you eat with another, then, remember not only the value to your body of what is set before you, but also the value of maintaining a proper respect for your host.

## 37

If you take on a role that is beyond your powers, you not only disgrace yourself in that role, but you neglect the role that you were capable of fulfilling.

## 38

As, when walking about, you take care not to tread upon a nail or twist your foot, so likewise take care not to harm your ruling faculty. And, if we guard against this in every action, we shall set to work more securely.

## 39

Each person's body is a measure for his property, as the foot is for his shoe. If, therefore, you stop at this, you will keep the measure, but if you step beyond it, you are sure in the end to fall down a cliff; as in the case of a shoe, if you go beyond the foot, it comes first to be gilded, then purple and embroidered. For once you go beyond the measure there is no limit.

## 40

Straightaway from fourteen years upwards, women are addressed as 'lady' by men. And so when they see that there is nothing else than to become the bed-fellows of men, they begin to beautify themselves, and place all their hopes in that. It is worthwhile, therefore, that we should take trouble to make them realize that they are honoured for nothing other than appearing well behaved and modest.

## 41

It is the mark of a want of natural talent to spend much time on things relating to the body, as in exercising a great deal, in eating and drinking a great deal, and often emptying one's bowels and copulating. These should be done in passing; and you should turn all your attention to the care of your mind.

## 42

When someone acts badly towards you, or speaks badly of you, remember that he is acting or speaking in that way because he thinks that it is appropriate for him to do so. Now, it is not possible that he should follow what appears good to you, but rather, what appears so to him, so that if he judges wrongly, he is the person harmed since he too is the person deceived. For if any one should suppose a composite judgement to be false, the composite judgement is not harmed, but he who is deceived about it. Setting out, then, from this principle, you will be gentle with a person who reviles you, for you will say on each occasion, 'It seemed so to him.'

## 43

Everything has two handles, by one of which it may be carried, and by the other not. If your brother wrongs you, do not take it by this handle, that he is wronging you (for this is the handle that it cannot be carried by), but by the other, that he is your brother, that he was brought up with you, and then you will be taking it by the handle by which it ought to be carried.

## 44

These arguments do not follow: 'I am richer than you, therefore I am superior to you'; 'I am more eloquent than you, therefore I am superior to you.' No, these are the arguments that follow: 'I am richer than you, therefore my property is superior to yours'; 'I am more eloquent than you, therefore my style is superior to yours.' But *you*, after all, are neither property nor style.

## 45

Does someone take his bath quickly? Do not say that he does it badly, but that he does it quickly. Does any one drink a great quantity of wine? Do not say that he drinks badly, but that he drinks a great quantity. For, unless you understand the judgement from which he acts, how should you know that he is acting badly? And thus it will not come to pass that you receive convincing impressions of some things, but give your assent to different ones.

## 46

Never call yourself a philosopher, nor talk a great deal amongst laymen about philosophical principles, but do what follows from those principles. Thus, at a banquet, do not say how people ought to eat, but eat as one ought. For remember how Socrates had so completely set aside all ostentation that when people came to him wanting to be introduced by him to philosophers, he took them along and introduced them, so well did he bear being overlooked. So that if talk should arise amongst laymen on some philosophical principle, remain, for the most part, silent; for there is a considerable danger that you will immediately vomit up what you have not yet digested. And when someone one tells you that you know nothing and you are not nettled by it, then you may be sure that you are setting to work at your task. For sheep do not bring their fodder to the shepherds to show how much they have eaten, but digest their food internally, and produce wool and milk externally. And so you likewise should not display your principles to laymen, but rather show them the actions that result from these principles once they have been digested.

## 47

When you have become adapted to the simple of life in bodily matters, do not pride yourself upon it; nor, if you drink only water, be saying on every occasion, 'I drink only water.' And if at any time you want to train yourself to endure hardship, do it for your own sake, and not for the world; do not embrace statues, but, when you are violently thirsty, take a little cold water in your mouth, and then spit it out and tell nobody.

## 48

The condition and character of a layman is that he never expects either benefit or harm from himself, but solely from externals. The condition and character of a philosopher is that he expects all harm and benefit from himself. The signs of one making progress are that he censures no one, praises no one, blames no one, accuses no one, never speaks of himself as being anybody, or knowing anything; when he is obstructed or hindered in anything, he accuses himself; and, if he is praised, he laughs within himself at the person who is praising him; and, if he is censured, he makes no defence. But he goes about like an invalid taking care not to disturb any part of him that is healing before it is perfectly fixed. He has rid himself of all desire; he has transferred his aversion to those things only which are up to us but contrary to nature. He is moderate in his impulses towards all things. If he appears foolish or ignorant, he does not care, and, in a word, he keeps guard against himself as his own enemy, and one lying in wait for him.

## 49

When a person shows himself vain at being able to understand and interpret the works of Chrysippus, say to yourself, 'If Chrysippus had not written obscurely, this person would have had no occasion for his vanity. Now what do I want? To understand nature and follow her. I seek for someone then, to interpret her, and, hearing that Chrysippus does so, I go to him. But I do not understand his writings. I seek, therefore, for a person to interpret them.' Thus far there is nothing to be vain about. And when I find the interpreter, what remains is to make use of what has been transmitted. This alone is the thing to be proud of. But, if what I admire is the mere act of interpretation, what else have I ended up as but a grammarian instead of a philosopher? Except, indeed, that instead of interpreting Homer I interpret Chrysippus. So when somebody says to me, 'Read me some Chrysippus', I blush rather than feel proud, when I cannot show him actions that are in agreement and harmony with Chrysippus' words.

## 50

Whatever rules you have set for yourself, abide by them as so many laws, and as if it would be an impiety for you to transgress them; and pay no heed to what any one says of you, for this, in the end, is no concern of yours.

## 51

How much longer will you wait before you think yourself worthy of the best things and transgress in nothing the distinctions laid down by reason? You have received the philosophical precepts that you should assent to, and you have given your assent to them. What sort of a teacher, then, are you still waiting for, that you should delay setting yourself right until he comes? You are no longer a boy, but a grown man. If now you are negligent and idle, and always making one delay after another, and setting one day after another as the time when you will begin to pay attention to yourself, then you will fail to realize that you are making no progress, but will continue to be a layman, both in life and in death. From this moment, then, you should consider yourself worthy of living as a grown man and one who is making progress; and let whatever appears to be best be an inviolable law to you. And if you meet with anything that is burdensome or sweet, or glorious or inglorious, remember that now is the time of the contest, and the Olympic games have arrived, and that you cannot defer things any longer, and that it rests on a single day and a single action whether your progress is lost or maintained. That was how Socrates became the man he was, by heeding nothing but his reason in all that he encountered. And even if you are not yet a Socrates, you should live as one who does indeed wish to be a Socrates.

## 52

The first and most necessary area of philosophy is the one that deals with the application of principles, such as 'We ought not to lie'; the second deals with demonstrations, for instance, 'How is it that we ought not to lie?'; the third confirms and analyses the other two, for instance, 'How comes it that this is a demonstration?' For what is a demonstration, what is logical consequence, what contradiction, what truth, and what falsehood?' The third area of study, then, is necessary on the account of the second, and the second on the account of the first. But the most necessary, and that on which we should dwell, is the first. But we do the reverse. For we spend all our time on the third topic, and employ all our effort that, and entirely neglect the first. Therefore we speak falsely, but are quite ready to show how it is demonstrated that one ought not to speak falsely.

## 53

On every occasion we ought to have these thoughts at hand:

> Lead me, Zeus, and thou, O Destiny,
> To wheresoever your decrees have assigned me.
> I follow cheerfully; or if my will should fail,
> Base though I be, I must follow still.

> 'Whoever yields duly to necessity we deem
> Wise among men, and wise in things divine.

> 'Well, Crito, if this is what pleases the gods, so be it.'

> 'Anytus and Meletus can kill me, but they cannot harm me.'

# FRAGMENTS

## I

What does it matter to me, says Epictetus, whether the universe is composed of atoms or uncompounded substances, or of fire and earth? Is it not sufficient to know the true nature of good and evil, and the proper bounds of our desires and aversions, and also of our impulses to act and not to act; and by making use of these as rules to order the affairs of our life, to bid those things that are beyond us farewell (which, perhaps, are incomprehensible to the human mind, but even if one should suppose them to be wholly comprehensible, still, what good does it do to comprehend them?) And must it not be said that those who accredit these things as necessary to the thinking of a philosopher are giving themselves trouble to no purpose? Is, then, the Delphic admonition, 'Know thyself', superfluous? – 'Surely not', the man replies. – What, then, does it mean? If one told the singer in a chorus to know himself, would he not attend to the order by paying regard to his partners in the chorus and taking care to sing in harmony with them? – 'Yes.' – And likewise with a soldier or a sailor. Do you suppose, then, that man is a creature who has been made to live all by himself, or for society? – 'For society.' – By whom? – 'By Nature.' – As to what Nature is, and how she governs the universe, and whether she really exists or not, these are things that we need not busy ourselves with any further now.

## 2

He who is discontented with what he has and what has been granted to him by fortune is a layman in the art of life. But he who bears it nobly, and acts rationally with regard to all that arises from it, deserves to be acknowledged as a good man.

## 3

All things obey and serve the universe, both earth and sea and the sun and the other stars, and the plants and animals of the earth. Our body likewise obeys it, both in sickness and health (when the universe wills) and when young and old, and as it passes through all other changes. It is therefore reasonable also that what depends on ourselves, that is to say, our judgement, should not be the only thing to strive against it. For the universe is powerful, and superior to ourselves, and has taken better counsel on our behalf than we can, by embracing us too in its governance in conjunction with the whole. Moreover, to act against it is to align ourselves with unreason, and achieving nothing but futile harassment, embroils us in pains and sorrows.

## 4

Of all things that are, god has laid down that some are within our powers, and some are not. Within our power is the finest and most excellent of things, and that through which he himself is happy, the capacity to make use of impressions. For when this capacity is rightly exercised, it is freedom, peace, cheerfulness, constancy, and justice too, and law, and self-control, and virtue in its entirety. But god has placed all else beyond our power. Therefore we also should come to be of one mind with god, and, dividing matters in this fashion, lay claim by every means to what is within our power, but what is not within our power we should entrust to the universe, and if it should have need of our children, or our country, or our body, or anything else whatever, we should gladly yield it up.

## 5

Who amongst us does not admire the saying of Lycurgus the Lacedaemonian? For when he had been blinded in one eye by one of his fellow-citizens, and the people handed the young man over for him to take whatever vengeance he might wish, Lycurgus refrained from vengeance, but educated him instead and made a good man of him, and brought him into the theatre; and, when the Lacedaemonians wondered at this, he said, 'This man was insolent and violent when I received him from you, and I am restoring him to you as a decent man and a good citizen.'

## 6

But this above all else is the function of nature, to bind our impulses to, and bring them into harmony with, our impression of what is fitting and beneficial.

## 7

It is the part of thoroughly mean-spirited and foolish men to suppose we shall be despised by others, unless, by every possible means, we harm the first enemies we come across; for we are inclined to say that a man can be recognized as contemptible by his incapacity to do harm; but he is much better recognized as such by his incapacity to be of help.

## 8

Such was, and is, and will be, the nature of the universe, and it is not possible that things should happen otherwise than they now do; and not only has mankind participated in this change and transformation, and the other living creatures, but the divine beings also, and, by Zeus, even the four elements, which are transformed and changed upwards and downwards, as earth becomes water, and water air, and air in turn is transformed into ether; and the same manner of transformation takes place from above in a downward direction. If a man endeavours to turn his mind towards these things, and to persuade himself to accept of his own free will what cannot be avoided, he will live a measured and harmonious life.

## 9

The way things look to the mind (what philosophers call 'impressions') have an immediate psychological impact and are not subject to one's wishes, but force human beings to recognize them by a certain inherent power. But the acts of approval (what philosophers call 'assents') are voluntary and involve human judgement. So, when some terrifying sound comes from the sky

or from a falling building, or when sudden news comes of some
danger, or something of this sort happens, even the wise person's
mind is necessarily affected, shrinks back, and grows pale for a
moment, not because he forms a judgement that something bad
is about to happen, but because of certain rapid and unconsidered movements which prevent the mind and reason from
functioning properly. But soon the wise person in that situation
does not give approval to (that is, 'he does not assent to, or
confirm by his judgement') 'this type of impression' (that is, the
fact that things look terrifying to the mind), but rejects them
and dismisses them completely, and sees in them no reason why
he should be afraid. They say that this is the difference between
the mind of the foolish and wise person. The foolish person
thinks that those things that initially strike the mind as dreadful
and horrifying really are what they first appear, and, as if they
were properly to be feared, he approves them by his assent 'and
confirms them by his judgement' (the word that the Stoics use
when they discuss this topic). But the wise person, although
affected superficially and briefly in colour and expression 'does
not assent', but keeps the consistency and firmness of judgement
which he has always had about things that look like this to the
mind, namely that they are not proper objects of fear at all, but
that they frighten with a false face and empty terror.

## 10

I have heard Favorinus say that the philosopher Epictetus said
that most of those who seemed to be practising philosophy were
philosophers of this kind: 'no action, only words'. There is an
even stronger expression which he often used, according to
Arrian, in the writings that he composed about Epictetus'
discourses. Arrian said that Epictetus noticed a man who had
lost all sense of shame, who had misguided energy, bad habits,
was self-confident and relied on his power of speech, and
concentrated on everything except his moral character. Epictetus
saw that a man of this kind was also tackling philosophical
subjects and methods, taking up physics and studying dialectic
and beginning to enquire into many philosophical topics of that
kind. He used to appeal in the name of gods and men, and, in
the middle of this appeal, he would attack this man in these
words: 'Man, where are you putting these things? Look carefully

to see if the jar is clean. If you put these things into your mind, they are ruined. If they rot, they become urine or vinegar or perhaps something worse than this.' Surely, there is nothing more important or truer than this statement: what the greatest of philosophers is conveying in this way is that the writings and teachings of philosophy, when they have been poured into a false and corrupt man, like liquids poured into a dirty and debased container, are altered, changed, spoiled, and (as he himself, in rather Cynic style, says) become urine or perhaps something fouler than urine.

The same Epictetus, as we have heard from the same Favorinus, used to say that there are two vices which are much more important and offensive than all the others: namely the inability to put up with things and to control oneself; that is, when we do not put up with and bear things that we should bear, and when we do not keep away from those objects and pleasures which we should keep away from. 'So', he said, 'if someone could hold these two words in his heart and live by them, controlling himself and keeping a watch on himself, he would certainly be largely faultless and would live the most peaceful kind of life. These two words, he used to say, are 'bear' and 'forbear.'

## II

When Archelaus sent for Socrates and said that he would make him rich, Socrates told the messenger to take back this reply: 'Four quarts of barley-meal can be bought at Athens for an obol, and the springs run with water. If what I have is not sufficient for me, yet I am sufficient for it, and thus it becomes sufficient for me. Do you not perceive that Polus did not act the part of Oedipus the King with a finer voice or any more pleasure than he acted Oedipus at Colonus, the vagrant and beggar? And shall a man of noble character show himself worse than Polus, and not perform well in any role that the deity imposes upon him? Shall he not imitate Odysseus, who was no less distinguished in rags than in a fine purple robe?'

## 12

There are some people who can be very ill-tempered in a gentle way, and, apparently without anger, act in just the same way as those who are completely carried away by their anger. We should guard, therefore, against the error of such people, as being much worse than that of violent anger. For people who are inclined to violent anger are quickly sated with their revenge, whereas the others stretch out their anger for a considerable time, like those suffering a light fever.

## 13

'But', someone says, 'I see those who are noble and good dying of hunger and cold.' – And do you not also see those who are not noble and good dying of luxury and imposture and vulgarity? – 'Yes, but it is shameful to depend on another for one's support.' – And who, poor wretch, depends on himself alone for his support, except indeed the universe? The man who blames providence because the wicked are not punished, but are strong and rich, is doing much the same as if, when they had lost their eyes, he said that they had not been punished because their nails were sound. I for my part say that there is much more difference between virtue and property than there is between eyes and nails.

## 14

... bringing forward those intractable philosophers who think that pleasure is not natural, but something that follows upon things that are natural, such as justice, self-control, and freedom. Why is it, then, that the soul rejoices in the lesser goods of the body, and finds peace in them, as Epicurus says, and yet does not take pleasure in its own goods, which are the greatest? And yet nature has given me a sense of shame; and I often blush when I catch myself saying something shameful. It is this emotion that will not allow me to lay down pleasure as the good, and the end of life.

## 15

The women at Rome have Plato's *Republic* in their hands, because he prescribes a community of women; for they attend merely to the words of the author, and not to his intention. For he does not tell one man and one woman to marry and live together, in the wish that there should be a community of wives subsequently, but he abolishes that kind of marriage and introduces another kind to replace it. And, in general, people delight in finding excuses for their own faults. Yet philosophy says, it is not right even to stretch out a finger without some reason.

## 16

One must know that it is not easy for a man to come to a judgement, unless he should state and hear the same principles every day, and at the same time apply them all to his life.

## 17

When we are invited to an entertainment, we take what we find; and if any one should bid his host set fish or cakes before him, he would be thought absurd. Yet, in the world we ask the gods for what they do not give us, and still do so despite the many things which they have in fact given us.

## 18

They are pretty fellows indeed, said Epictetus, who value themselves on things that are not in our own power. 'I am a better man than you', says one, 'for I have a great deal of land, and you are half-dead with hunger.' 'I am of consular rank', says another; another, 'I am a governor', another, 'I have a fine head of hair.' Yet one horse does not say to another, 'I am better than you, for I have a great deal of fodder and all that barley; and I have gold bridles and embroidered saddle-cloths'; but 'I am swifter than you.' And every creature is better or worse, because of its own virtue or vice. Is man, then, the only creature that has no virtue of his own? Must we then look to hair, and clothes, and ancestors?

## 19

Those who are sick are displeased with a physician who offers them no advice, and think that he has given them up. And why should one not assume the same attitude towards a philosopher and so conclude he is despairing of one's recovery to a right way of thinking, if he tells one nothing that will be of use?

## 20

Those whose bodies are in good condition are able to withstand heat and cold; and so, likewise, those whose souls are in the right condition can bear anger, and grief, and immoderate joy, and all other emotions.

## 21

It is right to praise Agrippinus on this account, that, although he was a man of the highest worth, he never praised himself but blushed even if another praised him. He was a man of such character, said Epictetus, that he would write in praise of every hardship that befell him; if he had a fever, in praise of fever; if he suffered disrepute, in praise of disrepute; if he was exiled, in praise of exile. And once, when he was just about to dine, a messenger interrupted him with news that Nero had ordered him go into exile: 'Well, then', said Agrippinus, 'we will dine at Aricia.'

## 22

Agrippinus, when he was governor, would try to persuade those whom he sentenced that it was proper for them to be sentenced. 'For it is not as their enemy', he said, 'or as a robber, that I cast my vote against them, but as their protector and guardian, just as the physician likewise encourages the man he is operating on and persuades him to submit himself to treatment.'

## 23

Nature is admirable, and, as Xenophon says, 'fond of her creatures'. At any rate we love and take care of our body, which is of all things the most unpleasing and the filthiest. For if we were obliged, for just five days, to take care of our neighbour's body, we could not bear it. For only consider what it would be, when we get up in a morning, to clean the teeth of another, and after he had attended to a certain necessary function, to wash those parts of him. In reality, it is wonderful we should love a thing which demands such services day after day. I stuff this sack, and then I empty it again. What is more troublesome? But I must serve god. Therefore I stay, and bear to wash and feed and shelter this paltry miserable body; and when I was younger, there was another charge which it assigned to me, and I bore it. And when nature, which gave us our body, takes it away, will you not bear that? 'I love it,' say you. But is it not nature, as I was saying just now, that has given you your very love for it? And yet this same nature also says, 'Let it go now, and have no further trouble.'

## 24

If a man dies young, he finds fault with the gods [because he is dying before his proper time, whereas if a man fails to die when he is old, he too finds fault with the gods] because, at the time when he ought to be at rest, he is encumbered with the troubles of life. But nevertheless, when death approaches, he wishes to live, and sends for the physician, and bids him to spare no trouble or zeal. People are extraordinary, he said, wishing neither to live nor to die.

## 25

When you attack someone agressively and threateningly, remember to tell yourself beforehand that you are not a wild animal; and then you will never do anything savage, and so live your life through without having to repent or account for yourself.

## 26

You are a little soul, carrying a corpse, as Epictetus used to say.

## 27

We must discover, he said, an art of assent, and in the area of impulse, we must keep our attention fixed so that it is exercised with reservation, and with regard to social demands and the merit of the case; from desire we must abstain altogether, and we must not seek to avoid anything that is not in our power.

## 28

The dispute, he said, is about no ordinary matter, but madness or sanity turns on it.

## 29

There is nothing you should give such thought to in everything as what is safe: for it is safer to remain silent than to speak; and to refrain from saying what will be empty of sense and full of reproach.

## 30

A ship ought not to be fixed to one small anchor, nor life to a single hope.

## 31

For both our legs and our hopes, possibility must govern our stride.

## 32

It is more necessary for the soul to be cured than the body; for it is better to die than to live badly.

## 33

The pleasures that come most rarely give the most delight.

## 34

If one should overstep the mean, the most enjoyable things would become the least so.

## 35

No man is free who is not master of himself.

## 36

Truth is something immortal and eternal. It bestows upon us, not a beauty that time will wither, nor a freedom of speech which the sentence of a judge can take away, but rather it bestows what is just and lawful, distinguishing this from what is unjust and exposing it.

# NOTES

The Discourses are referred to by book, chapter and paragraph alone. References to the Introduction (= Introd.) are to the numbered paragraphs. For scholarly references not otherwise identified, see pp. xxiv–xxv.

## Discourses

**Prefatory Letter** This letter, written separately from the Discourses, was attached to them as a preface in ancient times: see Introd. 3.

1.1 Epictetus stresses the idea that it is a key characteristic of human beings that, as rational animals, we are able to examine and 'make correct use' of our impressions (the way things 'appear' to us) instead of acting instinctively or unthinkingly in line with our impressions: see Introd. 8 and 11. Epictetus often uses as ethical exemplars political figures who face with equanimity punishment and ill-treatment by Roman emperors, e.g. Plautius Lateranus, executed by Nero (19–20), Agrippinus banished by him (his estate in Aricia lay on his way to exile, 28–32), and Thrasea Paetus (26) and Helvidius Priscus, executed by Nero and Vespasian respectively. The latter two were actually adherents of Stoicism, but Epictetus extracts a Stoic message from all these cases, i.e. the contrast between what is and is not 'up to us' (Introd. 8). Rufus, here (27) and elsewhere, is Musonius Rufus, Epictetus' Stoic teacher.

1.2 On Helvidius Priscus (19–24) and Agrippinus (12–18), see note to 1.1. On Epictetus' thinking about the importance of rehearsing to play the ideal (human) 'role' (prosopon), see Introd. 14, and ref. in Introd. n. 17. Philosophers, esp. Cynics and Stoics, but not all adult males, regularly have beards in this period (29). In 18 the 'purple' is the stripe at the edge of the toga worn as a distinguishing mark by Roman senators.

1.4 Chrysippus (c. 280–c. 206 BC) was the great systematizer of Stoic philosophy, and wrote many textbooks, of which Epictetus cites one,

*On Impulse* (*hormē*) (14), which relates to Epictetus' key theme (Introd. 8). The equanimity in misfortune of the aged Socrates (24) (Plato, *Crito* 43d) is contrasted with the responses of epic and tragic figures (Priam, Oedipus) in similar situations (25–6): see further, on Epictetus' ideas about tragedy, note on 1.28.

1.5 The Academic Sceptics (descendants of Plato's Academy) denied the possibility of knowledge: see LS 68–70, and Burnyeat (1983), ch. 3.

1.6 On the picture given here of distinctively human capacities and on the understanding of divine providence, see Introd. 10–11, and refs in Introd. n. 12. The work of Pheidias at Olympia is a famous gold and ivory statue of Zeus (23).

1.7 The Stoics regarded logic (together with physics, i.e. the study of nature) as a prerequisite for a full understanding of ethics; and Epictetus tries to bring home the relevance of logical reasoning to right practical judgement (see A. A. Long, 'Dialectic and the Stoic Sage', in Rist (1978), ch. 4). 'Equivocal' premises involve ambiguities, and 'hypothetical' premises involve assumptions or conditions.

1.8 Epictetus' point is that, although an understanding of logic is a key part of a full human education (thus it is better to understand a formal argument, or syllogism, than an informal argument, or enthymeme), it is dangerous for ethically uneducated people to copy philosophers, such as Plato, in trying to acquire expertise in logic and language which they are not equipped to use properly.

1.9 Among the implications of our sharing 'divine' rationality (Introd. 11) is that, while not committing suicide to avoid (what is usually regarded as) misfortune, we should not cling to life if we can no longer fulfil our proper role in life (Socrates' attitude, as shown in Plato, *Apology* 28e and 29c, is taken as exemplary, 23–4). On Stoic grounds for suicide, *see* LS 66G and H.

1.11 Epictetus uses this quasi-Socratic dialogue to bring out the Stoic points: (a) that (properly expressed) love of one's kin (*philostorgia*) is natural to human beings (see LS 57E, F), and (b) that the proper therapy for (apparent) misfortune is to change one's beliefs about good and bad (35–8; cf. Introd. 6).

1.12 On the Stoic idea of 'god' expressed here, *see* Introd. 11.

1.14  See note on 1.12; 'god' for Stoics is providential rationality, embodied (or immanent) both in the universe as a whole and in each human being (as a rational animal).

1.15  In Stoic theory, the psychological and physical life of an animal is directed by its governing or controlling part (*hegemonikon*), which in human beings is rational (Inwood (1985), 27–41). The life 'according to nature' is the goal of Stoic life, taken to mean the life of an ethically developed human being (LS 57A, 59D, 63C).

1.16  For the Stoic idea that human beings, as rational animals, have a special status in the providential shaping of the universe and that plants and animals exist for the sake of human beings, see LS 54N, P, 57F(5). *See* further R. Sorabji, *Human Minds and Animal Morals: The Origins of the Western Debate* (Duckworth, London, 1993), ch. 10.

1.17  On the Stoic idea of philosophy as the integrated study of logic, physics, and ethics, see LS 26B–E. On the picture of distinctively human capacities given in 20–9, *see* Introd. 11, and ref. in Introd. n. 12.

1.18  In Stoic theory, all human actions, emotions and desires are 'rational' in that they express beliefs (i.e. they have 'propositional content'). Passions (*pathe*), such as anger, rest on false beliefs about what is valuable and 'what are matters of indifference'; the wise person does not regard pain as a bad thing (so he does not groan 'inside', 19); *see* LS 58 and 65, and Introd. 8 and 12.

1.19  A tribune (24) was a Roman magistrate; Nicopolis, where Epictetus set up his school in later life, was founded by Augustus, and the priesthood of Augustus was a significant public office there (26–9).

1.20  On attending to 'impressions' (7–11, 15), see Introd. 8. 17–19: Epicurus (341–271 BC), the founder of the philosophical school which was the principal competitor of Stoicism, claimed that pleasure (sometimes characterized as pleasure 'of the flesh', *sarx*) was the chief good for human beings: see LS 21 G(1), N.

1.22  The Stoics believed that human beings, as rational animals, have the natural capacity, in the form of 'preconceptions' (*prolepseis*), to acquire ethical and other types of knowledge, but that they need to be educated to learn how to apply these preconceptions (such as the idea of good) properly and 'according to nature'. *See* LS 40N, S, T and (on ethical development) 59D.

**1.23** Epicurus (see note on 1.20) presented involvement in politics and, according to this passage (though not all ancient evidence), marriage as incompatible with the pursuit of peace of mind, though he laid great stress on the value of friendship: see LS 22D(1), E, F, H, O and Q(5). 'Mouse' (4) was the name of Epicurus' favourite slave-boy, who studied philosophy with his master.

**1.24** Epictetus imagines philosophers being sent as spies to Rome, perhaps because the emperor Domitian banished them around 90 AD. For his idealization of the Cynics, founded by Diogenes, see Introd. 5.

**1.25** If we can no longer play the 'role' that is consistent with our nature as rational animals, it is still 'up to us' whether to commit suicide or not; cf. 1.9.

**1.26** See notes on 1.7, 1.8: for Socrates' advice not to live an 'unexamined life' (18), see Plato, *Apology* 38a.

**1.27** The ethical problem of how to examine our impressions properly (in a way that is consistent with virtue) is more important than the purely intellectual problem raised by Pyrrho and the Academic Sceptics, whether we can gain knowledge from our impressions (see note on 1.5; and, on Pyrrho, *see* LS 1–3, 71–2). Sarpedon's statement (8) is based loosely on Homer, *Iliad* 12.324–5, 328.

**1.28** Typically, people act in line with their (misguided) impressions, e.g. Euripides, *Medea* 1078–9 (7); the real 'tragedy' in such cases is not the supposed disasters that result, but the fact that their impressions are misguided and that they act in line with these. See Introd. 10.

**1.29** Socrates is taken as an exemplar of someone who faces apparent disaster in the knowledge that nothing matters except what is 'up to us'; there are references to Plato, *Apology* 30c (18), *Crito* 43d (19), *Phaedo* 116d, 117d (65–6).

**2.1** The 'freedom' of 22–8 is that which comes from wishing only that which is 'up to us'; this idea of freedom develops the argument of Plato, *Gorgias* 466d–468e; *see* further 4.1. The idea that Socrates wrote a great deal (though not perhaps for publication, 32–3) conflicts with the usual ancient view that he wrote nothing.

**2.2** Socrates as an exemplar, again; 8–9 is loosely based on Xenophon, *Apology* 2–3; **15** cites Plato, *Apology* 30c. **14** is deliberately omitted, as being a meaningless interposition.

**2.4**   The idea that women should be the common property of men was proposed in the utopian political theories of Plato (*Republic* 457d–464b), and Zeno (LS 67B[4]); here (8), the idea is just put forward as a sophistical excuse. Archedemus (10–11) is either an ancient commentator on Aristotle's *Rhetoric* or a Stoic teacher (or both); he is not a well-known figure.

**2.5**   The point about playing and the ball (15–17, 20) seems to be a variant of the Stoic idea that virtue is a matter of 'playing the game well' not playing just to win: see Cicero, *On Ends* 3.22 and 24 (virtue compared to acting a role or dancing well). In 18–19 the reference is to Plato, *Apology* 27a–e and to the question of the orthodoxy of Socrates' belief in gods or semi-gods (*daemones*). The idea in 24–9 is that we should think of ourselves as part of a larger (providentially shaped) universe, not as something 'detached', if we are to form a correct understanding of what is 'natural': see Introd. 11.

**2.6**   On 'matters of indifference', *see* Introd. 12; on 9–15, see final sentence of note on 2.5 and LS 55, 58. In 16–17, *peristaseis* in Greek signifies both 'circumstances' in general and 'difficult circumstances'.

**2.7**   For this view of divination (prophesying the future, for instance, by examining the livers of sacrificial victims or bird-signs), cf. 1.17.18–19, and note Epictetus' contrasting 'prophecy' in 1.17.20–4. In 8, the point is that what matters ethically is our intention or choice (*prohairesis*), not the outcome.

**2.8**   See Introd. 11, and note on 1.16. Although the Stoic god is sometimes described as a 'designer' or 'craftsman' (as in 19–21), this divinity is immanent (the inner working of providential rationality) and not separate and transcendent: see LS 46A, 54A–B. In 18–20 reference is made to the sculptor Pheidias' statues of Zeus at Olympia and of Athena at Athens, the latter of which held a symbol of victory (*Nike*).

**2.9**   In 20–1, 'Jew' seems to mean 'Christian', i.e. someone baptized and distinctive for her or his consistency between faith and practice; the confusion between Jew and Christian is not uncommon in the Roman empire at this time.

**2.10**   See Introd. 14; on the role of 'human being' (1–6), see notes on 1.16, 2.5 (final sentence) and 2.6.

**2.11**   On 1–12, see note on 1.22; hence, ethical disagreement was seen by Stoics as the starting-point of debate designed to lead to knowledge

(13–25) and not as a basis for maintaining relativism or scepticism, as it was by some ancient philosophers.

**2.12**   Socrates presented his method of one-to-one dialogue as a means of 'shared search' for the truth: see Introd. 5, and refs in Introd. n. 3. The reference in 5 is to Plato, *Gorgias* 474a (also 472c). The argument of 17–24 is strongly reminiscent of Plato's Socrates: cf. *Apology* 29e–30b and *Protagoras* 312–13. Epictetus, like other philosophers, was banished from Rome by Diocletian in AD 89 (17, 25).

**2.13**   In 14 and 24, Antigonus, Alexander, Philip (all kings of Macedonia), and the (Thirty) Tyrants (who ruled Athens in 404 BC), are listed as supreme rulers, Zeno and Diogenes the Cynic as philosophers.

**2.14**   The comparison of philosophers, contemplating the order of the universe, to spectators at a festival (23–5) is well known to Antiquity and is traced back to Pythagoras (sixth century BC); cf. 1.6.19–21.

**2.15**   Epictetus presupposes the standard Stoic ideas: (a) that virtue expresses itself in consistency of judgement and character (LS 61A), and (b) that virtue/wisdom is like health or 'good tone/sinew' (*eutonia*), whereas vice/folly is like sickness or 'poor tone/sinew' (*atonia*) (LS 65R, S, T).

**2.16**   On 15–17, cf. note on 2.5 (first sentence). The fountain of Dirce (30–3) is at Thebes, Nero's baths and the Marcian aqueduct at Rome, the 'puny stones' and 'pleasing rock' are the Acropolis at Athens and the fine buildings on it, including the Parthenon. Heracles (44–5) performed his labours at the command of Eurystheus, who stayed at home; Theseus punished the robbers Procrustes and Sciron. The Stoics used such mythical heroes as prototypes of the wise person's wish to benefit humanity by virtuous action (Cicero, *On Ends* 3.66).

**2.17**   The main theme of this discourse is that logic (or dialectic), the first of the three standard parts of Stoic education (with physics and ethics), is valuable, if approached in the right spirit, in helping us to apply our preconceptions properly (cf. 1.22). It can be used to aid progress in the three areas into which Epictetus subdivides ethics (14–18): (a) the study of the proper objects of desire (*orexis*); (b) the guidance of our impulse to action (*horme*) towards 'appropriate acts' (*kathekonta*); (c) the examination of the impressions (*phantasiai*) to which we should give assent (*sunkatathesis*). Cf. note on 3.2. Epictetus cites Euripides' *Medea* 790ff. (19–22) in connection with the first topic, that of forming a proper conception of what is good; Euripides' *Medea* was a favoured subject in Stoic ethics from Chrysippus onwards because several of the protagonist's speeches express analysis of her psychological and ethical state. See 1.28.7, and C. Gill, 'Did Chrysippus understand Medea?', *Phronesis* 28 (1983), 136–49.

**2.18** On the 'Master' (18), see 2.19.1–4. The 'Liar' (cf. 2.17.34) is a stock logical problem and the 'Silent One' is an attempted solution to a stock fallacy. 20–1 refers to Plato, *Laws* 854b; 22 refers to Plato's presentation (*Symposium* 218a–219c) of Socrates as refusing to make love to the handsome young Alcibiades, despite being encouraged to do so by the young man.

**2.19** Epictetus presents himself as able to do no more than to report the subtle responses of other Stoic thinkers to the problems raised by the 'Master' argument (he compares himself to a grammarian or literary historian in this respect, 7–10). But in ethics the mere ability to report is not enough; you have to make ethical principles integral to your life and character if you are to become a real Stoic and not just someone who reports Stoic doctrines (20–4).

**2.20** On Academic Sceptics, see note on 1.5; the question whether Scepticism is a position you can live by (28–34) was often raised in Antiquity also: see Burnyeat, in Burnyeat (1983), ch. 6. The Epicurean position on the value of social involvement is more complex than is suggested here (6–20): see note on 1.23, and LS 22. But Epicureans did not share the Stoic view that shared rationality makes all human beings naturally disposed to benefit each other (6–7; cf. LS 57F). They denied that the gods took any interest, or intervened, in human affairs (23; cf. LS 23), but did not think that this belief was incompatible with virtue as they understood this (LS 23B and D and 21B[6]).

**2.21** On the idea of 'therapy' implied here (15, 22), see Introd. 6. For the idea that logic is a necessary prerequisite of proper ethical training, see note on 2.17.

**2.22** 'Friendship' (*philia*) in Greek covers family relationships (32) as well as our idea of 'friendship'. For the Stoics, there could be no real friendship that was not based on virtue (LS 67P). 11 refers to Euripides, *Alcestis* 691; 14 to Euripides, *Phoenissae* 621–2. Alexander's lost loved one (17) was Hephaestion. 23 refers to the origin of the Trojan War: that Paris ran off with Helen, the wife of his host/friend Menelaus.

**2.23** On the Stoic belief that rhetoric, or the art of expressive speech, like logic/dialectic, should be subordinate to the overall goals of philosophy (including ethical ones) and not practised for its own sake, see LS 31. The Stoics saw vision as an active, not a passive, capacity (3–4). 20–2 suggests that Epicurus' presentation of the flesh (*sarx*) as the basis of judgement (in knowledge and ethics) is incompatible with his brave indifference to bodily pains at his deathbed: see LS 16, esp. D; 21, esp. G(1); N; and 24D. 42 refers to Cleanthes' *Hymn to Zeus*.

**2.24** 23 refers to Homer, *Iliad* 2.25; 26 to Achilles' speeches in *Iliad* 9.

**2.26** Cf. 6 with 2.12.5 and note on 2.12.

**3.1** Philosophers at this period (and not all adult males) tend to have beards (24), but it is the more general removal of male bodily hair (e.g. from legs, 42), that Epictetus is criticizing here, and not just shaving the beard. Polemo (14) later became head of the Academy. 19–20 is based on Plato, *Apology* 28e; cf. 22–3 with 1.2, 17, 22, 30; 38 quotes Homer, *Odyssey* 1.37–9.

**3.2** For this threefold subdivision of ethics, which seems to be original to Epictetus, see note on 2.17 (also Inwood (1985), 115–25). Given the Stoic belief in the interconnection of the areas of philosophy, logic and physics are presumably relevant to all these three subdivisions of ethics, but logic seems to have been applied especially to the third (5–6). In 13–16, Antipater is a well-known Stoic, Archedemus a less well-known Aristotelian or Stoic, Crinis an obscure Stoic.

**3.3** On the view of the ethical status of family connections expressed here, see Introd. 14.

**3.5** The closest surviving parallels to the comment in 14 are Xenophon, *Memorabilia* 1.6.8, 14; and Plato, *Protagoras* 318a. 17: Protagoras and Hippias were sophists who were contemporary with Socrates and who taught rhetoric.

**3.7** A commissioner (literally 'corrector') is an imperial official given special responsibilities. As elsewhere, Epictetus gives a very unsympathetic and misleading picture of Epicureanism. On Epicurean views of the flesh (3–10), see note on 2.23; in fact, Stoics and Epicureans shared the view that both body and soul (*psuche*) were material entities. 12 reflects Epicurus' view that justice is only a social convention, though observing this convention helps to maintain one's peace of mind (LS 22D (2)), also 22A–B. On 19–20, see note on 1.23.

3.8 In 4 a 'convincing impression' (*phantasia kataleptike*) is one which self-evidently confers knowledge of the object in question (LS 40). Italicus (7) is otherwise unknown; presumably, he had been urged to be more 'philosophical' in responding to his situation and resented the thought of being 'philosophical' like the odd, low-class Epictetus.

3.10 2–3: *The Golden Verses* 40–4, ascribed to Pythagoras but almost certainly much later; for nightly self-scrutiny of this type, cf. Seneca, *On Anger* 3.36.

3.11 4: Homer, *Odyssey* 14.56–8.

3.12 This discourse seems to be critical of the ostentatiously ascetic lifestyle of some Cynics: Diogenes allegedly hardened himself by embracing statues naked in cold weather (2), and the travelling Cynic teacher may be the one who carries round the object described in 9. 'Setting up a palm' (2, 9) seems to mean climbing a pole with only hands and feet. Epictetus' advice in 7 recalls Aristotle's advice about learning to 'hit the mean' in action, desires and emotions (*Nicomachean Ethics* 2.9, 1109b1–7); for Socrates' advice (15), see note on 1.26.

3.13 The Stoics see human beings as material objects, composed of the same elements as the universe and dispersing into these at death (15); they also see the universe as having a life-span, punctuated by periodic conflagrations (4–5), a belief connected with their idea of god as the 'designer' or creative 'fire' (LS 46). All the ancient philosophical schools offered to provide peace of mind and freedom from fears such as that of death (for a review of strategies, see Cicero, *Tusculan Disputations*, esp. Book 1); 9–17 recalls that of the Epicureans, as presented by Lucretius, *The Nature of the Universe* 2.37–61, 3.978–1023, but conceived in Stoic terms; 20–3 seems to belong to a separate discourse which has become attached to this one; 23 refers to a lecturer spitting at his audience in over-enthusiasm.

3.14 These comments are unconnected and there is an incomplete sentence in 9. On Socrates' cross-examination as designed to remove conceit (9), see Plato, *Sophist* 230a–d.

3.15 8: Euphrates was a Stoic lecturer; see also note on 48. For the attitude to role-playing here (i.e. rehearse to play *one* role, that of a philosopher), see Introd. 14. 14: Galba was assassinated in AD 69 (the 'year of the four emperors') after a brief period as emperor.

**3.17** 4: Philostorgus was an unknown person prepared to gain wealth by sleeping with Sura, presumably Palfurius Sura, a senator under the Flavian emperors.

**3.18** The point of 5 is that you are only 'harmed' in the respect in which you 'go wrong': i.e. going wrong ethically is the only type of being harmed. The position recalls that of Socrates, e.g. Plato, *Gorgias* 472d–479d.

**3.20** 5: Epictetus may refer to his own lameness. Menoeceus gave up his life for his native city, Thebes. 7: Admetus' father refused to die to save the life of his son. 12–15: this represents an extreme version of the attitude towards 'matters of indifference' (including death) discussed in Introd. 12.

**3.21** The point of 12–16 is that to lecture on key Stoic doctrines (*theoremata*) without making them fundamental to one's life is like approaching the ritual Mysteries of the cult of Demeter at Eleusis without having gone through the necessary preliminary initiations. Also (17–21), the 'Mysteries' (i.e. key doctrines) are being revealed to everyone, without the preliminary training or 'therapy' (20), i.e. modification of beliefs, provided, in different ways, by the teaching-methods of philosophers such as Socrates, Diogenes and Zeno. See Introd. 5–6; and for the comparison of key philosophical truths with 'Mysteries', Plato, *Symposium* 210–11.

**3.22** This discourse idealizes the Cynic as philosophical teacher and exemplar of the philosophical life: see Introd. 5 and 14. For the image of philosophers as spies (24, 38), cf. 1.24.3–10. 30 refers to Homer, *Iliad* 10.15, 91, 94–5; 31 to 23.289. 72 refers to *Iliad* 2.25; 92 to *Iliad* 2.24, 25; 95 to Cleanthes' *Hymn to Zeus*; 108 to *Iliad* 6.492–3.

**3.23** 19: probably Dio Chrysostom, a famous public speaker at this time. 20: Lysias and Isocrates were orators in the fifth to fourth centuries BC. 21–2: cf. Plato, *Apology* 30c, *Crito* 46b. 23: recitations in the houses of rich men were common in the Roman empire; 'Quadratus' is used as a type-name for hosts of such recitations. 25: Plato, *Apology* 17c. 27: the Stoics believed that the rays of the sun consisted of vapour drawn up to feed its fires. 30: for the idea of philosophy as therapy, see Introd. 6.

**3.24** 13: cf. Homer, *Odyssey* 1.3, 17.487. 14–15: for Stoic idealization of Heracles, cf. Cicero, *On Ends* 3.66; for a contrasting (tragic) view of Heracles' relationships with his family, see Sophocles, *Trachi-*

*niae.* 18: cf. Homer, *Odyssey* 5.82. 37–8: Epicurus saw pleasure as the highest human good (though he did not mean what is presented as pleasure here); see LS 21, esp. 21B(5). 43: grief, envy and pity are standardly seen as 'passions' (emotions based on false beliefs) by the Stoics: see LS 65E(4). The Stoics valued family and friendly affection (*philostorgia*; see note on 1.11), while denying the ethical validity of the passions, such as grief, that are normally associated with this affection. 70: Philip, Alexander, Perdiccas, kings of Macedon; 'the great king' of Persia. 105: the first comment ('I knew that my son was mortal'), attributed to the fifth-century BC philosopher Anaxagoras, among others, became famous in Hellenistic and Roman philosophy as an expression of Stoic (or, more broadly, philosophical) fortitude against grief. 117: Caesar = the Roman emperor; the Capitol, a hill of Rome which was the site of major temples; 'taking auspices', ritual acts performed by priests (who are also public officials) to determine the gods' will.

3.26 14: for this criticism, cf. 3.2.5–6 and note on 3.2. The criticism is directed at those who use logic in connection with the third topic in Epictetus' programme (the avoidance of error, and trying to gain complete consistency in judgement), before understanding properly the first, the proper objects of desire and avoidance (18). The images of 15–18 convey this defect of pursuing advanced technicalities without grasping (ethical) fundamentals; 'measuring mere dust and ashes' (18) presumably signifies useless reasoning, or reasoning devoted to transient 'externals'. 30–3: Heracles and Odysseus are repeatedly used by Stoics as ethical exemplars (see 3.24.13, 18); for 33, cf. Homer *Odyssey* 6.130.

4.1 For the conception of 'freedom' involved here (by contrast with political or legal 'freedom'), see note on 2.1; the idea that only the wise person is 'free' in this sense is a commonplace of Stoic ethics. 19–20: cf. Menander, *Th. ˈˈˈˈed One* (fragment); Thrasonides seems to be a mercenary soldier, G. his slave. 29–31 (also 156): quotations from letters ascribed to Diogenes the Cynic. 33: the 5 per cent tax is levied in Rome on those holding high public office. 41–6: on 'preconceptions' and their application, see note on 1.22. 57: the consul is preceded by twelve attendants (lictors) carrying *fasces* (rods); Roman senators wear the *toga praetexta* (with a purple edge). 86–90: the main idea here is that the only way to protect ourselves from fear is to remove the valuation of 'matters of indifference' (including those specified in 87), which threaten to 'tyrannize' our judgement. Thus, paradoxically, by surrendering my wishes to god (the providential rationality embodied in the course of events), we can achieve the only real freedom; cf. LS 55 and 58J. The metaphor of the soul (*psuche*) as a citadel (*akropolis*), which may be taken over by false beliefs and 'tyrannized' by them, goes back to Plato *Republic* 560b–c, 572e–573b, 574d–575a. 104–9: this develops the comparison of the human being in the universe with a spectator at a festival (see note on 2.14). 114: the idea that Diogenes' life was changed by introduction to philosophy by Antisthenes (*c.* 445–*c.* 360 BC) is a common one in this period. 123: on Helvidius Priscus, see note on 1.1. 131: Cleanthes' *Hymn to Zeus*, lines often cited by Epictetus. 132–7: for the idea that those who have trained to be wise do not need to think about these questions because the answer has become obvious, see 1.2.13–18. 150: on making oneself a 'slave' to Felicio, as Epaphroditus did, see 1.19.17–23. 153–5: Diogenes the Cynic is presented as a citizen of the universe (*kosmopolites*); on the (various types of) significance of this idea for Stoics, see LS 67A, K, L; and M. Schofield, *The Stoic Idea of the City* (Cambridge University Press, Cambridge, 1991). 159–60: Plato, *Symposium* 219e–221b, *Apology* 32c. 163: Plato, *Phaedo* 117; 163–6: Plato, *Crito* 45c–d, 47d, 54a. 164: Plato, *Apology* 32b; 172: Plato, *Phaedo* 64a, *Republic* 361e.

4.2 10: For Thersites, an ugly common soldier who challenged Agamemnon, the leader of the Greeks in the Trojan War, see Homer, *Iliad* 2.212–77.

4.3 12: Masurius and Cassius were distinguished legal experts in the early second century AD.

4.4 16: these are titles of actual books by Stoic thinkers; they also correspond to the first two topics in Epictetus' programme of ethical instruction (see note on 2.17). 21–2: cf. Plato, *Crito* 43d, *Symposium* 219e–221b, *Phaedo* 60d. The Academy and Lyceum were public gymnasiums where Socrates engaged in dialogue with people and where Plato and Aristotle later set up their philosophical 'schools' (research centres). 23–8: see Introd. 10. 34: Cleanthes' *Hymn to Zeus*: Gyara (or Gyaros), an island used as a place of exile.

4.5 3: Thrasymachus (Plato, *Republic* 1); Polus and Callicles (Plato, *Gorgias*); Socrates' wife and son (possibly, Xenophon, *Memorabilia* 2.2). 14: 'to strangle lions' is a heroic act, as though one of Heracles'; embracing statues is an act of ostentatious toughness, ascribed to Diogenes (see 3.12.2). 15: a modification of a paradoxical poetic fragment (from Euripides, *Cresphontes*), urging us to grieve at birth, rather than death, as the beginning of bad things. 17: presumably, the point here is that, because Nero was a bad emperor and Trajan a good one, his coins (bearing the imprint (*charakter*) which symbolizes the properly 'human' quality, 16, 18) must also be rejected. 19–20: the beeswax used in leather sewing was commonly called 'the cobbler's apple' and apparently looked like an apple. 25–7: see note on 4.1.86–90. 29: in Greek myth, these two brothers (sons of Oedipus and Jocasta) became enemies and killed each other. 33: see Xenophon, *Memorabilia* 2.2, and other (dubious) ancient anecdotes. 37: this proverb reflects Spartan lack of success in Asia Minor (Turkey), where Ephesus is situated.

4.6   18: on the shades of difference in meaning between these (and related) terms connected with the impulse to action in Stoic theory, see Inwood (1985), 224–42. 20: an anecdote told several times by ancient authors about Antisthenes the philosopher and Cyrus, king of Persia in the fifth to fourth centuries BC. 32: Pythagoras, *Golden Verses* 40 (see note on 3.10). 33: phrases from the *Golden Verses* ascribed ironically to the type of person that Epictetus is criticizing. The Stoics thought the wise person (though not others) could legitimately lie on some occasions.

4.7   6: 'Galileans' presumably means 'Christians' (see note on 2.9). 30: Plato, *Apology* 32c–d.

4.8   17–20: Euphrates combined Stoic teaching, unusually, with successful public speaking: see 3.15.8. 21: Hephaestus, blacksmith god, here presented as wearing the smith's characteristic felt cap. 32: Homer, *Odyssey* 11.529–30. 36: a garden of Adonis (like a modern greenhouse) was used to 'force' plants in early spring.

4.9   6: Aristides and Euenus wrote erotic stories.

4.10   13: cf. 3.2.1–5, and notes on 2.17, 3.2. 14–17: see Introd. 11; cf. Seneca, *On Tranquillity of Mind* 11.3–4. 21: these are marks of being a Roman consul (for the rods, see note on 4.1.57) or other magistrate and person of great wealth; the 'suppers in baskets' are the 'dole' (*sportula*) given by Roman patrons to their clients. 31: the quoted words are taken from Homer's description of Achilles, after the death of Patroclus (*Iliad* 24.5), and the three men are close friends of his. In *Iliad* 18.95–100, Achilles famously accepted that his own death would come soon after his vengeance on the killer of Patroclus. For Epictetus' attitude to these epic/tragic situations, see note on 1.28. Epictetus' implied criticism of Homer's Achilles follows that of Plato, *Republic* 387d–388d. 33: Automedon was the charioteer of Patroclus and Achilles. 35: Homer, *Iliad* 19.321.

**4.11** 13: Epictetus criticizes over-enthusiastic philosophers, presumably Cynics, who rejected the customary Greek and Roman emphasis on cleanliness, and who thus anticipated some early Christian ascetics. 19: Plato, *Symposium* 174a, 175c–e, 217–18, 222a–b. 20: Aristophanes, *Clouds* 103, 179, 225: i.e. Aristophanes' evidence (in his very hostile comedy about Socrates, 423 BC) is of no value. 30: Xenocrates was head of the Academy (the school founded by Plato) and Polemo became head (cf. 3.1.14).

## Handbook

References to *Diss.* are to the *Discourses*. On the form of the work, see Introd. 2.

1. On the central role of this point for Epictetus, see Introd. 8; and *Diss.* 1.1 See also, on the threefold educational programme, notes on *Diss.* 2.17 and 3.2.

2. On the ideas of delaying the formation of desire, until ethical education is well advanced, and of wishing only 'with reservation', see Inwood (1985), 119–26.

15. Heraclitus (sixth to fifth century BC) was a pre-Socratic philosopher who was much admired by the Stoics.

17. On the attitude to role-playing, see Introd. 14.

29. This chapter is virtually identical with *Diss.* 3.15: see note on this.

30. See Introd. 14.

31. See Introd. 11. Polyneices and Eteocles, brothers, killed each other for royal power (see 4.5.29). Libations and sacrifices are typical rituals of Greek and Roman religion.

32. See note on *Diss.* 2.7. The principles of duty to country or to friend do not need to be established by divination since they are morally self-evident; also, they were confirmed by the most famous source of prophecy, the oracle of Pythian Apollo at Delphi.

49. For criticisms of this general type, see notes on *Diss.* 2.17 and 2.19.

52. The criticism of focusing on logical analysis at the expense of more fundamental parts of philosophy is similar to *Diss.* 3.2.6, though the threefold division of philosophical topics corresponds precisely neither to that of 3.2 (see notes on 2.17 and 3.2) nor to the classic Stoic programme of logic, physics and ethics.

53. Cleanthes' *Hymn to Zeus*; Euripides fragment 965 in Nauck's edition; Plato, *Crito* 43d; Plato, *Apology* 30c–d; all except the Euripides are favourite quotations in *Diss.*

## Fragments

These are passages drawn from other ancient writings (principally Stobaeus' anthology of philosophical doctrines) which are said to be by Epictetus, and which seem to be based on lost versions by Arrian of Epictetus' teachings. As stated in the Note on the Text (p. xxviii above), only fragments now thought by scholars to be probably or possibly by Epictetus are included. The numbering is that of Schenkl (1916).

1. This apparent rejection of physics in place of ethics goes beyond what we find in *Diss.*; but we would expect to find Epictetus insisting in the case of physics (the study of nature), as well as logic, that this must go hand in hand with ethical development (see, e.g., notes on *Diss.* 2.23, 3.2).

3. This passages uses *kosmos* ('universe', 'order') in place of 'god', a standard Stoic idea (LS 44F, 54, esp. A, B, E, H), but in other respects resembles the thinking about 'god' in *Diss.*

4. Cf. note on fragment 3.

5. Lycurgus was the legendary founder of the distinctive Spartan constitution, admired by ancient philosophers for its ordered legal structure and ethically educative character.

8. For the Stoic idea that the natural world is constituted by, and transformed back into, the four elements, see LS 47A; note on *Diss.* 3.13.

9. This passage is presented by Aulus Gellius (19.1.14–21) as a summary of an extract from Book 5 of Arrian's *Discourses* of Epictetus; the phrases given in inverted commas seem to be quotations; the passage is also quoted in Augustine, *City of God* 9.4. On impression and assent, see Introd. 8; on the idea of involuntary reactions (which fall short of being 'passions' i.e. emotions based on false beliefs), see LS 65X; and on the wise person's 'good emotions' (*eupatheiai*), see LS 65F, W.

10. This passage is also taken from Aulus Gellius (17.19); the phrases in inverted commas are likely to derive from Epictetus. On the central point, see note on fragment 1.

11. Archelaus was king of Macedon; Polus a famous actor of the fourth century BC; *Oedipus the King* and *Oedipus at Colonus* are two surviving tragedies by Sophocles; Odysseus is disguised in rags in Homer, *Odyssey* 14–21.

15. This is a fair comment on the proposals in Plato, *Republic* 457d–464b, which are also adopted by Zeno in his *Republic* (LS 67B(4)). Plato's scheme for his ideal state abolishes marriage and private property for the ruling class, and thus replaces standard socio-economic structures altogether in the attempt to portray justice in its ideal form.

21. See note on *Diss.* 1.1.

22. See fragment 21. The idea follows closely Plato, *Gorgias* 476a–481b, esp. 475d.

23. Cf. Xenophon, *Memorabilia* 1.4.7.

27. See note on *Handbook* 2.

# GLOSSARY

Some key terms of Stoic philosophy used in the Introduction and Notes are given here in transliterated form, together with their usual English translations and a brief explanation.

ADIAPHORA   *matters of indifference, indifferents*; conventional good things of life, regarded as of no value compared with virtue, the only real good.

AGATHON   *good*; proper object of desire and choice, identified with virtue (*arete*).

ANTHROPOS   *human being, mortal, man*; used by Epictetus to express an ethical ideal and as a generalized form of address, suggesting that each of us should live up to this ideal.

APATHEIA   *absence of passion* (see *pathos*), *peace of mind*; the state of mind characteristic of the Stoic ideal wise person.

APHORME   *impulse not to act, aversion*; opposite of HORME.

APOPROEGMENA   *dispreferred/disvalued things*, e.g. sickness, poverty, death; opposite of *proegmena*.

ASKESIS   *training*; disciplined practice designed to enable development towards full virtue.

ATARAXIA   *absence of disturbance, peace of mind*; a key part of the Epicurean idea of happiness, characteristic of the Epicurean wise person.

ATONIA   *absence of tone/sinew*; weakness of ethical character.

ENKLISIS   *aversion*; opposite of *orexis*, properly directed only at what is ethically bad.

EPH' HEMIN   *up to us, in our power*; that which falls within human agency and the power of choice, contrasted by Epictetus with 'externals'.

EUDAIMONIA *happiness, well-being*; taken by all Greek thinkers to be the supreme good and proper goal of human action (identified by Stoics with virtue).

EUPATHEIA *good feeling/emotion*; the calm feeling, consistent with right reason, that is characteristic of the wise person.

EUTONIA *good tone/sinew*; strength of ethical character.

HEGEMONIKON *controlling or governing part*; control centre of an animal's psychological (and psychophysical) life; in effect, the brain, though placed by the Stoics in the heart; in human beings thought to be rational in its functioning.

HORME *impulse to act*; motivation to action.

KATHEKONTA *appropriate acts, proper functions*; natural and socially approved acts which make up a life in which a human being makes progress towards complete virtue.

KATORTHOMATA *perfect acts*; completely right acts performed in the right way and state of mind by a completely virtuous person.

OIKEIOSIS *appropriation, familiarization, self-extension*; the process of development by which an animal makes the world 'its own' (*oikeios*); in human beings, a process of ethical development which leads ultimately to a sense of community with all human beings, as rational animals.

OREXIS *desire*; properly directed only towards virtue.

PATHOS *passion*; an intense or excessive emotion, based on a false judgement about what is valuable.

PHANTASIA *impression, appearance*; the way something 'appears' to animals (including human animals, in whom impressions are rational in character).

PHANTASIA KATALEPTIKE *cognitive impression*; one which self-evidently confers knowledge of the object in question.

PHILOSTORGIA *affection*; especially directed towards children or other family-members.

PROHAIRESIS *choice, capacity for choice*; used by Epictetus as a general term to signify human rational functions, especially 'attending to' impressions and giving (or withholding) 'assent'.

**PROHAIRETA/APROHAIRETA** *things that fall within/outside the sphere of choice.*

**PROEGMENA** *preferred/valued things*; conventional good things, e.g. health, material possessions, life, which can legitimately be 'selected' but which do not have the absolute value which belongs only to virtue, and therefore should not be 'chosen' for their own sake.

**PROKOPE** *progress*; i.e. ethical progress towards full wisdom or virtue.

**PROLEPSIS** *preconception*; general idea, such as 'good' or 'virtue', that human beings are naturally adapted to form.

**PROSOPON** *role, character*, literally *mask*; family or social role or status.

**SUNKATATHESIS** *assent*; approval or 'saying yes' to the content of impressions.

**SOPHOS** *wise person*; the perfectly virtuous person, the ethical norm.

**THEOS** *god*; identified with providential rationality.

See further Glossary in LS vol. 1, pp. 489–92; and, on Stoic psychological terms, Inwood (1985), esp. 111–26 and 224–42 (for full references, see pp. xxiv–xxv).

# THE DISCOURSES AND THE CRITICS

As stated in the Introduction 15–17, Epictetus' teachings, presented by Arrian, have attracted interest from his own day to the present. The extracts given here mostly illustrate contemporary scholarly responses to Epictetus and provide further analysis of some of the features of his thought emphasized in the Introduction. The final extract gives a striking example of the way in which Epictetus' writings have helped one modern reader to confront psychological torture in a wartime prison.

A. A. Long, a well-known scholar of later Greek philosophy, in a general introduction to Epictetus' work, relates key features of the style and ideas of the *Discourses* to Epictetus' conception of teaching (A. A. Long, 'Epictetus and Marcus Aurelius', in J. Luce, ed., *Ancient Writers: Greece and Rome* (Charles Scribner's Sons, New York, 1982), 993–4, 994–5. This essay is to be reprinted in A. A. Long, *Stoic Studies* (Cambridge University Press, Cambridge, forthcoming)). On the idea of ethical philosophy as therapy, see also Introd. 6.

The Epictetus whom Arrian encountered regarded himself as an old man (1.10.13); but though self-deprecating (2.6.24), he was clearly renowned as a teacher and visited or consulted by many prominent people. Recent studies have shown that his pupils were largely upper-class young men who would expect to succeed, like Arrian, in public life; and this helps to explain the treatment of moral themes in terms that would have more practical relevance to potential senators than to slaves or tradesmen. Examples of how one should evaluate a consulship, for instance, or threats of imprisonment or execution recur time and again. They would be otiose if Epictetus were addressing a low-born audience. 'Today a man was chatting to me about a priesthood of Augustus' (1.19.26); someone says, 'I am a senator and friend of Caesar; I have been consul and I have many slaves' (4.1.8).

The starting-point of Epictetus' teaching was very likely the reading and exposition of a passage from a famous Stoic philosopher (1.26.1; 2.14.1; 2.21.11), but he constantly warns against mistaking academic knowledge for moral expertise. A man should pride himself not on solving the 'Master' argument (a notorious problem in logic) but on resisting sexual desire (2.18.18). The meaning of 'education' is understanding that we are answerable for our moral purpose but not for our bodies, our relations, or our country (1.22.9). Facility in formal argument is necessary only in so far as it contributes to the moral life (1.27). If someone tells us that death is an evil, we must have at hand the argument that real evil should be avoided, but death is simply something inevitable.

Open-ended inquiry or theoretical questions such as the basis of sense perception (1.27.17) did not belong to Epictetus' conception of philosophy. In many of his discourses he simply assumes knowledge of basic Stoic principles and exhorts his hearers to apply them in their lives. But the exhortation can properly be called philosophical because it is always based on reasons and inferences from propositions that, he assumes, any reasonable man must grant to be true and perspicuous. All men have conceptions of good and evil (2.11.3), but they differ in their opinions about what things are good and the opposite. The task of philosophy is to examine and confirm the criteria for settling such disputes (2.11.23-4). That rationality, as conceived by the Stoics, must be this criterion follows from the fact that we are men and not beasts. If Epicurus claims that bodily pleasure is the good, we have only to point out that his doctrine fails to square with his own behaviour – a life devoted to reasoning and seeking to improve the human condition (1.20.17; 2.20.6ff.) . . .

In his methods of teaching Epictetus is at his most effective as a shock psychologist. His *Discourses* abound in acute analysis of mental states and problems. Suppose a man wants to change his mode of life but fears that old drinking companions will think badly of him for avoiding their company. Well, says Epictetus, he must make a choice. He can't have it both ways. 'If you don't drink with those you used to drink with you can't be liked by them as much as before; so choose whether you want to be a boozer and likeable to them or sober and not likeable' (4.2.7). In presenting the demands of the moral life he uses metaphors and examples that may alternate between hyperbole and bathos but rarely fail to seize attention and banish complacency. A man is really making moral progress if he bathes 'as someone who keeps his word' and eats 'as a man of integrity' (1.4.20). An adulterer is as useless as a *man* as a cracked saucepan, and deserves to be thrown on the dunghill (2.4.4). A 'coward and weakling' is really only a 'corpse' (1.9.33). Life itself is a game, or a military command, or an athletic contest: Socrates played the ball well, though it consisted of imprisonment, exile, drinking poison (2.5.19). 'This man has won the first round. What will he do in the second? What if it's blazing hot? What if he's at Olympia?' (1.18.21).

Following the model of Cynic philosophers, who strongly influenced him, Epictetus uses the word 'man' as what we should strive to be but most of us are not. We tend to act as if we were 'runaway slaves' (1.29.62); but we should consider 'who we are' (2.10.1). Of himself and his pupils he says: 'when we can't even fulfil the profession of man we take on that of the philosopher besides; that's a load like someone unable to lift ten pounds wanting to hold the stone of Atlas' (2.9.22). Yet as our models and heroes we should take Socrates or the Cynic Diogenes. The tone of admonition can be caustic, the standard of excellence is utterly uncompromising, but those who are to be judged by it are ourselves and not others. As one interlocutor says:

> They are thieves and robbers. What is being a thief and a robber? They have gone astray regarding good and evil. Should one get angry with them or pity them? Point out the error and you will see how they give up their mistakes. But if they don't see, they have nothing better than their own opinion.
>
> (1.18.3–4)

That is the Socratic thesis that no one does wrong deliberately. Perhaps it seems naive only if one has a naive view of moral knowledge.

Matthew Arnold – and he is by no means alone – observed that 'it is impossible to rise from reading Epictetus or Marcus Aurelius without a sense of constraint and melancholy, without feeling that the burden laid upon man is well-nigh greater than he can bear' (*Essays in Criticism: First Series* (Macmillan, London, 1910), p. 346). The reader must judge for himself. Epictetus does not stretch out a helping hand, perhaps. He gives us reasons for thinking we have the means to help ourselves. His strength as a moralist lies in the fact that he tells us what those reasons are. He pays us the great compliment of presenting an image of humanity that is intelligible in the light of reason. Courtesy demands that we offer him reasons if we reject it.

F. H. Sandbach, late Professor of Classics at Cambridge University, identifies Epictetus' belief that what matters most in life is 'up to us' as the central feature of his version of Stoic philosophy (*The Stoics* (Chatto & Windus, London, 1975), 165–7). See also Introd. 8 and 12.

Freedom is a word ever recurring in Epictetus. From his personal experience he had learned that although the body might be enslaved, a man could be master of his own thought and make his own decisions and judgements. The mind, he says, is free: man can decide what he wants. Various ideas present themselves or are suggested by others, and happiness depends on the way they are treated. The right way is not to think that things in the external world, which includes one's own body, are good or bad, not to want them or to fear them, but to accept them. One cannot control these things; one must take them as they come. 'Do not try to make what happens happen as you wish, but wish for what happens in the way it happens and then the current of your life will flow easily' (*Handbook* 8).

Essentially what man controls, or in a sense what man is, is his *prohairesis*, his moral purpose or basic choice of principle. Epictetus is the first Stoic known to have made this an important technical term. By it he means a general attitude towards life, an assignment of value which determines the way in which we 'treat our presentations'. This phrase was often used by him, and he takes it for granted that it will be understood. It would seem that what he had in mind was something like this: we receive from the outside world presentations, for example 'there is a gold ring', or 'my son is ill'; within us is a power of 'treating' these, by which we may judge that the gold ring is desirable or that our son's illness is a bad thing. These judgements are wrong; one ought to say 'the ring is unimportant' and 'my son's illness does not harm me'. If a man has the right general principles and holds to them, he will judge as he ought to judge. Not only will he be unaffected by desire and regret, unmoved by the pleasures and pains of the outer world, he will also maintain the independence of his thought, never allowing himself to be lured or forced into conduct that his conscience would not approve.

> 'Then you philosophers inculcate contempt for the governors of the state?' Heaven forbid! Which of us teaches men to dispute the rulers' rights over what is in their power? Take my wretched body, take my property, my reputation, those who are near me. 'Yes, but I want to rule your thoughts too.' And who has given you that power? How can you overcome another man's thought? 'I shall overcome it by intimidation.' You do not know that thought can be overcome by itself, but by nothing else. (*Discourses* 1.29.9–12)

Although he accepted the orthodox view that there were differences in the normal values of external things, Epictetus' sharp distinction between them and man's internal life led to a certain depreciation of those values. He saw moral life more in terms of gladly accepting all that happened to one than in those of trying to acquire the things that accord with human nature. For Chrysippus health, prosperity, a family, things for which a human being normally and properly has a preference, were for the most part correct objects of choice; only in unusual circumstances might his reason tell him that they should be forgone. Epictetus' position was summed up in his slogan *anechou kai apechou*, 'bear and forbear' or 'sustain and abstain'. One must tolerate, as being for the universal good, all those experiences that the world calls misfortunes, and one must not have any emotional attachment to the things that one cannot control. 'Do not admire your wife's beauty and you will not be angry if she is unfaithful'; at life's banquet do not want the dish that is not yet before you and do not try to detain it as it passes away (*Discourses* 1.28.11; *Handbook* 15). The orthodox Stoic would not disagree, but constant insistence gives this negative aspect a new emphasis. Not that Epictetus would have admitted his ideal to be a negative one: it was a positive determination to go freely and willingly along with the divine power that ordered all things for the best. This is an aspect not to be forgotten, for if it is overlooked there is a danger of seeing Epictetus as a man who renounces the world, confident in his own self-sufficiency. In fact he completely accepts the world, sure that its goodness is intelligible to its maker. If the individual suffers, his suffering serves a purpose for the universe as a whole, that great city of which he is a member. His reason, being an offshoot of the universal reason which is god, must approve all that god does:

> What else can I, a lame old man, do but sing a hymn of praise to God? If I were a nightingale, I should do as a nightingale; if I were a swan, I should do as a swan. But now I am a rational being: I must sing the praise of God. This is my work, and I shall not desert this post so long as I am assigned it, and I call on you to join in this same song. (*Discourses* 1.16.20–1)

A. A. Long pursues the psychological and ethical issues raised by Epictetus' stress on the power of human beings to 'use impressions correctly'. He suggests that Epictetus can offer a way of resolving the tensions that arise from this claim ('Representation and the Self in Stoicism', in S. Everson, ed., *Psychology, Companions to Ancient Thought*, 2 (Cambridge University Press, Cambridge, 1991), 114–16). See also Introd. 8–10.

> On the one hand, Epictetus says that a good life consists in using one's representations correctly, and that this is a faculty that human beings possess. This thesis suggests that we are able to take

stock of our representations, interpret their content and accept or reject courses of action that they propose. It implies that responsibility, praise and blame, rest not with our representations but with the use that we make of them. On the other hand, he also says that people cannot fail to act in accordance with their representation of what is dominantly in their interests. He speaks of representations as being good or bad (1.28.10). His examples of Medea and the figures of the *Iliad* impute to people whose ethical principles are unsound corresponding representations that induce their assent. Their horse has already bolted. What correct use could Medea have made of the representation that she should prefer revenge to her children's life?

The tension between these points of view is undeniable. Yet it is a tension which needs to be recognized and addressed in any serious ethical inquiry. The two viewpoints I have just identified in Epictetus' thought correspond to a standing problem for ethical psychology. On the one hand we hold people responsible for wrongdoing, on the presumption that it was in their power to resist unethical impulses – our version of the requirement to use representations correctly. At the same time our theories of upbringing, education and social welfare are strongly influenced by the belief that people's desires and interests, and hence their representations or occurrent mental states, are strongly shaped by the kind of world they are offered. To the question 'Is blame or pity the more appropriate response to the wrongdoer?', Epictetus answers 'pity' (1.28.9).

Epictetus lets the tension emerge, but he does not leave matters there. To resolve it, to the extent that it can be resolved, he advances his own version of living 'an examined life'. I want briefly to consider two of his principal recommendations, both of which turn on resources he thinks anyone can employ in 'using representations'. As I run through these, the reader may find it helpful to imagine Medea as listening in.

First, he suggests various ways in which we can detach ourselves from our representations. For instance, instead of immediately assenting to a representation, we can engage it in dialogue, saying: 'Wait for me a bit, representation; let me see who you are and what you are about; let me test you' (2.18.24–6). Representations of wrong courses of action are prone to give us attractive pictures of what will follow for us if we act upon them. We should forestall such pictures by opposing to the first representation 'a fair and noble one', which will give us the incentive to chuck out its predecessor. Alternatively, offered the representation of something pleasurable, we should first reflect on the duration of the pleasure and then compare that to the time subsequent to the pleasure and the possible self-revulsion we shall experience during this later time (*Handbook* 34).

Both of these strategies incorporate the two viewpoints I mentioned above, but in ways that seek to resolve the tension between them. Epictetus is not saying that we can ever act independently of representations. He preserves the thesis that people act on the basis of what appears suitable to them (as Medea does), but insists that action need not be based upon first impressions. Once we have learned that first impressions do not always present us with what, on reflection, we really want for ourselves, we can use that knowledge to produce alternative representations and thus enlarge the scope of what it is open to us to do.

But Medea might say that she has no such knowledge. Epictetus has a response to this objection which introduces the second recommendation I want to discuss. Like earlier Stoics, he holds that all human beings normally develop into persons who have 'preconceptions' (*prolepseis*) of what is good and bad. This does not mean that they have correct understanding of basic ethical truths, but rather that it is part of human nature to acquire such concepts as the profitability of what is good, the desirability of one's own happiness, and the identification of happiness with the possession of what is good (see 1.22.1). Where human beings typically go wrong, according to Epictetus, is in the way they fit or fail to fit representations of particular circumstances to preconceptions. Medea can be asked to consider whether her intention to kill her children accords with her general views of what is good for her, i.e. whether her current representation coheres with her preconception of her own well-lived life.

This test – one of consistency – will be ethically inefficacious if a person finds no discrepancy between his current representations and long-term beliefs and aspirations. The Stoics, however, would not be impressed by this objection, since they take internal conflict or inconsistency to be the hallmark of unhappiness (Stobaeus 2.75.11/LS 63BI). The unhappy person, on their view, fails to get what he wants or gets what he does not want. In other words, his desire for happiness is constantly at odds with his immediate impressions of what he should seek or avoid. If happiness is a consistent life, free from disappointment and frustration, and happiness is everyone's long-term goal, it makes excellent sense to invite the unhappy person to interrogate his representations and ask whether his impulse to pursue this or that objective matches up with his desire for happiness.

It should now be clear why Epictetus identifies ethical sensibility with the correct usage of representations.

Christopher Gill brings out the moral rigour of Epictetus' thinking on what it means to play your 'role' in life (Greek *prosopon*, Latin *persona*) by contrasting Epictetus 1.2 with another Stoic discussion of this topic. This is Cicero, *De Officiis* (*On Duties*), 1.107–25, based on the ideas of Panaetius (*c.* 185–*c.* 110 BC), who offers a less austere version of Stoic ethics than Epictetus does ('Personhood and Personality: the Four-*Personae* Theory in Cicero, *De Officiis* I', *Oxford Studies in Ancient Philosophy* 6 (1988), 187–9. See also Cicero, *On Duties*, ed. M. T. Griffin and E. M. Atkins (Cambridge University Press, Cambridge, 1991)). See also Introd. 14.

It is instructive to compare with Cicero's discussion of Cato (and of the second *persona* in general) a discourse by Epictetus on the topic: 'how may a man maintain what his *prosopon* requires (*to kata prosopon*) on every occasion?' (1.2). On the face of it, Epictetus' discourse is designed to illustrate a thesis which is central to the Panaetian theory: that each person should maintain his own specific *persona/prosopon*. And his illustration of this thesis, in terms of the contrasting reactions of Agrippinus Paconius or Helvidius Priscus, on the one hand, and of more ordinary men on the other, to situations of political danger, seems to imply the same conclusion as that drawn by Cicero in his illustration of Panaetius' thesis. That is, that different *prosopa* (or, more precisely, different appraisals of what one's *prosopon* requires) carry with them different obligations, so that what is right for Agrippinus or Helvidius is not right for someone of a different character. Indeed, it seems reasonable to think that Epictetus had the Panaetian theory in mind. But he deploys this theory in a significantly different way. For one thing, in Cicero's discussion the presentation of the two types of person (the rigid, or rigorous, and the flexible) is relatively neutral, even, awkwardly, in the case of the scrupulous and unscrupulous generals (*On Duties* 1. 108–9). Cicero modifies this neutrality in the case of Cato, but even there he does not explicitly champion Cato's stance (112). But, in Epictetus' discussion, there is a marked, and increasingly overt, favouring of the rigorous position, which is more powerfully articulated throughout, and with which Epictetus eventually seems to identify himself. From an early stage in the discourse, the less rigorous position is illustrated in humiliating examples: holding out a chamber-pot to someone (that is, acting as his slave), sitting in the senate silent 'as a jug', stepping naked into the gymnasium with amputated genitals (8–10, 24–5). The issue, as Epictetus poses it, is whether one is prepared to 'lower oneself' and calculate external values (that is, values other than virtue); it is a question of the value you place on yourself and the price at which you are prepared to 'sell yourself' (that is, to sell your capacity for rational moral choice, *prohairesis*). And Epictetus makes it increasingly clear where he stands on this issue, urging us not to sell ourselves 'cheaply' (*oligou*), and affirming that he would rather lose his neck than the philosopher's beard that is the expression of his *prosopon* (28–9, 33).

Associated with this general difference of attitude between the two discussions is a difference in the interpretation of the notion of living in accordance with one's *prosopon*. At first, in Epictetus' discourse, it looks as though this notion is being used neutrally, as in Panaetius' theory: different people have different *prosopa*, and each of us should choose to act 'in accordance with his own *prosopon*', whatever that is (7–8). But later, the notion of living *kata prosopon* seems to be reserved for those who make the rigorous response; and it is suggested that anyone who consistently tries to live *kata prosopon* will come to feel that he must make this response. Although Epictetus acknowledges that, at any given moment, a person may not be fully prepared for this response, so that it is 'inappropriate' (*meden prosekonta*) for him, he also urges us, whatever our natural capacities or deficiencies, to 'undergo a winter-training' to bring ourselves to the point where this response is appropriate (30–7). His advice presupposes the classic Stoic view that, as human beings, we are all, at some level, naturally capable of living in accordance with the virtuous rationality that constitutes our human nature. In effect, then, the advice to maintain our own specific *prosopon* is converted into the advice to maintain our universal *prosopon* as human beings. To put the point in different terms, while he advises us to live consistently with our 'personality', the only expression of personality he seriously commends is the one which will also embody our 'personhood', the status of rational moral agency we are all capable of assuming. He also emphasizes that the embodiment of personhood may demand a more than conventional level of response, in certain situations, and may require that a person 'stand out' or 'shine out' (*diaprepei*) from his society as a whole.

So, although Panaetius and Epictetus seem to offer very similar advice ('maintain your own *prosopon*'), there are significant differences in the way they interpret this advice. While Epictetus includes in his discussion some at least of the roles that figure in *On Duties* (those of magistrate and philosopher, one's own role, and our common human role), he stresses much more the idea that the other roles should, in effect, be subordinated to our common human role. He also envisages (as Panaetius seems not to have done) that the enactment of this human role may make rigorous demands on us, which are greater than, and sometimes different from, those which conventional attitudes dispose us to accept.

US Vice-Admiral James Stockdale tells how he was helped to survive the psychological pressures of being a prisoner of war in Vietnam, between 1965 and 1973, by recalling, and trying to live by, the principles of Epictetus, which he had studied at Stanford University a few years earlier ('Courage Under Fire: Testing Epictetus's Doctrines in a Laboratory of Human Behavior', the text of a speech given at King's College, London on 15 November 1993, at the invitation of Professor Richard Sorabji; Hoover Essays No. 6 (Hoover Institute, Stanford University, Stanford, 1993)). James Stockdale and his wife Sybil tell the respective stories of their experiences in this war in *In Love and War* (US Naval Institute Press, Annapolis, 1991).

The only good and evil that means anything is right in your own heart, within your will, within your power, where it's up to you. *Handbook* 32: 'Things that are not within our own power, not without our Will, can by no means be either good or evil.' *Discourses*: 'Evil lies in the evil use of moral purpose, and good the opposite. The course of the Will determines good or bad fortune, and one's balance of misery and happiness.' In short, what the Stoics say is 'Work with what you have control of and you'll have your hands full.'

What is not up to you? Beyond your power? Not subject to your will in the last analysis? For starters, let's take 'your station in life'. As I glide down toward that little town on my short parachute ride, I'm just about to learn how negligible is my control over my station in life. It's not at all up to me. I'm going right now from being the leader of a hundred-plus pilots and a thousand men and, goodness knows, all sorts of symbolic status and goodwill, to being *an object of contempt*. I'll be known as a 'criminal'. But that's not *half* the revelation that is the realization of your own *fragility* – that you can be reduced by wind and rain and ice and seawater or *men* to a helpless, sobbing wreck – unable to control even your own bowels – in a matter of *minutes*. And, more than even that, you're going to face fragilities you never before let yourself believe you could have – like after mere minutes, in a flurry of action while being bound with tourniquet-tight ropes, with care, by a professional, hands behind, jackknifed forward and down toward your ankles held secure in lugs attached to an iron bar, that, with the onrush of anxiety, knowing your upper body's circulation has been stopped and feeling the ever-growing induced pain and the ever-closing-in of claustrophobia, you can be made to blurt out answers, sometimes correct answers, to questions about anything they know you know.

'Station in life', then, can be changed from that of a dignified and competent gentleman of culture to that of a panic-stricken, sobbing, self-loathing wreck in a matter of minutes. So what? To live under the false pretence that you will forever have control of your station in life is to ride for a fall; you're asking for disappointment. So make sure in your heart of hearts, in your inner self, that you treat your station in life with *indifference*, not with contempt, only with *indifference*.

And so also with a long long list of things that some unreflective people assume they're assured of controlling to the last instance: your body, property, wealth, health, life, death, pleasure, pain, reputation. Consider 'reputation', for example. Do what you will, reputation is at least as fickle as your station in life. *Others* decide what your reputation is. Try to make it as good as possible, but don't get hooked on it. Don't be ravenous for it and start chasing it in tighter and tighter circles. As Epictetus says, 'For what are tragedies but the portrayal in tragic verse of the sufferings of men who have admired things external?' In your heart of hearts, when you get out the key and open up that old rolltop desk where you really keep your stuff, don't let 'reputation' get mixed up with your *moral purpose* or your *will power*; they *are* important. Make sure 'reputation' is in that box in the bottom drawer marked 'matters of indifference'. As Epictetus says: 'He who craves or shuns things not under his control can neither be faithful nor free, but must himself be changed and tossed to and fro and must end by subordinating himself to others.'

I know the difficulties of gulping this down right away. You keep thinking of practical problems. Everybody has to play the game of life. You can't just walk around saying, 'I don't give a damn about health or wealth or whether I'm sent to prison or not.' Epictetus took time to explain better what he meant. He says everybody should play the game of life – that the best play it with 'skill, form, speed, and grace'. But, like most games, you play it with a ball. Your team devotes all its energies to getting the ball across the line. But after the game, what do you do with the ball? Nobody much cares. It's not worth anything. The competition, the game, was the thing. The ball was 'used' to make the game possible, but it in itself is not of any value that would justify falling on your sword for it.

Once the game is over, the ball is properly a matter of

indifference. Epictetus on another occasion used the example of shooting dice – the dice being matters of indifference, once their numbers had turned up. To exercise *judgement* about whether to accept the numbers or roll again is a *willful* act, and thus *not* a matter of indifference. Epictetus' point is that our *use* of externals is not a matter of indifference because our actions are products of our will and we totally control that, but that the dice themselves, like the ball, are material over which we have no control. They are externals that we cannot afford to covet or be earnest about, else we might set our hearts on them and become slaves of such others as control them.

These explanations of this concept seem so modern, yet I have just given you practically verbatim quotes of Epictetus' remarks to his students in Nicopolis, colonial Greece, two thousand years ago.

Reprinted from *Courage Under Fire: Testing Epictetus's Doctrines in a Laboratory of Human Behavior* by James Bond Stockdale with the permission of the publisher, Hoover Institution Press. Copyright © 1993 by the Board of Trustees of the Leland Stanford Junior University.) This extract also appears in J. B. Stockdale, *Thoughts of a Philosophical Fighter Pilot* (Hoover Institution Press, Stanford, California, 1995), 185–201, esp. 190–2.

# SUGGESTIONS FOR FURTHER READING

Hijmans, B. L., Jr, *Askesis: Notes on Epictetus' Educational System* (Van Gorcum, Assen, 1959): focuses on Epictetus' conception of ethical education.

Inwood, B., *Ethics and Human Action in Early Stoicism* (Oxford University Press, Oxford, 1985): a detailed study of Stoic ethics and psychology.

Long, A. A., 'Epictetus and Marcus Aurelius', in J. Luce, ed., *Ancient Writers: Greece and Rome* (Charles Scribner's Sons, New York, 1982), 985–1002: a lucid and helpful introduction to both thinkers. To be reprinted in A. A. Long, *Stoic Studies* (Cambridge University Press, Cambridge, forthcoming).

Long, A. A., *Hellenistic Philosophy*, 2nd edn (Duckworth, London, 1986): a clear survey of the main Hellenistic philosophies.

Long, A. A., ed., *Problems in Stoicism* (Athlone Press, London, 1971): a collection of important scholarly essays on Stoic philosophy.

Long, A. A., and D. N. Sedley, *The Hellenistic Philosophers*, 2 vols (Cambridge University Press, Cambridge, 1987). Vol. 1, *Translations of the Principal Sources with Philosophical Commentary*; vol. 2, *Greek and Latin Texts with Notes*. The standard modern source-book for Hellenistic philosophy.

Matheson, P. E., *Epictetus: The Discourse and Manual*, translated with introduction and notes, 2 vols (Oxford University Press, 1916).

Oldfather, W. A., *Epictetus: The Discourses*, edited with a translation. Loeb Classical Library, 2 vols (Harvard University Press, Cambridge, Mass., 1946): useful introduction as well as sound translation and notes.

Rist, J. M., ed., *The Stoics* (University of California Press, Berkeley, 1978): a collection of scholarly essays on Stoic philosophy.

Sandbach, F. H., *The Stoics* (Chatto & Windus, London, 1975): informative survey of the main Stoic theories and thinkers, including Epictetus.

White, N. P., *The Handbook of Epictetus* (Hackett, Indianapolis, 1983): a good translation of the *Handbook* with a thoughtful introduction and notes.

Xenakis, J., *Epictetus: Philosopher–Therapist* (E. J. Brill, The Hague, 1969): a survey of Epictetus' aims as a philosopher and teacher.

# ACKNOWLEDGEMENTS

The editors and publishers wish to thank the following for permission to use copyright material:

Cambridge University Press for material from A. A. Long, 'Representation and the Self in Stoicism' from S. Everson, ed., *Psychology: Companions to Ancient Thought 2* (1991);

Hoover Institution Press for material from James Bond Stockdale, *Courage Under Fire: Testing Epictetus's Doctrines in a Laboratory of Human Behavior*. Copyright © 1993 by The Board of Trustees of the Leland Stanford Junior University;

Macmillan Publishing Company for material from A. A. Long, 'Epictetus and Marcus Aurelius' from *Ancient Writers: Greece and Rome*, T. James Luce, Editor in Chief, Vol. II, Charles Scribner's Sons, pp. 985–1002. Copyright © 1982 Charles Scribner's Sons;

Oxford University Press for material from Christopher Gill, 'Personhood and Personality: The Four-Personae Theory in Cicero, De Officiis I', *Oxford Studies in Ancient Philosophy*, Vol. 6, 1988, pp. 169–99;

The Estate of F. H. Sandbach for material from *The Stoics*, Chatto & Windus, 1975, pp. 165–7.

Every effort has been made to trace all the copyright holders but if any have been inadvertently overlooked the publishers will be pleased to make the necessary arrangement at the first opportunity.